Global Communication & International Relations

HOWARD H. FREDERICK

University of California, Irvine

Wadsworth Publishing Company
Belmont, California
A Division of Wadsworth, Inc.

TO MY WIFE, CLAIRE, AND DAUGHTER, CARRIE,

WHO HAVE SUSTAINED ME,

&

TO THE MOVEMENTS FOR PEACE, HUMAN RIGHTS,

SOCIAL JUSTICE, AND ENVIRONMENTAL PRESERVATION,

THAT HAVE INSPIRED ME.

Printed in the United States of America
1 2 3 4 5 6 7 8 9 10—97 96 95 94 93

Library of Congress Cataloging-in-Publication Data
Frederick, Howard H.
  Global communication and international relations / Howard H. Frederick.
    p.   cm.
  Includes bibliographical references and index.
  ISBN 0-534-19344-7
  1. Communication in international relations.   I. Title.
  JX1395.F73   1992
  327.1'7—dc20
                                                                    92-4890
                                                                    CIP

Sponsoring Editor: *Cynthia C. Stormer*
Marketing Representative: *Steve Simmons*
Editorial Associate: *Cathleen S. Collins*
Production Editors: *Kay Mikel and Kirk Bomont*
Manuscript Editor: *Laurie Vaughn*
Permissions Editor: *Mary Kay Hancharick*
Interior and Cover Design: *E. Kelly Shoemaker*
Cover Photo: *Imtek Imagineering/Masterfile*
Art Coordinator: *Lisa Torri*
Interior Illustration: *Diphrent Strokes*
Photo Editor: *Larry Molmud*
Typesetting: *Shepard Poorman Communications Corporation*
Printing and Binding: *Malloy Lithographing, Inc.*
Photo credits: **p. 18,** British Museum; and **p. 21,** Giraudon/Art Resource, NY.

Foreword

The year was drawing to a close as I read the manuscript of this book. It was a year of momentous, unpredictable, swift, and puzzling changes. It began with the war in the Persian Gulf, a calamity celebrated as victory. Six months later in Moscow a coup backfired in a victory that led to calamity. Each of these played out in a global arena. Hundreds of millions witnessed them and were deeply involved. I wondered what made these events different from the usual gradual shifting of historical ground. Why did they unloose landslides that swept over familiar territory and changed the historic landscape?

It occurred to me that after the long-accelerating accumulation of information and communication developments, there came a change in the nature of change. I called it "instant history." It is not only reporting but also making history. It happens when selected images and messages of a crisis are transmitted live, in real time, and evoke a reaction in time to influence the course of the very events they communicate.

It seemed to me that this is a major transformation in the way we show, talk about, and manage our affairs. But, unless we learn to use these crisis-management skills in new ways, it is likely to exacerbate and sharpen our techniques of mind-management and thought-control.

Where is the background, the knowledge, the analysis necessary to understand the potentials and hazards of the new global communications? I wondered. And then I discovered that much of it can be found in this book.

After an introduction that places the subject in an appropriately broad evolutionary and historical context, we are launched on a global journey. We travel through concepts and theories of information and communication; economic, technological, legal, and organizational aspects and contending approaches to the study of communication; the important but little-known UNESCO debate (and debacle) about an international information and communication order; and the "centerpiece" of the book, communication in peace and war. We arrive at the present predicament well equipped with facts, arguments, and directions for further study and action.

This tour de force is timely and necessary. The new communication systems are becoming ever more concentrated in ever fewer global power centers. At the same time, they increasingly pervade every home, vehicle, and place of work, and involve every person every day. That confronts the citizen with a new challenge: How do we participate in the making of policies shaping not only our culture and perspectives but increasingly our history and fate? There is no more profound and difficult challenge as we approach the twenty-first century. This book will help prepare us to meet it.

George Gerbner
Dean-Emeritus
Annenberg School of Communication

Preface

Throughout history, channels of communication have played instrumental roles in *exacerbating tensions*. Today the media of communication face the challenge of how to *promote peace, build confidence among nations and peoples, and strengthen understanding*. Accelerated by the rapid advances in electronic technologies, global information relations have become central to international relations in general.

Global communication has become a serious field of study at colleges and universities, and students of the next century must understand its history, theory, and policy implications. Such courses are usually taught in departments of political science, international relations, and communication at the advanced undergraduate and graduate levels. Students typically come to this course with some background in history, political science, international affairs, or communication theory. But the field is so controversial and important that even lay audiences now are questioning the role of communication and information in the conduct of peace and war.

Because our field is so dynamic, those of us who teach these courses are usually caught in a bind. Either we use a combination of two or three incomplete and expensive books, or we laboriously produce photocopied anthologies and periodical readings, or we use no textbook at all. The problem with all of these approaches is that they lack an integrated approach to substance and theory. There are some good edited anthologies, ones that could be used as supplemental reading in this course, but my book is currently the only integrated textbook in the burgeoning field of global communication.

Approach

In this textbook I try to be theoretical, historical, and policy oriented. My goal has been to produce a comprehensive, research-oriented, academically rigorous treatment of communication that will not go quickly out of date. I have tried to touch all the bases while at the same time giving the student many references for further study.

My text employs three approaches, two procedural and one normative. First, the book takes a comprehensive approach that attempts to include all the subject matter that a properly prepared student of global information relations should have for his or her examinations or career. From history to technologies, from law to policy, this book tries to cover the gamut of controversies, issues, and subject matter that informs enlightened debate and inquiry in this field.

Second, this work employs a "contending theories" approach. Where there is dispute, such as in the questions of Western news hegemony in the Third World, geostationary satellite spacing, or communication and human rights, contending viewpoints and evidence are presented.

Finally, the text takes a normative approach favoring the use of global communication for peace and international understanding and opposing its use for destabilization and disinformation. This gives the student an opportunity to form his or her own opinions and to justify them using the works cited in the many footnotes.

In summary, I have tried to make this book both rigorous and applied. I hope such an integrated approach will lead more students into the field and will give college instructors an easier way of presenting such a complex and diverse subject.

Content

One of the problems with studying global communications is its diversity. We study it at the intersection of international relations, political science, communication theory, sociology, psychology, anthropology, philosophy, ethics, and electronic technology. The student must master fields as diverse as culture, national development, foreign policy and diplomacy, conflict and conflict resolution, technology, news flow, national sovereignty, ideology, political systems, regulation and policy, human and civil rights, ideological confrontation, war and peace, and propaganda and influence, among other important subjects. Only a fully integrated textbook can accomplish this goal.

This is a rigorous and research-oriented treatment of the topic. In fact, the book has substantially more references than any other communication textbook I know. Now we all know that a great number of references does not necessarily result in a high-quality textbook—it simply offers some concrete evidence that this book is comprehensive in coverage and thoroughly grounded in research. You will find that the book is firmly rooted in the history of our field, that it draws on research and writing going back decades. With these thoughts in mind, let me outline some of the specifics of content coverage.

First, the study of global communication does not pretend to include *intercultural communication*, which "occurs whenever a message produced in one culture must be processed in another culture,"[1] or *cross-cultural communication*, "when institutions and individuals speak across cultural boundaries without personal interaction."[2] A firm grounding in these fields is important for anyone studying global

[1]Richard E. Porter and Larry A. Samovar, "Basic Principles of Intercultural Communication," in *Intercultural Communication: A Reader,* 6th ed., ed. Richard E. Porter and Larry A. Samovar (Belmont, CA: Wadsworth, 1991), p. 6.

[2]Alex S. Edelstein, "Steps towards Theory in Intercultural and International Communication." Paper presented at Conference on Intercultural and International Communication, Fullerton, California, March 1990.

communication, but they are well treated by other authors.[3] Nor does this book address the study of comparative mass communication systems, communication and development, or communications engineering.[4]

I have written this book with ten chapters so that it can be covered in one ten-week quarter. Spreading the assignments over a sixteen-week semester is ideal. The instructor should start with the first two chapters, but thereafter the order is not as important as is adapting the content to the needs of the student and to the events happening in the world at the time. This book works well with television excerpts, newspapers, readings, or group work on ongoing world conflicts.

Most students are already "amateur experts" in the field by virtue of watching so many thousands of hours of global television coverage. So Chapter 1, "A Preview," begins by drawing on some of the knowledge and experiences that students already have. They come to this class with an interest in global society, with concerns for population growth, the clash of cultures, and changing conceptions of community. Chapter 1 contains real-life examples and dramatic statistics to draw them into the substance of the course while anticipating the content areas of the book.

Drawing on the forgotten and unwritten history of our field, Chapter 2, "The History of Long-Distance Communication," explores how global communication evolved, beginning with biblical accounts of communication among peoples, and running through ancient times, through the Middle Ages, to our own era of the Pony Express, transatlantic cable, and the origins of the present world communication order.

Chapter 3, "A World of Communication," describes the interaction of information and communication both within and between national societies. In this chapter I give special attention to what today's "information society" means and to the growing disparities between the world's information-rich and information-poor populations. Also in this chapter, I detail the worldwide "infocomm" industries, address the question of the "global village," and give examples of enormous changes occurring throughout the world. The chapter concludes with a spotlighting of the complaints of people around the world about their communication systems.

---

[3]See *International Encyclopedia of Communications*, s.v. "Intercultural Communication." Some of the excellent texts include: Molefi K. Asante, E. Newmark, and C. A. Blake, eds. *Handbook of Intercultural Communication* (Beverly Hills: Sage, 1979); R. W. Brislin, K. Cushner, C. Cherrie, and M. Yong, *Intercultural Interactions: A Practical Guide* (Beverly Hills: Sage, 1986); Fred L. Casmir, ed., *Intercultural and International Communication* (Washington, DC, 1978); Pierre Casse, *Training for the Cross-Cultural Mind* (Washington, DC: Social Intercultural Educational Training and Resources, 1981); Edward T. Hall, *Beyond Culture* (Garden City, NY: Doubleday, 1976); Dan Landis and R. W. Brislin, *Handbook of Intercultural Training* (Elmsford, NY: Pergamon, 1983); and Larry A. Samovar and Richard E. Porter, *Intercultural Communication: A Reader*, 6th ed. (Belmont, CA: Wadsworth, 1991).

[4]See *International Encyclopedia of Communications*, s.v. "Development Communication" and "Communication and Development"; and Special Issue of *Communication Research Trends* 9 (3, 1988/89). Some important texts include: Robert Hornik, *Development Communication: Information, Agriculture, and Nutrition in the Third World* (New York, 1987); Daniel Lerner, *The Passing of Traditional Society: Modernizing the Middle East* (Princeton: Free Press, 1958); David McClelland, *The Achieving Society* (Princeton: Free Press, 1961; Hamid Mowlana and Laurie J. Wilson, *The Passing of Modernity: Communication and the Transformation of Society* (New York: Longman, 1990); Lucian W. Pye, ed., *Communications and Political Development* (Princeton: Princeton University Press, 1963); Everett M. Rogers, *Modernization among Peasants* (New York, 1968); Everett M. Rogers, *Diffusion of Innovations* (Princeton: Free Press, 1962); and Walt W. Rostow, *The Stages of Economic Growth: A Non-Communist Manifesto* (Cambridge: Cambridge University Press, 1960).

Chapter 4 outlines "The Channels of Global Communication." It provides a description of various channels of global communication. Of course, it includes descriptions of the technologies, using appropriate maps, graphs, or illustrations. But unlike many books that limit their descriptions to "hardware," my book goes on with a description of the "software" of global communications, especially language, emigration, transportation, and interpersonal channels. Most significantly, I give the student an overview of the diverse organizational actors in the fields of global communication and information.

Chapter 5, "The Dimensions of Global Communication," gives the student a menu of those issues that make our field so important and controversial today. These include national sovereignty, transnationalization, deregulation and privatization, the free flow of information, news values, media imperialism, communication policies, trade in services, protection and licensing of journalists, and codes of ethics. The issues are presented provocatively so that the student might be more willing to stake out his or her own position.

Chapter 6, "Communication, Information, and 'New World Orders,'" takes the student into that emotion-charged arena of the global information debates. In this chapter, the role of the United Nations and the Non-Aligned Movement, the rise of the New International Economic Order, and the New World International Information and Communication Order are examined. The chapter's focus is primarily on the activities of UNESCO and the role of the United States in global information relations.

No comprehensive survey of global communication is complete without a firm grounding in "Contending Theories of Global Communication," the seventh chapter. Here I describe the various theories that inform global information relations, beginning with social–psychological theories and ranging all the way up to relevant macro-level theories. In some ways this is the hardest chapter in the book because it forces the student to think theoretically, to distinguish between "good" and "bad" theories, and to differentiate those theories that take a comprehensive approach from those that only explain a small portion of the variation in the real world.

Chapter 8, "Communication in War and Peace," is the centerpiece of this book. The student has the most grist for the learning mill here, applying whatever conflicts might be happening at the time of instruction to the concepts and models presented. I examine how channels of global communication have been used throughout history to exacerbate international tensions. I also outline a spectrum of "communication in foreign affairs" that ranges from peaceful relations between societies, through contentious international relations, to high intensity conflict and the role of the military in communication. It is here that the student comes to grips with the language of conflict, the role of diplomacy, the influence of public opinion, and the impact of the mass media on international relations.

Chapter 9, "Global Communication and Information Law," challenges the student to come to terms with world-order values, such as human rights, sovereignty, and security, as they relate to global communication. For most students, this is totally new material, so the chapter begins with an outline of the fundamental principles of international law in general and a survey of those major international regulatory instruments that deal with communication.

The last chapter, entitled "Global Communication as We Enter the Twenty-First Century," gives me a chance to challenge the student to consider emerging social, political, and economic concepts that will pervade global information relations for years to come. Especially important here is the growth of world public opinion and of global civil society.

Acknowledgments

This book has been an enormous undertaking, one that has taken more than four years of effort and a decade of thought and research. To begin with, I'd like to thank the hundreds of students I have taught for inspiring me to be a better teacher and to put what I have to offer in a more usable format. My students have been a continuing inspiration.

Major portions of this work were completed during two academic research exchanges. I would like to thank the International Research and Exchanges Board (IREX) for funding me to conduct research on the international law of communication in the German Democratic Republic during 1986. My colleagues' respect for and knowledge of international law contributed invaluably to my work. I am especially grateful to my *Betreuer* Wolfgang Kleinwächter, who helped me to see the difference between opportunism and idealism under socialism.

I also want to thank the J. William Fulbright Foreign Scholarship Board for the opportunity to teach this subject and carry out research at the University of Salzburg, Austria, during the fall and winter of 1989–1990. My colleagues in Salzburg, particularly Kurt Luger, Josef Trappel, Benno Signitzer, Hans-Heinz Fabris, and Ursula Maier-Rabler, were so supportive during my long absence from home. I wrote most of this book from my office overlooking the Papageno-Platz. From my Salzburg vantage point I was able to participate in the dramatic events in Prague, Berlin, and Leipzig.

I also want to express my gratitude to two Iranians who have sustained me mightily throughout my academic life. They are Hamid Mowlana, whom I consider mentor, and Abbas Malek, with whom I sweated through my doctoral work. These two colleagues helped me look at global information relations from a fresh vantage point. I will never forget their insistence that I forget about "Marxism and other Western fallacies" and look for authentic development models rooted in peoples' real experience.

One organization deserves special thanks. I first attended the biennial meetings of the International Association for Mass Communication Research (IAMCR) as a graduate student. From that day forward, IAMCR has given me a supportive environment in which to develop myself as a communication researcher. Because it is the only truly worldwide communication research association, I have met colleagues from Albania to Zimbabwe. For their invaluable advice and support, I am especially indebted to Peggy Gray, James Halloran, George Gerbner, Cees Hamelink, Olof and Charly Hultén, Vaclav Slavík, Karol Jakubowicz, Jose Marques de Melo, Kaarle Nordenstreng, Rafael Roncagliolo, Michael Traber, and Robert White.

I want to express my thankful appreciation to the following friends who have sustained me throughout the trials and tribulations of a turbulent professional career: Caren Deming, William Wente, Rose Goldsen, Fred Jandt, Josep Rota, Vibert Cambridge, Peter Bruck, Anne Cooper-Chen, Arnaldo Coro, Peter Franck, Enrique Gonzalez Manet, Ralph Izard, John Lent, Gerald Sussman, Vincent Mosco, Janet

Wasko, Omar Oliveira, Colleen Roach, Churchill Roberts, Kusum Singh, Dallas Smythe, Jake Soderlund, Joseph Straubhaar, Elizabeth Thoman, and Peter Waterman.

The quality of a textbook depends greatly on the quality of the pre-publication reviews by professors around the country. The following persons greatly enhanced the development of this book through their thoughtful and constructive reviews: Douglas Boyd, University of Kentucky; Randall Clemons, Mercyhurst College; Paul B. Davis, Truckee Meadows Community College; Edward Kolodziej, University of Illinois; Hamid Mowlana, The American University; William Meyer, University of Delaware; Churchill Roberts, University of West Florida; and Gerald Sussman, Emerson College.

And finally, my heartiest thanks to the outstanding people at Brooks/Cole: Cynthia C. Stormer, Cathleen S. Collins, E. Kelley Shoemaker, Lisa Torri, Mary Kay Hancharick, Larry Molmud, Carline Haga, Kirk Bomont, and Kay Mikel.

Howard Frederick

Contents

1

A PREVIEW   1

2

THE HISTORY OF LONG-DISTANCE COMMUNICATION   15

3

A WORLD OF COMMUNICATION   47

4

CHANNELS OF GLOBAL COMMUNICATION   85

5

THE DIMENSIONS OF GLOBAL COMMUNICATION   119

6

COMMUNICATION, INFORMATION, AND "NEW WORLD ORDERS" 158

7

CONTENDING THEORIES OF GLOBAL COMMUNICATION 187

8
COMMUNICATION IN WAR AND PEACE   219

9
GLOBAL COMMUNICATION AND INFORMATION LAW   244

10
GLOBAL COMMUNICATION
AS WE ENTER THE TWENTY-FIRST CENTURY   267

1

A Preview

INFORMATION IS THE OXYGEN OF THE MODERN AGE. BREEZES OF ELECTRONIC BEAMS FLOW THROUGH THE IRON CURTAIN AS IF IT WERE LACE. TRYING TO CONTROL THE FLOW OF INFORMATION IS A HOPELESS, DESPERATE CAUSE. THE GOLIATH OF TOTALITARIAN CONTROL WILL RAPIDLY BE BROUGHT DOWN BY THE DAVID OF THE MICROCHIP.

Ronald Reagan to the English Speaking Union, 1989[1]

HE'S BEEN IN HIS STUDY A LOT WATCHING CNN. WELL, CNN IS DOING ALL THESE INTERVIEWS WITH MIDDLE EAST EXPERTS. SOME IDEA MIGHT POP UP THAT THE PRESIDENT COULD USE.

Aide to President Bush during a crisis in Lebanon[2]

SEEN AND HEARD AROUND THE WORLD

The phone rings early at the Swiss stockbroker's office in Zurich. On the line is a client from Hong Kong, nearing the close of his business day, who wants to buy foreign currencies on the Swiss market. The broker takes the order, hangs up, and calls another office by computer. Within a minute he transfers funds from one bank to another. He completes the transaction and sends a verification by electronic mail to Hong Kong.

A sophisticated remote-sensing satellite scans a seemingly desolate country 800 kilometers below. It takes detailed pictures, stores them on board, and then transmits them into waiting antennas in South Dakota. An analyst from a transnational corporation buys those images and discovers what seem to be valuable mineral deposits in the middle of that vast land. He notifies his business colleagues, who dispatch their agent to buy exploration rights to the land.

Fire breaks out in an apartment in Malmö, Sweden, and a worried Swede dials the emergency fire department number. Before dispatching his crew, the dispatcher types a few commands into his computer, connecting by satellite to a computer in

Cleveland, Ohio. Using data stored in the United States, within seconds he prints out street maps and other important information to help the fire fighters.[3]

In Moscow, the television camera zooms in on an army veteran of the Afghanistan war. On a wide screen a few meters away, he sees the image of an American veteran of the Vietnam war. Using simultaneous translators, the two men exchange war stories and share their hopes for a new world free from foreign interventions.

A staff person at PeaceNet Sweden (PNS) is sitting at a computer terminal when an urgent message flashes across her screen: Soviet tanks are heading toward Leningrad. The frightening news about the Soviet coup came from reporters at the Northwest News Service, a small agency in what is now called St. Petersburg. Unable to reach the West through Moscow because of clogged international phone lines, the Russian reporters filed their stories over local lines to a computer bulletin board system in Estonia that had a computer link with PeaceNet Sweden. PNS quickly forwarded those dispatches to GreenNet, its London-based partner, and to computer networks around the world.

These are not images from the future. They are examples of how global communication technologies are being used today throughout the world.

A WORLD OF COMPULSIVE COMMUNICATORS: BIOSPHERE AND SOCIOSPHERE

The green-blue orb we call "Earth" is a spherical body 12,700 kilometers in diameter and 40,000 kilometers in circumference. The Earth has a solid, rocky crust, and its atmosphere, made up mainly of nitrogen and oxygen, is barely one hundred kilometers thick. Its near-circular orbit keeps it within 150 million kilometers of the Sun. Our Earth is dynamically active, with plates of solid rock moving about, colliding, and causing earthquakes and volcanic eruptions.

The Earth's *biosphere*, extending only eight to ten kilometers into the atmosphere and into the soil, is made up of exposed continents, ocean basins, water, and atmosphere, all capable of supporting and sustaining life. The biosphere has been a stable system and, until the "greenhouse effect" and the "ozone crisis," has been balanced for millions of years. The atmosphere trails off to almost nothing within 150 kilometers of the ground, which means that most people are closer to space than they are to their national capitals! On a planetary scale, this thin biosphere is not unlike the fuzz clinging to the surface of a peach.

About two million years ago, the species called *Homo sapiens* emerged. In the New Stone Age less than ten thousand years ago, there were already ten million of us. We were ingenious users of tools living a cooperative life that favored the evolution of technology and the development of social institutions. For millennia no changes occurred. Then suddenly, four thousand years ago, our numbers began to increase. Two thousand years ago, we reached 250 million. A thousand years ago, we began to overrun our Earth. Figure 1-1 is a "cosmic calendar" in which we can see history depicted as though life on Earth were only one year long.

Why has this extraordinary growth happened? It was not due to any special human physical features or planetary changes.

The difference between the life of a skin-clad hunter leaving a cave with a spear over his shoulder to hunt mammoth, and a smartly dressed executive driving along a motorway in New York, London or Tokyo, to consult his computer print-out, is not due to any further physical development of body or brain during the long period that separates them, but to a completely new evolutionary factor.[4]

That factor is *communication*. Through communication, humans transmit their successes and failures, insights and mistakes, commonplace facts or extraordinary strokes of genius to each other and, most importantly, to future generations. We spend one-third of our waking life consuming mass media. A large part of the remaining two-thirds of our lives is spent in interpersonal communication with other people.

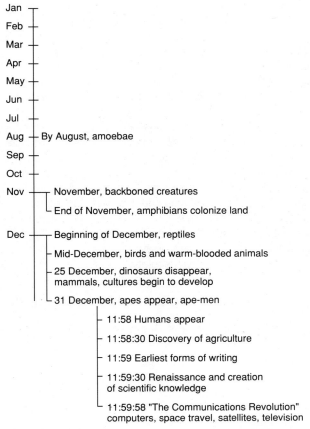

FIGURE 1-1   Cosmic Calendar. If human history were only one month long, the "Communications Revolution" occurred just before midnight on the last day of the month.

SOURCE: Adapted from David Attenborough, "Life on Earth," Episode 10, "The Compulsive Communicators"; and Joseph Pelton, "The Technological Environment," *Toward a Law of Global Communication Networks,* by the American Bar Association, ed. Anne W. Branscomb, p. 47. Copyright © 1986 by Longman Publishing Group. Reprinted with permission from Longman Publishing Group.

No other beings on earth are so communicative and in such need of informing others and being informed.

This compulsion to communicate has made it possible for us to speak of a *sociosphere*. Like the biosphere with its moving plates and colliding continents, Earth's sociosphere is dynamically active, with ideas moving about, crashing into one another, and causing social earthquakes and revolutionary eruptions. It is difficult to underestimate how important communication has been in the evolution of our species and in the progress we will make in the future.

If we could see the flow of news and information around the world from some comfortable perch in space, it would look much like the human circulatory system—a multilayered organism connected by a continuous flow throughout the system. The veins are filled with indistinguishable bits and bytes of data. We see arterial satellite links and undersea cables that span the continents. Filling these arteries daily are hundreds of hours of television programs, millions of individual phone calls, trillions of bits of data. Silver-winged, cigar-shaped projectiles ferry countless people across vast expanses of water and land. Small paper objects with colored marks in their upper right corners traverse difficult journeys across mountains and seas from sender to receiver. Most remarkable of all, virtually none of this existed only a few generations ago.[5]

But there is also a dark side to this story. Information technologies also threaten the life of the biosphere and sociosphere. The same technologies that brought us the image of the earth rising over the moon and instantaneous worldwide communication are propelling the current arms race. Although communication and computing technology have created a rudimentary planetary nervous system, they also control the deployment of weapons of mass destruction. Just as the optical scope increased the killing power of the rifle, new information technologies have electronically multiplied the destructive power of the means of destruction. Technology is two-sided. To use the biological metaphor again, information and communication are both the lifeblood and the viruses of modern society.

WHY STUDY GLOBAL COMMUNICATION?

Many factors—both positive and negative—point to the growing importance of global communication in the world of the twenty-first century.

World Population Explosion

There are more communicating human beings on this planet than ever before (see Figure 1-2 and Table 1-1). At the beginning of our century, there were 1.5 billion people on our planet. Now there are 5 billion people—up from 3.6 billion only sixteen years earlier. By the year 2000 there will be over 6 billion people on earth; by 2025, 8.5 billion. Demographers estimate that the world population is expected to double by the middle of the 21st century, from 5.3 billion to 11.6 billion people, and to stabilize ultimately shortly after the year 2200. The world's future population growth will be dramatically concentrated in today's less developed regions, according to the report. Africa has been and will continue to be the fastest growing area, with its

TABLE 1-1
Fifteen Most Populous Countries
(1988 Estimates)

Country	Population
China, People's Republic	1,103,980,000
India	796,600,000
Soviet Union (1988 boundaries)	344,580,000
United States	246,330,000
Indonesia	174,950,000
Brazil	144,430,000
Japan	122,610,000
Pakistan	105,410,000
Nigeria	104,960,000
Bangladesh	104,530,000
Mexico	82,730,000
Germany (united)	77,800,000
Vietnam	64,230,000
Italy	57,440,000
United Kingdom	57,080,000
World total	5,076,000,000
Developed countries	1,210,000,000
Developing countries	3,867,000,000

SOURCE: *UNESCO Statistical Yearbook 1990* (Paris: UNESCO, 1990), pp. 1–5 to 1–8.

TABLE 1-2
World's Largest Population
Agglomerations, 1990 and 2000
(millions)

	1990	2000
Tokyo/Yokohama	26.9	29.9
Mexico City	20.2	27.9
Sao Paulo	18.9	25.3
Seoul	16.2	22.0
Bombay	11.8	15.4
New York	14.6	14.6
Osaka–Kobe	13.8	14.3
Rio de Janeiro	11.4	14.2
Calcutta	11.7	14.1
Greater Buenos Aires	11.5	12.9
Moscow	10.4	11.1
Los Angeles	10.0	10.7

SOURCE: *The World Almanac* (New York: World Almanac, 1990), p. 774.

population stabilizing, according to the medium-fertility extension, at 3.2 billion people, nearly five times its 1990 size (see Table 1-2). The sheer size of this population explosion increases the volume of communication between and among people and cultures.

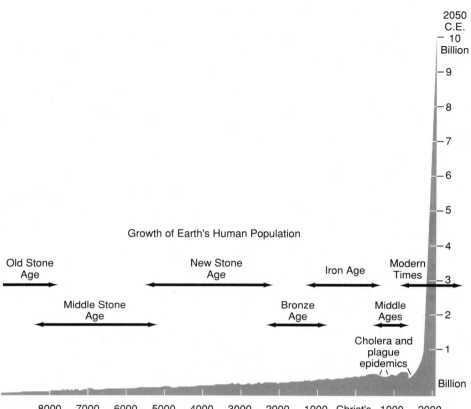

FIGURE 1-2 World Population Explosion. There are more communicating human beings on this planet now than ever before.

Geopolitics Now Gaiapolitics

World War II finally ended in 1990. The four victorious powers and the two German states negotiated a war settlement forty-five years after the end of hostilities. Coupled with the global environmental crises, this dramatic historical development is causing a "paradigm shift" in how we see our world. Geopolitics is giving way to *gaiapolitics,* a worldwide political movement on behalf of the biosphere we call Earth.

Where geopolitics may have forestalled atomic war, it is the task of gaiapolitics to stop impending ecological disaster. Since 1850, more than a third of the world's forests have disappeared. Since the turn of the century, one-sixth to one-third of the planet's plant and animal species have disappeared. Burning of fossil fuels has increased thirty times. Production of carbon dioxide and fluorocarbons is changing our atmosphere, and the greenhouse effect is affecting our climate with a rise in temperature and sea level.

Today's global problems are substantially different from any that the world has faced before. They are shaped by increasing ecological and economic interdependence spawned by a century of tremendous technological change. Proliferation of nuclear weapons, imbalanced use of resources leading to hunger and poverty, the destruction of the ozone layer: These and many other problems are so immense and have such geographically dispersed effects that they prohibit effective solutions on a local or even national scale. As a result, global cooperation and communication are essential in order to identify and forge solutions to these problems. Communication is intrinsic to global cooperative efforts, and communication technologies available today can greatly speed and enhance these efforts.

Increased Cross-Cultural Communication

Coupled with the vast population increase, people today have much more contact than ever before with the diverse cultures of the world. For thousands of years, people lived within the confines of the village. The only contact people had with foreigners was through traveling caravans or perhaps a once-in-a-lifetime pilgrimage to a shrine. Only seventy-five years ago global communication was limited to the personal and diplomatic contacts between national elites.[6] Today people travel to the furthest corners of the globe and encounter strikingly different cultural values and assumptions. We now even speak of bicultural or multicultural individuals, people who live simultaneously in different cultural milieus. As an example, a Japanese business executive from a traditional family may work at an auto assembly plant in Tennessee.

Changing Conception of Community

What we call "community" used to be limited to face-to-face dialogue among people in the same physical space, a dialogue that reflected mutual concerns and a common culture. Today, neither community nor dialogue is restricted to a geographical place. Modern media have expanded our sense of place by reallocating space and time. In the past, personal relationships relied on meeting at a cafe, signing a contract together, shaking hands, or interacting in the village square. With the advent of the fax machine, telephones, international publications, and computers, personal and professional relationships can be maintained irrespective of time and place. Today we are all members of international "non-place" communities.

> Communication relationships are no longer restricted to place, but are distributed through space.[7]

In the past few decades, we can point to the emergence of a *world public opinion*. Throughout the world there is a vast population of globally concerned citizens who daily follow events in the news and act locally while thinking globally. These citizens are concerned about such diverse global issues as disarmament and Middle East peace, the greenhouse effect, the Olympic games, and movements for democracy around the world. Increasingly global media sources arise to satisfy their needs for accurate and speedy news.

Today we can even speak of *global civil society,* that part of our lives that is neither market nor government but that is inundated by them. Before border-crossing technologies became widespread, the globe's diverse civil societies had difficulty uniting into broader alliances. Today new technologies foster communication among the widest variety of the planet's nongovernmental and not-for-profit organizations in the fields of human rights, consumer protection, peace, gender equality, racial justice, and environmental protection, not to mention the church and other voluntary organizations. This significant development in the history of human communication can profoundly affect the course of international affairs. I shall discuss this further in the final chapter.

Greater Centralization of Control

Partially as a result of the growing communication among and between people around the world, another, more ominous, development is taking place. A handful of immense corporations dominate the world's mass media. If present trends continue, by the turn of the century

> five to ten corporate giants will control most of the world's important newspapers, magazines, books, broadcast stations, movies, recordings and videocassettes.[8]

These "lords of the global village" exert a homogenizing influence over ideas, culture, and commerce. As Bagdikian writes, true freedom of information requires three conditions: the opportunity to read and watch whatever is available, a diversity of sources to choose from, and media systems that provide access for those citizens who wish to reach others.[9] For the most part, democratic countries provide the first condition, but the increasing concentration of media ownership and control are threatening the second two.

Information Explosion

The sheer quantity of information grows in leaps and bounds. We speak of our era as the Information Age. About half of all workers in the United States today are in some way involved in information processing. Information is expanding at an exponential rate.

If we take all the information available in the year 1 C.E. as one unit, it took 1,500 years for the amount of information to double in size by the dawn of the scientific revolution. It took another 250 years for the store of data to double once more. At the turn of our century, information had once again doubled. The next doubling took in only fifty years (see Figure 1–3). Then the curve steepened. The 1950s saw a spectacular doubling of knowledge in ten years. Doubling occurred again by 1967 and, in only six years, by 1973.[10]

This rapid pace continues unabated. Current estimates of the rate at which world knowledge doubles range from eighteen months to five years![11] (Figure 1–3 shows the most conservative estimates.) In other words, between the time a science or engineering student enters and graduates from a university, the core knowledge doubles in size. At the five-year rate, in less than seventy years we should know a million times more than we do today!

As information grows, many problems occur. People do not receive the right

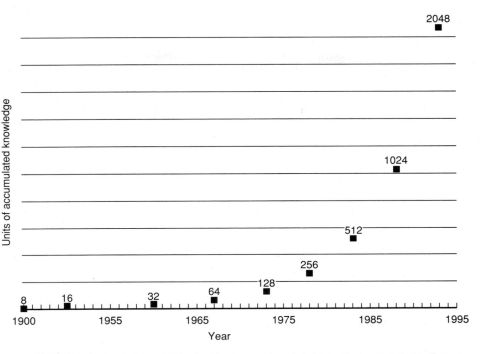

FIGURE 1-3 Accumulated Knowledge (assuming one unit in the year 1 C.E.). The quantity of information produced over human history is doubling at an exponentially accelerating rate.

information at the right time. They may not be aware the information exists or may not know where to look for it. Vital information may well be buried in a mass of extraneous information. Access to information does not necessarily lead to knowledge, let alone wisdom.

Changes in Technology

In the digital age, there is no longer a technological distinction between voice, text, data, and video services. The arrival of satellites has meant that the cost of services is no longer related to distance or terrain. New technologies such as fiber optics have virtually eliminated traditional technical limitations in the provision of services. With the globalization of networks, there is no longer a clear demarcation between many national and international networks. The speed and capacity of communications technologies has outpaced our wildest expectations. From the telegraph wire of the 1840s to the fiber-optic cable today, our ability to send and receive messages across the distances of land and space has increased astonishingly.[12] Fortunately, transmission capacity has exceeded service demand. We do not yet know what new types of communications technology will be developed, but given the tremendous growth rate of the information and communication sector—30 to 50 percent yearly—we can be certain of one thing: Growth will continue exponentially, shrinking distance, collaps-ing time, and lowering costs.

Yet the communications revolution has not benefited all of humankind equally. There are enormous and ever-growing disparities between those who have informa-tion and those who lack information. These differences exist within countries and between genders. They exist between cities and the countryside. They exist between the rich countries and the poor countries. In fact, information abundance is a reality only for an exclusive club of nations and elites within those nations.

Greater Dependence on Global Communication

Throughout the world on any given day about 600 million newspapers are produced. Eighty thousand broadcasting stations transmit programming to 1 billion viewers and to 2 billion listeners, and more than 100 news agencies produce more than 40 million words. Over 700 million telephones transmit voice, data, and pictures through more than one hundred communications satellites and through hundreds of thousands of miles of cable. Every day, several million computers store, process, and distribute untold megabytes of information.

We depend upon global communication flows for our information about the world. The greater the distance—both physical and cultural—we are from another group, the greater we rely on others to collect and bring us information. Each person in the chain of information that connects a newspaper reader or television viewer to a world event will make judgments about what to transmit. The farther we are from an event or a culture, the greater the cumulative biases that will creep into our perceptions.[13]

The growth in global communications has led to a change in the way peoples and nations build coalitions and networks based upon their organizational affiliations and trade and communication patterns. In times past, transaction clusters formed within local and regional boundaries—for example, medieval Europe, the Arab world, China and Japan, West African kingdoms, the Caribbean slave and sugar econo-mies. But the increased speed and reliability of communication technologies has led to different affiliations today. This is particularly true in the rise of nongovernmental organizations (NGOs) as world actors. Previously isolated from one another, NGOs are flexing their muscles at the United Nations and other world forums as their power and capacity to communicate increase.

The United States Is the World's Most Communicating Nation

The United States is the largest producer, processor, storer, and exporter of infor-mation in the world. It dominates world information flows from television programs to data bases. With its technological advantages, the United States is the most advanced information society on the planet today. Not only does it dominate the world's movie and TV screens, its culture and ideology also deeply penetrate the consciousness of people around the world. The lofty ideals of democracy and free-dom, as well as the material values of consumerism and affluence, capture the global imagination. Not only does the United States communicate abundantly *to* the rest of the world, but the "brain drain" of talent *from* other countries also means that people are bringing valuable information and skills to the United States.

Greater Interdependence and Democracy

Nearly every issue in this book involves the growing interdependence of nations and peoples. There is no longer such a marked distinction between domestic and international issues. National governments can no longer shield their populations from events happening throughout the world. Economies have been inextricably intertwined. Military alliances are entangling and permanent. Private individuals have become "citizen diplomats" in a world that grows smaller all the time. Today's developments challenge the prevailing assumptions of the past. Nation–states are no longer the only actors on the world stage. Nonstate actors, such as transnational corporations, nongovernmental organizations, lobbying bodies, liberation organizations, and even private individuals, all have important roles to play.

We are moving into a "new world order." The age of democracy may have had its beginnings in the French and the American revolutions, but only today is it finally reaching the hearts and minds of sympathetic populations around the world. This "preferred" world order of democratic change depends heavily on the efficiency of communication systems. Communication media do not merely report violations and victories of human rights; there is also a growing realization that *communication and information are central to human rights.*

Impact of Communication on Peace and War

For centuries, channels of communication have played instrumental roles in exacerbating tensions. Today the media of mass communication face the challenges of how to bring about peace, build confidence among nations, and strengthen international understanding. Accelerated by the rapid advances in electronic technologies in the last twenty years, international information relations have become central to international relations in general. More than fifty thousand nuclear warheads sit idly waiting to destroy the planet. Virtually all of them are in the possession of the United States and the Commonwealth of Independent States (primarily Russia, Ukraine, and Kazakhstan). Many of these warheads are capable of unleashing ten to twenty times the destructive power dropped on Hiroshima in 1945. Nuclear weapons tests continue in the dozens per year. Launch-on-warning missiles can reach their destinations in less than ten minutes. In 1984, some 256 serious launch-on-warning errors occurred. At the same time, more than seven thousand peace groups in the United States were working for a world free from the fear of nuclear devastation.[14] Both the war machines and the peace movements rely on communication.

WHAT IS GLOBAL COMMUNICATION?

The field of global communication is that intersection of disciplines that studies the transborder communication of values, attitudes, opinions, information, and data by individuals, groups, people, institutions, governments, and information technologies, as well as the resulting controversial issues arising from the structure of institutions responsible for promoting or inhibiting such messages among and between nations and cultures.

The preceding definition includes a broad category of communication transactions. Smith and Smith captured this sense in 1956 when they defined "international communication" as including

> the negotiations conducted by diplomats; the activities abroad by tourists and other agencies; the creation of impressions abroad by tourists and other migrants; the probably massive but generally unplanned impact of books, art works, and movies distributed in foreign countries; the international contacts of students, educators, scientists, and technical assistance experts; the negotiations and correspondence of international business interests; the activities of international missionaries and religious movements; the work of international pressure groups, such as trade unions, chambers of commerce, and political parties; international philanthropic activities . . .; the "propaganda of the deed" implicit even in the *un*publicized activities of leaders and collectivities, as perceived by various audiences and a great many other processes by which information and persuasion are consciously or unconsciously disseminated across national and cultural boundaries.[15]

The academic study of global communication has not enjoyed a firm disciplinary home. As a result, we often call global communication research and theory an *interdiscipline* because it lies at the intersection of so many diverse fields. Scholars from a wide variety of academic disciplines have contributed greatly to the study of global communication.[16]

Global communication emerged as a a field of study when it became possible to distinguish a body of knowledge and a corps of people to think about it. Just as we say that international law as a field of study did not exist before the nation–state system emerged after the Congress of Vienna, so we point to the emergence of global communication technologies in the nineteenth century as the origin of the field of global communication.

For years a small number of prescient authors saw the growing impact of communication on international politics. One of the earliest influential works was *Propaganda Technique In the World War,* published in 1927.[17] The study of global communication increased dramatically after World War II due to military considerations coupled with their economic and political implications.[18] Many of the important early contributions came from political science and international relations under the labels of "international political communication," "international persuasion," and "international integration."[19]

Like all social sciences, global communication as a field of study is influenced by contemporary history. More global communication research was written in the decade from 1945 to 1955 than in the previous thirty years.[20] Most of the research of the 1950s dealt with propaganda and the Cold War. By 1970, global-communication research had doubled again and had grown to include a great variety of subjects, especially comparative mass communication systems, communication and national development, and propaganda and public opinion.[21] Today, international communication research has emerged as one of the most active fields of communication research in general.

NOTES

1. President Ronald Reagan's Churchill Lecture to the English Speaking Union, Guildhall, London, June 13, 1989.

2. Maureen Dowd, "When a Crisis Hits, Bush Watches CNN," *San Francisco Chronicle,* August 11, 1989, p. A14.

3. John Eger, "The Global Phenomenon of Teleinformatics: An Introduction," *Cornell International Law Journal* 203 (1982): 210–217.

4. David Attenborough, *Life on Earth: A Natural History* (Boston: Little, Brown, 1979), p. 302.

5. For inspiring this biological analogy, thanks to Robert L. Stevenson and Steven Marjanovic, "A Look at Alternative News Sources" (Paper presented at the Biennial Conference of the International Association for Mass Communication Research, Prague, 1984).

6. Harold Nicolson, *Diplomacy,* 3rd ed. (London: Oxford University Press, 1963), cited in Davis B. Bobrow, "Transfer of Meaning across National Boundaries," *Communication in International Politics,* ed. Richard L. Merritt (Urbana: University of Illinois Press, 1972), p. 36.

7. Robert Cathcart and Gary Gumpert, "Media Communities/Media Cultures" (Paper presented at Conference on International and Intercultural Communication, Fullerton, California, March 1990).

8. Ben Bagdikian, "The Lords of the Global Village," *The Nation,* June 12, 1989, p. 805.

9. Ibid., p. 812.

10. See George Anderla, *Information in 1985* (Paris: Organization for Economic Cooperation and Development, 1973) and Alvin Silverstein, *Conquest of Death* (New York: Macmillan, 1979), p. 136. Another estimate by James Martin estimated that by 1800 information was doubling every fifty years; by 1950, every ten years; by 1970, every five years; by 2000, every three years. See James Martin, *Telecommunications and the Computer* (New York: Prentice-Hall, 1989), p. 12.

11. See also Robert Anton Wilson, "The Year of Fractal Chaos," *Magical Blend,* April 1990, p. 45–46. Wilson says futurist Jacques Vallee estimated that the amount of information today doubles every eighteen months.

12. The rate that data can be sent over the telephone lines has increased from 600 bits per second in the 1930s to today's fiber-optic standard of millions of bits per second. Soon telecommunications cables will probably transmit several trillion bits per second. See Martin, *Telecommunications and the Computer,* pp. 8–9.

13. Susan Welch, "The American Press and Indochina, 1950–56," in *Communication in International Politics,* p. 228.

14. A. J. S. Rayl, "The Peacemakers," *Omni Magazine,* January 1988, p. 66.

15. Bruce Lannes Smith and Chitra M. Smith, *International Communication and Political Opinion* (Princeton, NJ: Princeton University Press, 1956), p. 6.

16. In a survey of international communication scholars, twenty-five different specialties were indicated by the respondents. Ramona R. Rush and K. E. M. Kent, "Information Resource Use of International Communication Scholars," *Journalism Educator* 35 (April 1977): 50–52.

17. Harold D. Lasswell, *Propaganda Technique In the World War* (London: Kegan Paul, Trench, Trubner & Co., 1927), reprinted as *Propaganda Technique in World War I* (Cambridge, MA: MIT Press, 1971).

18. Bruce Lannes Smith, "Trends in Research on International Communication and Opinion, 1945–55," *Public Opinion Quarterly* 20 (1, Spring 1956): 182–195.

19. Kenneth Boulding, *The Image* (Ann Arbor, MI: University of Michigan Press, 1965); Bernard C. Cohen, *The Press and Foreign Policy* (Princeton, NJ: Princeton University Press, 1963); Karl W. Deutsch, *Nationalism and Social Communication: An Inquiry into the Foundations of Nationality* (Cambridge, MA: MIT Press, 1968); Karl W. Deutsch et al., *Political Community and the North Atlantic Area* (Princeton, NJ: Princeton University Press, 1957) and *International Political Communities: An Anthology* (New York: Anchor Books, 1966); Arthur Hoffman, ed., *International Communication and the New Diplomacy* (Bloomington, IN: Indiana University Press, 1968); Her-

bert Kelman, ed., *International Behavior* (New York: Holt, Rinehart and Winston, 1965); Richard L. Merritt, ed., *Communication in International Politics* (Urbana, IL: University of Illinois Press, 1972); Ithiel de Sola Pool, *Symbols of Internationalism* (Stanford, CA: Stanford University Press, 1951); James Rosenau, *Public Opinion and Foreign Policy* (New York: Random House, 1961); Ralph K. White, *Nobody Wanted War* (Garden City, NY: Doubleday, 1968).

20. Bruce Lannes Smith, "Trends in Research," pp. 182–195.

21. Hamid Mowlana, *International Communication: A Selected Bibliography* (Dubuque, IA: Kendall/ Hunt, 1971); and Hamid Mowlana, "Trends in Research on International Communication: 1950– 1970" (Paper presented at International Association for Mass Communication Research, Buenos Aires, September 1972). Some of the early important works included: W. Phillips Davison, *International Political Communication* (New York: Praeger, 1965); Wilbur Schramm, *Mass Media and National Development* (Stanford, CA: Stanford University Press, 1964); Heinz Dietrich Fischer and John C. Merrill, eds., *International Communication: Media, Channels, Functions* (New York: Hastings House, 1970); James W. Markham, *Voice of the Red Giants: Communications in Russia and China* (Ames, IA: Iowa State University Press, 1967); Frederick T. C. Yu, *Mass Persuasion in Communist China* (New York: Praeger, 1964); Walter B. Emery, *National and International Systems of Broadcasting* (East Lansing, MI: Michigan State University Press, 1969); and Leonard W. Doob, *Communication in Africa* (New Haven, CT: Yale University Press, 1961).

2

The History of Long-Distance Communication

In "Tower of Babel," Flemish painter Pieter Brueghel (BROY-gel) portrays the famous biblical legend of why there are so many different languages in the world. The story goes that King Nimrod presumptuously set out to build a tower high enough to reach heaven. His architects designed a brilliant structure that reached through the clouds, and laborers worked slavishly to fulfill the king's command. But when God observed this prideful and arrogant effort, he caused the people to speak in many tongues. Suddenly bricklayers could not give orders to workers. The king's overseers could not get anyone to obey their orders. The entire work force fragmented into warring groups of "foreigners." The tower itself became hopelessly bungled, and soon the whole immense project came to a halt.

"TEMPUS CENTRISM"

We often suffer from "tempus centrism," that particular human affliction that makes us think that it is in our time—*our* history—that the world is changing most rapidly.[1] The antidote to this is the *millennium perspective*—to look at the development of global communication and information over the centuries. Brueghel's painting reminds us that today's communication system—truly the largest machine on earth—is the result of generations of evolution. Yet surprisingly little has been written about the history of global communication.[2]

For millennia, people lived near one another in small communities. The few large cities were small by today's standards. People's kinship and friendship circles determined the extent of their worlds. The medieval peasant's entire life was spent within a radius of no more than thirty or forty kilometers from his or her place of birth.[3] Only wars, migrations, and traveling pilgrimages brought strange faces into these isolated communities.

Even in the early part of the twentieth century, the average person still lived in the countryside, knew of the world only through travelers' tales, and had very little contact with foreigners. At the height of British imperialism, only a few Britons had set foot outside England on the empire on which "the sun never set."[4] Long-distance communication moved at an agonizingly slow speed. In the 1830s, a letter from Europe to India might take five to eight months by sailing ship around the Cape—in each direction! It took as long as two years to send a letter and receive a reply.[5]

Until only a few decades ago, the few worldwide communication channels that did exist rested in the hands of the military, the wealthy, and the governing elite. From the days of Solomon and Sheba to the reign of Queen Elizabeth I, postal service was reserved for the use of royalty and the rich. Only in the sixteenth century did the need of the emerging merchant class for a reliable communications medium drive a wedge in the royal mail monopoly.

Beginning in the mid-nineteenth century, the world's media landscape has been totally transformed. As Figure 2-1 shows, the demand and capability of new communications technologies has risen exponentially since the invention of the telegraph. The figure also illustrates how recent these developments have been. Telegraphic cables arrived on the scene in 1870; World War I saw the first experiments with international radio. The first undersea telephone cable between the United States and Europe was laid in 1956, and the first communications satellite was launched in 1962.

Yet as we saw in the last chapter, these events happened only a few seconds ago in the millennium perspective. Technology has advanced so rapidly that today's communication channels compel us to be citizens of the world. We have opinions about religion in Iran. We know what ideals drove the Chinese student movement toward democracy. We make judgments about the U.S. invasion of a small Caribbean island, about secret aid to mercenary soldiers, about nuclear arms talks, about democracy in Eastern Europe. Indeed, one of the most important effects of this technological revolution is that today many people are concerned with subjects that previously were the domain of the few.

MAPS AS INTERNATIONAL COMMUNICATION CHANNELS

For all our advanced technology, we sometimes react to world events with the narrow vision of our ancestors. Ancient stereotypes and biases take much longer to die out than the short time we have had reliable global communication channels. Nowhere are these distortions better seen than in our maps—mental and physical—of what we have conceived the world to be. Indeed, maps were some of the first channels of international communication.[6]

For centuries, our knowledge of faraway peoples and places depended on reports and maps from courageous (and sometimes foolhardy) sailors. Twenty-eight hundred years ago, the Greeks had become accomplished mariners and had colonized large portions of the eastern Mediterranean. The first book on geography showed a circular, flat Earth surrounded by water. The Romans learned geography from the Greeks and used this knowledge to reach the Red Sea, the Persian Gulf, and even northern India.[7]

Early maps reflected not only what explorers found but also what they hoped (or feared) to find.[8] The third-century Roman grammarian Gaius Julius Solinus told of horse-footed humans with ears so long the flaps covered their entire bodies, making clothing unnecessary. One-eyed savages downed mead from cups made from their

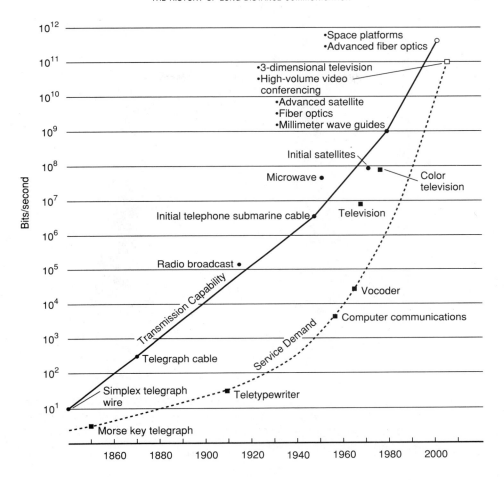

FIGURE 2-1 **The Development of Telecommunications (service demand versus transmission capability). The capacity of telecommunications technologies has risen exponentially since their invention 150 years ago, and it still exceeds demand.**

SOURCE: From *Toward a Law of Global Communications Networks*, by the American Bar Association, ed. Anne W. Branscomb, p. 39. Copyright © 1986 by Longman Publishing Group. Reprinted with permission from Longman Publishing Group.

parents' skulls. These depictions of foreigners found their way onto maps until the eighteenth century.[9]

During the thousand-year period of the Middle Ages in Europe, cartographers added little new knowledge to their visions of the world.[10] They relied heavily on mythology and the Bible and depicted the Earth as a flat disk with Jerusalem at the center. Only six hundred years ago, Portuguese seafarers still believed that south or west of Cape Bojador in Africa there were wild storms, huge reptiles and strange human creatures. Maps showed fierce griffins and people without heads, men with dogs' heads and six toes, horned pygmies, "cyclopeans" with only one eye and one foot, and Amazons with tears made of silver.[11]

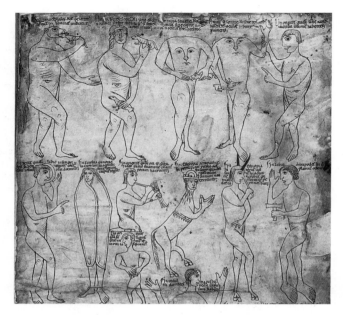

The *Arnstein Bible* (1175) depicts a twelfth-century monk's misperceptions of people living in other lands. Despite advances in communication technologies, we still have distorted perceptions of "foreigners."
SOURCE: From the "Arnstein Bible" ca. 1175. By permission of the British Library.

How do our maps compare today? Of course, our ability to map our planet has increased dramatically in the last few decades. Satellite images of our earth's surface give us a pride of place. Yet many of our "mental maps" of the world today still portray stereotyped images of "foreigners."

HOW TO OVERCOME SPACE

For most of history, the average person rarely traveled more than a few days' ride from home. The dialect spoken in one village was unintelligible fifty miles away.[12] Yet even in ancient days, knowledge and ideas traveled great distances; imperial bureaucrats administered great empires spread over thousands of kilometers of far-flung territory. How were these remarkable feats accomplished?

Among the rowdy deities who lived on Mount Olympus, the Greeks believed, there lived one god who ruled communication. His name was Hermes. (The Romans called him "Mercury;" the Incas, "Chasqui.") The result of a union between Zeus and the daughter of Atlas, Hermes was not only the symbol of inventive spirit and grace, he was also the personification of agility, cleverness, and craftiness. Hermes was always in a hurry; painters represented him with a winged cap, and jewelers minted him as the patron saint of travelers.

TRAVEL AS COMMUNICATION

Throughout history people have communicated across the globe as tourists and merchants. Figure 2-2 is a map showing intercontinental trade routes in the ancient

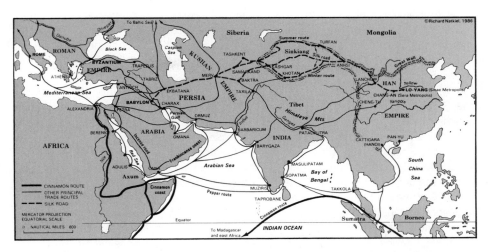

FIGURE 2-2 Intercontinental Trade Routes in the Ancient World. Despite dangers and hardships, merchants and tourists traveled vast distances in ancient times. The Silk Route and the Cinammon Route were the most important highways of their time.

SOURCE: *Atlas of Maritime History* (Greenwich, CT: Bison Books, 1986), p. 19.

world. To write his famous history of the Greco-Persian war, the Greek historian Herodotus personally visited many of the areas in Persia, and, like a cultural chauvinist of today, he reacted with shock to the strange customs of Egypt.

One reason more people did not take to the road was that travel was so arduous and dangerous. The rutted roads, always dusty or muddy, carried a flow of peddlers, bandits, merchants and traveling entertainers. In Europe, a day's journey on horseback was about fifty kilometers; with a packtrain, about fifteen kilometers.[13]

Until the mid-fifteenth century, very few Europeans succeeded in traveling beyond what is now known as the Middle East. One Venetian trader, Nicolo de Conti, penetrated all the way to Indonesia and returned to tell about it. Here is how he described Java:

> The inhabitants of these islands are more inhuman and cruel than any other nation, and they eat mice, dogs, cats and all other kinds of unclean animals. They exceed every other people in cruelty. They regard killing a man as a mere jest . . . [14]

Amerigo Vespucci, after whom America is named, described the inhabitants of the New World:

> We found the whole land inhabited by people entirely naked, the men like the women without any covering of their shame. . . . Having no laws and no religious faith, they lived according to nature. . . . When they fight they slaughter mercilessly. Those who remain on the field bury all the dead of their own side, but cut up and eat the bodies of their enemies.[15]

In 1271, in the company of his father and uncle, the great Venetian explorer Marco Polo left Italy "to carry the word of God" to Asia. Remarkably, his *Travels* was the primary source for the European image of the Far East for six hundred years.

After four years of arduous travel, Marco Polo's party reached the city of Shan-tu, the summer capital of the Mongol emperors near present-day Beijing. There they met for the first time the great Lord of Lords, Kublai Khan, whose grandfather, the fearsome Genghis Khan, had swept over the entire face of Asia, from the China Sea to the Baltic Sea.

Marco Polo and his entourage were not sure what fate lay in store for them. But the Polos had nothing to fear. The Great Khan's earlier exploits into the nether realms of Western Asia and Eastern Europe had made him familiar with Europeans and their customs. Kublai Khan saw in Christianity a civilizing influence for his people. When the Polos arrived, they were both expected and welcomed![16] Polo's account stood virtually alone as a description of the Far East until supplemented by the chronicle of the Jesuit missionary Matteo Ricci, which appeared in 1615.

Few travelers of any age have ventured so widely as Ibn Battuta, who, beginning in Mecca in 1326, wrote the most exhaustive account of the Moslem world in the later Middle Ages. For thirty years he journeyed through North Africa, the Middle East, East Africa, Central Asia, India, Southeast Asia, and possibly China. He followed the tradition of describing a pilgrimage to the holy places of Arabia. The extended nature of his journeys blurred this objective, however, and his account expanded into a depiction of the known world beyond Europe.

It was sometimes hard to distinguish between fact and reality in early stories. One of the most widespread and influential tall tales of the Middle Ages was about a legendary Christian king named Prester John whose dominion, it was believed, lay somewhere in southwest Asia or northeast Africa, just beyond the Islamic empire. Europe's leaders sought to form an anti-Moslem alliance with him. Europeans were enthralled by reports of his heroic struggles against the "infidels."

Around 1165, in a colossal case of Byzantine disinformation, some clever scribe circulated through the courts of Europe a letter allegedly written by Prester John. Prester John "reported" that his abode was one of peace and justice and was the home of "men with horns, one-eyed, men with eyes before and behind; centaurs, fauns, satyrs, pygmies, giants forty ells high, Cyclops . . . " Prester John's kingdom was included on medieval maps for several hundred years, and Pope Alexander II in the twelfth century even sent a letter to him by a messenger, who never returned.[17]

During this period the Catholic Church launched a number of military expeditions to "protect" Jerusalem from Moslems. Collectively known as the Crusades, these campaigns "can be seen in retrospect as a major chapter in the evolution of international communication."[18] The Church organized and promoted participation in the Crusades through oral and written communications throughout Europe. The Crusades expanded the volume and extended the range of trading routes in the Eastern Mediterranean. Communication with Asia was improved as missionaries were sent to the Mongol khans to persuade them to join an alliance against Islam.

Interestingly, the spread of Islam was also due in large measure to the extensive travel network of caravans and sea transportation. Scholars and intellectuals traveled all over the Moslem world seeking and bringing religious knowledge. Long-distance Moslem communication was stimulated through the *hajj*, or pilgrimage to Mecca.

Not until the eighteenth century did the leisure time available to Europe's aristoc-

The Crusades can be seen as a major chapter in the history of global communication. Here Pope Urban II arrives in France and preaches his call for a crusade at the Council of Clermont in 1095.

SOURCE: Roman de Godefroi de Bouillon, 1337. Giraudon Art Resource, New York.

racy lead to a fashion for travel among the wealthier classes. In Europe, students were encouraged to spend a year at a foreign institution. In Britain was born the idea of the "Grand Tour": an educational journey that consisted of a year or two of travel and learning in the major cities of western Europe. But it was not until the industrial revolution that long-distance tourism became attractive to more than the privileged elite.[19]

HUMAN COURIERS

For secure communication, nothing can surpass human legpower. Ancient messengers were given some mnemonic device such as a notched stick to indicate numbers of days or warriors. The ancient Incan empire, which never developed the wheel, relied on trained messengers, known as *chasquis*, who carried the *quipu*, a knotted string with complex messages. Spanish *conquistadores* reported that not only financial information and private correspondence, but even poetry were as easily expressed by *quipus* as by writing.[20]

Couriers carried the triumphant and the mundane. According to legend, in 490 B.C.E. a Greek soldier named Phidippides ran the 36.2 kilometers from the site of the Battle of Marathon to Athens, where he died after announcing the Greek victory over the Persians. The modern "marathon" commemorates this feat. We know that a "courier" was among the list of everyday professions in Mesopotamia during the

third millennium B.C.E. There is evidence that the rulers of Sumeria had regular channels through which they could communicate through the territories and transmit dispatches to particular officials and individuals.[21]

Emperor Augustus of Rome developed an elaborate courier system using
horses, carriages, and relay stations. Messengers could travel about thirty-five kilometers per day. The Romans even had an "express service." News of the revolt of
the Rhine army traveled over the Alps in winter to Rome in nine days at the incredible
rate of about 250 kilometers per day.[22]

ANCIENT POSTAL SERVICES

For a trifling charge, and with no other participation than throwing the letter in a post
box, we can be reasonably sure our message will travel to almost any other person
on the globe with speed, certainty, and security. Under the Universal Postal Union,
the world has been united as a single postal territory.

About 3800 B.C.E., King Sargon of Babylon established the world's first postal
service under the command of a postmaster general named Urduk, who trained the
mail carriers. Urduk gave maps to his couriers showing every road and footpath
between the Tigris and Euphrates Rivers to guide the couriers in their delivery of clay
tablets. If the runners were attacked by robbers, they would release pigeons with an
emergency message to send out a rescue party.[23]

Under Cyrus the Great in the sixth century B.C.E. the Persians inaugurated a
postal service that still ranks as a major achievement. The Greek historian Herodotus
counted 111 relay stations for mounted couriers on the Sardis-Susa road alone, a
route of about 2,500 kilometers.

The Battle of Marathon, fought in 490 B.C.E. on a plain northeast of Athens,
was a victory for the Greek forces as they repelled the Persian invasion. It was also a
triumph for Persian mail technology. Herodotus writes of the stalwart mail carriers of
the Persian King Cyrus as they carried messages to the Persian army battling the
Greeks. The final line of his description is still used by the U.S. Postal Service:

> There is nothing in the world which travels faster than these Persian couriers.
> . . . *Nothing stops these couriers from covering their allotted stage in the*
> *quickest possible time—neither snow, rain, heat, nor darkness.*[24] [Emphasis
> added]

The Romans imitated the Persian postal model and created an extensive highway system to facilitate troop movements, travel, trade, and communications. Papyrus, parchment, and wax tablets were used for correspondence. Postal relay
stations were large and numerous; each station kept forty horses and grooms.
Speed was about seventy-five kilometers per day, and there were accurate fixed
times for delivery and collection.[25] Although government posts carried only official
letters, commercial posting companies served merchants and other citizens. The
average daily post covered 50 to 80 kilometers per day, and occasional express
riders covered 150 kilometers per day. The confidence with which Paul wrote to the
early Christians in various parts of the empire indicates that the service was soon
used for private letters as well.

After Rome's central authority collapsed, however, reliable mail in western

Europe nearly disappeared. Pilgrims, preachers, soldiers, merchants, and jugglers became the sole agents of long-distance communication.

> News was as slow as feet and horses' hoofs; when it did arrive, it passed from mouth to mouth and was apt to end up as myth and legend.[26]

Yet the great merchant cities of Venice and Bruges preserved a regular postal service that could cover seven hundred kilometers in about seven days.[27] Monastic orders operated a postal service to exchange news and goods among convents.[28] Charlemagne created postal routes that united Italy, Germany, and Spain. Under the protection of the French kings, the University of Paris operated the first extensive postal network from the thirteenth century until the end of the eighteenth, carrying letters between students and their parents throughout France. When the Arabs brought paper to Europe[29] just before the Renaissance, it stimulated a boom in official, commercial, ecclesiastical, and private correspondence.

While postal service languished in Europe, Marco Polo reported that the Mongols of Kublai Khan had an elaborate postal system. Indeed, to China must go the honor of having established the world's first postal system. Three thousand years ago postal runners delivered news and letters to many Chinese towns and villages. Around 500 B.C.E. Confucius wrote about the Imperial Post.[30] By Polo's time, no fewer than 200,000 horses and 10,000 post offices some forty kilometers apart constituted the trunk routes of a well-developed system.[31]

Modern postal service began in 1464, when French King Louis XI set up a network of relay stations using horses and mounted couriers.[32] England opened a similar service in 1481, and many of the Italian and German city–states followed suit. By 1516 international postal service between Berlin and Vienna was available to the wealthy. In Britain a royal postal service begun in 1525 was limited to governmental use.[33] Among the oldest of the private systems was that begun in 1450 by the Thurn and Taxis families of Venice for the Holy Roman Empire; it was, in effect, a franchise financed by an annual fee. By the nineteenth century, however, the practice of granting royal franchises had been discontinued in favor of royal monopolies whose revenues went directly to the crown.[34]

Early mail service in the American colonies was irregular, haphazard, and for the most part in private hands. For a fee of one penny, colonists could post mail abroad with the captains of merchant ships. Mail arriving from Europe was typically stored at harbor saloons for pickup. In 1672 monthly mail service was inaugurated between Boston and New York City. In 1683 the first post office was set up in Philadelphia, and a postal service was begun that connected Maine to Georgia.[35]

How fast were these early postal services? News of the Battle of Barnet in 1471 traveled the 200 kilometers to Cerne Abbas in one day, and news of the landing of Queen Margaret at Bamborough in 1462 traveled the 520 kilometers to London in five days. In 1482 Edward IV could expect a series of riders to carry news over a distance of 320 kilometers in two days.[36] As late as 1833 a letter in England could reach only two hundred kilometers in one day. By 1900 the daily span of the postal service was six hundred kilometers.[37]

Even "airmail" was known to the ancients. Carrier pigeons have been used to send messages since before the time of Christ. King Solomon improved on land mail by exchanging letters with the Queen of Sheba by means of messenger pigeons in

An Austrian mail courier doffs his cap as he carries a sealed envelope to its recipient. (From an old Viennese playing card.)

SOURCE: *Old Post Bags* (D. Appleton & Co., 1928), p. 36.

about 1000 B.C.E. The Arabs established airmail service with pigeons in the twelfth century.[38] Pigeons were also used successfully to carry news during the 1848 revolt in France.[39] Flying at an average speed of 70 kilometers per hour, pigeons could fly up to 1,000 kilometers in a day. But these tireless and reliable transporters depended on the weather. Only when the telegraph came into being did carrier pigeons begin to lose their importance. Nevertheless, during the two world wars in the twentieth century, the signal corps of every army made extensive use of mobile pigeon units. Carrier pigeons turned out to be the only reliable means of communication during the 1992 civil war among the former Yugoslav republics.[40]

LONG-DISTANCE SIGNALING

Signaling is the transmission of information by any means other than the unaided human voice. Signals can be visual, audible, or electrical and can be made using such means as lighted torches, smoke, flags, lamps, drums, guns, telegraph, telephone, and radio. Electrical signals transmitted quickly over great distances have become known as *telecommunications*.

The first "long-distance" communication must have been shouting across valleys. Swiss and Austrian mountain dwellers still yodel across steep valleys. The exertion was great, the distance traveled short, and the messages quite simple. The

Persian emperor Cyrus the Great, a great innovator in long-distance communication, set up a series of towers staffed by men with loud voices and big lungs. Using a megaphone of animal skins, the men relayed the message along the entire length of the system. One herald's voice was louder than fifty men together! His name was Stentor, from which we still describe a loud voice as "stentorian."[41] This type of "voice telegraph" was used by the Roman Consul Scipio to transmit news of the siege of Numantia in 133 B.C.E. According to Caesar, the Gauls could send "voicegrams" over 270 kilometers in twelve hours. Fifteen hundred years later, the Spanish invaders said they found the same system in use in South America—stentorian transmitters stationed atop wooden towers.[42] As late as 1910 the voice telegram was still in use in Albania.[43]

Another signaling device is the fire tower. Aeschylus reports that in about 1000 B.C.E. the watchman in the tower of Atreus heard of the fall of Troy within one night via fire signals across a distance of five hundred kilometers.[44] This "firegram" started on a mountain overlooking the victorious battle. To transmit a predetermined message, towers along the route lit their flames as soon as they saw the previous tower's flame ignite. The Greek historian Polybius, in the second century B.C.E., describes a Greek system in which the position and number of torches could represent letters of the alphabet.[45] The Chinese used firegrams along the 10,000-kilometer Great Wall.[46] Message complexity was limited to a single, predetermined meaning.

During the summer of 1588 an armada of 130 Spanish ships advanced into the English Channel. On the English shore, fire beacons and columns of smoke passed the word that the Spanish were about to attack. From Plymouth to London, the message took twenty minutes to travel 320 kilometers. Forewarned, English sailors ran to their ships to begin the fight that would defeat the Spanish fleet and end Spain's domination of the sea.[47]

If there were "firegrams," there were also "watergrams." A kind of "water telegraph" used a cylindrical vessel in which floated a perpendicular shaft painted with symbols indicating messages. Both sender and receiver had identical devices on high hills. At the signal of a torch on one hill, same-volume faucets on both hills were opened simultaneously. When the torch was extinguished, the faucets were shut off. The resulting water line in the vessel then indicated the desired message.[48]

North American native peoples are famous for their smoke signals. Built on the highest available land and covered with damp green grass, these fires produced a dense column of white smoke that could be seen seventy-five kilometers away. Using a blanket, the sender could vary the amount of smoke released and could send a few simple messages. Today a column of smoke often means a call for help.[49]

Africans developed a long-distance signaling system of "talking drums." Some African languages rely on intonation and complex rhythm for meaning. High pitch and low pitch also have different meanings. So a hollow log with differing diameters and thicknesses could imitate tonal variations and make sounds resembling a native dialect. To a person familiar with the language, these sounds can successfully transmit messages about eight kilometers. Sending a message over longer distances required a coordinated set of relays.[50]

A North American equivalent to talking drums was the "talking cannons" along the Erie Canal and the Hudson River. Posted 12 to 16 kilometers apart, in 1825 they

The "firegram" could transmit a predetermined message from tower to tower across hundreds of kilometers.

SOURCE: *Mensch und Medien* (Stuttgart: AT Verlag Aarav, 1985), p. II-116.

carried a simple message (that the first boat had entered the Erie Canal) 584 kilometers, from Buffalo to New York City, in eighty minutes![51]

But none of these signaling channels is reliable and secure. There was no way to direct a message to a chosen receiver or to keep the sender's location secret. Weather and darkness could and did close down the system. Such "line-of-sight" channels cannot travel through obstructions or around corners.

During the French Revolution, so the legend goes, French engineer Claude Chappe needed investment capital to develop his "optical telegraph." He tried to convince the National Constituent Assembly, the supreme French revolutionary body, of the optical telegraph's usefulness in transmitting the news of ongoing battles with monarchist troops. In front of the entire Assembly, Chappe demonstrated how the remarkable machine worked. As he left, wondering whether his efforts would be successful, the next applicant, a Monsieur Guillotin, rolled his apparatus— and a sheep shaven at the neck—into the Assembly, also in search of funds![52]

Chappe constructed towers about eight to fifteen kilometers apart and mounted on each a pivoted beam with arms at each end. With a telescope, each tower operator could see and relay the incoming beam-arm signals. Using rope pulleys, the arms could transmit 196 different symbols. Chappe's first operational line was put into operation in 1794 between Paris and Lille. The first message, news of the French victory over the Austrians in Belgium, was delivered to Paris within one hour. The French built these stations in all directions out of Paris, and other European countries copied them. By the end of the eighteenth century, optical telegraphs were in use from the English Channel to the Swiss border.[53]

The optical telegraph's capacity was small: On one given day in 1832, one hundred words were transmitted from Berlin to Koblenz. Despite its limitations, however, the military saw the great utility in this invention and reserved it for the army. When the system was finally surpassed by the electric telegraph in 1852, France was covered with a network of 556 semaphore stations stretching a total distance of 4,500 kilometers.[54]

Torches raised, faucets on adjacent hills released water from "watergram" vessels simultaneously. When the torch was extinguished and the water turned off, marks on a floating shaft could be read.

SOURCE: *Mensch und Medien* (Stuttgart: AT Verlag Aarav, 1985), p. II-114.

TRANSPORTATION MEDIA

The spread of postal communication—indeed, of all physical communication, including books and newspapers—depended greatly on the development of transportation media. In Johannes Gutenberg's time it was possible to publish books and even newspapers with the latest news, but their timeliness was compromised if they arrived weeks late. So it is no accident that long-distance print communication depended first of all on the development of the transportation media. Many newspapers still carry names like "Post" and "Courier" in their titles—from the *Hamburger Morgenpost* to the *Daily Mail* to the *Corriere della Sera*.

Already in antiquity, merchants had developed paths and roads that reached far and wide.[55] As early as the Bronze Age in Europe (2000 B.C.E.), the so-called Bernstein (Amber) Highway ran from Italy through Austria to Denmark. From the third century B.C.E., caravans used the long and dangerous Silk Road to transport

Chappe's optical telegraph was used longest in North Africa, where it was not replaced by the electrical telegraph until 1859. Here, an installation in Algeria.
SOURCE: *Telecommunication Journal* 32 (1, 1965), p. 33.

goods to and from Antioch, in present-day Syria, to Chang'an (Xian) in China. The Incas, who never developed the wheel, had a vast network of roads extending from present-day Quito 3,680 kilometers south to Santiago de Chile.

Even before the Incas, perhaps as early as 3000 B.C.E., the civilizations of Egypt, Mesopotamia, and the Indus Valley developed roads, first for pack animals and then for wheeled vehicles. Beginning in the sixth century B.C.E., the Persians linked existing highways to form the "Royal Road" from Ephesus to Susa, and in the third century B.C.E. the Chin dynasty in China established a country-wide network of roads. Trade routes for the export of gold and ivory (and later for slaves) extended from Africa to Asia and Europe. The Romans were the greatest road builders of the ancient world. They built a durable road network totaling 90,000 kilometers that reached from the Sahara desert to Scotland and from the Atlantic to the Persian Gulf.

Centuries passed before any attempt was made to reconstruct the Roman road system. Indeed, the roads decayed so much during the Middle Ages that travel was difficult and dangerous. Until the Industrial Age, European travel was no faster than in Roman times. In the sixteenth century a coach and horses took one month to travel from Paris to Toulouse.[56] Not until Mussolini and Hitler launched road construction programs in the 1930s can we say that there was again a truly continental road system in Europe.

The introduction of the steam railroad meant that physical communications

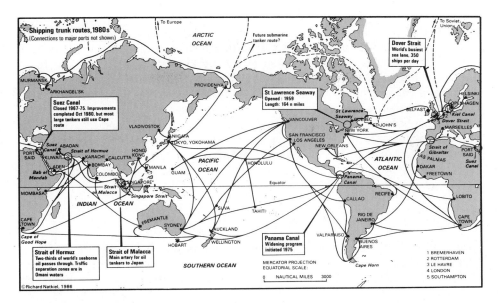

FIGURE 2-3 **The bulk of the world's maritime traffic traverses the few channels shown on this map.**

SOURCE: *Atlas of Maritime History* (Greenwich, CT: Bison Books, 1986), p. 249.

could travel at the breakneck speed of forty kilometers per hour. A product of industrial development, railroads first appeared in the early nineteenth century in England, France, and the United States. By mid-century, they proved superior to canals, turnpikes, and steamboats; their use spread all over Europe; and they had a crucial impact on the history of the telegraph. By the early decades of the twentieth century, nearly 1.4 million kilometers of railroad had been built in the world, with some in nearly every nation.[57]

Colonization from ancient times through the age of imperialism depended entirely on the quality of the long-distance communication links between metropolitan and colonial centers. Colonization always followed the paths of the transportation media, namely roads, sea-lanes, and railways. (Figure 2-3 is a map of the world sea lanes we use today.) As technologies improved, "time distance" became the proper measure in colonial administration (not the number of miles, but the number of hours needed to transport a message).[58] Today's advanced telecommunications networks have reduced "time distance" to milliseconds.

One short-lived (1860–1861) but glamorous means of reducing "time distance" in the American West was the pony express, a rapid mail delivery system connecting the United States from Missouri to California. Until the pony express, the Overland Mail Company, using stagecoaches and teams of horses and drivers, could cover the distance in about twenty days, but Overland's business losses threatened the service.[59] Given the desire to keep California in the Union during the Civil War and the record losses of the Overland Mail, by 1860 the Post Office Department was under pressure to find an alternative.

One upstart cargo company promised to carry letters the 3,000 kilometers between Saint Joseph, Missouri, and Sacramento, California, in ten days, half the time taken by Overland Stage—a speed that thrilled Americans. The company established 190 relay stations fifteen to twenty kilometers apart along a route through Nebraska, Wyoming, and Nevada. The riders, who each traveled about 100 kilometers, carried the mail at a cost of $5 an ounce.[60] The speediest means of communication of its day, the pony express relied on lightweight riders willing to risk the summer heat, winter snow, and native peoples upon whose land the route trespassed. The fastest time of delivery was seven days and seventeen hours, when the ponies carried President Lincoln's Inaugural Address to San Francisco in 1861.[61] For all its fame, the pony express lasted less than two years, when telegraph lines uniting East and West were joined.

PRINT MEDIA

Ideas and images in books have been important channels of reliable, though slow, transnational communication. They depend, of course, on literacy. How slowly print communication penetrated many parts of the world is revealed by the fact that only a few generations ago it was exceedingly rare in Africa to see something written on paper. McLuhan cites Prince Modupe's first encounter with the written word in a missionary's study in West Africa:

> The one crowded space in Father Perry's house was his bookshelves. I gradually came to understand that the marks on the pages were *trapped words*. Anyone could learn to decipher the symbols and turn the trapped words loose again into speech. . . . I shivered with the intensity of my desire to learn to do this wondrous thing myself.[62]

The first book was probably the *volumen*, a roll of papyrus sheets pasted together. The Romans had booksellers and long-distance lending libraries. Diffusion was restricted to rich amateurs, collectors, scholars, and later students and clerks. Because of these restrictions and widespread illiteracy, public reading aloud was the most common form of publishing and dissemination of ideas.

The next stage in the history of the book was stitching sheets into the *codex*. Much better suited to administrative work and record keeping, the codex did not need to be rolled out. Early Christians used the papyrus codex to disseminate the Bible. From the fourth century, for more than a thousand years, manuscripts of bound vellum in the hands of clerks (especially Moslem and Jewish librarians) preserved the history and experience of generations. Books were sacred; becoming a copyist was next to becoming a priest in bestowing honor on a family. Illuminators (illustrators) were prized assets of courtly patricians. University libraries came into being by the thirteenth century.

Books were in great demand, but hand copying limited their availability. As time progressed, new sectors of society took up reading, especially nobles, merchants, and magistrates. They had little use for Latin and religious texts and wanted technical books and books of imagination in the vernacular.

Three factors led to printing in Europe: new technological discoveries, the availability of paper, and public demand. Printing prospered in Europe much more than in

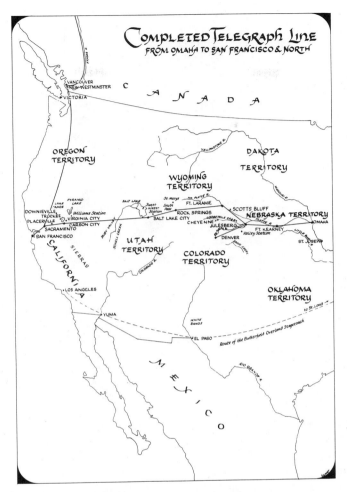

The legendary Pony Express was put out of business in its second year by the first completed telegraph line from Omaha, Nebraska, west to San Francisco and north to Vancouver, British Columbia.

SOURCE: P. Ault, *Wires West* (New York: Dodd, Mead, 1974), p. 56.

China, where it was discovered, because it used a vastly simpler alphabet and served a society in the midst of rapid economic and social development.[63] The spread of printed literature was due in large measure to the entrepreneurship of the publishers. Printing was amazingly successful. By 1500, some estimates put the number of books in Europe at 20 million in a population of only 100 million, most of whom were illiterate. A great deal of European history since that time is connected with the spread of printed books.

By 1600, printing runs of individual books reached 2,000 to 3,000 copies, a considerable output with hand presses. Magisterial ordinances also limited the number of volumes a printer was allowed to produce. As a result, book prices remained

44 *Tauolette e Libri per li Putti*

A seventeenth-century bookseller hawks his wares through the Italian countryside.

SOURCE: *The Bookseller*. From Annibale Carracci, *Le arti di Bologna*, 1646, plate 44. Facsimile, Rome: Edizioni dell'Elefante, 1966. Reprinted with permission.

at the level where only the wealthier classes could afford them. Thus, until the early nineteenth century, books reached only a small proportion of the population. How fast did these works spread throughout Europe? Dante's *Divine Comedy* (1320) took more than three centuries to make its way throughout the continent; twenty years sufficed for Cervantes's *Don Quixote de la Mancha* (1605).

What made it possible for print media to be so widely diffused? The difference was made by mechanization—the steam-driven papermaking machine and press. Although movable type had been used as early as the sixth century C.E. in China, Gutenberg's movable metal type made possible the eventual development of what we know today as the newspaper. The Enlightenment of Germany, Methodism in England, and revolution in France all converged to generate the demand for books for the masses.[64] Between 1800 and 1820 a series of inventions revolutionized printing: the metal press, the foot-operated cylinder press, and the steam press. When Napoleon went into exile on Elba in 1814, more pages could be printed in an hour than had been possible in a day fifteen years earlier. By 1830 publishing had been revolutionized. Printed matter was now cheap. Literacy extended through all levels of the population for the first time in history. The production of books, magazines, newspapers, and business periodicals grew to meet the demand. In 1827 Goethe was able to say, "the epoch of world literature has arrived."[65]

The Germans were newspaper pioneers in Europe. Forerunners of newspapers

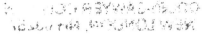

Copying texts by hand was one of the most revered professions prior to the development of mechanical printing.

SOURCE: *Mensch und Medien* (Stuttgart: At Verlag Aarav, 1985), p. I-148.

were published in the fifteenth century in Nuremberg, Cologne, and Augsburg. In the sixteenth and seventeenth centuries, rudimentary newspapers spread throughout Germany and appeared elsewhere in Europe—Venice in 1562, the Low Countries in 1616, Britain in 1620, and France in 1631.

Toward the end of the eighteenth century, newspapers began to spread internationally to such an extent that European powers, fearing the infection of foreign ideas and ideology, concluded the Treaty of Karlsbad in 1819 to regulate the transborder flow of printed material.[66] But Gutenberg's invention had already caused revolutionary changes throughout Europe, allowing widespread dissemination of information even to remote corners of the world.[67]

ELECTRIC TELEGRAPH

The first experiments to transmit messages electrically over wires were undertaken in several countries. In 1753, Charles Marshall built an alphabetic signaling system that used a wire for each character. The Spaniard Francisco Salvá y Campillo developed a similar system.[68] By 1774, the Swiss scientist Georges-Louis Lesage demonstrated the

The oldest known drawing of a printing shop (Lyon, 1499) shows the divisions of labor between the seated owner and his workers. The book shop is owned by the publisher. And typical of its time, dancers of death appear in the background.
SOURCE: *Mensch und Medien* (Stuttgart: At Verlag Aarav, 1985), p. I-156.

first electrical message-transmission device. A piano-type device with twenty-four letters was connected by isolated wires to a second piano. Depressing a lettered key on one machine caused the same key to vibrate on the other. Electricity was volatile and dangerous, so for years Chappe's optical telegraph was preferred. But by 1833 the German scientists Carl Friedrich Gauss and Wilhelm Weber, using the knowledge of Michael Faraday, demonstrated a telegraph that used only two wires.[69]

Although it had been discovered elsewhere, the American Samuel Morse made the two-wire device a success.[70] Morse devised a system whereby an operator could use a switch, or "key," to supply short pulses of electric current through a long-distance wire from a battery to print dot-and-dash symbols of the Morse code. Demonstrated first in New York in 1838, on January 1, 1845, the machine successfully sent the message "What hath God wrought" from Baltimore to Washington. Morse's receiver was widely adopted. He sold stock, and small telegraph companies sprang up in the eastern, southern, and midwestern United States. Within one year there were 1,445 kilometers of telegraph lines in the country.[71] In 1851 the Stock Exchanges of London and Paris were connected.[72]

SUBMARINE CABLES

In 1842 Morse tested the possibility of sending electric impulses through an underwater cable. By 1850 a single strand of copper wire coated with a rubberlike substance called "gutta-percha" was laid between Dover, England, and Calais, France.[73] Only a few messages passed through it before a fisherman trawled it up and claimed he had found a new kind of seaweed with "gold" in the middle.[74]

Another American, Cyrus W. Field, enthusiastically pursued the idea of undersea cable to connect Europe and the United States with speedy and reliable submarine

In 1809 S. T. von Soemmering demonstrated an electrochemical telegraph with a piano-like keyboard to members of the Munich Academy of Science.
SOURCE: *Telecommunication Journal 32* (January 1965), p. 31.

links. In 1857 British and American naval ships began laying a copper-core wire over the 4,000 kilometers between Ireland and Newfoundland. But disaster struck, and the cable snapped due to an inattentive brake operator. Refusing to accept defeat, Field once again raised money for a new cable. Huge storms and more breaks foiled this second attempt. Finally, on July 17, 1858, a third try was successful. By October 20, 1858, more than seven hundred messages had crossed the Atlantic, including Queen Victoria's message to President Buchanan. Although exciting to all the world, the cable's capacity was very small: It took sixty-seven minutes to transmit the Queen's ninety-word message.[75] Then the cable suddenly failed again.

For seven long years, Field again raised funds for a new attempt. In 1865, with improved cable and the largest steamship in the world, he set out from Ireland, but after 2,000 kilometers the wire snapped. One year later, on July 27, 1866, he succeeded in laying the cable again. He even succeeded in recovering the cable he had attempted to lay in 1865, so there were now two cables under the Atlantic. By the end of the century, other companies laid dozens of Atlantic cables to North, Central, and South America. Even the much wider Pacific had been crossed several times. In 1903 President Theodore Roosevelt was able to send a message circling the entire globe in nine minutes.[76]

TELEPHONE

Today's most frequently used medium of global communication is the telephone. The invention of the telephone is usually credited to Alexander Graham Bell, but the first

The telegraph made its appearance during the American Civil War. Here, soldiers run the wire out from a signal telegraph train.

SOURCE: *Telecommunication Journal 32* (January 1965), p. 281.

device that could transmit sound electrically was built in 1861 by the German Johann Philip Reis. The first telephonic words were: *"Das Pferd frißt keinen Gurkensalat."* ("Horses don't eat cucumber salad.")[77] His machine generated little interest in Germany, so it can be said that Bell invented the first operational telephone. Bell's lab had been built by his assistant, Thomas A. Watson. Together they experimented with a "harmonic telegraph" that varied a steady electrical current. In 1876, while working on a transmitter designed to send sound to another room where Watson was, Bell accidentally spilled a container of battery acid and cried out: "Mr. Watson, come here—I need you!" Watson, hearing this cry through the new invention, raced to his aid, and thus began the history of the telephone.

The telephone was first exhibited in 1876 at the Philadelphia Centennial Exhibition, and by 1878 the first long-distance telephone exchange was set up in New Haven. With astounding speed, the telephone network extended through North America and Europe in the last two decades of the nineteenth century. By 1885 the European member states of the International Telegraph Union had at their disposal 1,168 telephone switching centers, with 68,845 connections annually, making more than 92 million local calls and 5 million long-distance calls. Urban lines totaled 306,632 kilometers, but interurban lines totaled only 304 kilometers.[78] At the end of the century, about 2 million telephone instruments were in operation.[79]

By merging telephone and radio technologies, in 1927 the U.S. company AT&T and the British Post Office were able to establish the first voice service between New

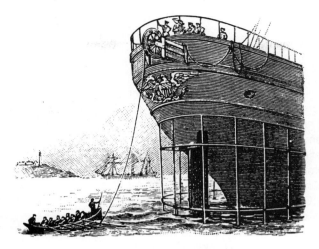

In 1858 Cyrus W. Field succeeded in laying the first Atlantic cable. It broke after three months of operation.

SOURCE: P. Ault, *Wires West* (New York: Dodd, Mead, 1974), p. 97.

York City and London. Powerful radio transmitters propelled the signal through the air from Long Island to Scotland.[80] The price for a three-minute call: $75. Today there are approximately 400 million telephones worldwide, with 155 million in the United States alone.

RADIO-TELEPHONY

To operate, the telephone, telegraph, and undersea cable all required wires to be stretched over vast distances. As Cyrus Field had discovered, laying cable over such spans caused tremendous problems. So attention turned to finding a long-distance medium that did not rely on wire.[81]

Guglielmo Marconi is known as the father of the wireless. In 1894, in his father's garden in Bologna, Italy, Marconi was able to send radio signals over three kilometers. He offered his wireless communication system to the Italian government, but it was not interested. Marconi's mother encouraged him to try England, and in London in 1896 he patented his system and secured backing for it. He first demonstrated its utility by sending messages between two Italian ships twenty kilometers apart. Governments around the world sought him, and he became a celebrity. How far could the signal travel? On December 12, 1901, Marconi was able to send a message over the 3,540–kilometer distance from England to America. His famous experiment showed that a radio-wave signal sent from a tower in Cornwall, England, could be received by a kite-suspended antenna in Saint John's, Newfoundland.[82]

The Marconi system used the dots and dashes of the Morse code, but Canadian-born engineer Reginald Fessenden was convinced that voice and music could also span vast distances. On Christmas Eve of 1906 wireless operators around the Atlantic Ocean listening for Morse code suddenly heard a speech, phonograph music, and greetings from Fessenden transmitting from Massachusetts. The earliest propaganda radio broadcasts date from 1923.[83]

NEWS AGENCIES

The distribution of international news was unpredictable at best until the early nineteenth century. In the pre-telegraphic era, news traveled by word of mouth, by letter, or by transported newspaper, all of which traveled slowly.

Early entrepreneurs were able to profit from control of long-distance information. The story goes that in 1815 Baron Nathan Mayer Rothschild exploited the fragile state of international communication by becoming one of Europe's best-informed bankers through a unique long-distance connection. A rider came directly from the killing fields at Waterloo to the London stock exchange with a message. Rothschild immediately began to sell his stock, causing everyone to believe that Wellington had lost to Napoleon and that Rothschild was the first to know. The result was panic trading at depressed prices; Rothschild then bought up everything he could for a penny. When the official news of Wellington's victory arrived in London after much delay, it was too late for the speculators. They were ruined, and Rothschild had increased his fortune a thousandfold. His only cost: creating the appearance of the first news.[84]

Three men are usually recognized as the founders of the international news agencies: Charles Havas, Bernhard Wolff, and Julius Reuters.[85] In 1825, using messenger pigeons, the optical telegraph of Chappe, semaphores, and the mails,[86] Havas established a news service for individual subscribers that carried reports from Belgium and England.[87] Havas was even able to break the French government's optical telegraph code and to win numerous news "exclusives." In 1835, Havas created the world's first news agency, which carried his name for more than a century. The fight against time led Havas to the electric telegraph, which he installed in 1848.[88]

Impressed by Havas' success, two of his employees set off to capture their own portions of the growing market. In 1849 Berlin newspaper publisher Bernhard Wolff started publishing stock market news and daily reports from Paris, London, Amsterdam, and Frankfurt. He founded the Telegraphische Correspondenz Bureau Wolff, which supplied German newspapers for nearly a century until the Nazis closed it down in World War II.[89]

Another enterprising German and former Havas employee, Julius Reuter, found that messenger pigeons could beat Rothschild's couriers. At the time, the French telegraph line stopped in Brussels, while the German wire halted one kilometer away at Aachen, on the Belgian–Prussian border. To get vital stock market quotations from the Paris stock exchange to Berlin and back, in 1849 Reuter established his own commercial service. His carrier pigeons beat the mail train from Brussels to Aachen by seven hours. He in turn put the market quotes on the Aachen–Berlin wire well ahead of any competition.[90] When the telegraph line finally was extended across the border in 1851, Reuter, realizing that his service was no longer useful, transferred himself to London to take advantage of the recently installed Calais–Dover cable.[91] By the end of the year he was transferring financial news among Paris, Berlin, and London. He added a general news report in 1858 and organized a worldwide exchange of news in 1870.[92]

Beginning in 1856, the three agencies exchanged stock market information, but in 1859, Reuter, Havas, and the German Wolff agency reached an agreement to exchange news from all over the world. The arrangement was known as the League of Allied Agencies, or the "Ring Combination." Reuter received the concession for the British Empire, North America, states along the Suez route to Asia, and most of Asia and the Pacific, including China and Japan. Havas received the French empire, southern Europe, South America, and parts of Africa. Wolff received what was left in Europe, including Prussia, the North German Confederation, south Germanic states, Austria–Hungary, Scandinavia, and the Slavic states.[93] This combination led to odd circumstances. For example, until 1914 people in the United States and Latin America received their news of each other from a French news agency.[94]

Indeed, during this time we might say that the United States suffered from the same kind of "news imperialism" that many Third World nations complain about today. The "big three" agencies presented European news favorably and without contradictions. But of America, in the famous words of Kent Cooper,

> these agencies told the world about Indians on the warpath in the West, lynchings in the South, and bizarre crimes in the North. For decades, nothing credible to America was ever sent.[95]

Originally, the United States was excluded from the "Ring Combination," but Yankee ingenuity began long-distance news gathering quite early. One industrious American used a unique method to gather international news. To gain a time advantage over other newspapers, Daniel Craig would sail out to incoming ships, prepare his reports using interviews from the passengers and crew, and send them back to the New York Herald using messenger pigeons.[96]

The American news agency Associated Press attributes its foundation to the telegraph. Morse's telegraph line functioned well by the late 1840s, but it was a cause of great concern to New York newspapers. Correspondents throughout the country sent their dispatches eastward to a single receiving facility in New Jersey that served all the newspapers in New York City. Each paper assigned a reporter to listen and copy down the news as it came over the wire from that paper's correspondent. But the reports were read aloud by the telegraph operator, and all the press corps present could overhear it. Worried also about the expense of sending a reporter from each newspaper to cover the Mexican War, the New York papers agreed to establish their own news agency and to pool their information.[97] Thus in 1848 arose the giant of all news agencies, the Associated Press.[98]

Reuter realized he was in for trouble in the United States because this exclusivity effectively locked other competing agencies out of the business. Reuter convinced his cartel partners to let Associated Press into the deal, but AP was not formally admitted until 1887, and it was confined to North America.

HISTORY OF PROPAGANDA

A history of global communication must include one of its most pernicious aspects, propaganda. The desire to persuade another person is a part of human nature; its methodology evolved about 500 B.C.E. in the Greek science of *rhetorike*. Public speeches were specially important in the ancient public sphere because politicians depended on the decisions of the inexpert public. Therefore, politicians made great use of the "power of the word" to construct the opinion of the masses. The word *demagogue* ("leader of people") comes from those Greek politicians who led their people through rhetoric.

The influence of propaganda also made it possible for the ancient Romans to establish the power of the Roman Empire. The Roman hallmark was the construction of a "cultural image" so grandiose that the entire imperial population could grasp its magnificence. Conquered peoples were not only offered military protection, but also were inculcated with the Roman world view, art, and architecture. The Roman state's power was symbolized by resplendent buildings, its Kaisers through literature and sculpture, and its world view through theater. Julius Caesar was able to construct a powerful Kaiser-image through the most original of communication channels, the coin. Caesar's famous slogan *"Veni, vidi, vici"* is still heard around the world.

The propagation of the faith can also be seen as a long-term propaganda effort by the church. Early Christianity targeted Roman slaves, the poorest population segments, and conquered peoples. Propaganda methods were relatively simple but reached a vast public. Parables and metaphors such as "the eye of the camel" and the "shepherd and his flock" mediated a powerful and emotion-laden message within an easily understood message. In the fourth century, Christ on the cross became Christianity's main symbol. The secret symbol of the fish was used throughout the Roman empire as propagandistic graffiti to alert the population of the presence and size of the believer community.

The invention of mass printing was an important threshold for propaganda. In the middle of the fifteenth century, this new communication channel played a crucial role in the great battle between the Roman Catholic Church and Martin Luther. One of the most important achievements of the Reformation was the publication of the Bible in the German vernacular. Luther's pamphlets and flyers were printed by the thousands and carried throughout the entire Northern European population. Building upon the growing dissatisfaction with the Catholic Church, Luther reached his audience in its own language. His famous "95 Theses" were posted on paper on the door of the church in Wittenberg and reproduced in quantities previously unheard of in Europe.

To combat the dramatic advance of the Lutherans, in 1622 Pope Gregory XV formulated a systematic plan for the propagation of the Roman Catholic faith. Its purpose was to bring people to accept Christ voluntarily. Thus, the Pope defined two of the main goals of modern propagandists—to control and guide public opinion and to have indirect influence on the behavior of the masses.

Despite its religious and imperial roots, the further development of propaganda was greatly accelerated by the secular press. All sides in Europe's Thirty Years' War used printed propaganda. The great century of revolutions, which started in 1776, was accelerated by improved printing technology that could disseminate propaganda ideas faster and more efficiently, especially after the increases in literacy. Even illiterates could be reached with cartoons and other visual material. Propaganda played a special role in the American Revolution. The revolutionary ideology was diffused throughout the colonial population through newspapers, books, and pamphlets. Publicists used such events as the Boston Tea Party to excite American hatred of British repression. Print media were also significant in bringing people to the side of the revolutionists. The fervor of the storming of the Bastille was symbolized through the patriotic music of "The Marseillaise." French publicists, using the colors red, white, and blue, designed distinctive costumes for the representatives of the revolution. Later, Napoleon's use of propaganda rivaled only the Roman emperors in pretention.

The nineteenth century, distinguished by its technical advances, also saw the rise of the propaganda of democracy. In the "war to end all wars," propaganda skillfully manipulated human emotions, often twisting moral and conceptual value beyond recognition. Scientists and citizens alike were shocked at this development. As Lasswell wrote:

> There is little exaggeration in saying that the world War led to the discovery of propaganda by both the men in the street and the man in the study.[99]

The nature of war was transformed in the age of mass production and mass communication. Battles were no longer fought in distant battlefields but in the hearts and minds of the various national publics. The onset of World War I found a highly developed information and communication infrastructure already existing in Europe. Books, newspapers, posters, flyers, public speech, and radio now served to manipulate public opinion. The first airplanes even rained mass-printed flyers behind enemy lines. War on such a scale required mobilizing both the military and information power. As Lasswell wrote:

> International war propaganda rose to such amazing dimensions . . . because the communication of warfare necessitated the mobilization of the civilian mind. No government could hope to win without a unified nation behind it, and no government could have a united nation behind it unless it controlled the minds of the people.[100]

During World War I, propaganda media often created exaggerated enemy and ally images and deliberately stirred up hatred against opponents. In this "service," media workers frequently broadcast fictitious, often imaginative, but highly effective atrocity stories. Stereotypes and enemy images permeated all types of media, from entertainment programs to scientific literature and *belles lettres*. Enemy images stressed the cruelty, barbarity, and inhumanity of the opponent and at the same time justified national sacrifices and unwavering patriotism at home. At the same time, "Great War" propaganda also deified the ally, sought support among neutral neighbors, and tried to destroy the morale of enemy forces.

Vladimir Lenin and Woodrow Wilson were the "Great Communicators" of the war. In press statements and appearances, Wilson was able to make a distinction between the German leadership and the German people, and thereby to drive a public-opinion wedge into the German war effort. Through his vision of a better, more just, and peaceful world, he eventually won a large portion of German public sympathy.

CONTINUITY AND CHANGE IN INTERNATIONAL COMMUNICATION

Despite the advent of new communications technologies, the problems of communication between and among peoples and nations remain unchanged. The basic structure and function of communication remains the same: Just as before, people today want to inform, they want to be informed, and they want to communicate. The revolution in technology has not changed this. For centuries, missionaries were sent to distribute information. Spies were sent to collect information. And ambassadors were sent to communicate. What is new today? Direct-broadcast satellites, broadcasting television programs from space, are the new missionaries. Remote-sensing satellites are the new spies. And the Moscow–Washington "hot line" and fax machines are the new diplomats. All perform the same functions as before.[101]

The renowned anthropologist Margaret Mead agreed. After reviewing the growth of human communication systems from cave painting to satellite broadcast, she concluded:

> I think it can be maintained that all of our modern methods of communication amplify, expand, or contract earlier methods of communication but never have wholly displaced them, and that every one of these earlier methods of communication not only exists today but provides a kind of template on the bases of which new methods of communication can be elaborated.[102]

NOTES

1. Thanks to Dr. Elise Boulding for this enlightening concept.

2. One treatment can be found in Llewellyn White and Robert D. Leigh, "The Growth of International Communications," in *Mass Communications*, 2nd ed., ed. Wilbur Schramm (Urbana, IL: University of Illinois Press, 1960), pp. 70–75.

3. R. H. Hilton, *A Medieval Society: The West Midlands at the End of the Thirteenth Century* (New York: Wiley, 1966), p. 6, quoted in Robert Brentano, "Western Civilization: The Middle Ages," in *Propaganda and Communication in World History: The Symbolic Instrument of Early Times*, vol. 1, ed. Harold D. Lasswell, Daniel Lerner, and Hans Speier (Honolulu: University Press of Hawaii, 1979), p. 554.

4. Colin Cherry, *World Communication: Threat or Promise? A Socio-technical Approach*, rev. ed. (Chichester, England: Wiley, 1978), p. 26; see also Colin Cherry, "On Communication before the Days of Radio," *Proceedings of the IRE* (Institute of Radio Engineers) 50 (1, 1962): 1143–1145.

5. Philip D. Curtin, *Cross-Cultural Trade in World History* (Cambridge, England: Cambridge University Press, 1984), p. 252.

6. A. G. Hodgkiss, "Maps as a Medium of Communication," in *Understanding Maps: A Systematic History of Their Use and Development* (Folkestone, UK: Dawson, 1981), pp. 11–24. Hodgkiss applies information theory to mapmaking. For example, he refers to "cartographic noise" to explain such distortions as sea monsters on early maps.

7. *International Encyclopedia of Communications*, s.v. "Exploration."

8. Michael Parfit, "Mapmaker Who Charts Our Hidden Mental Demons," *Smithsonian*, May 1984, pp. 123–131.

9. John Noble Wilford, *The Mapmakers* (New York: Vintage Books, 1981), p. 35.

10. Ptolemy's *Geography* became available to Western readers through translation only in 1406. See *International Encyclopedia of Communications*, s.v. "Exploration."

11. Barbara W. Tuchman, *A Distant Mirror: The Calamitous 14th Century* (New York: Ballantine, 1978), p. 58.

12. As Chaucer relates, a group of fourteenth-century London merchants shipwrecked on the north coast of England were jailed as foreign spies! James Burke, "Communication in the Middle Ages," in *Communication in History: Technology, Culture, Society*, ed. David Crowley and Paul Heyer (New York: Longman, 1991), p. 68.

13. Tuchman, *A Distant Mirror*, p. 56.

14. Cited in J. H. Parry, *European Reconnaissance: Selected Documents* (New York: Walker and Co., 1968), p. 47.

15. Cited in Parry, *European Reconnaissance*, pp. 187, 189.

16. Cherry, *World Communication: Threat or Promise?* p. ix.

17. Igor de Rachewiltz, *Papal Envoys to the Great Khans* (Stanford, CA: Stanford University Press, 1971); *Prester John and Europe's Discovery of East Asia* (Canberra, Australia: Australian National University Press, 1972); Robert Silverberg, *The Realm of Prester John* (Garden City, NY: Doubleday, 1972); Vsevolod Slessarev, *Prester John: The Letter and the Legend* (Minneapolis: University of Minnesota Press, 1959; and Alvin F. Harlow, *Old Post Bags: The Story of the Sending of a Letter in Ancient and Modern Times* (New York: Appleton, 1928), p. 28.

18. *International Encyclopedia of Communications*, s.v. "The Crusades."

19. Horst W. Opaschowski, *Tourismus Forschung* (Opladen, FRG: Leske & Budrich, 1989); Valene L. Smith, ed., *Hosts and Guests: The Anthropology of Tourism* (Philadelphia, PA: University of Pennsylvania Press, 1977); and Louise Turner and John Ash, *The Golden Hordes: International Tourism and the Pleasure Periphery* (London: Constable, 1975).

20. Marcia Ascher and Robert Ascher, "Civilization without Writing: The Incas and the Quipu," in *Communication in History*, pp. 36–42; Harlow, *Old Post Bags*, p. 11; *International Encyclopedia of Communications*, s.v. "Americas, Pre-Columbian"; and Harold Osborne, *Indians of the Andes: Aymaras and Quechuas* (New York: Cooper Square, 1973), p. 103.

21. Jacob J. Finkelstein, "Early Mesopotamia, 2500–1000 B.C.," in *Propaganda and Communication*, vol. 1, p. 52.

22. *International Encyclopedia of Communications*, s.v. "Roman Empire."

23. G. Allen Foster, *Communication: From Primitive Tom-Toms to Telstar* (New York: Criterion Books, 1965), p. 58; and Harry Edward Neal, *Communication from Stone Age to Space Age* (New York: Messner, 1974), p. 121.

24. Herodotus, *The Histories*, trans. Aubrey de Sélincourt (Harmondsworth, Middlesex, UK: Penguin Books, 1972), p. 556.

25. Cherry, *World Communication: Threat or Promise?* p. 32.

26. Manuel Vásquez Montalbán, *Historia y Comunicación Social* (Madrid: Alianza Editorial, 1985), p. 33.

27. Tuchman, *A Distant Mirror*, p. 56.

28. Vásquez Montalbán, *Historia y Comunicación Social*, pp. 47–48.

29. When the Arabs defeated Chinese forces in Samarkand in 751 C.E., they captured Chinese papermakers and brought the technology to North Africa. It eventually arrived in Spain around 1150, in Italy in 1270, and in Germany in 1390. In the twelfth century, France acquired the new material made in Spain but did not produce it until the fourteenth century. Vásquez Montalbán, *Historia y Comunicación Social,* pp. 47–48.

30. Gordon C. Baldwin, *Talking Drums to Written Word: How Early Man Learned to Communicate* (New York: Norton, 1970), p. 143.

31. *The Travels of Marco Polo* (New York: Liveright, 1953), p. 165.

32. Neal, *Communication*, p. 122.

33. Foster, *Communication*, pp. 61–62.

34. *American Academic Encyclopedia*, s.v. "Postal Services."

35. Neal, *Communication*, p. 124. See also Alex L. Braake et al., ed., *The Posted Letter in Colonial and Revolutionary America, 1628–1790* (State College, PA: American Philatelic Research, 1975); LeRoy R. Hafen, *The Overland Mail, 1849–1869: Promoter of Settlement, Precursor of Railroads* (New York: AMS Press, 1969); George E. Hargest, *History of Letter Post Communication between the United States and Europe, 1845–1875*, Smithsonian Studies in History and

Technology no. 6 (Washington, DC: Smithsonian Institution Press, 1971); Harlow, *Old Post Bags;* F. George Kay, *Royal Mail: The Story of the Posts in England from the Time of Edward IV to the Present Day* (London: Rockliff, 1951); and Frank Staff, *The Transatlantic Mail* (Lawrence, MA: Quarterman, 1980).

36. C. A. J. Armstrong, "Some Examples of the Distribution and Speed of News in England at the Time of the War of the Roses," in *Studies in Medieval History Presented to Frederick Maurice Powicke*, ed. R. W. Hunt, W. A. Pantin, and R. W. Southern (Oxford, England: Clarendon Press, 1948), pp. 439, 447, 448, quoted in Robert Brentano, "Western Civilization: The Middle Ages," in *Propaganda and Communication,* vol. 1, p. 554.

37. Werner Hadorn and Mario Cortesi, *Mensch und Medien: Die Geschichte der Massenkommunikation*, vol. 2 (Stuttgart, FRG: AT Verlag Aarau, 1986), p. 26.

38. Dagmar Metzger, "Von den Bildern in der Höhle zu den Daten auf der Bank," *Geo Wissen* (2, 1989): 124.

39. Foster, *Communication*, p. 60; and Neal, *Communication,* p. 117.

40. Carol J. Williams, "Carrier Pigeons Make Comeback in War," *Los Angeles Times,* January 11, 1992, p. A3. See also Arthur C. Bent, *Life Histories of North American Gallinaceous Birds* (Washington, DC: U.S. Government Printing Office, 1932; reprint, New York: Dover Publications, 1963); Derek Goodwin, *Pigeons and Doves of the World*, 2nd ed. (Ithaca, NY: Comstock Publishers Association, 1977); and Wendell Levi, *Encyclopedia of Pigeon Breeds* (Jersey City, NJ: T. F. H. Publications, 1965) and *The Pigeon* (Sumter, SC: Levi, 1974).

41. Neal, *Communication,* p. 136.

42. Harlow, *Old Post Bags,* p. 10.

43. Hadorn and Cortesi, *Mensch und Medien,* vol. 2, p. 114; and Vásquez Montalbán, *Historia y Comunicación Social*, p. 14.

44. Harlow, *Old Post Bags*, p. 11.

45. Polybius, *The Histories*, Book X (Bloomington: Indiana University Press, 1962); and Jack Coggins, *Flashes and Flags: The Story of Signaling* (New York: Dodd, Mead, 1963), pp. 13–14.

46. Metzger, "Von den Bildern," p. 123.

47. James Jespersen and Jane Fitz-Randolph, *Mercury's Web: The Story of Telecommunications* (New York: Atheneum, 1981), p. 15.

48. Hadorn and Cortesi, *Mensch und Medien*, vol. 2, p. 115.

49. Jack Coggins, *Flashes and Flags*, pp. 13–14.

50. Neal, *Communication*, p. 134; and *International Encyclopedia of Communications*, s.v. "Africa, Precolonial."

51. Harlow, *Old Post Bags*, p. 12.

52. Pierre Etaix, producer, *I Write in Space* (Paris: La Geode/Flach Films, 1988). Film.

53. Anthony R. Michaelis, "From Semaphore to Satellite," *Telecommunication Journal* 32 (1, 1965): 32; and 32 (2, 1965): 86; and Hadorn and Cortesi, *Mensch und Medien*, vol. 2, p. 118.

54. Michaelis, "From Semaphore to Satellite," 32 (1, 1965): 31. The last operating optical telegraph was replaced in 1859 in Algeria.

55. William Albert, *The Turnpike Road System, 1663–1840* (Cambridge, England: University Press, 1972); *American Academic Encyclopedia*, s.v. "Roads and Highways"; *International Encyclopedia of Communications*, s.v. "Silk Road"; Ryoichi Hayashi, *The Silk Road and the Shoso-in*, trans. Robert Ricketts (New York: Weatherhill, 1975); and Jan Myrdal and Gun Kessle, *The Silk Road*, trans. Ann Henning (New York: Pantheon, 1979).

56. Hadorn and Cortesi, *Mensch und Medien*, vol. 2, p. 19.

57. *American Academic Encyclopedia,* s.v. "Railroads."

58. *International Encyclopedia of Communications*, s.v. "Colonization."

59. Gerald J. Cullinan, *The United States Postal Service* (New York: Praeger, 1973), pp. 74–75.

60. Wayne E. Fuller, *The American Mail: Enlarger of the Common Life* (Chicago: University of Chicago Press, 1972), p. 100; and Cullinan, *The United States Postal Service*, p. 78. See also G. D. Bradley, *Story of the Pony Express: An Account of the Most Remarkable Mail Service in Existence, and Its Place in History*, 4th ed. (Chicago: McClurg, 1923); Arthur Chapman, *The Pony Express: The Record of a Romantic Adventure in Business* (New York: Putnam, 1932; reprint, 1972); and Raymond W. Settle and Mary L. Settle, *Saddles and Spurs: The Pony Express Saga* (Harrisburg, PA: Stackpole, 1955; reprint, 1972).

61. Neal, *Communication*, p. 126.

62. Marshall McLuhan, *Understanding Media: The Extensions of Man* (New York: New American Library, 1964), p. 84.

63. T. F. Carter, "Paper and Block Printing: From China to Europe," in *Communication in History*, pp. 83–93.

64. See Elizabeth Eisenstein, "The Rise of the Reading Public," in *Communication in History*, pp. 94–102.

65. Johann Wolfgang von Goethe, *Goethes Werke*, vol. 12 (Hamburg, FRG: Christian Wegner, 1953), p. 362. See also *Schriften zur Literatur*, vol. 14 (Zurich, Switzerland: Artemis, 1950), pp. 908–916. Translation by the present author.

66. Wolfgang Kleinwächter, "The Interrelationship of the Introduction of New Communication Technology and the Need for International Regulation," in International Journalism Institute, *New Communication Technology and International Law: Procedings [sic] of an International Seminar of Experts within the UNESCO Participation Program, 20–21 September 1987* (Prague: International Journalism Institute, 1988), p. 10.

67. Smith, Anthony, *The Newspaper: An International History* (London: Thames and Hudson, 1979).

68. Hadorn and Cortesi, *Mensch und Medien*, vol. 2, p. 119; and Metzger, "Von den Bildern," p. 124.

69. Metzger, "Von den Bildern," p. 124; and Hadorn and Cortesi, *Mensch und Medien*, vol. 2, p. 120.

70. Daniel Czitrom, "Lightning Lines," in *Communication in History*, pp. 127–131.

71. Metzger, "Von den Bildern," p. 124.

72. Cherry, *World Communication*, p. 34.

73. Jespersen and Fitz-Randolph, *Mercury's Web*, p. 44.

74. Anthony R. Michaelis, "From Semaphore to Satellite," 32 (1, 1965): 36. A second cable laid the following year operated for many years.

75. Pierre Frédérix, *Un Siècle de Chasse aux Nouvelles* (Paris: Flammarion, 1959), p. 65, quoted in Esteban López-Escobar, *Análisis del "Nuevo Orden Internacional de la Información"* (Pamplona, Spain: Ediciones Universidad de Navarra, S.A., 1978), p. 45. Another report believes the transmission took sixteen hours! See Jespersen and Fitz-Randolph, *Mercury's Web*, p. 47. Frédérix also cites a Havas dispatch that a twenty-three–word telegraphic transmission took thirty-five minutes.

76. Neal, *Communication*, pp. 145–149; and Jespersen and Fitz-Randolph, *Mercury's Web*, p. 49.

77. Metzger, "Von den Bildern," p. 125.

78. Michaelis, "From Semaphore to Satellite," 32 (4, 1965): 164.

79. This development accelerated as the century progressed: in 1900, 1.9 million; 1920, 19.6 million; 1938, 39.2 million; 1946, 60.8 million; 1963, 161.1 million; 1973, 312.9 million; 1983, 600 million; 1987, 700 million. See H. Haschler and W. Paubel, *Die Internationale Fernmeldeverein [The International Telecommunication Union]*, (Berlin, GDR: Staatsverlag der DDR, 1977), p. 19, quoted in Wolfgang Kleinwächter, *Weltproblem Information* (Berlin, GDR: Dietz, 1989), p. 17. See also Henry M. Boettinger, *The Telephone Book: Bell, Watson, Vail, and American Life, 1876–1976* (Croton-on-Hudson, NY: Riverwood, 1977; rev. ed., New York: Stearn, 1983); John

Brooks, *Telephone: The First Hundred Years* (New York: Harper & Row, 1976); Ithiel de Sola Pool, *The Social Impact of the Telephone* (Cambridge, MA: MIT Press, 1977); and J. Edward Hyde, *The Phone Book: What the Telephone Company Would Rather You Not Know* (Chicago: Regnery, 1976).

80. Michaelis, "From Semaphore to Satellite," 32 (4, 1965): 163.

81. See Stephen Kern, "Wireless World," in *Communication in History*, pp. 186–189.

82. Hugh G. J. Aitkin, *Syntony and Spark: The Origins of Radio* (New York: Wiley, 1976); Orrin E. Dunlap, *Marconi: The Man and His Wireless*, rev. ed. (New York: Macmillian, 1937; reprint, New York: Arno, 1971); and W. P. Jolly, *Marconi* (New York: Stein & Day, 1972).

83. *International Encyclopedia of Communications*, s.v. "Radio."

84. Kleinwächter, *Weltproblem Information*, p. 11.

85. J. Rosewater, *History of Cooperative Newsgathering in the United States* (New York: Appleton, 1930); Oliver Gramling, *AP: The Story of News* (New York: Kennikat Press, 1940); Kent Cooper, *Barriers Down: The Story of the News Agency Epoch* (New York: Kennikat Press, 1942); J. A. Morris, *Deadline Every Minute: The Story of United Press* (Garden City, NY: Doubleday, 1957); Kent Cooper, *Kent Cooper and the Associated Press: An Autobiography* (New York: Random House, 1959); and Frédérix, *Siècle de Chasse aux Nouvelles*.

86. A. Dubuc, "Charles-Louis Havas (1983–1858), Organisateur de la Première Agence International d'Information," *EdeP*, (18–19, 1958): 23–27, quoted in López-Escobar, *Análisis del "Nuevo Orden Internacional,"* p. 36.

87. Clifford R. Weigle, "The Rise and Fall of the Havas Agency," *Journalism Quarterly* 19 (1942): 277–286.

88. Hadorn and Cortesi, *Mensch und Medien*, vol. 2, p. 123.

89. Ibid., p. 123.

90. Frédérix, *Siècle de Chasse aux Nouvelles*, p. 38, quoted in López-Escobar, *Análisis del "Nuevo Orden Internacional,"* p. 41.

91. López-Escobar, *Análisis del "Nuevo Orden Internacional,"* p. 41.

92. Graham Storey, *Reuters: The Story of a Century of News Gathering* (New York: Crown, 1951).

93. The entire agreement signed by the "big three" may be found in Esteban López-Escobar, *Análisis del "Nuevo Orden Internacional,"* pp. 46–48; and Frédérix, *Siècle de Chasse aux Nouvelles*, pp. 76–78. See also White and Leigh, "The International News-Gatherers," in *Mass Communications*, p. 77; and Robert W. Desmond, *The Information Process: World News Reporting to the Twentieth Century* (Iowa City, IA: University of Iowa Press, 1978).

94. J. Laurence Day, "U.S. News Coverage of Latin America: A Short Historical Perspective" (Paper presented at Conference on Latin America, Philadelphia, 1984), p. 2.

95. Cooper, *Barriers Down*, p. 9.

96. Gramling, *AP*, pp. 11–12.

97. López-Escobar, *Análisis del "Nuevo Orden Internacional,"* pp. 50–51.

98. Neal, *Communication*, pp. 141–142.

99. Harold D. Lasswell, *Propaganda Technique in World War I,* 1971, p. 10, cited in Garth Jowett and Victoria O'Donnell, *Propaganda and Persuasion* (Newbury Park, CA: Sage, 1986).

100. Lasswell, *Propaganda Technique*, p. 10.

101. Wolfgang Kleinwächter, "Continuity and Change in the International Law of Mass Communication" (Paper presented at the Symposium on Media Accountability under International Law, sponsored by the National Lawyers Guild and the Union for Democratic Communications, Los Angeles, June 14, 1989).

102. Margaret Mead, "Continuities in Communication from Early Man to Modern Times," in *Propaganda and Communication*, vol. 1, p. 29.

3

A World of Communication

After defining some terms, global communication and information are examined from two levels—within national societies and between national societies. Communication and information activities in all societies reflect the needs and aims of prevailing social forces and manifest the dominant goals of that society. This chapter contains an outline of what today's "information society" means in concrete terms. The growing disparities between the world's information-rich and information-poor populations are examined. The chapter also contains a treatment of the question of whether a "global media village" exists. This chapter concludes with a discussion of the complaints of people around the world about their communication systems.

DEFINITIONS

The academic field of *global communication* is that *intersection of disciplines* that studies the *transborder transfer* of values, attitudes, opinions, *information*, and *data* by individuals, groups, people, institutions, governments, and *information technologies* as well as the resulting controversial *issue areas* that arise from the structure of institutions responsible for promoting or inhibiting such messages among and between nations and cultures.[1]

Communication is studied at the *intersection of disciplines*, particularly communication theory, sociology, psychology, anthropology, philosophy, ethics, international relations, political science, and electronic technology. Global communication is a field of study that encompasses many *issue areas,* including culture, national development, foreign policy and diplomacy, conflict and conflict resolution, technology, news flow, national sovereignty, ideology, comparative mass communication systems, regulation and policy, human and civil rights, ideological confrontation, war and peace, and propaganda and influence.

Transborder usually refers to communication across national frontiers. This could also include intercultural communication, which means the transfer of messages between members of different cultures, who may even reside within a country's national frontiers.

It is also necessary to distinguish between *international* communication and *global* communication. The former refers to communication between and among nation-states and connotes issues of national sovereignty, control of national information resources, and the supremacy of national governments. As we approach the next century, it is clear that nation-states are increasingly in competition with important non-state actors such as nongovernmental organizations (NGOs) and transnational ("beyond" the nation-state) corporations (TNCs). The present author prefers the term *global communication* because it goes beyond the bounds of individual countries and emphasizes communication between and among peoples.

How are *information* and *communication* defined? The "MacBride Report" made the following distinction:

> Information is often basically considered to be the signs or coded messages transmitted in one direction from a source to a receiver, while communication corresponds more to the complexity of the phenomenon of various interchanges, through signs and symbols, between individuals and communities.[2]

Communication, as used in this book, is the *process* of exchanging news, facts, opinions, and messages between individuals and people; *information* is the *product*, that is, the various contents and output of media, cultural activities, or industries.[3]

Data are similar to information, but with one very significant difference. Data are representations of facts, concepts, objects, and events in unprocessed format, whereas *information* consists of processed data.

> Data and information do not transmit facts, events, topics, persons, etc., per se, they transmit messages. War activities, criminal behaviour, and physical money do not flow across borders, but messages about war, crime, and money.[4]

International *information technologies* can be classified by their functions. Technologies exist that

Capture, such as remote-sensing satellites, radar systems, electronic cameras, VCR systems, videodiscs, and optical-character-recognition devices.

Transport, such as coaxial cable, fiber-optic cable, microwave links, communication satellites, cellular mobile radio, laser beams, facsimile transceivers, videophone, electronic teleprinters, and modems.

Store, such as memory chips, magnetic film, tape, holography, laser emulsion, and microfilm.

Process, such as integrated circuits, computer software, and peripheral equipment.

Retrieve, such as high-definition TV, teletext, videotex, pay TV, and on-line data bases.[5]

Some economic and geographical terms, used in this text to compare and contrast countries, are clarified here. UNESCO classifies the world's economies into two categories: *Developed* nations (about one-fourth of the world's population) include all European countries (except Yugoslavia and Albania), the United States, Canada, the

Commonwealth of Independent States, Japan, Israel, New Zealand, Australia, and South Africa. The *developing* economies (about three-fourths of the population) constitute the rest of the world.[6]

Although they have lost a great deal of their meaning in the present era and reflect a Eurocentric bias, the following terms are also used: The *First World* is the industrialized "free-market" democracies of Europe, North America, Japan, Australia, and New Zealand, as well as South Africa. The *Second World*, now a somewhat archaic term, referred to the centrally planned economies of Eastern Europe and the USSR, China, and Vietnam. The term *Third World* refers to those countries, constituting three-quarters of humankind, that have remained outside the first two worlds. "Third World" has become primarily an economic term, used for poor and non-industrialized nations in preference to such arcane words of the past as "underdeveloped" or "backward."[7]

COMMUNICATION WITHIN NATIONAL SOCIETIES
Communication and National Identity

Nations and people can actually be defined in terms of communication. A map of North America shows a line running from the Pacific more or less straight across the continent on the Forty-ninth Parallel for some 2,500 kilometers. The line then dips and follows the contours of lakes, rivers, and waterways until it reaches the Atlantic Ocean. A person on the ground is not going to find some gap in the earth separating Manitoba and Saskatchewan from North Dakota!

A map of the communication flows within and between the United States and Canada—a map that shows arrows of various thicknesses indicating volume of flow—shows a distinct "division" demarcating the two countries. Message traffic originating in North Dakota tends to flow eastward toward Minnesota and the U.S. side of the Great Lakes, following the transcontinental railway, microwave, and highway networks. Similarly, if we could see every phone call made, every letter sent, and every journey undertaken, we would find that the flow map of Saskatchewan and Manitoba points eastward, toward Toronto and Ottawa.[8]

What we observe on the northern plains, we also observe along the Maine–Quebec border and along the California–Mexico border. What distinguishes one village from another is not just lines on a map but also the outlet of that village's communication flow. Messages from Tijuana, Baja California, flow largely south toward Mexico City. From San Diego, "upper" California, messages flow northward and eastward. By making flow maps indicating direction and volume, one can see that "countries turn out to be clusters of population, united by grids of communication flows and transport systems, and separated by thinly settled or nearly empty territories."[9] (See Figure 3-1.) Even in areas such as Tijuana and San Diego, where dense populations are separated by only the thinnest, most porous of walls, traffic lines go generally in different directions.[10]

Therefore, *boundary* can be defined as "an area where the settlement densities and traffic densities decline quite sharply."[11] If a boundary is set arbitrarily across a living communication community or an interdependent cluster of settlements,

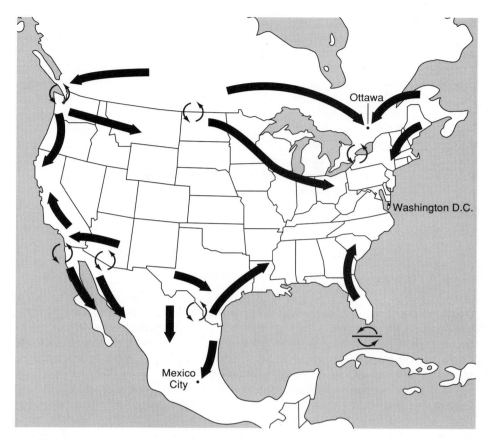

FIGURE 3-1   Communication Flow Map of North America. Nations can be defined by their communication flows. Relatively little communication flows across national frontiers compared to the flow of communication within a nation and toward the national capital. Note that there has been a virtual blockade on communication flows between Cuba and the United States for more than thirty years.

chances are that boundary will cause resentment and resistance. In some densely populated regions, for example, between Pakistan and India, the boundary purposely does not cut across communication communities.

Boundaries define countries. A *country* is an area with a highly interdependent communication community not separated by sharp internal boundaries. A country typically is both a unified economic and communication community. A message from the capital is likely to be disseminated with equal frequency throughout the territory of a country. Trade and economic policies are promulgated throughout the entire territory of a country. People in such interdependent entities have a feeling of mutual identification, of being "in the same boat."[12]

In time, a country can constitute a *people*, groups of individuals "united together by a high ability to communicate." They communicate not just on a few topics, but on many different ones. A people has a history, shared experiences, and customs. They can predict one another's behavior. In contrast, "a *foreigner* is a person whose responses we find it difficult to predict."[13] We place boundaries at those points where we find it hard to recognize the communication habits of the others and where we cannot predict their behavior.

A *state* is an area within which certain laws can be enforced because people obey them voluntarily. States are those areas where compliance to laws is high. "When a country, a people, and a nation coincide by and large," we have the modern *nation–state.*[14]

As examples, today's Poland is made up of almost all Polish-speaking, Catholic, ethnic Poles.[15] Within Poland there is a high level of communication; mutual predictability; ease of organization; and economic, political, and social interaction. Poland is one example where the terms *people, culture, state and nation–state* largely coincide. However, if one examines such multilingual and multicultural countries as Canada, Cyprus, India, and Sri Lanka, the definitions also apply very well in those countries.

Some of the most interesting examples of communication and nationalism are the so-called "forbidden nations." The peoples of these nations have contiguous territory and a unified language and culture, but they do not live in nation–states of their own choosing. Some have lost their sovereignty; others never had it.

Within Europe alone, there are at least fifteen "forbidden nations." These include Brittany and Languedoc in France; Euzkadi and Catalonia in Spain; Scotland, Wales, Cornwall, and the Isle of Man in Great Britain; Sardinia, Friuli, and the Ladin Dolomites in Italy; the Grisons in Switzerland; Friesland in the Netherlands; the Faeroe Islands in Denmark; and Lapland in Finland, Norway, and Sweden (see Figure 3-2.) Macedonia in Yugoslavia, Corsica in France, Galicia in Spain, and many others could also be included. In all these cases, the culture and language do not correspond with that of the dominant state authority.[16] Some, like the Basque people of Euzkadi, have waged a bitter struggle for independence. Others, like the Welsh and Scots, have limited their pro-independence activities to debating forums. Still others, like the Sorbs in Germany, live somewhat autonomously (and often uneasily) within a larger national framework. A fourth group, like the Manx from the Isle of Man, have virtually lost their self-identity. Throughout the world dozens of "forbidden nations" are struggling for identity and recognition, united under the banner of an "alternative United Nations" called the Unrepresented Nations and Peoples Organization.[17] (See Table 3-1 for a list of nations involved in this organization in 1991.)

Communication and Social Forces

Canadian political economist Harold Innis was one of the earliest authors in communication research to credit the powerful impact of technology on culture. In his *Empire and Communications* and *The Bias of Communication*, Innis demonstrated the reciprocal influence of communication, culture, and politics throughout history.[18] Indeed, information and communication within national societies reflect the needs, interests, and aims of prevailing social forces. The channels and content of a nation's media cannot be viewed in isolation from the conditions in which they arise. In every society, media are controlled by certain groups and are used to perpetuate the dominance of certain groups both within that society and in relation to other societies in the world. Just as U.S. media are infused with free-market ideology and filled with

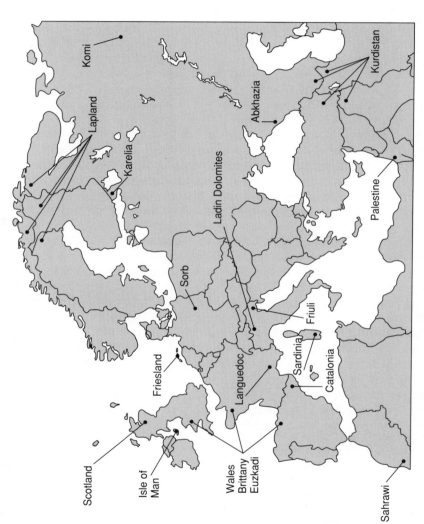

FIGURE 3-2   Throughout the world dozens of "forbidden nations" are struggling for sovereignty and security.

TABLE 3-1
Unrepresented Nations and Peoples Organization:
Nations and Peoples Invited to the Second General Assembly, 1991

Abkhazia	Greek Minority in Albania*
Acheh*	Hawaii
All Indian Pueblo Council (AIPC)	Inner Mongolia
Amazonia	International Indian Treaty Council
Armenia*	Iraq Terkleri*
Assyria*	Komi
Assembly of First Nations (Canada)	Kurdistan*
Australian Aborigines*	Latvia*
Belau*	Maasai
Bougainville*	Mari
Burmese Karen National Union	Mohawk Nation
Chechenskaya*	Onondaga Nation
Cherokee Nation of Oklahoma	Republic of South Moluccas*
Chittagong Hill Tracts*	Samiland
Cordillera*	Sarawak
Crimea*	Taiwan*
East Timor	Tataristan*
East Turkestan*	Tibet*
Eritrea	West Papua*
Estonia	World Council of Indigenous Peoples
Georgia*	Zanzibar*

*Members of the Unrepresented Nations and Peoples Organization

SOURCE: Unrepresented Nations and Peoples Organization, 1991

commercial advertisements, media throughout the world reflect the ruling ideas prevalent in their societies.[19] As Judge Learned Hand once stated, "The hand that rules the press, the radio, the screen, and the far-spread magazine rules the country."[20]

Throughout the world, the allocation and conduct of power are associated with the control of information resources. Information is power in a double sense: it is a commodity with both intrinsic and exchange value, and power can be exercised only through communication and information channels. Increasingly, power depends on access to information, control of its processing, and knowledge of its application in decision making. If knowledge is power, then nations controlling information are indeed powerful.

Technology is not politically neutral. Quite the contrary, it plays an important role in the international distribution of power and the exercise of political, social, and economic controls. Like all products of human labor, technology has a social origin. Its development is connected with certain social needs, purposes, and practices as perceived by centers of power.

As Hamelink quips, "the barrel of a gun can, if one insists, be used to stir one's tea. It is, however, better at killing, and will certainly be used primarily for that application."[21] Technologies "can foster liberation or deepen dependency and domination, depending on the objectives of and social environment in which they are applied."[22]

Classifying Communication within National Societies

National media systems cannot exceed the limits permitted by the nation's society; on the other hand, they cannot lag very far behind. Because media systems are

social in origin and decidedly not neutral, writers have sought to categorize communication systems around the world.

Free press versus controlled press

In this scheme, media can be either controlled systems with explicit rules (authoritarian) or free and open, self-determined, autonomous, and nonrestrictive, with a minimum of rules (libertarian). In reality, there is a spectrum of systems rather than a
polar dichotomy. Journalists and media workers experience varying degrees of
autonomy and restriction.[23] Freedom of communication means different things in different societies, but it is possible to describe one society as *freer* than another.

Most democratic countries have laws governing libel, obscenity, invasion of privacy, and antitrust. But only the United States enjoys the protections afforded by the
First Amendment. Many otherwise "free-press" countries often have censorship,
prior-restraint, judicial gag orders, and legal limits on who can practice journalism. For
example, in Austria, special "press judges" can impose prior-restraint orders against
the press. In Belgium, the title "professional journalist" can only be used legally by
people who meet certain qualifications. The Italian government subsidizes newsprint
purchases, telephone services, and mail deliveries of newspapers.

Even under the First Amendment, in the United States a battery of laws restricts
the circulation of certain kinds of content in the interests of national security, foreign
policy, border control, trade protectionism, or other concerns.

Here are some of the kinds of communication content controlled or forbidden in
the United States:

Defamation: One may not expose another person to public hatred, shame, contempt or disgrace, or induce an evil opinion of another person.

Privacy: These laws prohibit appropriation of another's name or likeness, unreasonable intrusion upon another's seclusion, publicity that unreasonably
places another in a false light before the public, and unreasonable publicity
given to another's private life.

Obscenity: Mass media come under a bewildering assortment of content restrictions regarding obscenity. "Indecency" is banned from American airwaves.

National security and state secrets: The government forbids disclosure of information that might compromise the national security.

Deceptive advertising: The Federal Trade Commission regulates misleading
advertising, and the Federal Communications Commission monitors loud-
ness, number, and separation of commercial advertisements.

World communism: The McCarran-Walter Immigration Act bars entry of aliens
who "advocate the economic, international, and governmental doctrines of
world communism . . . "

Political propaganda: The Foreign Agents Registration Act forbids registered
agents from disseminating "political propaganda," defined as any communication content intended to "influence a recipient . . . with reference to
the political or public interests, policies, or relations of a government of a
foreign country . . . or with reference to the foreign policies of the United
States. . . . "[24]

In a similar vein, in 1987 Merrill computed a Control Inclination Index (CII) for
fifty-eight countries around the world. (See Table 3-2.) The CII did not reflect actual

TABLE 3-2
Merrill's 1987 Control Inclination Index

Strict control	Moderate control	Little control
German Democratic Republic	Ivory Coast	South Africa
People's Republic of China	Hungary	Philippines
Iraq	Pakistan	New Zealand
Syria	Argentina	Norway
Tunisia	Ecuador	India
Cuba	Guyana	Sweden
Peru	Nigeria	Australia
Bulgaria	Poland	Japan
Jordan	Portugal	Netherlands
Paraguay	Bangladesh	United Kingdom
Ethiopia	Indonesia	Federal Republic of Germany
USSR	South Korea	Mexico
Lebanon	Austria	Greece
Angola	Denmark	Canada
Czechoslovakia	Turkey	United States of America
Yugoslavia	Chile	
Egypt	Costa Rica	
Panama	Guatemala	
Central African Republic	Sudan	
Zimbabwe	Finland	
Malaysia	Spain	
Kuwait		
Bolivia		

control; rather, it reflected governmental inclination to control the media based on attitudes on six factors: in-country licensing of journalists, international licensing, identification cards or accreditation, university education, in-country codes of ethics, and international codes of ethics.[25]

Four "theories" of the press
Drawing and expanding on the authoritarian–libertarian dichotomy, one of the most influential books in the field of communication was a slender volume published in 1956 called *Four Theories of the Press*. Although not "theories" in the traditional sense, these four "approaches" to the press—authoritarian, libertarian, communist, and social responsibility—imprinted a set of social categories on communication researchers for more than three decades.[26]

Authoritarianism. Authoritarianism, in the political sense, is the insistence by a government authority on total submission to its will. The authority may be that of a leader, an elite, or a party. In the authoritarian system, mass communication champions the state and government and promotes regulated economic, political, and social development. Media serve as educators and propagandists for the ruling power elite. Journalists serve at the whim of the elite and have only as much freedom as the leadership allows.

Libertarianism. Arising in Europe in the period between the Reformation and the French Revolution, and drawing especially on English and American revolutionary political thought, libertarianism places rational human beings at the center of the universe. A libertarian press presents the diverse "truths" of a society, however fragmented they may be in a pluralist community. Libertarians have faith that an unfettered press will present all the viewpoints necessary for a democratic society.

Communism.   Deriving from the writings of Marx and Engels as elaborated by Lenin, communism sees the world as a perpetual struggle between two main classes: the capitalists, who own the productive resources, and the workers, who must work for wages in order to survive. Communism also signifies a centralized political system, collective ownership of the means of production, central economic planning, and rule by a single political party. In a communist system, media function as collective agitators, propagandists, and organizers toward these goals. What is important is not the "truth," but rather transmission of social policy.

Social responsibility.   The social responsibility approach goes beyond libertarian- ism. Inspired largely by the 1947 Hutchins Commission on Freedom of the Press, this approach reaches back to Thomas Jefferson, who, in his comments about the draft Bill of Rights, stated:

> The people shall not be deprived of their right to speak, to write or otherwise to publish anything but the false facts affecting injuriously the life, liberty, property or reputation of others, or affecting the peace of the confederacy with foreign nations.[27]

In other words, Jefferson believed in *freedom with responsibility*. Viewing the excesses of a free and sometimes irresponsible press in the first half of this century, the Hutchins Commission maintained that the obligation of social responsibility must be imposed on the media.

Non-ideological classification

The preceding systems of classifications have many inherent problems. Mowlana recognized the problems with these classification systems and designed a non-ideo- logical schema that accounts for many aspects of variation in the world's communi- cation systems.[28] (See Figure 3-3.) He criticized earlier models for overgeneralizing at the cost of careful consideration of diversity. There are many countries, he says, whose media systems have aspects of all four "approaches." Practically all media systems can claim to be "socially responsible." Mowlana proposed eight broad areas that classify both message formation and distribution: types of ownership, types of control, sources of operation, disposition of income and capital, complexity of media bureaucracy, perceived purpose, number and circulation of messages, and types of content.

The Information Society

Dramatic changes are sweeping our world. Many have their cause or effect in the information and communication sectors. Here are some examples.

- More than a third of America's $5.5 trillion GNP is generated from ideas rather than from manufactured goods.[29]

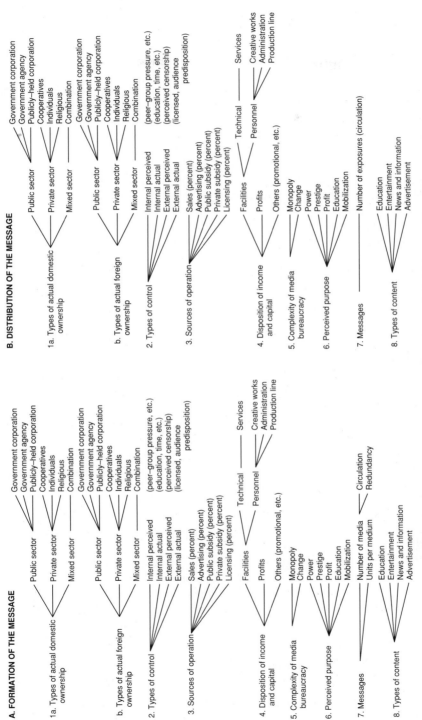

A. FORMATION OF THE MESSAGE

1a. Types of actual domestic ownership
- Public sector
  - Government corporation
  - Government agency
  - Publicly-held corporation
  - Cooperatives
- Private sector
  - Individuals
  - Religious
  - Combination
- Mixed sector
  - Government corporation
  - Government agency
  - Publicly-held corporation
  - Cooperatives
  - Individuals
  - Religious
  - Combination

b. Types of actual foreign ownership
- Public sector
- Private sector
- Mixed sector

2. Types of control
- Internal perceived
- Internal actual
- External perceived
- External actual
  - (peer-group pressure, etc.)
  - (education, time, etc.)
  - (perceived censorship)
  - (licensed, audience predisposition)

3. Sources of operation
- Sales (percent)
- Advertising (percent)
- Public subsidy (percent)
- Private subsidy (percent)
- Licensing (percent)
  - Facilities
  - Technical — Services
  - Personnel — Creative works / Administration / Production line

4. Disposition of income and capital
- Profits
- Others (promotional, etc.)

5. Complexity of media bureaucracy
- Monopoly
- Change
- Power

6. Perceived purpose
- Prestige
- Profit
- Education
- Mobilization

7. Messages
- Number of media
- Units per medium — Circulation / Redundancy

8. Types of content
- Education
- Entertainment
- News and information
- Advertisement

B. DISTRIBUTION OF THE MESSAGE

1a. Types of actual domestic ownership
- Public sector
  - Government corporation
  - Government agency
  - Publicly-held corporation
  - Cooperatives
- Private sector
  - Individuals
  - Religious
  - Combination
- Mixed sector
  - Government corporation
  - Government agency
  - Publicly-held corporation
  - Cooperatives
  - Individuals
  - Religious
  - Combination

b. Types of actual foreign ownership
- Public sector
- Private sector
- Mixed sector

2. Types of control
- Internal perceived
- Internal actual
- External perceived
- External actual
  - (peer-group pressure, etc.)
  - (education, time, etc.)
  - (perceived censorship)
  - (licensed, audience predisposition)

3. Sources of operation
- Sales (percent)
- Advertising (percent)
- Public subsidy (percent)
- Private subsidy (percent)
- Licensing (percent)
  - Facilities
  - Technical — Services
  - Personnel — Creative works / Administration / Production line

4. Disposition of income and capital
- Profits
- Others (promotional, etc.)

5. Complexity of media bureaucracy
- Monopoly
- Change
- Power

6. Perceived purpose
- Prestige
- Profit
- Education
- Mobilization

7. Messages
- Number of exposures (circulation)

8. Types of content
- Education
- Entertainment
- News and information
- Advertisement

FIGURE 3-3 Mowlana's paradigm for comparative analysis of mass media systems categorizes media systems functionally by message formation and distribution.

SOURCE: *International and Intercultural Communication*, by H. D. Fischer and J. C. Merrill, pp. 478–479. Copyright © 1976 by Hastings House Publishers. Reprinted with permission.

- By the year 2000, Japan's production of information technology and services will represent more than 20 percent of its GNP. [30]
- Electronic funds transfers have reached $9 trillion annually—equal to two-thirds of the world's GNP. Six of every seven transferred dollars are transferred electronically. [31]
- American Airlines earns more revenue from its computerized reservation system—most of which is run by English-speaking operators out of the Dominican Republic—than from its traditional airline business. [32]
- Many of the world's most sophisticated industrial products are assembled by the world's lowest-paid industrial workers. More than a quarter of a million non-Japanese Asians, primarily young women, assemble the components of the information age at wages that cannot support a family. [33]
- With the capability to move vast quantities of data under the sea through optical fibers, data processing is moving to where labor costs are lowest. Calls between Osaka and Tokyo may well be switched in San Francisco. More likely, calls between Los Angeles and San Francisco will be switched in Japan. [34]

While some nations languish in the "pre-electronic" age, other nations are quickly leaving the industrial age behind and entering the information age. Telecommunications services grew by 800 percent worldwide in the 1980s. According to UNESCO, the total world information and communication economy in 1986 was $1,185 billion, about 8 to 9 percent of total world output, of which $515 billion was in the United States.

As shown in Table 3-3, modern communications are divided into three components. The *media* are the producers of information content. They include the press and publishing and recording industries as well as television, radio, and cinema. The *service industry* is the sector that actually processes and disseminates information. It includes computing services, data processing, software, on-line data bases, computer communications services, postal services, and telecommunications common carriers (telephone, telegraph, telefax, and so on). Finally, the *equipment industry* manufactures the capital goods needed for the other two sectors. These manufacturers can be divided into data processing and office automation equipment, telecommunications equipment, electronic and non-electronic (e.g. photographic) products, testing instruments, navigation equipment, computer-assisted design and manufacturing equipment, and "components" (which are actually input for other products).

The telecommunications equipment and services market is one of the fastest growing internationally. For example, the equipment component of Table 3-4 accounts for a 13-percent share in exports of manufactured goods and is growing at a 15-percent annual rate. [35] Computer services are growing at a 24-percent annual rate. [36] Many knowledgeable observers believe that communications and information will one day become the world's largest single industry—a distinction now held by agriculture. [37]

The U.S. government estimates that more than two-thirds of the U.S. work force is now engaged in information-related jobs, and telecommunication equipment and services are the United States' third largest export. [38] Almost half the Gross National Product of the 14 most industrialized countries, and one-quarter of all international trade,

TABLE 3-3
Information and Communication Economy by Sectors, 1986
(in billions of dollars)

	World	U.S.	Japan	EEC	Others
Media	315	140	65	70	40
Services	380	180	50	90	60
Equipment	400	165	108	92	35
Components	90	30	30	15	15
Total	1185	515	253	267	150

SOURCE: Institut pour le Développement de l'Audiovisuel et des Telecommunications en Europe, contribution to *World Communication Report* (Paris: UNESCO, 1989), p. 83.

comes from services.[39] The growth is not limited to the developed countries. A number of countries in Asia and Latin America have developed national electronic industries of some scope. Electronic products account for 20 to 50 percent of the manufactured exports in Singapore, Malaysia, the Philippines, Taiwan, and South Korea.[40]

The implications are tremendous. As the Economic Commission for Europe has written,

the construction of new integrated digital telecommunication systems and networks represents an investment in infrastructure perhaps as important for industrial and economic development as were earlier investments in railways, roads and electricity transmissions.[41]

The most widespread development has been in *informatics* (the automation of telecommunications and the linkage of data transmissions to computers for analysis). Together with word processing and computerized management, informatic systems have totally transformed finance, banking, business management, and public management.

The role of communications technologies in economic development has been studied for decades.[42] The macroeconomic impact is difficult to determine, but it is "sensed intuitively that telecommunications are much more important than generally suspected, and have major multiplier effects on development."[43] Summarizing the research, one writer has said: "If trade is the lifeblood of an economy, then telecommunications can truly be regarded as the nervous system of both the economy and society."[44] For example, a very strong correlation exists between gross national product and telephone density.[45] In the social-service sector, new telecommunications technologies assist in everything from health care delivery to educational administration. In the economy, these technologies facilitate more efficient production and marketing systems, reduce business transaction costs, help counteract rural-to-urban migration, substitute for travel, contribute to social change, assist in national development, and improve the overall quality of life.

Genesis of the Information Society

The term *information society* is used to describe the transformation within certain national societies that have undergone the "information revolution." Bell sees three kinds of societies:

In *preindustrial* societies . . . the labor force is engaged overwhelmingly in the extractive industries, including mining, fishing, forestry, agriculture. Life is primarily a game against nature. . . . *Industrial* societies are goods-producing societies. Life is a game against fabricated nature. The world has become technical and rationalized. . . . A *post-industrial* society is based on services. Hence, it is a game between persons. What counts is not raw muscle power, or energy, but information.[46] [Emphasis added]

Four factors distinguish the information economy:

1. The economy is primarily oriented to service rather than to manufacturing; the knowledge industry predominates.
2. The labor force is no longer dominated by people operating machines (machine operatives), but by people manipulating information (information operatives).
3. The economy is no longer based on cash flow, but on credit flow.
4. The economy is primarily transnational rather than national; trade has expanded beyond national borders.

There are three prerequisites to reaching this stage:

1. There must be an extensive computer communications ("telematics") infrastructure.
2. There must be a wide range of service industries that sell information as a commodity or in which information is the primary component.
3. There must be a national system of social, economic, and political stimulus to the service industries.

What enterprises make up the "information economy" in practice? On the *service* side, these industries include electronic and print media, advertising, education, telecommunications services, parts of finance and insurance, libraries, consulting, maritime transport, travel and tourism services, components of engineering and construction, and research and development firms. On the *goods* side, industries include computer, communications, and electronic equipment manufacturers; office and business machines; measuring and control instruments; and printing presses. We must not forget that every firm has an "information services" component. Firms hire "information labor," require information input, have information overheads. So in addition to the information services and information goods industries, there is the "internal information" produced and consumed by "noninformation" firms.[47] (See Table 3-4.)

Marc Porat has the distinction of first pointing this out authoritatively. He demonstrated the following in a 1977 report for the U.S. Department of Commerce:

The [United States] is now an information-based economy. By 1967, 25 percent of GNP originated in the production, processing, and distribution of information goods and services. In addition, over 21 percent of the GNP originated in the production of information services by the private and public bureaucracies for purely international uses. By 1970, close to half of the U.S. workforce was classified as "information workers," holding a job where the production, processing, or distribution of symbols is the main activity.[48]

TABLE 3-4
Inventory of Information Occupations

INFORMATION PRODUCERS

Scientific and Technical: chemists, physicists, physical scientists, civil engineers, electrical and electronic engineers, mechanical engineers, metallurgists, mining engineers, industrial engineers, biologists, zoologists, bacteriologists, pharmacologists, agronomists, statisticians, mathematicians,
economists, sociologists, anthropologists

Market Search and Coordination Specialists: commodity brokers, purchasing agents and buyers,
technical salespeople and advisors, insurance and stock brokers, business services advertising
salespeople, auctioneers

Information Gatherers: workstudy officers, surveyors, inspectors, testers

Consultative Services: architects and town planners, drafters, medical practitioners, dietitians and
nutritionists, optometrists, systems analysts, computer programmers, accountants, barristers, advocates, and solicitors, education methods advisors, commercial artists, designers

Information Producers: authors, composers

INFORMATION PROCESSORS

Administrative and Managerial: judges, head teachers, legislative officials, government administra-
tors, general managers, production managers, government officials

Process Control and Supervisory: clerks of works, flight and ship navigating officers, transport and
communications supervisors, dispatching/receiving clerks, clerical and sales supervisors, supervisors and general foremen

Clerical and Related: auditors, stenographers, typists, and teletypists, bookkeepers, cost computing
clerks, wage clerks, finance clerks, stock records clerks, material and production planning clerks,
correspondence and reporting clerks, receptionists and travel agents, library and filing clerks, statistical clerks, coding clerks, proofreaders

Educators: university and higher education teachers, secondary teachers, primary teachers, pre-
primary teachers, special education teachers

Communication Workers: journalists and writers, stage directors, motion picture, radio, and television
directors, storytellers, producers, performers

INFORMATION INFRASTRUCTURE OCCUPATIONS

Information Machine Workers: photographers and camera operators, teleprinter operators, card and
tape-punching machine operators, bookkeeping and calculating machine operators, automatic
data processing machine operators, office machine operators, office machine repairers, sound and
vision equipment operators, compositors and typesetters, printing press operators, stereotypers
and electrotypers, printing engravers, photo-engravers, bookbinders, photographic processors

Postal and Telecommunications: mail carriers, mailsorters, messengers, telephone operators, radio
and television repairers, telephone and telegraph installers and repairers, telephone and telegraph
linespersons, broadcasting station operators

TABLE 3-5
Percentage of Labor Force in
Information Industries in
Selected Countries by 1980–82

Country	Percentage
United States	46
Australia	42
United Kingdom	41
New Zealand	40
Japan	38
Sweden	36
FRG	35
Hungary	32
Finland	30

SOURCE: *Trends in the Information Economy* (Paris: OECD, 1986); and sources cited in *World Communication Report* (Paris: UNESCO, 1989), pp. 110–111.

The Organization for Economic Cooperation and Development (OECD) has calculated this figure to be more than 30 percent in most developed countries.[49] (See Table 3-5.)

Porat wrote that the economy was traditionally divided into three sectors: agriculture, industry, and services. Viewing the revolutionary changes in the economy after World War II, he added a fourth sector—information—which included teachers, selected managers, selected clerical workers, selected professionals (accountants, lawyers), and people who work at information machines (computer and telephone operators). The criterion for inclusion in this fourth sector was whether the information-handling aspect of the job overshadowed the noninformation aspects. Figure 3-4 is a graphical depiction of the four-sector aggregation of the U.S. work force from 1860 through 1980.

According to Porat, in Stage I (1860–1906) agriculture dominated the U.S. work force. In Stage II (1906–1954) the industrial work force was pre-eminent, reaching a peak of 40 percent in 1946. This was the period we might call "industrial" society. In Stage III (1954–present) information workers became the largest sector of the economy. By 1978 the number of industrial workers had declined to only 25 percent of the U.S. labor force, while information workers made up about 47 percent of the work force.[50]

This revolutionary development in the world economy is known by many terms. Driven by the marriage of two technologies—computers and communications—in the United States we call it the "information society." The Harvard Program on Information Resources Policy coined the word *compunications* to describe the technological nexus. The French use the words *telematique* or *informatique*. The famous Nora–Minc report, commissioned by the French government, called it "l'informatisation de la société."[51]

The information revolution has had a tremendous impact on the labor movement and on the "smokestack" industries. Core industries such as steel, automotive, and

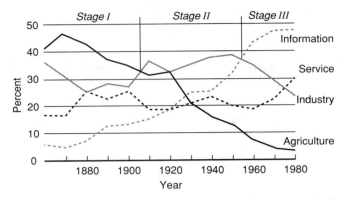

FIGURE 3-4   Four-Sector Aggregation of the U. S. Work Force, 1860–1980 (using median estimates of information workers). By 1954 the labor force was predominantly in the information sector.

SOURCE: Marc Uri Porat, *The Information Economy: Definition and Measurement*, No. 77–12(1) (Washington, DC: Office of Telecommunications, Department of Commerce, 1977).

textiles have increasingly been replaced by electronics, aerospace, and banking, where information processing is the essential characteristic. Wide-ranging changes have occurred in the labor force. Traditional manufacturing used to require high input from labor and machinery, but little information. New industries require just the reverse. Even today's manufacturing industries are requiring increasing input of information; about 10 percent of the manufacturing work forces in West Germany, Japan, and Sweden are information occupations.[52]

COMMUNICATION BETWEEN NATIONAL SOCIETIES

Just as the gap is increasing between the world's rich and the world's poor, there are growing disparities between the *information-rich* and the *information-poor* of the world. This is true even within the United States, where the gap between those who can access communication services and use information strategically and those who cannot is likely to increase.[53]

Researchers have collected a large body of evidence to confirm this trend. They have also pointed to the far-reaching consequences. Summarizing this research, Hamelink argues that

current international information structures promote dependence between nations, legitimize existing economic disparities, and contribute to the cultural synchronization of the world.[54]

Called the "largest machine in the world," the world telecommunications network is one of the marvels of the twentieth century. Yet it is no exaggeration to say that 90 percent of this network serves only 15 percent of the world's nations.[55] Many nations and peoples have not yet entered the era of electronic technologies. The United States, Western Europe, and some ASEAN (Association of Southeast Asian Nations) countries have experienced the most far-reaching innovations of new technology. But most Third World nations are so far behind in the high technology race that the perpetual debt crisis will probably prohibit them from ever overcoming this technology chasm. Even within societies and between men and women, social inequalities are worsening due to uneven access to new communication technologies.

The World's Info-Rich and Info-Poor

The world is divided between the haves and the have-nots. Even within a single nation, wide disparities exist between rich and poor, urban and rural, men and women. The people of the "First World" make up only a quarter of the world's population, yet they control half its income. The poorest fifth of the world's population earns only 2 percent of the world's GNP. This gap is over twice as large as it was thirty years ago.[56]

The world of communication is also divided into the haves and the have-nots, or the *info-rich* and the *info-poor*.[57] The nations with a huge proportion of info-poor people start at a great disadvantage in terms of development. As Hans Singer has said:

> If you do not have information to begin with, or know what new information could be assembled, initial inferiority is bound to be sharpened and perpetuated. This unequal bargaining position will affect all relations whether labeled aid, trade, investment, transfer of technology, technical assistance, or any other.[58]

UNESCO published its first comparative worldwide survey of media in 1962. Dozens of similar analyses have shown that the disparities have not changed.[59] In virtually every medium, the gaps are dramatic. There are some rudimentary measuring sticks for communications development. UNESCO set basic standards for newspapers, radio, and cinema: Every country should have 100 newspaper copies, 50 radio receivers, and 20 cinema seats for every 1,000 inhabitants.[60] Remarkably, the latest statistics reveal that only one developing country, Cuba, has met all three minimum standards.

Newspapers

Around the world each day, more than 8,500 newspapers publish over 575 million copies. The developed countries account for 70 percent of total newspaper production. Although developing countries, with three-quarters of the world's population, own about one-half of the world's daily newspapers, they can manage only 30 percent of the world's newspaper output.[61] In 34 countries and territories, no daily general-interest newspapers are published.[62] Another thirty nations had only a single newspaper. Eighteen countries had ten or fewer daily newspaper copies available per one thousand people. (The United States has 259.)[63]

Daily newspaper circulation in the developed countries was over 406 million copies, more than twice the 169 million copies in the developing countries. But in per capita terms, the disparity was more than sevenfold.[64] The UNESCO-recommended minimum is 100 copies per 1,000 people. Even in Europe, Albania, Spain, and Portugal have not yet met this standard. The only developing countries to reach this level were Mexico, Suriname, and fifteen island nations.[65] Overall, developed countries had 337 daily newspaper copies per 1,000 inhabitants, whereas the developing countries averaged only 43 copies, less than one-half the UNESCO-recommended level.[66] These statistics do not account for the great differences between urban and rural populations. Nor do they reflect the extraordinarily high cost of subscriptions. In India, Thailand, and the Philippines, an annual subscription to a newspaper represents eleven to twenty days' work for a teacher.[67]

Books

Book production has increased dramatically around the world. In the developed countries, book production increased from 225,000 titles a year in 1955, to 451,000 in 1970, to 613,000 in 1988. In the developing countries, book production climbed dramatically from 44,000 in 1955, to 70,000 in 1970, to 221,500 in 1988 (a threefold increase in the last eighteen years).[68]

Yet the Third World's share of total world book production continues to remain disproportionately low. The developed countries (with 25 percent of world population) accounted for 73 percent of the total book production. The developing countries (with 75 percent of world population) accounted for only 27 percent.[69] (See Table 3-6.)

Illiteracy and cost are major restrictions on the spread of books. Illiterates make up 60 percent of the population in Africa, 40 percent in Asia, and 25 percent in Latin America. Most books, even paperbacks, are very expensive compared to the incomes of most people in the world. Virtually all lending libraries in the Third World are in the metropolitan centers and thereby exclude populations living in the countryside.

Another glaring disparity is the differences in distribution of book titles per million inhabitants. In the developed countries, there were 507 book titles per million people (0.5 per 100 people) in 1988, but in the developing countries this figure was only 57 (0.06 per 100 people), a ratio of almost 9 to 1. But this figure masks vast differences. For every one hundred Americans, there were two new book titles yearly (four times the "developed countries" average), whereas every one hundred Danes had twenty-two new book titles! In areas with great population increases, there has been a net decline in book titles per inhabitant. Overall, after peaking in 1970, the world has suffered a decline in books per capita from 187 per million in 1970 to 164 per million in 1988.

About 65 percent of the world's population experiences an acute book shortage.[70] The increasing demand for scientific, technical, and educational books and the shortage of printing paper requires most developing countries to import increasing quantities of books from the developed countries of the West. However, the flow of books from the developing countries to the developed world remains slight. Essentially, the flow of books between the two groups is a one-way flow, with increasing concentration of the publishing industry in a few multinational corporations. The United States of America, Great Britain, and Germany are among the largest exporters of books. Europe alone accounts for 53 percent of total world book production. (See Table 3-7.)

The leading book exporters are Great Britain and the United States, which benefit from the increasing use of English as a second language. Translations also play an important part in the international flow of printed materials. Of the 167 authors most frequently translated between 1961 and 1984, only 3 came from outside Europe and North America.[71]

TABLE 3-6
Book Production in Number of New Titles, 1988

	Total titles	Titles per million people	Distribution percentage
World	834,500	164	100.0
Developed countries	613,000	507	73.5
Developing countries	221,500	57	26.5
Africa	12,000	20	1.5
Asia	154,000	68	24.0
Europe	456,000	584	54.6
Oceania	12,000	462	1.4
North America	106,000	390	12.7
Latin America and Caribbean	48,000	122	5.8

SOURCE: *UNESCO Statistical Yearbook 1990* (Paris: UNESCO, 1990), pp. 6–11.

TABLE 3-7
Export of Books and Pamphlets, 1985 (in thousands of dollars)

Country	Export amount
United Kingdom	612,323
United States	591,358
Federal Republic of Germany	340,127
France	241,545
Spain	235,230
Italy	158,500
Netherlands	149,182
Japan	145,430

SOURCE: Compiled by UNESCO from COMTRADE (UN Statistical Office), *World Communication Report* (Paris: UNESCO, 1989), p. 500.

Cultural Paper

In the developed world, the consumption of newsprint and printing or writing paper (called "cultural paper") was 28.0 million metric tons and 49.9 million metric tons, respectively, in 1988. In the developing countries, it was a meager 3.8 million and 6.0 million, respectively. Developed countries consumed 88 percent of the total world production. Europe and North America alone consumed 75 percent of the world's cultural paper.[72] Yet these statistics disguise even greater disparities. Although Africa consumed 400,000 metric tons of newsprint in 1988, 60 percent of that was concentrated in three countries (South Africa, Egypt, and Nigeria).

The typical person in the developed countries consumed 65 kilograms of cultural paper each year, while the average Third World person consumed only 2.5 kilograms. Remarkably, with a yearly consumption of 140 kilograms, North Americans consumed more than twice as much cultural paper as people in other developed countries. The average North American consumes more newsprint in four days than the average African does in one year.[73] The *Los Angeles Times* buys more newsprint each year than does all of Sweden. Readers of the *Los Angeles Times* exceed the African yearly per capita average each Sunday.[74] By contrast, in Cuba newsprint is so scarce and expensive that only one newspaper can print daily.[75]

More than 80 percent of world paper production originates in Canada, the United States, Japan, Scandinavia, Russia, and Germany. Eighty percent of world consumption goes to twelve countries, with the United States occupying first place with 11 million tons (forty percent of the world amount), followed by Japan with 3 million (ten percent).[76]

Paper production is one of the most energy-intensive industries. To produce one ton of paper, one to two tons of black coal or one ton of natural gas is required. Energy costs make up 15 to 50 percent of every paper product.[77] Although the Third World produces no more than 6 percent of all pulp, some countries have increased their production considerably in the last few years, especially the Philippines, China, South Korea, India, and Brazil.

Cinema

Production and distribution of cinematic films is a major area of global information flow. Disparities in this area are not in the production of films. In fact, in 1987 the developed countries produced 1,900 films, and the developing countries produced 2,140.[78] India leads the world, with 806 films and exports to 80 countries.[79] (See Table 3-8.)

What is remarkable here is that the United States, while not the largest *producer*, continues to be the single largest *exporter*. Together, the United States, France, Italy, Great Britain, and Germany account for 80 to 90 percent of all exported films.[80] Together with music and television, movie exports make up the United States's second largest trade surplus after aircraft. By the year 2000, half the revenue from American entertainment media will be earned abroad.[81]

Only twenty countries around the world have met the UNESCO-recommended standard of 20 movie seats per 1,000 people.[82] Cinema seating capacity in the developing countries averaged only 7 per 1,000 inhabitants, as compared to 50 in the developed countries.[83] Nevertheless, annual cinema attendance in developing countries is 7,670 million, in comparison to 6,530 million in the developed countries. In the developed countries, there is a declining trend in both seating capacity and annual attendance since the 1970s, due largely to the advent of large-scale cable and broadcast television and the VCR. However, in the case of the developing countries, while annual cinema attendance has grown 60 percent from 1970 to 1987, cinema facilities have not kept pace with population growth, and television is beyond the reach of the masses.[84]

Radio

The one area where the developing countries have made substantial progress in reducing disparities is in radio receivers. The transistor revolution in the 1960s, coupled with plummeting prices and increasing illiteracy in the Third World, raised the number of radio receivers. Between 1970 and 1987, the number of radios in the world increased more than 250 percent; the developing countries' share rose 600 percent. Per capita penetration has improved in the developing world, too. The number of receivers per 1,000 inhabitants in the developed countries was 1,006 in 1988, while in the developing countries it was 173, a 6-to-1 discrepancy. In 1970, this ratio was 14 to 1.[85] (See Table 3-9.)

But the disparity between the developed and developing worlds is still substantial. In 1988 the developed countries accounted for almost two-thirds of radio receivers in the world, with North America and Europe alone having about 57 percent of the world's receivers. In fact, the average North American had access to two radio receivers each. In spite of the remarkable growth in absolute numbers of radio sets in certain countries and regions, the penetration of radio receivers still remains very uneven. In Africa, so dependent on radio, there were only 165 radios per 1,000

TABLE 3-8
Ten Leading Producers of
Feature Films, 1987

Country	Number of feature films
India	806
USA	578
Japan	286
USSR	156
France	133
Thailand	134
Hong Kong	130*
Italy	116
Turkey	96
Mexico	82

*The figure for Hong Kong is from 1986.

SOURCE: *UNESCO Statistical Year-book 1990* (Paris: UNESCO, 1990), pp. 9-3 to 9-6.

TABLE 3-9
Radio Broadcasting Receivers, 1988

	Number (million)	Receivers per 1,000 people
World Total	1,891	370
Africa	101	165
America	691	985
Asia	543	181
Europe (excluding the former USSR)	531	683
Oceania	25	984
Developed countries	1,215	1,006
Developing countries	676	173
Africa (except Arab states)	66	142
Asia (except Arab states)	527	180
Arab states	51	245
North America	545	2,008
Latin America/Caribbean	146	339

SOURCE: *UNESCO Statistical Yearbook 1990* (Paris: UNESCO, 1990), pp. 6–20.

people, up from 102 per 1,000 in 1980.[86] In the Third World, the number of sets per 1,000 inhabitants ranges from about 25 (Burkina Faso) to 323 (South Africa) in African countries and from 40 (Haiti) to 1,080 (Netherlands Antilles) in Latin America and the Caribbean. Twelve developing countries still fall below the UNESCO-recommended minimum standard of fifty radios per 1,000 people.[87]

Developed countries operate two-thirds of the world's 37,850 radio transmitters,[88] including three-fifths of the medium-wave and 90 percent of the FM transmitters. Of approximately 13,000 FM transmitters in the world, almost half are installed in Europe, and one-third in Canada and the United States. The United States alone has three times more FM transmitters than all developing countries together.[89] These statistics do not reflect the fact that hundreds of transmitters in the Third World are actually repeaters for signals originating in the developed countries. Although the developing countries have made some progress in terms of radio receivers, they have not done so in terms of radio transmitters.

In terms of exports of radio receivers, the bulk of production rests in the hard-currency countries of Asia, followed by Europe and the United States. (See Table 3-10.)

Television

The number of television sets in the developing countries has increased over fourfold during the period from 1975 to 1988, whereas in developed countries it increased about 1½ times. Yet the developing world's considerable increase was accompanied by rapid population growth. As a result, per capita penetration increased at the same rate in most parts of the world.

The developed countries had 77 percent of the television receivers and 84 percent of the television transmitters in the world, while the developing world had only

TABLE 3-10
Value of Export
of Radio Receivers, 1985
(in thousands of dollars)

Country	Export value
Japan	$2,630,932
Singapore	497,484
Korea	497,107
Hong Kong	424,787
Federal Republic of Germany	228,931
United States	101,166
Belgium	97,023
Austria	96,373
France	94,118
United Kingdom	41,095

SOURCE: COMTRADE (U.N. Statistical Office), *World Communication Report* (Paris: UNESCO, 1989), p. 506.

TABLE 3-11
Television Receivers per Capita, 1988

	Total in millions	Per 1,000 people
World Total	756	148
Africa	17	28
Americas	279	398
Asia	160	53
Europe (including the former USSR)	289	372
Oceania	11	411
Developed Countries	585	485
Developing Countries	171	44
Africa (excluding Arab states)	7	14
Asia (excluding Arab states)	152	52
Arab States	19	90
North America	214	790
Latin America/Caribbean	64	149

SOURCE: *UNESCO Statistical Yearbook 1990* (Paris: UNESCO, 1990), pp. 6–22.

23 and 16 percent, respectively. The number of receivers per 1,000 inhabitants was 485 in the developed countries, as compared to only 44 in the developing countries—more than a 12-to-1 ratio. In 1988 North Americans enjoyed eighteen times more television receivers than the developing-world average and more than twice as many as Europe.[90] (See Table 3-11.) Almost half the world television audience is in the United States of America and the Commonwealth of Independent States.[91]

Per capita penetration of televisions is also very uneven. While every two to three people in most developed countries have a television receiver, in Latin America there are seven persons per set, in Asia more than eighteen, and in Africa thirty-six. In the least developed countries, the disparity is acute. In thirty-six countries of the world, there are fewer than 10 television receivers per 1,000 people, with thirteen countries having only 3 or fewer. Sixteen countries had only one television transmitter; dozens still have no color transmissions. In Africa, two-thirds of the countries have fewer than 10 television receivers per 1,000 inhabitants.[92]

Throughout the world, many countries depend heavily on imported television programming, primarily from the United States or, to a much lesser extent, Western Europe or Japan. Most of these programs are entertainment and sports programs. (See Table 3-12.)

Video

Non-broadcast video (videocassettes) appeared on the world scene only in the late 1970s. Non-broadcast video is an increasingly significant alternative to official and commercial control of media systems around the world. There are four "video-rich" areas: Japan and Southeast Asia, the Arab world, Western Europe, and North America. Most developing countries lag far behind in non-broadcast video. (See Table 3-13.)

TABLE 3-12
Imported Television Programming in Selected Countries, 1986
(percent of total programming)

Country	Percent of total programming	Country	Percent of total programming
Below 10%			
USA	2	India	8
Japan	6	USSR	8
China	8		
Between 11% and 30%			
Indonesia	12	Cuba	24
Philippines	12	Czechoslovakia	24
Republic of		Netherlands	25
Korea	12	Hungary	26
Pakistan	16	Bulgaria	27
France	17	Vietnam	28
United		Belgium	29
Kingdom	17	Yugoslavia	29
Italy	17	Ethiopia	30
Federal		German	
Republic of		Democratic	
Germany	20	Republic	30
Australia	21	Norway	30
Between 31% and 50%			
Canada	32	Turkey	39
Syria	33	Argentina	40
Venezuela	33	Nigeria	40
Mexico	34	Sri Lanka	40
Egypt	35	Denmark	43
Sweden	35	Austria	43
Finland	37	Chile	44
Kenya	37	Democratic	
Uganda	38	Yemen	47
Brazil	39	Malaysia	48
Greece	39	Ivory Coast	49
Portugal	39		
Over 50%			
Senegal	51	United Arab	
Algeria	55	Emirates	65
Singapore	55	Ecuador	66
Tunisia	55	Iceland	66
Ireland	57	Brunei	70
Mauritius	60	Peru	70
Cyprus	60	Zaire	70
Zimbabwe	61	New Zealand	73

SOURCE: Dietrich Berwanger, *Television in the Third World: New Technology and Social Change* (Bonn, FRG: Friedrich Ebert Stiftung, 1987), cited in *World Communication Report* (Paris: UNESCO, 1989), p. 148.

TABLE 3-13
Availability of Videocassette Recorders,
Top Ten and Bottom Ten Countries, 1988

TOP TEN		BOTTOM TEN	
Country	% of households	Country	% of households
Japan	70%	El Salvador	9%
Lebanon	65	Hungary	8
Hong Kong	64	Poland	7
Bahrain	64	Argentina	7
Australia	63	Uruguay	6
United Kingdom	60	Chile	5
United States	59	Bulgaria	4
Canada	58	Barbados	4
Bermuda	55	China	2
Saudi Arabia	52	USSR	1

SOURCE: *Screen Digest*, November 1988, cited in *World Communication Report* (Paris: UNESCO, 1989), pp. 159–160.

Records and tapes

Sound recordings have become one of the most influential means of disseminating culture around the world.[93] Americans spent $35 billion in 1990 on records, tapes, and CDs.[94] Of the $14 billion yearly sales reported (conservatively) in UNESCO statistics, 69 percent takes place in only five countries: the United States, Japan, Germany, Great Britain, and France. The top ten consumers of records and tapes (all developed countries except Brazil) account for 80 percent of all sales worldwide. (See Table 3-14.) Of course, pirated copies are rampant and are not included in these figures.

Advertising

There is no area of communications where the disparities are more dramatic than in advertising. The United States alone spends 1½ times more on advertising than the other 64 countries listed in the 1986 UNESCO statistics. Only seventeen countries in the world had a Gross National Product larger than total U.S. advertising expenditures.[95] At $102 billion in 1986, this figure was about equal to Mexico's entire foreign debt. (See Table 3-15.)

Eleven transnational advertising agencies control more than half of the world's advertising budget. Only nineteen firms account for two-thirds of the world total. (See Table 3-16.)

Most ad agencies in the Third World are foreign-owned, mostly by owners in the United States. Even Western European agencies suffered from predominantly foreign ownership: Ninety percent of Germany's largest agencies and more than seventy percent of those in Belgium, Italy, and Britain are United States–owned.[96]

Satellites

Today there are 184 communications satellites in geosynchronous orbit. Of these, only seventeen satellites have been launched by developing countries (four by India;

TABLE 3-14	TABLE 3-15
World Sales of	World Advertising
Records and Tapes, 1985	Expenditures, 1986
(in millions of dollars)	(in millions of dollars)

Country	Amount of sales	Country	Advertising expenditures
World Total	14,000.0	United States	102,140
United States	4,651.1	Japan	18,309
Japan	1,972.9	United Kingdom	8,222
Federal Republic of Germany	1,199.6	Federal Republic of Germany	8,094
United Kingdom	1,089.1	Canada	4,797
France	678.6	France	4,475
Canada	487.2	Italy	3,075
USSR	384.9	Spain	3,002
Brazil	239.1	Australia	2,380
Netherlands	232.7	Brazil	1,958
Australia	228.8	Rest of world	15,463

SOURCE: International Federation of Phonogram and Videogram Producers and affiliated organizations, cited in *World Communication Report* (Paris: UNESCO, 1989), p. 162.

SOURCE: *World Advertising Expenditures*, 21st ed. (New York: Starch INRA Hooper Inc., and International Advertising Association), cited in *World Communication Report* (Paris: UNESCO, 1989), p. 500.

three each by Colombia and Indonesia; two each by Brazil, Mexico, and a consortium of Arab nations; one by China.) The United States and the Commonwealth of Independent States have the largest satellite networks, including domestic civilian and worldwide military communication. They have fifty-four and forty-five geosynchronous satellites, respectively. INTELSAT has twenty-six (including reserves) and INTERSPUTNIK three. The United States and the Commonwealth of Independent States, with only 15 percent of the world's population, use more than 50 percent of the geostationary orbit. The Third World uses less than 10 percent.[97]

Satellite-delivered radio and television services are available only in forty countries. These include twenty countries each from the developing and developed nations. However, except for India, Indonesia, Mexico, Brazil, and China, which have their own satellite broadcasting services, in all other developing countries these services are received through leased satellite services. (This does not include the dozens of countries lying under domestic signals, such as the Caribbean and Central American countries lying under United States satellite footprints.) With the exception of Mexico, no developing country broadcasts television programming directly to a developed country.

Telephone

Although cable, direct broadcast satellite, packet switching, and a host of other innovations have improved service and lowered costs in the developed nations, telephone technology available in the developing nations is still primitive, nonexistent,

TABLE 3-16
Leading Advertising Agencies, 1988 Billings (in billions of dollars)

Agency	Billings
Dentsu Inc.	9.45
Young & Rubicam	5.39
Saatchi & Saatchi	5.04
Backer Spielvogel Bates	4.68
McCann-Erikson	4.38
FCB-Publicis	4.36
Ogilvy & Mather	4.11
BBDO	4.05
J. Walter Thompson	3.86
Lintas	3.59
Grey Advertising	2.89
D'Arcy Masius Benton & Bowles	3.36
Leo Burnett	2.87
DDB Needham	3.02
WCRS	2.03
HDM	1.94
Roux, Seguela, Cayzac & Goudard	1.53
Lowe, Howar-Spink & Bell	1.32
NW Ayer	1.35

SOURCE: *Advertising Age*, cited in Peter Muzik, *Die Medien Multis* (Vienna: Verlag Orac, 1989), p. 268.

TABLE 3-17
Top Ten Countries in Telephone Lines

Country	No. of telephone lines
World total	405,848,805
United States	94,905,850
Japan	48,014,000
Federal Republic of Germany	27,221,756
France	24,803,609
Commonwealth of Independent States	24,540,000
United Kingdom	22,137,000
Italy	19,104,828
Canada	13,206,233
Spain	10,236,408
South Korea	8,625,000

SOURCE: International Telecommunication Union, *Yearbook of Common Carrier Telecommunication Statistics*, 16th ed. (Geneva: International Telecommunication Union, 1989).

or expensive. Not only are rates in developing countries higher for the same distance and time, but they are also higher between two points within developing countries than between developed and developing countries. Rates are higher for calls from a developing to a developed country (and from most developed countries to the United States) than for calls in the opposite direction. Such differences in tariffs, coupled with lower per capita incomes, perpetuate the imbalance in telephone traffic flows.

In 1987 the number of telephone lines in service in the developed countries was 347 million, as compared to 59 million in the developing world.[98] Five countries, with 15 percent of the world's population, accounted for more than half of the world's telephone lines. Ten developed countries, with 20 percent of the world's population, accounted for almost three-quarters of all telephone lines. (See Table 3-17.) The United States had as many telephone lines as all of Asia; the Netherlands, as many as all of Africa; Italy, as many as all of Latin America; Tokyo as many as all of Africa.

In terms of per capita telephone-line density, Western European countries had 42 lines per 100 inhabitants; Monaco led the list with 75 lines. In the United States, there were forty-one lines. About 50 countries have less than one telephone line per 100 people. More than 110 countries have fewer than 10 lines per 100 people. With the exception of Japan, South Korea, Hong Kong, Singapore, and the Arab nations, the developing countries of Africa and Asia have the lowest per capita telephone-line penetration, with most having one or fewer telephones per 100 inhabitants. Telephone coverage is also scant in South and Central American countries, where, except

TABLE 3-18
Top Ten and Bottom Ten
Countries in Telephone Lines, 1987

	Total no.	Density per 100 people
Monaco	20,800	74.29
Sweden	5,480,500	65.13
Denmark	2,711,000	52.86
Guernsey	29,219	52.66
Jersey	42,123	51.68
Switzerland	3,381,492	51.45
Canada	13,206,233	51.20
Finland	2,365,000	47.86
Norway	1,948,680	46.41
Iceland	113,134	45.80
Federal Republic of Germany	27,221,756	43.95
Central African Republic	3,902	0.14
Burundi	6,631	0.13
Burkina Faso	11,556	0.13
Niger	8,141	0.13
Burma	42,274	0.12
Bangladesh	89,000	0.10
Rwanda	6,561	0.10
Zaire	29,010	0.10
Mali	7,300	0.09
Chad	2,359	0.05

SOURCE: International Telecommunication Union, *Yearbook of Common Carrier Telecommunication Statistics*, 16th ed. (Geneva: International Telecommunication Union, 1989).

for the seven Caribbean island nations, there are fewer than ten telephones per one hundred inhabitants. These statistics mask rural-urban, gender, and racial differences. In most rural areas, where 60 to 70 percent of the population of the developing countries resides, the per capita telephone penetration is less than one per one hundred. Only 5 percent of India's villages have any telephone.[99] (See Table 3-18.)

Information on telephone-line density indicates availability of telephone services, but it does not show how much these services are used, especially for international calling. International traffic accounts for a considerable share of revenue and has a much larger growth rate than national traffic. Two major routes account for 80 percent of all world telephone traffic: the route between North America and Europe (60 percent) and the route between North America and Southeast Asia (20 percent).[100] Some interesting comparisons can be made between the volume of international calling in the countries with the highest and lowest percentages. Cyprus is the world's leader in international phone traffic per capita, presumably because of its role as a "monitoring post" for Middle East affairs and because it is an island. The United States is very low in per capita international calling despite a 20-percent yearly growth in this sector.[101] (See Tables 3-19 and 3-20.)

TABLE 3-19
International Calls by Selected Countries, 1986

Country	Thousands of pulses	Per capita international pulses
France	8,097,000	146.17
Sweden	7,533,344	902.08
Cyprus	1,094,309	1626.01
Morocco	963,503	42.42
Algeria	962,386	42.99
Hungary	853,000	80.25
Switzerland	802,000	123.57
Tunisia	479,580	64.43
United States	478,770	1.98
Federal Republic of Germany	468,198	7.68
Japan	320,000	2.63
Mexico	39,961	0.49
Egypt	27,300	0.55
China	17,660	0.01
Brazil	13,100	0.09
India	5,736	0.00
Iran	5,716	0.11
Thailand	4,698	0.08
Ethiopia	2,393	0.05
Pakistan	2,130	0.01
Cuba	1,500	0.14

SOURCE: *Yearbook of Common Carrier Telecommunication Statistics*, 15th ed. (Geneva: International Telecommunication Union, 1988), cited in *World Communication Report* (Paris: UNESCO, 1989), pp. 459–461.

Postal Services

Although most countries have extensive postal services, in some nations large proportions of the population are without postal service. (See Table 3-21.) Libya ranked worst in the world, with 80 percent of its population outside the postal network. The disparities are also great in the average number of inhabitants serviced by a post office. (See Table 3-22.) The cost of postage is escalating everywhere, but the burden was especially great in the developing world. The cost of one airmail letter from Hanoi to Los Angeles is equivalent to three days' salary for the typical Vietnamese government worker.[102]

Another remarkable comparison is the volume of international postal traffic. The United States leads the world, with 787 million international letters mailed. Yet the Netherlands was the highest in terms of per capita international mail received. One interesting anomaly is that Japan ranks low in this regard, presumably because of its linguistic insularity. (See Table 3-23.)

International Computer Communications

International computer communication is available to cities in more than one hundred countries. But it requires three basic preconditions: a reliable and universal electrical

TABLE 3-20
International Telex Traffic
by Selected Countries, 1986

Country	Telex minutes	Per capita
Federal Republic of Germany	188,698,410	3.09
United States	179,234,682	0.74
France	148,820,000	2.68
Netherlands	88,064,000	6.05
Belgium	73,421,445	7.40
Japan	51,181,000	0.42
India	50,663,000	0.06
Hong Kong	46,985,078	8.70
Spain	45,779,000	1.18
Denmark	41,743,000	8.15
Singapore	30,182,658	11.66
Brazil	20,100,000	0.14
China	12,360,000	0.01
Ethiopia	11,979,933	0.27
United Arab Emirate	10,746,745	7.65
Egypt	9,685,270	0.19
Venezuela	9,463,220	0.53
Malaysia	9,368,840	0.59
Algeria	8,415,000	0.37
Thailand	7,465,200	0.14
Iran	6,423,863	0.12
Cyprus	4,310,478	6.40

SOURCE: *Yearbook of Common Carrier Telecommunication Statistics*, 15th ed. (Geneva: International Telecommunication Union, 1988), cited in *World Communication Report* (Paris: UNESCO, 1989), pp. 462–464.

supply, noise-free and interference-free telephone lines, and reliable maintenance services. All these are lacking in much of the world.

Even in countries where telecommunication services are being expanded and upgraded, the new channels being installed have a much lower capacity than those operating in the First World. Despite its low cost, fiber-optic cable—the medium best suited to long-distance data flows—is not being installed for terrestrial telecommunications in the developing world. In countries where public data networks do exist, they are hampered by antiquated switching plants, incorrect or busy numbers, and slow transmission speeds—in addition to high price.

Ninety percent of the world's computers are found in fifteen of the world's most economically advanced countries.[103] Ninety-five percent of all computers are in the developed countries. Only 3.5 percent are in Latin America, 1.6 percent in Asia, and .5 percent in Africa.[104] Venezuela has about 1 computer for every 2,200 people. Brazil has 1 for every 6,000; Mexico, 1 for every 7,000; Bolivia, 1 for every 65,000.[105]

Even within the United States, information disparities exist. Millions of Americans cannot read or type, do not have access to computers, do not consume newsprint, cannot afford a book. White children are 2.5 times as likely to have home computers as African-American and Hispanic children.[106]

TABLE 3-21
Percentage of Population without Postal Services, 1986 (selected countries)

Country	% without postal service
Libya	80
Chad	76
Botswana	73
Saint Lucia	35
Ecuador	19
Paraguay	12
Argentina	11

SOURCE: *Statistique des Services Postaux* (Berne, Switzerland: Universal Postal Union, 1988), cited in *World Communication Report* (Paris: UNESCO, 1989), pp. 443–445.

TABLE 3-22
Average Number of Inhabitants Served by Post Office, 1986 (selected countries)

Country	Number served
United States	5,768
USSR	2,973
Federal Republic of Germany	3,423
France	3,195
Macau	50,000
Angola	64,661
Yemen	65,774
Mali	66,307
Ethiopia	86,956
Chad	161,875
Burundi	266,088

SOURCE: *Statistique des Services Postaux* (Berne, Switzerland: Universal Postal Union, 1988), cited in *World Communication Report* (Paris: UNESCO, 1989), pp. 443–445.

The rapid evolution in informatics and telecommunications technologies has made it possible to have data bases distributed around the world. (Table 3-24 contains information regarding the amount of computer equipment that various countries exported in 1985.) Distance no longer has a meaning where data are concerned. But many countries still lack the ability to build and offer their own data bases on the world market.

A WORLD OF COMMUNICATION CONTROVERSY

The statistics and social problems discussed in this chapter paint a gloomy picture. This widely verified situation has led to a crisis in such international organizations as UNESCO. Indeed, the majority of the world's nations actually called for a *rearrangement of the present information and communication order.* Their underlying complaints, as expressed in UNESCO's famous "MacBride Report," (Many Voices, One World), unites these diverse threads. Here are some of the MacBride Commission's recommendations:[107]

- Developing countries must take measures to establish or develop the essential elements of their communications systems.
- Networks should be set up to increase news flows.
- National book production should be encouraged and accompanied by the establishment of a distribution network.
- National production of broadcast materials can help overcome dependence on external sources.
- The communication component in all development projects should receive adequate financing.
- Nations must expand basic postal services and telecommunication networks.

TABLE 3-23
International Dispatch
of Letters, Selected Countries, 1986
(in thousands)

Country	International letters mailed	International letters per capita
United States	787,621	3.26
Netherlands	540,600	37.17
United Kingdom	516,200	9.11
Federal Republic of Germany	457,864	7.51
France	370,800	6.69
Italy	365,852	6.40
Canada	279,290	10.54
German Democratic Republic	254,180	15.28
Spain	249,559	6.43
Austria	238,352	31.80
India	242,906	0.30
Mexico	134,550	1.65
Japan	105,353	0.86
Pakistan	101,509	0.94
Philippines	101,288	1.79
Egypt	91,022	1.86
Bangladesh	72,701	0.69
Thailand	40,261	0.76
Indonesia	27,336	0.16
Brazil	24,142	0.17

SOURCE: *Statistique des Services Postaux* (Berne, Switzerland: Universal Postal Union, 1988), cited in *World Communication Report* (Paris: UNESCO, 1989), pp. 446–448.

TABLE 3-24
Export of Computer
Equipment, 1985
(in thousands of dollars)

Country	Export amount
United States	7,343,117
Japan	6,184,820
Federal Republic of Germany	2,904,975
United Kingdom	1,821,321
Ireland	1,391,145
Italy	1,368,389
France	1,109,227
Singapore	922,148
Netherlands	877,195
Sweden	613,014

SOURCE: Compiled by UNESCO from COMTRADE (U. N. Statistical Office) *World Communication Report* (Paris: UNESCO, 1989), p. 524.

- The world needs a major international research and development effort to increase the supply of paper.
- Tariffs for news transmission, telecommunications rates, and airmail charges for the dissemination of news and the transport of newspapers, periodicals, books, and audiovisual materials are one of the main obstacles to a free and balanced flow of information.
- The electromagnetic spectrum and geostationary orbit should be more equitably shared as the common property of mankind.
- Special attention should be devoted to obstacles and restrictions that derive from the concentration of media ownership.
- Effective legal measures should be designed to limit the process of concentration and monopolization.
- Attention must be paid to the communication needs of women.
- It is necessary to promote conditions for the preservation of the cultural identity of every society and to modify situations in many countries that suffer from cultural dominance.

NOTES

1. A similar definition was formulated by graduate students (including the present author) in Hamid Mowlana's Seminar in International Communications at American University in 1980–1981. Mowlana cites that definition in *Global Information and World Communication* (New York: Longman, 1986), p. 216.

2. International Commission for the Study of Communication Problems [MacBride Commission], *Many Voices, One World* [*The MacBride Report*] (Paris: UNESCO, 1980), p. 283. The book is out of print at UNESCO but can be obtained from the World Association for Christian Communication, 357 Kennington Lane, London SE11 5QY, United Kingdom, Tel: (071) 582 913 Fax: (071) 735 034, Email address: wacc@gn.apc.org.

3. Ibid., p. 283.

4. Cees J. Hamelink, "International Communication," in *Discourse and Communication: New Approaches to the Analysis of Mass Media Discourse and Communication*, ed. Teun A. van Dijk (New York: Walter de Gruyter, 1985), pp. 143–144.

5. Cees J. Hamelink, "Information Technology and the Third World" (Paper presented at the biennial conference of the International Association for Mass Communication Research, New Delhi, August 1986).

6. *UNESCO Statistical Yearbook* (Paris: UNESCO, 1990).

7. The term "Third World" was coined by the French sociologist Alfred Sauvy in 1952 at the height of the Cold War. See his *Théorie Générale de la Population*, 1966, translated as *General Theory of Population* (New York: Basic Books, 1970); and *Zero Growth?* (New York: Praeger, 1975).

8. This section draws heavily on Karl W. Deutsch, "The Impact of Communications upon the Theory of International Relations," in *Theory of International Relations*, ed. Abdul A. Said (Englewood Cliffs, NJ: Prentice-Hall, 1968), pp. 74–92. See also Marshall R. Singer, *Weak States in a World of Powers* (New York: Free Press, 1972), pp. 10–13.

9. Deutsch, "Impact of Communications," p. 75.

10. One interesting note is that the border between the United States and Mexico is the only international frontier where the First World and the Third World confront one another.

11. Deutsch, "Impact of Communications," p. 76.

12. Ibid., p. 76.

13. Ibid., p. 78.

14. Ibid., p. 81.

15. Ethnic Germans, Ukrainians, and Byelorussians make up less than 2 percent of the population.

16. See Donald Dewey, "Forbidden Nations," *TWA Ambassador*, January 1988, pp. 46+.

17. Offices of the General Secretariat are located at Post Box 85878, 2508 CN The Hague, Netherlands.

18. Harold Innis, *Empire and Communications* (Oxford: Oxford University Press, 1950; Toronto: University of Toronto Press, 1972); and Harold Innis, *The Bias of Communication* (Toronto: University of Toronto Press, 1951).

19. Karl Marx and Friedrich Engels, *The German Ideology*, ed. C. J. Arthur (New York: International Publishers, 1981); Armand Mattelart and Seth Siegelaub, eds., *Communication and Class Struggle*, 2 vols. (New York: International General, 1979 and 1983); Herbert I. Schiller, *Mass Communications and the American Empire* (Boston: Beacon Press, 1971); Herbert I. Schiller, *The Mind Managers* (Boston: Beacon Press, 1973); and Herbert I. Schiller, *Communication and Cultural Domination* (White Plains, NY: International Arts and Sciences Press, 1976).

20. Quoted in Ralph K. Allen, "Mass Media in Intercultural Communication," *Journal of Communication* 5 (1955): 72.

21. Cees J. Hamelink, "Is Information Technology Neutral?" in *Communication and Domination: Essays to Honor Herbert I. Schiller*, ed. Jörg Becker, Göran Hedebro, and Leena Paldan (Norwood, NJ: Ablex, 1986), p. 20. See also Herbert I. Schiller, *Communication and Cultural Domination*, pp. 46–67.

22. Enrique Gonzalez-Manet, *The Hidden War of Information*, Laurien Alexandre, trans. (Norwood, NJ: Ablex, 1988), p. 53.

23. John C. Merrill, "A Conceptual Overview of World Journalism," in *International and Intercultural Communication*, ed. Heinz-Dietrich, Fischer, and Merrill (New York: Hastings House, 1976), p. 20.

24. See Stephen R. Barnett, "United States Regulation of Transborder Speech," *Comm/Ent Law Journal* 9 (1987): 635–745; Morton Halperin in Susan Blank, "Opening America's Borders to a Free Flow of Information," *Civil Liberties*, Spring (1986): 1; David H. Weaver, Judith M. Buddenbaum, and Jo Ellen Fair, "Press, Freedom, Media, and Development, 1950–1979: A Study of 134 Nations," *Journal of Communication* 35 (2, 1985): 104–117; Achal Mehra, "Freedom Champions as Freedom Muzzlers: U.S. Violations of Free Flow of Information," *Gazette* 36 (1985): 3–20; and "Human Rights in the United States," special issue of *International Review of Contemporary Law* (1, 1990).

25. John C. Merrill, "Governments and Press Control: Global Attitudes on Journalistic Matters," *Political Communication and Persuasion* 4 (1987): 223–262; John C. Merrill, "Governments and Press Control: Global Views," *International Communication Bulletin* 23 (1–2, Spring 1988): 12; and *Current Issues in International Communication*, ed. L. John Martin and Ray Eldon Heibert (New York: Longman, 1990), pp. 110–112.

26. Fred S. Siebert, Theodore Peterson, and Wilbur Schramm, *Four Theories of the Press* (Urbana, IL: University of Illinois Press, 1956). These "theories" have attracted considerable controversy and attention. See particularly William A. Hachten, *The World Press Prism: Changing Media, Clashing Ideology* (Ames, IA: Iowa State University Press, 1981); Denis McQuail, *Mass Communication Theory*, 2nd ed. (Newbury Park, CA: Sage, 1987); John C. Merrill, *Media, Messages, and Men: New Perspectives in Communication* (New York: Longman, 1979); Whitney R. Mundt, "Global Media Philosophies," in *Global Journalism: Survey of International Communication*, 2nd ed., ed. John C. Merrill, (New York: Longman, 1991), pp. 11–27; Robert G. Picard, "Revisions of the 'Four Theories of the Press' Model," *Mass Communication Review* 10 (Winter–Spring 1982–1983): 1–2; William L. Rivers and Wilbur Schramm, *Responsibility in Mass Communication*, 3rd ed. (New York: Harper & Row, 1980); and Jan Servaes, "Beyond Four Theories of the Press" (Paper presented at the annual conference of the International Communication Association, New Orleans, 1988).

27. S. K. Padover, ed., *Thomas Jefferson on Democracy* (New York: Appleton-Century, 1953), p. 48.

28. Hamid Mowlana, "A Paradigm for Comparative Mass Media Analysis," in *International and Intercultural Communication* (New York: Hastings House, 1976), pp. 474–484.

29. Thomas McCarroll, "What New Age?" *Time*, August 12, 1991, p. 44.

30. *Michanizace a automatizace administrativy*, November 1987, back cover, citing Japanese Ministry of Foreign Trade and Industry figures, quoted in *Mass Communication Media in the World* 5 (1, 1988): 17.

31. Richard C. Beiard, "Telecommunications as an Engine of Economic Growth," (Washington, DC: U.S. Department of State, 1989).

32. Ibid.

33. Lenny Siegel and John Markoff, *The High Cost of High Tech: The Dark Side of the Chip* (New York: Harper & Row, 1985), pp. 179–201.

34. William H. Davidson, "Telecommunications Takes Off: While the U.S. Dithers, Other Nations Are Aggressively Modernizing to Compete," *Los Angeles Times*, February 26, 1989, p. IV3.

35. General Agreement on Trade and Tariffs, *International Trade, 1987–1988* (Geneva: GATT, 1989), p. 36.

36. United Nations General Assembly, *Development and International Economic Co-operation: Long-Term Trends in Social and Economic Development*, Doc. A/43/554 (New York: United Nations, 1988), p. 151.

37. Beiard, "Telecommunications as an Engine of Economic Growth."

38. "U.S. International Communication and Information Policy," *Gist* (Department of State), December 1988, p. 1.

39. Meheroo Jussawalla, "Can We Apply New Trade Rules to Information Trade?" in *International Information Economy Handbook*, ed. G. Russell Pipe and Chris Brown (Springfield, VA: Transnational Data Reporting Service, 1985), p. 11.

40. General Agreement on Trade and Tariffs, *International Trade, 1987–1988*, p. 37.

41. Economic Commission for Europe, *The Telecommunication Industry: Growth and Structural Change* (New York: United Nations, 1987), quoted in *World Communication Report* (Paris: UNESCO, 1989), p. 80.

42. Heather Hudson, *When Telephones Reach the Village: The Role of Telecommunications in Rural Development* (Geneva: International Telecommunication Union, 1984); Heather Hudson, *A Bibliography of Telecommunications in Socio-Economic Development* (Geneva: International Telecommunication Union, 1988); Heather Hudson, *Three Case Studies on the Benefits of Telecommunications in Socio-Economic Development: A Report to the International Telecommunication Union* (Geneva: International Telecommunication Union, 1983); Heather Hudson, Douglas Goldschmidt, Edwin B. Parker, and Andrew Hardy, *The Role of Telecommunications in Socio-Economic Development: A Review of the Literature with Guidelines for Further Investigations* (n.p.: Keewatin Communications, 1979); International Telecommunication Union, *Contributions of Telecommunications to the Earnings/Savings of Foreign Exchange in Developing Countries* (Geneva: International Telecommunication Union, 1988); and William Pierce and Nicolas Jequier, project coordinators, *Telecommunications for Development* (Geneva: International Telecommunication Union, 1983); Hamid Mowlana and Laurie J. Wilson, *The Passing of Modernity: Communication and the Transformation of Society* (New York: Longman, 1990), pp. 151–169.

43. *Telecommunications for Development*, cited in Economic Commission for Europe, *The Telecommunication Industry*, p. 155.

44. C. R. Dickenson, "Telecommunications in the Developing Countries: The Relation to the Economy and Society," cited in Hudson et al., *Telecommunications in Socio-Economic Development*, p. 7.

45. Economic Commission for Europe, *The Telecommunication Industry*, p. 156. Of course, correlation does not imply a causal relationship.

46. Daniel Bell, *The Coming Post-Industrial Society: A Venture in Social Forecasting* (New York: Basic Books, 1973), pp. 126–127.

47. See Marc Uri Porat, "Global Implications of the Information Society," *Journal of Communication* 28 (1, 1978): 70–81; Marc Uri Porat, *The Information Economy: Definition and Measurement*, vols. 1–9, OT Special Publication 77–12 (1) (Washington, DC: United States Department of Commerce, May 1977); G. Russell Pipe, "Introduction," in *International Information Economy Handbook*, p. ix; and Mark E. Hepworth, *Geography of the Information Economy* (London: Belhaven, 1989).

48. Porat, "Global Implications," p. 70.

49. UNESCO, *World Communication Report* (Paris: UNESCO, 1989), p. 79.

50. Porat, "Global Implications," pp. 70–81.

51. Simon Nora and Alain Minc, *Computerization of Society* (Cambridge, MA: MIT Press, 1980).

52. Organization for Economic Cooperation and Development, *Trends in the Information Economy*, Series on Information, Computer, and Communication Policy No. 11 (Paris: OECD, 1986), p. 15.

53. *Critical Connections: Communication for the Future*, OTA Report Brief (Washington: Office of Technology Assessment, U.S. Congress, 1990), p. 1.

54. Cees J. Hamelink, *Finance and Information: A Study in Converging Interests* (Norwood, NJ: Ablex, 1980), p. 7.

55. Anne W. Branscomb, "Global Governance of Global Networks," in *Toward a Law of Global Communications Networks,* ed. Anne W. Branscomb (New York: Longman, 1986), p. 6.

56. Ruth Leger Sivard, *World Military and Social Expenditures 1989*, 13th ed. (Washington, DC: World Priorities, 1989), p. 8.

57. Similar terms are used in Jill Hills, "The Telecommunication Rich and Poor," *Third World Quarterly* 12 (2, April 1990): 71–90. Most figures in this section are from the 1990 *UNESCO Statistical Yearbook* or from UNESCO's 1989 *World Communication Report*.

58. Hans Singer, "The Distribution of Gains from Trade Revisited," *Journal of Development Studies* 11 (1975): 377–382.

59. See "Disparities" (Part II, Chapter 6) and "Flaws in Communication Flows" (Part III, Chapter 1) in *Many Voices, One World* [*The MacBride Report*].

60. "More News Media Urged by UNESCO," *New York Times*, April 10, 1962, p. 4.

61. *UNESCO Statistical Yearbook*, 1990, pp. 6-13.

62. UNESCO, *World Communication Report*, p. 305.

63. *UNESCO Statistical Yearbook*, 1990, pp. 7-114 to 7-118.

64. *UNESCO Statistical Yearbook*, 1990, pp. 6-13.

65. The island nations were Bahamas, Barbados, Bermuda, Cayman Islands, Cook Islands, Cuba, Cyprus, French Polynesia, Guam, New Caledonia, Puerto Rico, Qatar, Singapore, Trinidad and Tobago, and the U. S. Virgin Islands.

66. *UNESCO Statistical Yearbook*, 1990, pp. 6-13.

67. Center for Research on Information, University of Rome, 1977, cited in Enrique Gonzalez-Manet, *The Hidden War of Information*, p. 11.

68. *UNESCO Statistical Yearbook* (Paris: UNESCO, 1989), pp. 6-11 to 6-12; and *UNESCO Statistical Yearbook*, 1990, pp. 6-11 to 6-12.

69. *UNESCO Statistical Yearbook*, 1990, pp. 6-12.

70. Hamid Mowlana, *Global Information and World Communication*, p. 77.

71. *UNESCO Statistical Yearbook*, 1990, pp. 7-110 to 7-113. They were Gabriel García Márquez (Colombia), R. Tagore (India), and Pablo Neruda (Chile).

72. *UNESCO Statistical Yearbook*, 1990, pp. 6-14 to 6-15.

73. *UNESCO Statistical Yearbook*, 1990, pp. 6-14 to 6-15.

74. *Mass Communication Media in the World* (4, 1990): 6.

75. *Mass Communication Media in the World* (5, 1990): 9.

76. *Mass Communication Media in the World* (6–7, 1989): 3. Despite its massive output, the United States still imports half its newsprint. *Mass Communication Media in the World* (4, 1990): 6.

77. Jörg Becker, ''Paper Technology and the Third World: Global Restrictions and Technical Alternatives'' (Paper presented at the biennial conference of the International Association for Mass Communication Research, Prague, 1984), appeared in *Papiertechnologie und Dritte Welt: Ökonomische Rahmenbedingungen und Technische Alternativen für die Produktion von Kulturpapier* (Braunschweig, FRG: Vieweg & Sohn, 1986).

78. *UNESCO Statistical Yearbook*, 1990, pp. 6–16.

79. *UNESCO Statistical Yearbook*, 1990, pp. 9–6.

80. *UNESCO Statistical Yearbook*, 1990, pp. 9–9 to 9–12.

81. Thomas B. Rosenstiel, ''The Selling of the U.S. Media: Have Foreign Buys Gone Too Far?'' *Los Angeles Times*, November 4, 1990, p. D10; and Carl Bernstein, ''The Leisure Empire,'' *Time*, December 24, 1990, p. 56.

82. *UNESCO Statistical Yearbook*, 1990, pp. 9–12 to 9–16. These countries are Argentina, Bulgaria, Canada, Cuba, Czechoslovakia, France, the former German Democratic Republic, Hungary, Malta, Mauritius, Montserrat, North Korea, Norway, San Marino, Singapore, St. Pierre and Miquelon, and Sweden. While not included in the UNESCO statistics, presumably Japan, South Korea, the United States, and the Commonwealth of Independent States should also be included.

83. *UNESCO Statistical Yearbook*, 1990, pp. 6–17.

84. *UNESCO Statistical Yearbook*, 1990, pp. 6–18.

85. *UNESCO Statistical Yearbook*, 1990, pp. 6–20.

86. *UNESCO Statistical Yearbook*, 1990, pp. 6–20.

87. *UNESCO Statistical Yearbook*, 1990, pp. 10–3 to 10–8. These countries are Bangladesh, Bhutan, Burkina Faso, Guinea, Guinea-Bissau, Haiti, Mali, Mozambique, Nepal, Somalia, Tanzania, and Yemen.

88. *UNESCO Statistical Yearbook*, 1990, pp. 6–19.

89. UNESCO, *Latest Statistics on Radio and Television Broadcasting* (Paris: UNESCO, Division of Statistics on Culture and Communication, Office of Statistics, 1987), p. 26.

90. *UNESCO Statistical Yearbook*, 1990, pp. 6–21 to 6–22.

91. Tapio Varis, *International Flow of Television Programmes* (Paris: UNESCO, 1985), p. 17.

92. *UNESCO Statistical Yearbook*, 1990, pp. 10–9 to 10–14.

93. Deanna Robinson, *Music at the Margins: Popular Music Production and Cultural Diversity* (Newbury Park, CA: Sage, 1990); James Lull, ed., *Popular Music and Communication* (Newbury Park, CA: Sage, 1987).

94. Bernstein, ''The Leisure Empire,'' p. 58.

95. These seventeen countries were Canada, Brazil, Mexico, France, the Federal Republic of Germany, Netherlands, Spain, United Kingdom, Czechoslovakia, the former German Democratic Republic, the former Soviet Union, Sweden, Switzerland, India, China, Japan, and Australia.

96. Graham Murdock and Noreene Janus, *Mass Communications and the Advertising Industry* (Paris: UNESCO, 1984).

97. International Telecommunication Union, *Twenty-ninth Report by the International Telecommunication Union on Telecommunication and the Peaceful Uses of Outer Space*, Booklet no. 38 (Geneva: International Telecommunication Union, 1990); and *World Communication Report* (Paris: UNESCO, 1989), p. 61.

98. All figures in this section are derived from International Telecommunication Union, *Yearbook of Common Carrier Telecommunication Statistics*, 16th ed. (Geneva: International Telecommunication Union, 1989). "Telephone lines" is a more valid statistic than "telephone sets" because the number of sets connected to a line can vary greatly from country to country.

99. Even in the United States, disparities exist. A Government Accounting Office (GAO) study reports that only 81.5 percent of Hispanics have telephone service, compared with 93.6 percent of whites. The average for all races was 92.2 percent in 1986. See "Telephone Communications: The FCC's Monitoring of Residential Telephone Service," GAO-RCED-86-146 (Washington: Government Accounting Office, June 1986), cited in *Global Electronics*, December 1986, p. 3.

100. Economic Commission for Europe, *The Telecommunication Industry*, p. 141.

101. Ibid., p. 141.

102. Lady Borton, Quaker service worker in Vietnam, private correspondence.

103. Joseph N. Pelton, "Toward an Equitable Global Information Society," in *International Information Economy Handbook*, p. 95.

104. UNESCO, Provisional Intergovernmental Committee of the Intergovernmental Program of Informatics, Principle [sic] Working Document, SC-84/CONF. 209/4 (Paris: UNESCO, 1984), cited in Gonzalez-Manet, *The Hidden War of Information*, Laurien Alexandre, trans., p. 3.

105. *Mass Communication Media in the World*, 4 (8, 1987): 1.

106. "Information Rich vs. Poor," *Global Electronics*, Issue 107, March–April 1991, p. 4, referring to U. S. Bureau of the Census data cited in the *San Jose Mercury News*, March 27, 1991.

107. In some cases the sentence structure has been altered for logical flow and fluidity. International Commission for the Study of Communication Problems, *Many Voices, One World* [*The MacBride Report*], (Paris: UNESCO, 1980).

4

Channels of
Global Communication

In his landmark book *International Political Communication,* Davison included a "comprehensive survey" of channels of world communication, listing news media; radio and television; satellites; books and publications; films, fairs, and cultural events; international travel; and organizational channels (such as embassies and international organizations).[1] Although he could be faulted for not including "old" technologies like the telephone and the telex, global technologies, such as the fax machine and computer communications, now exist. In addition, "nontechnological" channels, such as language, tourism, migration, and international organizations, must be included. This chapter is a survey of the various communications channels that link us together around the globe.

INTERPERSONAL CHANNELS

The Languages of World Communication

Languages are constantly evolving. Over the centuries, even over the last few decades, significant changes have occurred in the world's languages. Some writers see a Darwinian struggle of languages for survival, in which the stronger languages drive out the weaker ones.[2] Others argue that rapidly increasing world communication channels will eventually lead to a single predominant language.

How many languages are there today on the planet? Measuring this is fraught with difficulty. How can we speak of a single Chinese tongue? Isn't Quebecois different from French? Should Hindi and Urdu be counted together or separately? Should Indian English and American English, sometimes mutually unintelligible to the ear, be counted as one? Because of these problems, estimates of the total number of languages spoken somewhere today have varied from 2,500 to 7,000.[3]

If we examine languages with more than five million speakers, we find an astounding fact: Only ninety-five languages account for almost 98 percent of the world's population. That leaves less than 3 percent of our world speaking between 2,405 and 6,905 other languages, depending on how you count them. In fact, only seven languages account for more than half the world's population. (See Table 4-1).

What is the life span of a language? From prehistory to the present, languages live an average of 2,000 to 3,000 years. For every language that has died, two more have been born; for example, Latin spawned a score of descendants.[4] Rather than dying like endangered species, languages apparently have a tendency to proliferate. There are even several "Englishes" evolving quite independently throughout the world![5]

Why do some languages persist while others die? Language viability is linked to the size of the community using it. Languages with few speakers face extinction. Also, languages change over time. In hundred-year increments, languages remain relatively stable. But over a millennium, even such enduring languages as German and English have changed considerably.

Another factor is the "porosity" of language boundaries. *Physical discontinuities,* such as oceans or mountains, isolate such languages as Icelandic and Swiss Romansch and allow them to prosper undisturbed. We also find *familial boundaries* between languages. Sharing many cognates, French and Italian exchange mutual influence across the Franco–Italian frontier. But on Italy's eastern frontier, Italian and Slovenian are quite unrelated and thus influence one another less. Finally, significant *social boundaries,* such as class and racial divisions, can promote or inhibit this interactive process between and among languages.

How does a language spoken by few people (such as Icelandic) or a language under cultural pressure (such as Ukrainian or Estonian) survive in the modern age? LaPonce has an interesting answer to this question. He defines linguistic sustainability as a language's capability to sustain a university and its ability to administer a national government.

About 165 languages are "university capable," with a population of one million as the minimum needed to sustain a modern university teaching chemistry and history. However, some of these languages still do not sustain a university curriculum today. (For example, the eight million Andean speakers of Quechua have no university education in their language.) Yet even these 165 languages represent only 2 to 7 percent of all spoken tongues.

Each of the top ten languages in Table 4-1 is the official language of at least one national government. However, those lower on the list are less likely to be an official language of government. Smaller numbers of people are clearly associated with non-sovereign peoples.[6]

When people speaking different languages meet, the question of language dominance arises. Travelers often ask: What is the *lingua franca?* A lingua franca is any language used to communicate between people who speak different tongues. Literally "Frankish tongue," the expression initially was used to describe how Italian had combined with other trading languages during the Middle Ages.

The diversity and mutual unintelligibility of our planet's "natural" languages have led to attempts to create a worldwide "artificial" language. The first artificial language to enjoy widespread international acceptance was Esperanto, devised by Ludwik Lazar Zamenhof, a Polish ophthalmologist, in 1887.[7] Today there are about two million speakers of Esperanto in more than eighty countries.

How do we define language dominance? LaPonce proposes two criteria: languages of scientific progress and languages of political power. For example, 95

TABLE 4-1
Languages with at Least Five Million Speakers, 1989

Language	Million	% of world	Language	Million	% of world
Chinese[a]	1069	20.1	Sinhalese	13	0.2
English	443	8.3	Uzbek	13	0.2
Hindi	352	6.6	Cebuano	12	0.2
Spanish	341	6.4	Czech	12	0.2
Russian	293	5.5	Greek	12	0.2
Arabic	197	3.7	Malagasy	11	0.2
Bengali	184	3.5	Afrikaans	10	0.2
Portuguese	173	3.3	Byelorussian	10	0.2
Malay–Indonesian	142	2.7	Madurese	10	0.2
Japanese	125	2.3	Oromo	10	0.2
French	121	2.3	Bulgarian	9	0.2
German	118	2.2	Catalan	9	0.2
Urdu	92	1.7	Kurdish	9	0.2
Punjabi	84	1.6	Malinke–Bambara–		
Korean	71	1.3	Dyula	9	0.2
Telugu	68	1.3	Swedish	9	0.2
Tamil	65	1.2	Kazakh	8	0.2
Italian	64	1.2	Quechua	8	0.2
Marathi	63	1.2	Ruanda	8	0.2
Javanese	58	1.1	Akan	7	0.1
Vietnamese	57	1.0	Ilocano	7	0.1
Turkish	55	1.0	Khmer	7	0.1
Thai	48	0.9	Shona	7	0.1
Ukrainian	45	0.8	Somali	7	0.1
Polish	43	0.8	Tatar	7	0.1
Swahili	43	0.8	Uighur	7	0.1
Kannada	41	0.8	Xhosa	7	0.1
Gujarati	38	0.7	Zulu	7	0.1
Tagalog	36	0.7	Efik	6	0.1
Hausa	34	0.6	Finnish	6	0.1
Malayalam	34	0.6	Lingala	6	0.1
Persian	32	0.6	Luba–Lulua	6	0.1
Burmese	30	0.6	Minangkabau	6	0.1
Oriya	30	0.6	Panay–Hiligaynon	6	0.1
Romanian	25	0.5	Wolof	6	0.1
Sundanese	24	0.5	Yi	6	0.1
Assamese	22	0.4	Albanian	5	0.1
Dutch–Flemish	21	0.4	Armenian	5	0.1
Pashto	21	0.4	Danish	5	0.1
Serbo–Croatian	20	0.4	Kikuyu	5	0.1
Yoruba	18	0.3	Miao (Hmong)	5	0.1
Amharic	17	0.3	Mongolian	5	0.1
Ibo	16	0.3	Norwegian	5	0.1
Sindhi	16	0.3	Rundi	5	0.1
Azerbaijani	14	0.3	Santali	5	0.1
Hungarian	14	0.3	Slovak	5	0.1
Zhuang	14	0.3	Sylhetti	5	0.1
Fula	13	0.2	Tibetan	5	0.1
Nepali	13	0.2	Total over 5 million	5190	97.6

[a]Includes Mandarin, Wu, Cantonese, Min, and Hakka.

NOTE: Native plus nonnative speakers. Using 1990 population figure of 5,320 billion.

SOURCE: Sidney S. Culbert, "The Principal Languages of the World," *The World Almanac and Book of Facts* (New York: World Almanac, 1990), pp. 808–809. Reprinted by permission.

percent of all the world's chemical knowledge is in only six languages: English, Russian, Japanese, German, French, and Polish. Two languages–English and Russian–account for 82 percent of the total. (Because of the collapse of the Soviet Union and government subsidies to publishing, Russian will doubtless fall in rank.) As a measure of political power, LaPonce correlated military power (in this case, military expenditures) with language. About 60 percent of all military expenditures in the world are transacted in English, Russian, and Chinese.[8]

Throughout history a small number of languages, sometimes only one, have dominated. Latin became the lingua franca of Europe through the military might of Rome. For hundreds of years after the Roman empire collapsed, Latin was still the means of communication in politics, scholarship, religion, and culture.

Until about 1970, French came close to being the dominant international language, at least in affairs between governments, commerce, and the arts. Though still widely used, it continues to lose its influence to English. Even French scientists publish their results in English if they want to be read and cited. In the post–World War II era, English has increasingly assumed the role of dominant world language—especially the patois of American business English. While in the past there was considerable resistance to English, particularly in France and Latin America, today there are fewer complaints that speaking English is an affront to the cultural dignity of other countries.

International Transportation Media

For centuries it was dangerous and uncomfortable to travel at all. Traveling became easier only in the last 150 years with the development that began with the railroad and the steamship. Unaffected even by the Titanic disaster in 1912, by the mid-1920s more than 140 luxury liners were crossing the Atlantic regularly. Trains crisscrossed Europe from Portugal to Turkey and the Soviet Union. The invention of the automobile, coupled with the development of the road system, made long-distance travel by the middle classes possible throughout the pre–World War II era.

Long-distance air travel began with the passenger-carrying dirigibles, which carried thousands of people in Germany before World War I. The world's first propeller-driven passenger plane began service in 1919 from London to Paris. Today, about five hundred airlines operate around the world. People take jet travel for granted today, but it was not until 1958 that passenger jets crossed the Atlantic Ocean in a matter of hours. Such speed and comfort suddenly made remote areas accessible, especially Oceania, the Orient, South America, and Africa.[9]

Although the number of passenger ships has declined considerably, the maritime industry still transports people and goods over every ocean. The most heavily traversed channels of international shipping communication are the North Atlantic route between North America and northern Europe; the South American route, from the coasts of the United States and Canada to the coasts of South America; and the Mediterranean–Asiatic–Australasian route extending through the Mediterranean to Asia and Australia.[10] (See Chapter 2, Figure 2-3.)

Migratory and Diaspora Communication

Refugees have sought sanctuary in other countries for centuries, but the twentieth century has seen an explosion in migration. As many as forty million people have been uprooted from their homelands since 1940. The refugee problem has been most acute in Africa, the Middle East, Asia, and Central America. The term *Diaspora* first referred to Jewish migration, but many populations (for example, Palestinians, Kurds, and Armenians) now are forced to maintain "Diaspora communication" with their far-flung communities.[11]

TECHNOLOGICAL CHANNELS

Print Media

The most durable global communication channels are the print media, including books, newspapers, and periodicals that carry ideas to foreign audiences. Transporting heavy printed materials across national borders required heavy-duty transportation media, so it would be difficult to say that print media had a powerful global effect before about 1820. Today, however, print media are less limited by the weight of paper. Satellites now distribute images of the *Wall Street Journal,* the *International Herald Tribune, Die Zeit* and many other newspapers and periodicals to publishing houses around the world. A central production facility can transmit the entire contents of a newspaper, magazine, or paper—camera-ready—to printing plants around the world in a matter of hours.

Nor does publishing necessarily mean "hard copy." The once-"printed" page can now be distributed to computers or television sets via telephone lines, TV cables, videodiscs, or even over broadcast airwaves, and traditional print publishers have begun adapting or creating materials for new electronic publishing formats. The consensus seems to be that narrative works, such as novels and monographs, will continue to be published on paper. However, reference works, such as dictionaries and encyclopedias, will be increasingly available in electronic form.

International Postal Communication

Postal communication has become a near-universal medium of global communication. From the time a letter is dropped in a post box until it reaches its destination, it rarely is touched by human hands. Letter sorting is now entirely automated in most industrialized countries. Machines can even read the address on an envelope. Deregulation in the postal industry has led in many countries to private and public companies competing for express mail services that can deliver a package throughout the world in about two days. Electronic mail can now be transmitted from post office to post office, where it is reproduced in original form and then placed into the "physical mail." The home fax machine is becoming so ubiquitous in the United States that by the decade's end home faxes may replace the postal service for personal mail.

International Radio Broadcasting

Since its inception in the early 1920s, international radio broadcasting has become one of the most significant channels of international communication. In terms of numbers of hours per week, the major international radio broadcasters have grown from 7,834 in 1960 to 16,092 in 1988.[12] About one hundred countries broadcast news,

TABLE 4-2
World's Fifteen Leading External Radio Broadcasters, June 1991

Hours per week	Radio broadcasters
2,401	United States (Voice of America, Radio Free Europe, Radio Liberty, Radio Free Afghanistan, Radio Martí)
1,951	Soviet Union (Radio Moscow, Radio Peace and Progress)
1,537	China (Radio Beijing)
841	Federal Republic of Germany (Deutsche Welle and Deutschlandfunk)
778	United Kingdom (BBC)
593	Egypt (Voice of the Arabs)
535	PDR Korea (Radio Pyongyang)
472	India (All India Radio)
400	Iran (Radio Tehran)
398	France (Radio France International)
396	Spain (Spanish Foreign Radio)
392	Turkey
360	Cuba (Radio Havana Cuba)
338	Australia
336	Japan

SOURCE: British Broadcasting Corporation, International Broadcasting and Audience Research, June 1991, personal correspondence.

opinion, and entertainment to foreign listeners, providing a major source of information from abroad.[13] The United States, the Soviet Union, and China have been the major international radio broadcasters. (See Table 4-2.) Who listens to international radio broadcasts? Some very influential people. Huge international audiences sometimes follow every word of the BBC, Voice of America, and other stations. These audiences tend to be predominantly male, urban, younger, and well educated.[14]

International radio broadcasting relies on the remarkable characteristics of high frequency (HF), also known as "shortwave," radio waves to reach its audiences. These waves actually hit the solar-charged ionosphere, from which they are refracted to points thousands of kilometers away. Sometimes the signal bounces from earth back to the ionosphere for a second hop and more distance. This *skywave propagation* provides the only method of transmitting radio signals from land-based stations around the world (see Figure 4-1). Although the International Telecommunication Union (ITU) has reserved medium-wave (also known as AM) radio for domestic purposes, some countries also use the medium-wave frequencies for international broadcasting in violation of ITU regulations.[15]

Sharing the high-frequency bands with the official external broadcasters are 1.5 million amateur radio enthusiasts, known as "ham" radio operators. Ham radio communications are sent primarily by voice or by Morse code. There are even communications satellites—called the Oscar series—for amateur use. Although ham radio is primarily a hobby to most of the operators, amateur radio enthusiasts play an important role in emergency communication during disasters, revolutions, and war. For example, during the U.S. invasion of Grenada, the Pentagon excluded journalists, but ham operators on the island carried news and sometimes sounds of the fighting.[16]

Another technology for long-distance (and sometimes international) communica-

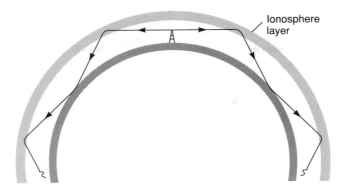

FIGURE 4-1 Skywaves radiate outward above the horizon into space. However, when they encounter the ionosphere, waves of certain frequencies are refracted back toward the earth. The return wave may bounce off the earth back to the ionosphere, then back to earth and so on, in a series of skips. This is the principle of "shortwave" broadcasting.

SOURCE: Reprinted with the permission of Charles Scribner's Sons, an imprint of Macmillan Publishing Company. Adapted from *From Spark to Satellite*, by Stanley Leinwoll. Copyright © 1979 Stanley Leinwoll.

tion is microwave radio. Particularly among island nations and mountainous regions, where laying cables is technically impossible or expensive, microwave radio "transceivers" (transmitter/receiver antennas) relay communications from point to point, usually no more than 50km between sites. One hundred of these transceivers are needed to cross the United States.

Many news agencies, as well as embassies and intelligence agencies, distribute information via another radio medium, international radioteletype (RTTY). Personal computers and other receivers store and print out huge quantities of textual information. This technology is widely distributed, especially among news agencies, weather services, and diplomatic telegrams. But RTTY is very slow—about 60 to 70 words per minute—and is often disturbed by atmospheric or solar activity.[17]

Satellite Telecommunications

The science fiction writer Arthur C. Clarke is credited with originating the concept of satellite telecommunications. In 1945, Clarke published an article outlining the fundamental technical considerations necessary to create earth–satellite–earth communications.[18]

A satellite can interconnect any number of stations that lie under the satellite's antenna beams (known as its "footprint") because they can see up to a third of the earth's surface at a time. When we say that a satellite communication is "insensitive to distance," we mean that all points on the earth's surface are about the same distance from the satellite: Communicating from Lima to Quito is virtually the same distance as from Lima to Montreal. But to send a signal around the world, satellite signals have to be "multihopped" from earth station to satellite to earth station to satellite to earth station (see Figure 4-2).

Geostationary satellites work especially well for countries on or near the

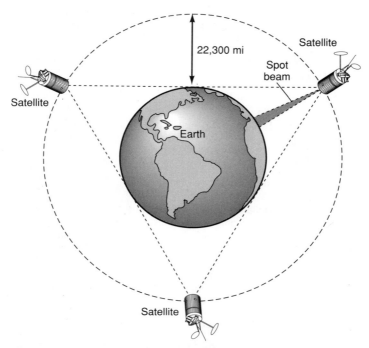

FIGURE 4-2   Satellite Global Coverage. Hypothetically, three communication satellites positioned at equidistant points on a circle above the earth's equator, 35,000 kilometers in space, would be able to relay signals to the entire globe.

SOURCE: From *Broadcasting in America*, 4th Ed., by Sydney W. Head and Christopher H. Sterling, p. 89. Copyright © 1982 by Houghton Mifflin Company. Used with permission.

equator. From that vantage point, satellites see those countries through a relatively thin layer of atmosphere. But for countries in the far northern or southern hemispheres, satellites have to "look" through a thick layer of dense atmosphere, which can weaken the signal and cause interference. For example, the Commonwealth of Independent States has much of its territory in the far northern hemisphere and has devised a solution using nongeostationary satellites. Using an elongated elliptical orbit that puts the satellite over the country for a longer time, tracking antennas follow the satellites coursing over the country. The primary disadvantage is the need for complex ground equipment to track the satellite, but the picture is clearer because the distance through the atmosphere is lessened.[19]

The first true communication satellite, Syncom III, broadcast the 1964 Tokyo Olympic Games.[20] In April 1965 INTELSAT placed into orbit the world's first commercial communications satellite. Known as "Early Bird," the satellite sat over the Atlantic and was capable of transmitting only 240 voice channels or one television channel. The global INTELSAT system now carries about 80 percent of the world's long-distance international telecommunications traffic.[21] Figure 4-3 is a diagram of the INTELSAT network.

One new technology is store-and-forward satellites, used by the military and the intelligence community for years.[22] Both the *contras* in Nicaragua and the RENAMO

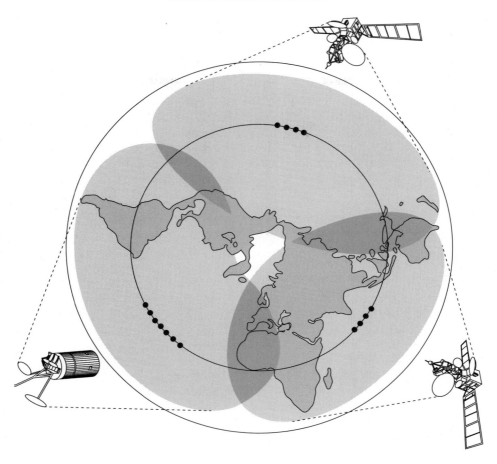

FIGURE 4-3   INTELSAT Global Satellite Network. In practice, INTELSAT needs many satellites to cover the earth's surface with strong television, telephone, and data channels.

in Mozambique have had access to this "data-burst" technology on the U.S. spy satellites. These satellites have a polar orbit of about 500 miles above earth and pass over every spot on the planet from two to four times daily. Packet data are transmitted via this satellite to either a tracking antenna or a briefcase-style portable station with a whip antenna.

International Cable Communications

In the early years, telegraphs and telephones were connected by open copper wire, known as "wire pairs," stretched along poles. Copper could carry one telephone conversation from New York to Denver even before amplifiers were invented. But wire pairs were susceptible to attenuation (fading) and leakage (hearing faint conversations from neighboring wires). So, to minimize leakage, wire pairs were twisted together in differing lengths, and amplifiers were added to boost signal strength.

It was also discovered that twisted wire cable can carry more than one voice by raising the frequencies of the human voice to a higher level. Different channels are raised in different amounts, a process called *multiplexing*. Signals are multiplexed through coaxial cable, which consists of thin copper wire centered by spacers inside a copper tube.

Although telegraphic communications have traversed submarine cables since the 1850s, the problems of building reliable underwater amplifiers and the frequent cable cuttings by trawlers made transatlantic voice transmission by cable impossible. It was not until 1956 that the first transatlantic telephone cable, the TAT-1, was laid.[23] Figure 4-4 shows the main oceanic telephone cable network.

Increasingly, thin strands of glass called *optical fibers* are replacing coaxial cable.[24] Optical fibers can be used to guide light in much the same way that coaxial cables guide lower-frequency electromagnetic radiation. Yet optical fibers are superior in every way: wider channel capacity, lower attenuation, longer distance between repeaters, immunity from outside interference, and lower leakage.[25] Already fiber optics can carry one-half billion bits per second, or about 8,000 simultaneous phone calls. It has been predicted that fibers will eventually be able to carry one trillion bits per second.[26]

The first transatlantic fiber cable between the United States, Great Britain, and France was called TAT-8. Used for telephone and video transmissions, it began operation in 1988 with the capacity to carry 37,000 phone calls simultaneously, twice the number of calls that are today exchanged between Europe and America.[27] TAT-9 now connects the United States, Canada, Britain, France, and Spain.[28] The first optical fiber cable linking Japan and the United States was activated in 1989. With a capacity of 40,000 simultaneous calls free of distortion and interference, the fiber optical cable replaces copper wire pairs that could handle only 6,000 calls.[29] Other submarine fiber cables currently in use connect England and Belgium, France and Corsica, and England and Scandinavia.

The Digital Revolution

Basically, information can be transmitted over any telecommunications medium in two ways: analog or digital. Analog transmission uses an electrical signal to represent the voice, picture, or data to be sent. If a voice is loud, the signal is strong. If the voice is soft, the signal is weak. This is the way medium-wave, or AM, radio is transmitted.

In digital transmissions, the information is translated into discrete binary digits (zeros and ones) known as *bits*. These bits can be transmitted unambiguously and saved exactly as transmitted. Even errors in transmission can be fully corrected. Sending digital computer data over phone lines requires a *modem* (a contraction of the words *modulate* and *demodulate*), which converts analog information into digital. Any communications—stereo music, television, copy machine output—can be converted into digital form. For example, in the modern telephone system, conversations are converted into digital form and transmitted by wire or optical fiber. Indeed, digital technology is also the basis for the computer, and this has led to the marriage of computers and communications, known as *telematics* or *informatics*.[30]

Virtually all the world's telecommunications channels started as analog devices.

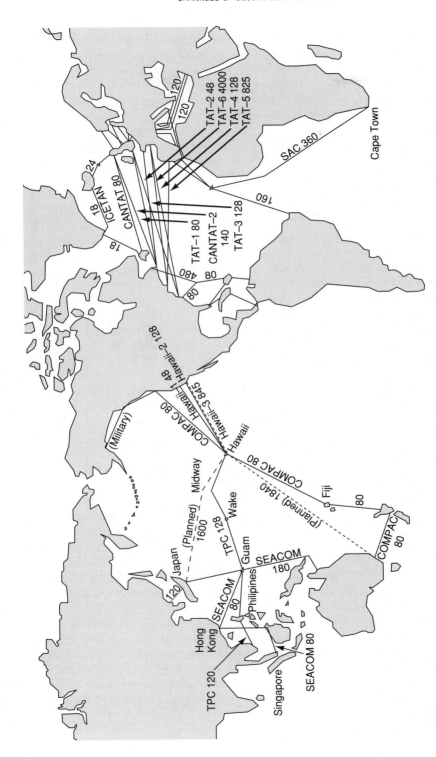

FIGURE 4-4 The main oceanic telephone cables. The numbers indicate the number of voice channels in a cable (without TAS 1).

But the inherent advantages of digital communications have led to a massive race to replace analog devices with digital technology. The world's public telecommunications networks will be totally digitalized by the turn of the century. This represents a massive reinvestment; high-volume and high-density areas are converted first. Some countries are digitizing their networks faster than others.

The worldwide digital revolution has led to a drive to create a global "integrated services digital network" (ISDN), which will eventually merge previously separate communications networks into new, high-capacity systems that include telephone, telegraph, teletext, fax, data, and video. ISDN will provide a common "digital pipe," covering the entire globe, for information of all types. With ISDN, a single common interface would connect the user to all types of networks and services.[31]

Computer Communications

The computer has been part of the driving force behind the digital revolution. In fact, it is increasingly difficult to distinguish whether a particular item is a computer or a telecommunications device. Computers have increased dramatically in capacity, speed, and reliability and have decreased dramatically in price in the last decade.[32]

Computers are used throughout the telecommunications process from production to reception, but the pivotal technological development has been the computerized switching network. The physical impossibility of linking every one of the world's 600 million telephones one to another made it necessary to create the global switching network, the system for routing calls along the worldwide system of satellite, microwave, and cable lines.

The computer has affected another area as well. Throughout the world people are communicating with previously unheard-of speed and reliability from their computers.[33] Worldwide computer-to-computer communication has brought about another technological development: the packet switching network. Ordinary telephone switching is not always the most efficient way for computers to communicate. Unlike telephone callers, computer communicators use the line not in a fairly steady stream of voice but in sudden bursts of data followed by long periods of inactivity. The most effective way of transmitting information in bursts is to organize the data into separate *packets*. We now find an elaborate network of "public data networks" (PDNs) connecting many countries around the world conforming to the ITU's "X.25" recommendations for packet switching.

Packets are really "electronic envelopes" into which data are placed. Just like a "physical envelope," a packet also needs a destination address and other control information. Sending the packet through the network has no effect on the contents; in fact, security measures keep the packets from being opened. Messages from one computer to another are cut up into several envelopes and are reassembled at the destination. Interestingly, there is no guarantee that the message packets will take the same route through the network or arrive at the same time! So "host" computers have packet assembly and disassembly (PAD) devices. Local computer users gain access to the PAD through leased lines or the public dial-up telephone network. On many networks, computer users can communicate throughout the world *for the price of a local telephone call!*[34]

Throughout the world, people are acquiring personal computers and joining international computer networks. In a computer network, individual stations called "nodes" are connected by coaxial cables, optical fibers, or standard telephone lines. Computers can communicate through a modem using regular telephone lines. But packet switching networks make use of *value-added networks* (VANs) such as SprintNet and Tymnet (United States), Datapac (Canada), Radio Austria (Austria), and British Telecomm (United Kingdom). The value-added carriers lease lines from common carriers and combine them with computer equipment of their own. They are dedicated solely to data.

A worldwide metanetwork of highly decentralized computer networks has arisen that democratize information flow, break down hierarchies of power, and make communication from top and bottom just as easy as from horizon to horizon. One such network has distinguished itself by specializing in the communication needs of the global Nongovernmental Organization (NGO) Movement. The *Association for Progressive Communication (APC),* or APC Networks, is the world's first computer communications system dedicated solely to peace, human rights, and environmental preservation. Comprising more than 20,000 subscribers in 95 countries, the APC Networks constitute a veritable honor role of organizations working in these fields, including Amnesty International, Friends of the Earth, Oxfam, Greenpeace, labor unions and peace organizations. There are APC partner networks in the United States, Nicaragua, Brazil, Russia, Australia, the United Kingdom, Canada, Sweden and Germany and affiliated systems in Uruguay, Costa Rica, Czechoslovakia, Bolivia, Kenya and other countries. The APC even has an affiliate network in Cuba providing the first free flow of information between the United States and Cuba in thirty years. Dozens of FidoNet systems connect with the APC through "gateways" located at the main nodes (see Figure 4-5).

Computer communicators use these networks for a variety of purposes. Communicators have established thousands of electronic "bulletin boards" or "conferences" specializing in subjects as diverse as fire fighting, peace, the environment, and magic. A bulletin board system allows a subscriber to read messages, exchange mail with other users, browse through materials stored in the system's reference library, and participate in on-line ("real-time" and "non–real-time") dialogues.[35] Computerists also use these networks for mail and banking and for purchasing airline tickets, examining the latest news, and looking up subjects in the encyclopedia.[36]

Other Technologies of Global Communication

The earliest form of electronic communication was the telegraph. There is now an enormous network of national and international telegraphy networks that, together with their associated telegraph switching centers, form the modern telex system, with its 1,500,000 subscribers in more than 120 countries.[37]

In the precomputer age, governments and businesses required highly reliable international communications. The telex grew out of the telegraph network and retains many of its limitations, including a restricted character set, no graphics, and slow transmission speed. It transmits only 50 to 150 bits per second (about 60 words per minute), compared to computer modems that can operate over leased telephone lines at 1.44 megabytes a second. Despite these limitations, telex grew

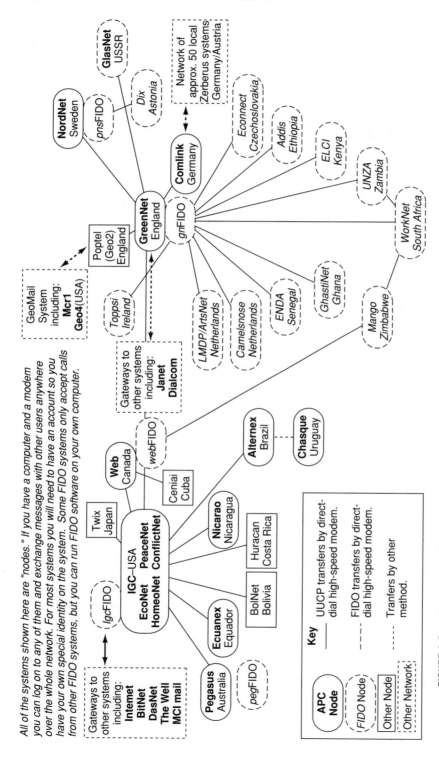

FIGURE 4-5 Association for Progressive Communications (APC) nodes and connected systems, January 1992. The APC constitutes the world's largest computer communications network dedicated solely to promoting human rights and preserving the environment. It serves the growing movement of nongovernmental organizations and citizen activists who "dial locally and act globally."

SOURCE: Association for Progressive Communication.

into a worldwide system for transmitting text electronically and still remains the only publicly available form of electronic mail service available in many countries.[38]

Then there is the telephone. Described as the "world's most complicated machine," the international telephone network consists of four main components:

1. *Instruments,* or handsets, to which are attached an endless array of answering machines, computers and other devices.
2. *Local loops,* which are the wire-pair cables that connect the subscriber's premises to the central telephone office. (There are several hundred million miles of local loops in the United States alone.)
3. *Switching facilities,* which enable a telephone to connect with virtually any other telephone in the world.
4. *Trunk networks,* which are worldwide transmission lines that consist of coaxial cables, microwave radio, satellites, undersea cables, and fiber optics.

Telephone costs have plummeted from £173 for a three-minute telephone call from the United Kingdom to the United States in 1927, to £9 in 1967, to £1.63 in 1983.[39] In 1992, the cost of a three-minute direct-dial call from the United States to the United Kingdom is £1.00 or $1.80.

Facsimile machines (also known as "telefax," or simply "fax") are sweeping the world and altering the way people conduct international relations. Driven by falling prices and the ability to send text and graphics across the country or around the world using ordinary telephone lines, fax machines, about the size of a small typewriter and costing as little as $350, are rapidly appearing in offices and homes. A fax machine can transmit a one-page document anywhere in the world in about 30 seconds, depending on the amount of detail. There are more than 2.5 million fax machines around the world, now surpassing the number of telex machines in use.[40]

Facsimile transmission is rapidly overtaking mail as the most rapid method for sending printed material. Fax machines scan a document and convert the dark marks into audible tones, which are then transmitted over standard phone lines to a receiving fax machine, which reconverts the tones and prints a copy of the document. Parallel with the development of the fax machine, computers can now scan and send text and graphics to other computers, where the text and graphics can be edited and printed.

INTERNATIONAL ORGANIZATIONS AND GLOBAL COMMUNICATION

International organizations are perhaps the most important arena where peoples, nations, and interest groups peacefully carry out modern international relations (see Figure 4-6). It is no accident that the oldest international organization in continuous existence is the International Telecommunication Union, founded in 1865. Although all international organizations are channels of global communication, the focus in this section is on those international organizations that specialize in communication.

There are two types of international organizations: *intergovernmental* and *nongovernmental.* Intergovernmental organizations (IGOs) are comprised of official representatives of national governments and liberation organizations. Nongovernmental organizations (NGOs) encompass private citizens and national interest groups.

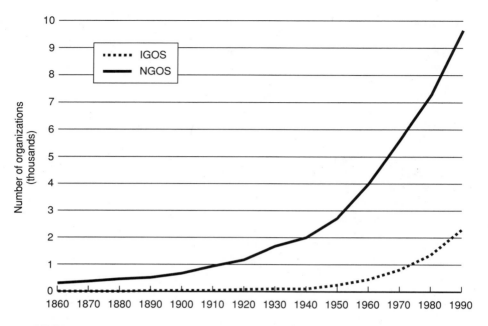

FIGURE 4-6 **Growth of International Organizations (cumulative status at end of decade). The oldest international organization in continuous existence is the International Telecommunication Union, founded in 1865. Since that time, the number of such organizations has increased dramatically.**

There has been a tremendous growth in the number of international organizations. This huge increase is due in no small measure to the development of modern communications technologies.[41] Altogether there are 8,960 conventional international organizations and other international bodies in the world today.[42] All communicate internationally, but 582 international organizations have communication as their central focus, and 1,190 international organizations specialize in general communications.[43] In this section, this complex network of organizations is divided by scope and function, beginning with the intergovernmental organizations.

United Nations Agencies

Although the United Nations Charter, signed in 1945 in San Francisco, does not mention communication *per se*, all United Nations agencies, whatever their mandates, are by definition involved in the global exchange of information within their respective areas.

Established in London in November 1945, the *United Nations Educational, Scientific, and Cultural Organization (UNESCO)*, is located in Paris. It is legally autonomous from the United Nations and reports to the General Assembly through the Economic and Social Council (ECOSOC).[44] UNESCO's purpose is to promote the cause of peace by increasing understanding among nations through education and research. Believing that ignorance leads to distrust and war, UNESCO's framers wrote the following famous words into the preamble of the UNESCO charter: "Since

Agencies of the United Nations Concerned with Global Communication

Centre for Telecommunications Development (CTD)
Committee on Information (CoI)
Committee on the Peaceful Uses of Outer Space (COPUOS)
General Agreement on Tariffs and Trade (GATT)
International Bank for Reconstruction and Development (IBRD) "World Bank"
International Civil Aviation Organization (ICAO)
International Frequency Registration Board (IFRB)
International Labour Organization (ILO)
International Maritime Organization (IMO)
International Programme for the Development of Communication (IPDC)
International Radio Consultative Committee (CCIR)
International Telecommunication Union (ITU)
International Telegraph and Telephone Consultative Committee (CCITT)
United Nations Centre on Transnational Corporations (UNCTC)
United Nations Commission on International Trade Law (UNCITRAL)
United Nations Conference on Trade and Development (UNCTAD)
United Nations Development Programme (UNDP)
United Nations Economic and Social Council (ECOSOC)
United Nations Educational, Scientific, and Cultural Organization (UNESCO)
United Nations Food and Agriculture Organization (FAO)
United Nations Fund for Population Activities (UNFPA)
United Nations General Assembly (UNGA)
Universal Postal Union (UPU)
World Health Organization (WHO)
World Intellectual Property Organization (WIPO)

war begins in the minds of men, it is in the minds of men that the defences of peace must be constructed."[45]

UNESCO's policy and financial decisions are made by the biennial General Conference. An Executive Board has oversight over the programs approved by the General Conference. The Secretariat carries out these programs and serves the two legislative bodies. UNESCO is led by a Director-General nominated by the Executive Board and appointed by the General Conference.

UNESCO has a broad mandate in the fields of social and economic development, scientific and technological cooperation, national culture and cultural heritage, and social sciences. Some of these non–communication-related program areas have clear-cut communication components.[46] But the "C" in UNESCO easily could also stand for *communication;* UNESCO has a specific mandate to develop the communication capacities of nations and to promote the free and balanced flow of information. UNESCO deals directly with international communication through programs in new technologies, textbooks, mass communication, research, and cultural and scientific exchange.[47]

Under UNESCO's Program Area called "Communication in the Service of Humanity" is the Communication, Information, and Informatics Sector. Within this sector, the Communication Division has two sections, Free Flow of Information and Communication Research, and Communication Development. The Free Flow Section seeks to promote freedom of information by removing obstacles to the free flow of information; by administering international agreements to remove customs duties on scientific, cultural, and academic materials (see Chapter 9, "International Communication and Information Law''); and by seeking to reduce postal charges and tele-communications rates. UNESCO started the now-independent *International Network of Documentation Centres on Communication Research and Policies (COMNET)*, which facilitates the exchange of information among communication research centers.[48] One of UNESCO's most prominent spin-offs is the *International Program for the Development of Communication (IPDC)*. Established in 1980 as a direct outgrowth of the communication debates, IPDC is now a fund-dispensing body that finances projects designed to increase the communication capacities of developing countries.

Founded in 1865, today's *International Telecommunication Union (ITU)* administers international legal agreements on international telecommunications; promotes the responsible use of telecommunications services; provides technical assistance to developing countries; administers programs financed by the United Nations Development Programme (UNDP); registers radio frequency assignments to avoid interference; coordinates development of space communications; encourages the lowest possible tariffs and rates; assists in the saving of human lives through telecommunications services; and undertakes studies, makes regulations, adopts resolutions, formulates recommendations, and collects and publishes information on telecommunications issues. Until the 1970s the ITU was primarily a forum for engineers and technicians; lawyers and politicians rarely made appearances. But with the increasing politicization of the information debate, the ITU moved into more political and legal areas.

Three ITU organs have temporary life spans. The *Plenipotentiary Conference* meets every five years, has the supreme authority, and can revise the ITU Convention. Two types of *Administrative Conferences*—Administrative Radio Conferences and Administrative Telegraph and Telephone Conferences—revise the Administrative Regulations, which govern the international operations of telegraph, telephone, and radio communications.[49] Finally, the ITU's *Administrative Council* facilitates the implementation of Administrative Regulations and oversees decisions of the Plenipotentiary Conference and other conferences or meetings of the Union.

The ITU has four permanent organs. The *General Secretariat*, in continuous existence since 1868, coordinates the activities of the other permanent organs and carries out the administrative duties of running a huge organization. The *International Frequency Registration Board (IFRB)* registers electromagnetic frequency assignments and satellite positions and provides advice on how telecommunication services can avoid interference. The *International Telegraph and Telephone Consultative Committee (CCITT)* issues recommendations on technical and tariff questions specifically related to telecommunication services other than radio communication. The *International Radio Consultative Committee (CCIR)* studies technical and operating questions relating specifically to radio communication and issues recommendations on them. The work of these latter three bodies has become increasingly politicized in recent years.

The *World Intellectual Property Organization (WIPO)*, located in Geneva, was established in its present form in 1967, but its origins go back to the 1883 Paris Convention and the 1886 Berne Union, which united in 1893. WIPO is responsible for administering the provisions of several dozen copyright conventions. Created in 1965 to act as a central source of grant funding and to coordinate development projects for the entire UN system, the *United Nations Development Programme (UNDP)* has been involved in virtually all aspects of communication development since the mid-1960s.[50] The *International Civil Aviation Organization (ICAO)* in Montreal makes policy in the field of international aviation. Its sister agency, the *International Maritime Organization (IMO)* in London, provides the international machinery for governments to cooperate on international merchant shipping and maritime communications. Established in 1874, the *Universal Postal Union (UPU)* in Berne operates according to the founding principle of a "single postal territory" for the reciprocal exchange of letters and guaranteed freedom of transit within the Union's member territories. The *General Agreement on Tariffs and Trade (GATT)* seeks to liberalize trade by reducing tariff and nontariff barriers. GATT is rapidly becoming involved with information and communication as it debates the question of "international trade in services."

Finally, two divisions of the *United Nations General Assembly (UNGA)* should be noted. The *Committee on the Peaceful Uses of Outer Space (COPUOS)* was established in 1959 to review international cooperation in the peaceful uses of outer space and to study how the United Nations might undertake programs toward that goal. The *Committee on Information (CoI)* oversees United Nations public information policies. The CoI meets several weeks each summer to produce a report of its work for the Fall meeting of the General Assembly's Special Political Committee. This report becomes the basis of a draft resolution on "Questions Relating to Information."

Other Regional and Intergovernmental Bodies

The *Organization for Economic Cooperation and Development (OECD)* in Paris is comprised of Japan and twenty-five industrialized countries of North America and Western Europe. OECD has been concerned with international information and communication issues, including transborder data flow and personal privacy, since the first expert group, the Data Bank Panel, was established in 1969.[51] Much of its work now takes place in the Committee for Information Computer and Communications Policy, which examines policy issues arising from the development and application of technology in these fields. Of special concern to OECD have been issues of transborder data flow and personal privacy.

An increasingly visible and important player in the North Atlantic community is the *Conference on Security and Cooperation in Europe (CSCE)*, known in the United States as the "Helsinki Process," which began with the signing of the Helsinki Final Act in 1975. Forged in the era of detente, the Final Act stressed that "confidence-building" can only come about with more "knowledge" and "wider understanding." The mass media play a positive role in bringing that about.[52] Information and communication provisions of the Final Act are subject to periodic reviews at an Information Forum.

One of the most influential forums in the communication and information debate is the *Non-Aligned Movement (NAM)*. The Non-Aligned Movement is not a chartered intergovernmental organization *per se*, but rather a periodic conference with a rotating leadership. It consists of more than one hundred member nations, most of them in Asia, Africa, and Latin America, and the Palestine Liberation Organization. Its name comes from being "not aligned" to big power blocs such as NATO or the former Warsaw Pact. Despite the disappearance of the bipolar world from which it originally drew its reason for being, the Movement's primary issues, such as global economic inequities, are still on the organization's agenda.

Satellite Consortia and Program Exchanges

The *International Telecommunications Satellite Organization (INTELSAT)*, with its headquarters in Washington, operates the most sophisticated satellite communications system in the world. Founded in 1964, INTELSAT maintains the *satellite space segment. Earth stations* are operated by telecommunications authorities in member countries and in other, nonmember user countries. INTELSAT thus operates two-thirds of all intercontinental message traffic and virtually all live transborder television communication.[53] INTELSAT's domestic service for *intra*national communication serves predominantly Third World countries.

INTELSAT's space monopoly is coming to an end. In 1984, President Reagan, on the advice of his Secretaries of State and Commerce, issued a "determination" that permitted private satellite systems to compete with INTELSAT. A consequence of the U.S. government's philosophy of deregulation, this decision was caused by pressure from the private sector to "open the skies" to competition.

INTELSAT's counterpart in the former socialist community is the *International Organization of Space Communications (INTERSPUTNIK)*, based in Moscow. Founded in 1971 by socialist governments, INTERSPUTNIK's aims are to operate a satellite communication system for member countries to exchange television and radio, telegraph and telephone. It uses satellites over the Atlantic and Indian oceans and has ground stations in Eastern European capitals, as well as in Hanoi, Ho Chi Minh City, Vientiane, Ulan Bator, Kabul, Algiers, Havana, Managua, Pyongyang, South Yemen, Damascus, and Luanda.

What INTELSAT and INTERSPUTNIK do for land communications, the *International Maritime Satellite Organization (INMARSAT)* does at sea. Based in London and established in 1979, INMARSAT has vastly improved maritime and aeronautical communication and has led to advances in safety of life at sea through communication; efficient management of ships; maritime, aeronautical, and mobile public correspondence services; and radio navigations capabilities. INMARSAT's coastal earth stations are owned and operated by INMARSAT members; shipboard antenna stations are owned and operated by shipowners. INMARSAT interfaces with public switched networks at coastal earth stations.

These satellite telecommunications networks have made possible the growth of regional television news and program exchanges. The *Asia-Pacific Television News Exchange (ASIAVISION)*, with headquarters in Kuala Lumpur, began this service in April 1984, when a group of Asian countries, including India, Pakistan, Bangladesh, Sri Lanka, Brunei, Malaysia, and Indonesia, began exchanging television news weekly through INTELSAT satellites over the Indian and Pacific oceans. Following a principle of "free to offer, free to receive or to refuse," ASIAVISION is now exchanging news daily. A second ASIAVISION network was also created linking China, South Korea, Japan, Hong Kong, Australia and New Zealand.[54]

Other Intergovernmental Organizations
Concerned with Global Communication

Association of South East Asian Nations (ASEAN)
Commission of the European Communities (CEC)
Conference on Security and Cooperation in Europe (CSCE)
Coordinating Bureau of the Non-Aligned Countries
Coordinating Committee for Satellite Communications (CCTS)
Council of Europe (CE)
Economic Commission for Europe (ECE)
European Communities (EC)
European Conference of Postal and Telecommunications Administrations (CEPT)
European Telecommunications Standards Institute (ETSI)
Intergovernmental Council for Coordination of Cooperation of Non-Aligned Countries in the Field of
    Information and Communication
International Green Number
League of Arab States (LAS)
Organization for Economic Cooperation and Development (OECD)

Postal Unions

African Postal Union (APU)
African Posts and Telecommunications Union (APTU)
Arab Postal Union (APU)
Asian-Pacific Postal Union (APPU)
Central African Posts and Telecommunications Conference (CAPTAC)
European Conference of Postal and Telecommunications Administrations (CEPT)
Nordic Postal Union (UPPN)
Organization for Cooperation of Socialist Countries in the Domain of Tele- and Postal Communication
    (OCTPC)
Pan African Postal Union (PAPU)
Postal Union of the Americas and Spain (PUAS)

Telecommunications Unions

African Postal and Telecommunication Union (APU/ATU)
African Posts and Telecommunications Union (APTU)
Arab Federation of Post, Telegraph, and Telephones
Arab Telecommunications Union (ATU)
Association of State Telecommunication Enterprises of the Andean Subregional Agreement (ASETA)
Caribbean Telecommunications Union (CTU) (proposed)
Commonwealth Telecommunications Organization (CTO)
Inter-American Telecommunications Conference (CITEL)
Middle East and Mediterranean Telecommunication Network
Organization for Cooperation of Socialist Countries in the Domain of Tele- and Postal Communication
    (OCTPC)
Pan-African Telecommunications Union (PATU)
Technical Commission for Telecommunications in Central America (COMTELCA)

Informatics Associations

African Institute of Informatics (IAI)
Asia-Pacific Telecommunity (APT)

(continued)

Comité de Acción para la Cooperación y Concertación Latinoamericana en Informática y Electrónica (CACIEL)
European Informatics Network
Intergovernmental Commission for Cooperation of Socialist Countries in the Field of Computer Technology (IGCCT)
International Computing Centre (ICC)
International Council for Computer Communication
Latin American Center for Studies in Informatics
Regional Center for Education in Information Science (CREI)
Regional Informatics Network of South Central Asia
Southeast Asia Regional Computer Confederation
World Information System on Informatics (WISI)

Satellite Consortia

African Satellite Telecommunications System (AFSAT)
Arab Satellite Communications Organization (ARABSAT)
Consortium for International Pacific Education and Communications Experiments by Satellite (PEACESAT)
COSPAS-SARSAT
Pan European Satellite Broadcasting Consortium
Radio Amateur Satellite Corporation (AMSAT)

Regional Program Exchanges

EUROVISION
Gulfvision
INTERVISION
Nordic Television Cooperation (Nordvision)

Broadcasting Associations

Throughout the world there is a vital network of broadcasting associations loosely grouped under the *World Conference of Broadcasting Unions (WCBU)*. The oldest are the two European associations formed after ideological differences split the *International Broadcasting Organization (OIR)*, which was founded in 1946.

The *European Broadcasting Union (EBU)*, based in Geneva, was founded in 1950. EBU promotes radio and television exchanges such as EUROVISION, coordinates research on broadcasting and information, and assists members in working within international communication law. Most of EBU's active members are public broadcasting companies.

EBU's complement in the former socialist community is the *International Radio and Television Organization (OIRT)*. When Western Europeans withdrew from the OIR and set up a separate European Broadcasting Union in 1950, the OIR moved to Prague, changing its name to OIRT in 1959. Like the EBU, OIRT facilitates relations between members and studies the practical and theoretical aspects of radio and television broadcasting.

Regional Broadcasting Associations

Arab States Broadcasting Union (ASBU)
Asian-Pacific Broadcasting Union (ABU)
Asian-Pacific Institute for Broadcasting Development (AIBD)
Asia-Pacific Telecommunity (APT)
Association of European Commercial Television (ACT)
Broadcasting Organizations of the Nonaligned Countries (BONAC)
Caribbean Broadcasting Corporation (CaBC)
Commonwealth Broadcasting Association (CBA)
Communauté des Radio Publiques de la Langue Française (CRPLF)
European Broadcasting Union (EBU)
Ibero-American Television Organization (IATO)
International Amateur Radio Association (IARU)
International Broadcasting Association (AIR/IAB)
International Catholic Radio and Television Association (UNDA)
International Council for Film, Television, and Audiovisual Communication (IFTC)
International Maritime Radio Association (IMRA)
International Radio and Television Organization (OIRT)
Islamic States Broadcasting Organization (ISBO)
Latin American and Caribbean Broadcasting Union (ULCRA)
Nordic Television Cooperation
North American National Broadcasting Association (NANBA)
Pan African Christian Broadcasting Association (PACBA)
Union of National Radio and Television Organizations of Africa (URTNA)
World Association of Community Radio Broadcasters (AMARC)
World Conference of Broadcasting Unions (WCBU)

In the Western Hemisphere, the *International Broadcasting Association (AIR/ IAB)*, headquartered in Montevideo, Uruguay, includes privately-owned broadcasting organizations from Latin America, plus some European countries. IAB's mandate is to defend the existence of private broadcasters and to represent their interests in international fora. Taking a different approach is the *Latin American and Caribbean Broadcasting Union (ULCRA)*, which has as members some public-interest stations. With help from UNESCO/IPDC, ULCRA promotes regional exchanges of television and radio programs.

In Asia, the *Asian-Pacific Broadcasting Union (ABU)* in Kuala Lumpur, in addition to organizing the ASIAVISION exchange, provides coordination and collaboration for broadcasting professionals. In the Middle East, the *Arab States Broadcasting Union (ASBU)* in Damascus was founded in 1969 under the auspices of the League of Arab States. ASBU's projects include the Arab Television News Service, a regional training center, exchanges of programs, copyright management, and Arabization of broadcasting terms. In Africa, the *Union of National Radio and Television Organizations of Africa (URTNA)*, in Dakar, Senegal, was founded in 1962 to assist in the development of radio and television in Africa. Of special importance is the *URTNA Program Exchange Center (URTNA-PEC)*. Based in Nairobi, this is Africa's answer to reducing the high level of dependency upon foreign programs and to sharing cultural and nation-building programs.

Two other organizations deserve mention. The *Broadcasting Organizations of the Nonaligned Countries (BONAC)*—with its headquarters in Belgrade, was founded in 1977 and is composed of broadcasting organizations from nonaligned countries. Finally, the *World Association of Community Radio Broadcasters (AMARC)*, based in Montreal, was created in 1988 to promote the promise and opportunity of community radio in the international arena. Its goals include establishing a new world information order based on more just and equitable exchanges among people; contributing to the expression of different social, political, and cultural movements; and supporting initiatives for peace, friendship among peoples, and democracy. AMARC works to recognize the fundamental and specific role of women in establishing new practices of communication, to use programming to promote sovereignty and independence of all peoples, and to build respect for people's distinct cultural identities.

News Agencies

There are more than one hundred news agencies around the world. More than mere purveyors of world events, many of the international press agencies have played a key role in shaping the issues so hotly debated in the field of international information relations.

Two of these agencies are based in New York. Founded in 1848 by six daily newspapers, the *Associated Press (AP)* is a nonprofit cooperative that transmits 2 million words daily to 15,000 outlets through some 1.3 million kilometers of leased wire, cable, land lines, and radio waves. Also headquartered in New York is *United Press International (UPI)*. Once the largest commercial news agency, it was surpassed by Reuters in 1984. On the brink of bankruptcy in 1986, UPI is slowly recuperating. With service in over one hundred countries, UPI's Latin American desk is still preeminent in that region despite its financial woes.

Two European giants are also in the top five. London-based *Reuters*, founded in 1851, has been the most financially successful agency. Some 90 percent of its revenues come from its business services. *Agence France Presse (AFP)* operates in more than 140 countries and transmits three million words daily in four languages (it ranks first in the Arab world).

Rounding out the top five is the Moscow-based international news agency *TASS*. Founded in 1917 during the Russian revolution, TASS has become one of the largest international news agencies and provides service to over one thousand newspapers, radio and television companies, magazines, agencies, ministries of information, and other government organs in 115 countries. It transmits in Russian, English, French, German, Spanish, Portuguese, and Arabic and has over one hundred foreign bureaus.

Often overlooked, the sixth-place (in terms of daily wordage) Spanish news agency *EFE,* based in Madrid, could quickly have become the world's second leading agency if it had succeeded in acquiring ailing UPI's Latin American services.[55]

Regional and alternative news agencies are growing in size and quality of information. The Latin American region illustrates the vitality of these outlets. The *Latin American Agency for Special Information Services (ALASEI)* in Panama, also known as the Latin American Features Agency, began operations in 1983 with participation by journalists' unions in ten Latin American countries as well as by regional organizations such as FELAP, ALAIC, and FELAFACS. ALASEI aims to gather and distribute information concerning the economic and cultural development of Latin America and

International and Regional News Agencies

Acción de Sistemas Informativos Nacionales (ASIN)
Agence France Presse (AFP)
Agencia Latinoamericana de Información (ALAI)
Agenzia Nazionale Stampa Associata (ANSA)
Arab Revolutionary News Agency (ARNA)
Asian-Pacific News Network (APNN)
Associated Press (AP)
Caribbean News Agency (CANA)
Deutsche Presse Agentur (DPA)
EFE
European Alliance of Press Agencies (EAPA)
Federation of Arab News Agencies (FANA)
Human Rights Media Services (HURMES)
Inforpaz
Inter Press Service (IPS)
Isis International Women's Information and Communication Service
Nonaligned News Agencies Pool (NANAP)
Organization of Asia-Pacific News Agencies (OANA)
Pacific Islands News Association (PINA)
PACNEWS
Pan African News Agency (PANA)
Reuters
TASS
Telegrafska Agencija Nova Jugoslavija (TANJUG)
United Press International
West and Central African News Agencies Development (WANAD)

the Caribbean. Also serving Latin America are the *Acción de Sistemas Informativos Nacionales (ASIN)*, a regional news exchange network between nineteen national news agencies; and the *Agencia Latinoamericana de Información (ALAI)*, based in Quito, Ecuador. Serving the Caribbean region in English is the *Caribbean News Agency (CANA)* in Barbados. Owned by media institutions themselves, CANA transmitted its first report in 1976, and its services are now received in the Caribbean by all newspapers and the majority of English-speaking radio and television stations in twelve English-speaking Caribbean countries and territories.

Several news services deserve special attention for the innovative and dynamic way they collect and disseminate news that too often fails to find a place among the Big Five.

One outgrowth of the information debates was the formation of the *Non-Aligned News Agencies Pool (NANAP)*, established in 1975 at the initiative of the Yugoslav news agency and under the auspices of UNESCO. With over fifty participating news agencies, *Telegrafska Agencija Nova Jugoslavija (TANJUG)* collects and disseminates news of more than ninety, mostly government-run national news agencies. It exchanges about 100,000 words daily among its ten distribution centers in Asia, Africa, Europe, and Latin America.

The world's best-known alternative press agency is *Inter Press Service (IPS)* with headquarters in Rome. Actually, in terms of its reach (900 clients in 90 countries), IPS is the sixth-leading news agency in the world. Founded in 1964, IPS distributes about 100,000 words daily in eleven languages to some five hundred newspapers in seventy countries from its world desk in Amsterdam, telecommunications headquarters in Rome, and regional centers in San Jose, Costa Rica; Kingston, Jamaica; Harare, Zimbabwe; Colombo, Sri Lanka; Tunis; New York; Bonn; and Vienna. IPS participates in scores of programs aimed at rural areas, social organizations, and schools. In addition to providing a daily and feature wire service, it supports networks of women journalists on all Third World continents, emphasizes cultural affairs in developing societies, operates a special children's news service, and has even launched a global network for reporting church activities in development. Remarkably, IPS is virtually invisible in the world's largest news market, the United States.

Publishers' and Editors' Associations

Another set of key players is the international publishers' and editors' associations. Bringing together more than one thousand publications, the *Inter-American Press Association, (IAPA-SIP)* in Miami was founded in 1942 to safeguard freedom of the press in the Americas; to promote and maintain the dignity, rights, and responsibilities of the journalism profession; and to foster a wider knowledge and greater interchange among the peoples of the Americas.

The oldest association in this category is the *International Publishers Association (IPA)* in Geneva. Founded in 1896 as the International Publishers Congress, IPA defends the freedom of publishers to publish and distribute the works of the mind and works to overcome literacy and book shortages. IPA helps attract adherents to the Berne Convention and the Universal Copyright Convention and assists in revising and drafting new copyright conventions. Its special goal is to keep the international flow of books free of tariffs and other obstructions.

The *International Federation of Newspaper Publishers (IFNP-FIEJ)*, founded in Paris in 1948, represents the newspaper publishing industry in Western Europe and North America. FIEJ's goals are to "promote the free flow of ideas by word and image, to safeguard the ethical and economic interests of newspapers" and to "defend freedom of information in cooperation with other international press organizations." The Barbados-based *Caribbean Publishing and Broadcasting Association (CPBA)* brings together publishers and broadcasters to discuss their common problems and to promote an independent and free media throughout the region. CPBA joins in efforts to fight threats to freedom of the press, works to improve standards of journalism education, and cooperates with other professional organizations.

Two other allies of publishers' and editors' associations have been very active in the information debates. The *World Press Freedom Committee (WPFC)* in Washington, DC, composed primarily of editors, publishers, and broadcasters, emerged in 1976 to unify the defenders of the free press against perceived attacks by UNESCO. WPFC sends representatives to intergovernmental media conferences and has particular influence within the United States delegation. *Freedom House*, based in New York, was founded in 1941 to combat Nazism and Fascism and counts more than four thousand members dedicated to strengthening free institutions, including the press, around the world. Freedom House publishes a yearly analysis of press freedom worldwide.

Publishers' and Editors' Associations

Association of South East Asian Publishers (ASEAP)
Caribbean Press Council (CPC)
Caribbean Publishing and Broadcasting Association (CPBA)
Commonwealth Press Union (CPU)
EEC Community of Associations of Newspaper Publishers (CAEJ)
International Book Committee (IBC)
International Federation of Newspaper Publishers (IFNP-FIEJ)
International Institute of Communication (IIC)
International Press Institute (IPI)
International Press Telecommunications Council (IPTC)
International Publishers Association (IPA)
Inter-American Press Association (IAPA-SIP)
Inter-American Publishers Group
Nordic Newspaper Publishers' Joint Board (NTS)
Pacific Area Newspaper Publishers Association (PANPA)
Press Foundation of Asia (PFA)

Journalists' and Press Workers' Associations

The best-known Western association is the *International Federation of Journalists (IFJ)* in Brussels. Splitting from the International Organization of Journalists in 1952, IFJ is composed of journalists' unions from Western and Western-oriented Third World countries. IFJ's aims are to safeguard freedom of the press and of journalists and to take action whenever the rights and liberties of the press and journalists are threatened. It coordinates collective action in support of any member union that requests international measures in accordance with the Federation's constitution.

IFJ's counterpart is the *International Organization of Journalists (IOJ)*, based in Prague. Founded in Copenhagen in 1946, IOJ was the successor to the International Federation of Journalists founded in Paris in 1926 and to the International Federation of Journalists of the Allied and Free Countries, formed in London in 1941. Composed of national trade unions and organizations, committees, and individual members from mostly socialist and Third World countries and territories, IOJ is the largest association of its kind in the world. It is particularly concerned with the physical protection of journalists and makes a special effort to be involved in such important issues as disarmament, human rights, racism, apartheid, and decolonization. Because of its association with the communist regime in Czechoslovakia, IOJ has been ordered out of the country, and its continued existence appears uncertain.

Some of the most visible actors in the information debates have come from Latin America. The *Latin American Federation of Journalists (FELAP)* in Mexico, founded in 1976, is composed of national organizations and unions. FELAP defends freedom of the press and access to information, works to improve working conditions, and treats the needs of journalists who are persecuted. Aligned with FELAP is the *Latin American Federation of Press Workers (FELETRAP)* in Buenos Aires. Founded in 1976 in Costa Rica during the first Latin American Congress of Press Workers, FELETRAP organizes press workers; promotes, defends, and represents press workers' interests vis-a-vis their employers and governments; defends and promotes the right of free and democratic organization of all press workers; and monitors respect for freedom of information and expression.

Journalists' and Press Workers' Associations

Afro-Asian Writers Association (AAWA)
Caribbean Association of Mediaworkers (CAMWORK)
Committee to Protect Journalists (CPJ)
Commonwealth Journalists' Association (CJA)
Confederation of ASEAN Journalists (CAJ)
Federation of Arab Journalists (FAJ)
Freedom House
International Federation of Journalists (IFJ)
International Organization of Journalists (IOJ)
International PEN
Latin American Federation of Journalists (FELAP)
Latin American Federation of Press Workers (FELETRAP)
Nordic Association of Journalists Unions (NJF)
Postal, Telegraph, and Telephone International (PTTI)
Union of African Journalists (UAJ)
World Press Freedom Committee (WPFC)

Catholic press organizations
Catholic Media Council (CAMECO)
Catholic Union of the Press in Africa (UCAP)
Communication Foundation of Asia (CFA)
East Asia Catholic Press Association (EACPA)
International Catholic Federation of Dailies and Periodicals
International Catholic Union of the Press (ICUP)
International Federation of Associations of Church Press
International Federation of Catholic Journalists (IFCJ)
International Federation of Catholic Press Agencies
Latin American Catholic Press Union (UCLAP)
Pan African Episcopal Committee for Social Communication (CEPACS)
Pontifical Commission for the Media of Social Communication (CPCS)
South Asian Catholic Press Association (SACPA)
South East Asian Catholic Press Association (SEACPA)

The *Caribbean Association of Mediaworkers (CAMWORK)* in Barbados was launched in Jamaica in 1986 to assist journalists and other media professionals in promoting an authentic Caribbean media identity. CAMWORK sponsors on-the-job training, conferences, and other fora designed to facilitate a dialogue about media in the region.

Perhaps the most broadly organized sector of journalists and press workers are those who work for Catholic publications. The *International Catholic Union of the Press (ICUP)*, based in Geneva, was founded in 1927. ICUP is made up of professional, international member federations and regional organizations. ICUP links Catholics who are influential in the press, as well as Catholic journalists, and represents the interests of the Catholic press at international meetings. It carries out research on press and religion and promotes the Catholic press in developing countries.

The *World Association of Christian Communication (WACC)* in London began in 1975. WACC counts as its members regional associations, individual members, and corporate members from churches, boards, and church agencies; councils of churches; publishing houses; religious programming services; publishers; educational institutions; film producers; and secular communication organizations.

WACC's aims are to promote "the more effective use of the media to communicate God's salvation in Christ for every aspect of human development and to proclaim the Christian Gospel with relevance to the whole of life." Its activities include communication development and research, especially in the Third World. It is concerned with the ethical and social aspects of communication and works to ensure that communication channels are used in support of a just and peaceful society.

Research Associations and Training Institutes

Founded in 1967 in London, the *International Institute of Communication (IIC)* promotes and disseminates research and policy studies about the impact of broadcast media on society. It is especially interested in investigating the social, political, economic, and cultural effects of new communications technologies. IIC also aims to improve professional competence and to eliminate the barriers to the free flow of information throughout the world.

News managers have a nonprofit, educational ally in the *International Press Institute (IPI)* in London. Founded in 1951 and composed of those responsible for editorial and news policies of newspapers and broadcasting systems, IPI's goals are to further and safeguard freedom of the press. IPI defends journalists from harassment and persecution around the world. It also conducts research on news flows, sources, and reporting and is one of the staunchest defenders of the free flow of information.

The world's largest professional organization in the field of communication research is the *International Association for Mass Communication Research (IAMCR)—Association Internationale des Études et Recherches sur l'Information (AIERI)*—founded in 1956 in Strasbourg. With more than 2,300 members in some seventy countries, the largest division within the IAMCR is the International Communication Section. Other sections focus on such areas as: bibliography, communication technology policy, gender and communication, history, law, political communication research, political economy, professional education, and sociology/social psychology. The association is a Class A nongovernmental organization before UNESCO.

Regional research associations carry out the bulk of global communication research around the world. In Africa, communication educators created the *African Council on Communication Education (ACCE)* in Nairobi in 1976. ACCE is composed of institutional members, such as communications training schools, and 200 individual members from twenty-five African countries. The *Latin American Communication Research Association (ALAIC)*, based in Brazil, is Latin America's most authoritative communication research grouping. The *International Centre of Advanced Communication Studies for Latin America (CIESPAL)* in Quito was founded in 1959 by UNESCO, the government of Ecuador, and Central University of Ecuador. CIESPAL provides advanced training in information science and journalism and carries out research on mass communication. The *European Institute for the Media* in Manchester analyzes media policies in Europe and trains media specialists. The *Nordic Documentation Centre for Mass Communication Research (NORDICOM)* counts as its members the communication research documentation centers of five Nordic countries. The *Central European Mass Communication Research Documentation Centre (CECOM)* in Krakow, founded in 1974, carries out information retrieval and

Research Associations and Training Institutes

Academy for Educational Development (AED)
African Council on Communication Education (ACCE)
Arab Regional Centre for Communication Research
Asian Institute of Journalism (AIJ)
Asian Mass Communication, Information and Research Center (AMIC)
Asociación Hispanoamericana de Centros de Investigación y Estudios de Telecomunicaciones (AHCIET)
Association Internationale d'Histoire des Telecommunications et de l'Informatique (AIHTI)
Caribbean Institute of Mass Communication (CARIMAC)
Center of Telecommunications for the Third World (CETTEM)
Center for Media and Valves (CMV)
Central European Mass Communication Research Documentation Centre (CECOM)
Centre for the Study of Communication and Culture (CSCC)
Clearinghouse on Development Communication (CDC)
European Institute for the Media
Instituto Para América Latina (IPAL)
International Association for Mass Communication Research (IAMCR)
International Centre of Advanced Communication Studies for Latin America (CIESPAL)
International Institute for Audio-Visual Communication and Cultural Development (MEDIACULT)
International Institute of Communication (IIC)
International Press Institute (IPI)
International Radio and Television University (IRTU)
Latin American Association of Communications Researchers (ALAIC)
Latin American Federation of Schools of Communication (FELAFACS)
Latin American Institute for Transnational Studies (ILET)
Latin American Institute of Communication Education (ILPEC)
Nordic Documentation Centre for Mass Communication Research (NORDICOM)
Pacific Telecommunications Council (PTC)

dissemination from Eastern European countries. The *Latin American Institute for Transnational Studies (ILET)* in Mexico and the *Instituto Para América Latina (IPAL)* in Lima carry out communications research directed at Latin American development and the impact of transnational corporations on the economy. The *Asian Mass Communication, Information and Research Center (AMIC)* in Singapore counts individual and institutional membership in thirty-nine countries and serves mass communication research in Asia through documentation, publications, research, seminars, and training. The *Centre for the Study of Communication and Culture (CSCC),* operated in London by the Society of Jesus (Jesuits), studies media and their influence from an ecumenical perspective, with special emphasis on religion and communication. The *Center for Media and Values* in Los Angeles carries out action-oriented research on everything from media and alcohol addiction to news coverage of war and peace.

NOTES

1. W. Phillips Davison, *International Political Communication* (New York: Praeger, 1965), pp. 327–338.

2. For much of the content of this section, I am indebted to J. A. LaPonce, "Language and Communication: The Rise of the Monolingual State," in *Communication and Integration in Global Politics,* ed. Claudio Cioffi-Revilla, Richard L. Merritt, and Dina A. Zinnes (Newbury Park, CA: Sage, 1987), pp. 183–207.

3. S. H. Muller, *The World's Living Languages: Basic Facts of the Structure, Kinship, Location and Number of Speakers* (New York: Ungar, 1964); J. A. LaPonce, *Langue et Territoire* (Quebec: Les Presses de l'Université Laval, 1984), cited in LaPonce, "Language and Communication," p. 185.

4. Those include French, Italian, Portuguese, Spanish, Romanian, Swiss Romansch, Provençal, Catalan, Sardinian, Ladino, Haitian, and Louisiana French.

5. Robert MacNeil's ten-part series, "The Story of English," produced by the British Broadcasting Corporation (UK) and the Public Broadcasting Corporation (USA), devotes entire episodes to such variants as Australian English, Indian English, and commercial English.

6. LaPonce, "Language and Communication," p. 192.

7. George Alan Connor, comp., *Esperanto, The World Interlanguage,* 2nd rev. ed. (New York: T. Yoseloff, 1966); Alexander Gode and Hugh E. Blaire, *Interlingua: A Grammar of the International Language,* 2nd ed. (New York: Storm, 1955); Rudiger Eichholz and Vilma Sindona Eichholz, comps., *Esperanto in the Modern World: Studies and Articles on Language Problems, the Right to Communicate, and the International Language, (1959–1982)* (Bailieboro, Ontario, Canada: Esperanto Press, 1982); Peter G. Forster, *The Esperanto Movement* (The Hague: Mouton, 1982); Mario Pei, *One Language for the World* (New York: Devin-Adair, 1961); and David Richardson, *Esperanto: Learning and Using the International Language* (Eastsound, WA: Orcas, 1988).

8. LaPonce, "Language and Communication," pp. 198–201.

9. Arthur John Burkart, *Tourism: Past, Present and Future,* 2nd ed. (London: Heinemann, 1981); Donald E. Lundberg, *The Tourist Business,* 6th ed. (New York: Van Nostrand Reinhold, 1990); and Woodrow McIntosh and Charles R. Goeldner, *Tourism—Principles, Practices, Philosophies,* 6th ed. (New York: Wiley, 1990).

10. Patrick Mitchell Alderton, *Sea Transport: Operation and Economics,* 2nd ed. (London: T. Reed, 1980); and Bruno Tavernier, *Great Maritime Routes: An Illustrated History,* trans. Nicholas Fry (New York: Viking Press, 1972).

11. *International Encyclopedia of Communication,* s.v. "Migration." See also *Diaspora: A Journal of Transnational Studies,* a forum for the "discussion of movements of people, capital, technology, ideas, and mass media across national borders."

12. "International Radio Broadcasting," in UNESCO, *World Communication Report* (Paris: UNESCO, 1989), p. 154.

13. Kim Andrew Elliott, "Too Many Voices of America," *Foreign Policy* (Winter 1989/1990), p. 113.

14. Donald R. Browne, *International Radio Broadcasting: The Limits of the Limitless Medium* (New York: Praeger, 1982), p. 331.

15. For example, BBC and Radio Moscow have long used medium-wave frequencies for international broadcasting. The United States uses AM radio for its Radio Martí programming aimed at Cuba. The International Frequency Registration Board of the ITU ruled: "[Radio Martí] is not in compliance with the intent and spirit of #2666 of the Radio Regulations [and] . . . the operation of this station is in contravention of . . . the regulations." See Karen Wald, "Cuba Battles for Sovereignty of the Airwaves," personal correspondence.

16. Judith Valente, "Beltsville Ham Monitors Grenada," *Washington Post,* October 28, 1983, p. 14. The FCC stepped in and issued warnings to news operations trying to contact the hams in Grenada because ham radio is not supposed to be used for commercial purposes.

17. Oliver P. Ferrell, *Confidential Frequency List* (Park Ridge, NJ: Gilfer Associates, 1984), p. 12.

18. Arthur C. Clarke, "Extraterrestrial Relays: Can Rocket Stations Give Worldwide Radio Coverage?" *Wireless World,* October 1945, reprinted in J. R. Pierce, *The Beginnings of Satellite Communications* (San Francisco: San Francisco Press, 1968), appendix 1, p. 37. Clarke did not patent his idea!

19. Richard Collins, *Satellite Television in Western Europe* (London: Libbey, 1990); Robert L. Douglas, *Satellite Communications Technology* (Englewood Cliffs, NJ: Prentice-Hall, 1988); Robert M. Gagliardi, *Satellite Communications,* 2nd ed. (New York: Van Nostrand Reinhold, 1991); Heather E. Hudson, *Communication Satellites: Their Development and Impact* (New York: Free

Press, 1990); Donald M. Jansky and Michel C. Jeruchim, *Communication Satellites in the Geo-stationary Orbit,* 2nd ed. (Norwood, MA: Artech House, 1987); Larry Martinez, *Communication Satellites: Power Politics in Space* (Norwood, MA: Artech House, 1985); Michael E. Kinsley, *Outer Space and Inner Sanctums: Government, Business, and Satellite Communication,* foreword by Ralph Nader; introd. by Nicholas Johnson (New York: Wiley, 1976); Ralph Negrine, ed., *Satellite Broadcasting: The Politics and Implications of the New Media* (London and New York: Routledge, 1988); David W. E. Rees, *Satellite Communications: The First Quarter Century of Service* (New York: Wiley, 1990); and Dennis Roddy, *Satellite Communications* (Englewood Cliffs, NJ: Prentice-Hall, 1989).

20. Charles-Noel Martin, *Satellite into Orbit,* trans. T. Schoeters (Toronto: George G. Harrap, 1965), p. 119.

21. Economic Commission for Europe, *The Telecommunication Industry: Growth and Structural Change* (New York: United Nations, 1987), p. 26.

22. John Schneidewind, "The Laptop Is Mightier than the Sword," *USA Today,* September 5, 1990, p. 8B.

23. Michael J. Goldey, "International Voice Communication," in *Toward a Law of Global Communications Networks,* ed. Anne W. Branscomb (New York: Longman, 1986), p. 63; and Economic Commission for Europe, *The Telecommunication Industry,* p. 75.

24. Dagmar Metzger, "Von den Bildern in der Höhle zu den Daten auf der Bank," *Geo Wissen* (2, 1989): 128.

25. Michael K. Barnoski, ed., *Fundamentals of Optical Fiber Communications* (New York: Academic Press, 1976); Paul S. Henry and Stewart D. Personick, eds., *Coherent Lightwave Communications* (New York: IEEE Press, 1990); N. S. Kapany, *Fiber Optics: Principles and Applications* (New York: Academic Press, 1967); N. S. Kapany and J. J. Burke, *Optical Waveguides* (New York: Academic Press, 1972); and Arthur F. Wickersham, *Microwave and Fiber Optics Communications* (Englewood Cliffs, NJ: Prentice-Hall, 1988).

26. Economic Commission for Europe, *The Telecommunication Industry,* p. 25.

27. *Mass Media in the World* (3, 1988): 18.

28. *Mass Media in the World* (5, 1988): 17.

29. *Mass Media in the World* (4–5, 1989): 38.

30. Martin S. Roden, *Analog and Digital Communication Systems,* 3rd ed. (Englewood Cliffs, NJ: Prentice-Hall, 1991); and William W. Wu, *Elements of Digital Satellite Communication* (Rockville, MD: Computer Science Press, 1985).

31. Rolf T. Wigand, "Integrated Services Digital Networks: Concepts, Policies, and Emerging Issues," *Journal of Communication* 38 (1, Winter 1988): 29–49; A. M. Rutkowski, "Integrated Services Digital Network: Issues and Options for the World's Future Communications Systems," in *Regulation of Transnational Communications: Michigan Yearbook of International Legal Studies, 1984,* ed. Leslie J. Anderson (New York: Clark Boardman, 1984), pp. 243–270; James Martin, *Telecommunications and the Computer* (Englewood Cliffs, NJ: Prentice-Hall, 1989), pp. 339–363; Peter Bocket et al., *ISDN, The Integrated Services Digital Network: Concepts, Methods, Systems* (Berlin and New York: Springer Verlag, 1988); John M. Griffiths et al., *ISDN Explained: Worldwide Network and Applications Technology* (Chichester and New York: Wiley, 1990); and Robert K. Heldman, *ISDN in the Information Marketplace* (Blue Ridge Summit, PA: Tab Professional and Reference Books, 1988).

32. Herman Heine Goldstine, *The Computer from Pascal to von Neumann* (Princeton, NJ: Princeton University Press, 1972); Fredrick J. Hill and Gerald R. Peterson, *Digital Systems: Hardware Organization and Design,* 3rd ed. (New York: Wiley, 1987); Tracy Kidder, *The Soul of a New Machine* (Boston: Little, Brown, 1981); N. Metropolis, J. Howlett, and Gian-Carlo Rota, eds., *A History of Computing in the Twentieth Century: A Collection of Essays* (New York: Academic Press, 1985); and Forrest M. Mims, *Siliconnections: Coming of Age in the Electronic Era* (New York: McGraw-Hill, 1986).

33. John S. Quarterman, *The Matrix: Computer Networks and Conferencing Systems Worldwide* (Bedford, MA: Digital Press, 1989).

34. James Martin, *Telecommunications and the Computer,* pp. 511–535.

35. The first systems are described in Steve Ciarcia, "Turnkey Bulletin Board Systems," *BYTE,* December 1985, pp. 93–103; Stuart Gannes, "New Medium for Messages," *Discover,* May 4, 1984, pp. 80–82; and Martin Lasden, "Of Bytes and Bulletin Boards," *New York Times Magazine,* August 4, 1985, pp. 34–42.

36. See Anne W. Branscomb, "Videotext: Global Progress and Comparative Politics," *Journal of Communication* 38 (1, Winter 1988): 50–59.

37. *Yearbook of Common Carrier Telecommunication Statistics,* 15th ed. (Geneva: International Telecommunication Union, 1988), cited in UNESCO, *World Communication Report,* pp. 462–464.

38. Economic Commission for Europe, *The Telecommunication Industry,* p. 76.

39. Economic Commission for Europe, *The Telecommunication Industry,* p. 40.

40. UNESCO, *World Communication Report,* p. 59.

41. *International Encyclopedia of Communications,* s.v. "International Organizations." The accompanying graph also includes organizations that have ceased to exist. See also Union of International Associations, *Yearbook of International Organizations, 1987–88* (Munich: K. G. Saur, 1987), vol. 1, app. 7, Table 4.

42. This includes conventional international bodies (federations of international organizations, universal membership organizations, intercontinental membership organizations, and regionally-oriented membership organizations) as well as other international bodies classified as Categories A–F in Union of International Associations, *Yearbook of International Organizations, 1987–88,* vol. 1, app. 7. This figure does *not* include the 7,632 internationally-oriented national organizations; 688 religious orders and secular institutes; 450 autonomous conference series; 1,620 multilateral treaties and intergovernmental agreements; or 2,414 dissolved/inactive organizations.

43. Organizations may be duplicated in these two categories. General communications also includes transportation, tourism, cargo expediters, and the like, which will not be covered here. Union of International Associations, *Yearbook of International Organizations,* vol. 3, Table 6.1.

44. The United States withdrew at the end of 1984, citing UNESCO's politicization of issues, anti-Western stands, and unrestrained expenses. The United Kingdom and Singapore withdrew at the end of 1985. Financial contributions by member nations are made according to a formula corresponding to a country's size and wealth. Before its withdrawal, the largest contributor was the United States, at 25 percent of the total budget, followed by the Soviet Union, Japan, the Federal Republic of Germany, France, the United Kingdom, Italy, and Canada. Together, these eight nations paid for 71 percent of UNESCO's operations. In contrast, the required two-thirds majority needed to approve the budget could be comprised of 108 nations contributing only 2.7 percent of the budget. C. Anthony Giffard, *UNESCO and the Media* (New York: Longman, 1989), p. 3.

45. Richard Hoggart, *An Idea and Its Servants: UNESCO from Within* (New York: Oxford University Press, 1978); Julian Huxley, *UNESCO: Its Purpose and Its Philosophy* (Washington: Public Affairs Press, 1948); William Preston, Jr., Edward S. Herman, and Herbert I. Schiller, *Hope and Folly: The United States and UNESCO, 1945–1985* (Minneapolis, MN: University of Minnesota Press, 1989); and James P. Sewell, *UNESCO and World Politics: Engaging in International Relations* (Princeton, NJ: Princeton University Press, 1975).

46. For example, the Division of Educational Sciences, Contents, and Methods applies media techniques in distance learning and new information technology in education. The Division of Population in the Sector of Social and Human Sciences carries out communication projects on population. Within the Science Sector, UNESCO established the Intergovernmental Informatics Programme (IIP) in 1986. UNESCO, *World Communication Report,* p. 5.

47. Together, these programs constitute Major Programme II, "Communication in the Service of Man," in UNESCO's overall Programme and Budget. UNESCO, *World Communication Report,* p. 3.

48. Research centers include the International Centre of Advanced Communications Studies for Latin America (CIESPAL) in Quito, Ecuador; the Nordic Documentation Centre for Mass Communication Research (NORDICOM) in Göteborg, Sweden; the Central European Mass Communication Research Documentation Centre (CECOM) in Krakow, Poland; the Asian Mass Communication, Information and Research Center (AMIC) in Singapore; the Caribbean Institute of Mass Communication (CARIMAC) in Kingston, Jamaica; the Arab Regional Centre for Communication Research in Damascus, Syria; and others in Egypt (two), Kenya, Senegal, Tunisia, Canada, Iraq, Lebanon, Austria, France, Portugal, Spain, and the United Kingdom.

49. There are two types of radio conferences—world and regional. The World Administrative Radio Conferences are known as *WARCs,* and the Regional Administrative Radio Conferences are known as *RARCs.* Conference agendas may be limited to one medium and one region.

50. By 1988 it had funded 729 communication projects, totaling over $289 million. UNESCO, *World Communication Report,* p. 11.

51. Jon Bing, ''The Council of Europe Convention and the OECD Guidelines on Data Protection,'' in *Regulation of Transnational Communications,* pp. 271–303.

52. Norbert Ropers, ''Information and Communication between East and West within the CSCE Process,'' in *Europe Speaks to Europe: International Information Flows between Eastern and Western Europe,* ed. Jörg Becker and Tamas Szecsko (Oxford: Pergamon Press, 1989), pp. 363–384.

53. Branscomb, *Toward a Law of Global Communications Networks,* p. 7.

54. Don M. Flournoy, ''Emerging from the Periphery: Satellite News Exchanges in the Third World.'' Paper presented at the International Association of Mass Communication Research, New Delhi, August 1986.

55. Soon Jin Kim, *EFE: Spain's World News Agency* (New York: Greenwood Press, 1989).

5

The Dimensions of Global Communication

The predicaments facing the world today are substantially different in scope and character from those of previous eras. They are shaped by the increasing ecological and economic interdependence spawned by a century of tremendous technological change. The proliferation of nuclear weapons, imbalanced resource use, hunger and poverty, the destruction of the rain forests, and the developing "greenhouse effect" pose such large problems and have such geographically dispersed effects as to limit the effectiveness of solutions developed on a local, or even a national, scale.

Communication and information are intrinsic to worldwide cooperative efforts and often play decisive roles in creating the conditions for peace, human dignity, justice, disarmament, and resolving other planetary problems. This chapter examines the scope and importance of worldwide communications as reflected in some of the most burning controversies. Several of the problems that constitute the leading issues in global information and communication relations will be reviewed.

THE GLOBAL VILLAGE AND THE "WAR OF IDEAS"

In the 1960s Canadian professor Marshall McLuhan popularized the notion of a "global village," a world interconnected by the marvels of electronic communication, in which the old social, racial, and ethnic barriers would break down. In his book *Understanding Media*, McLuhan asked whether a planetary communications network might not "make of the entire globe, and of the human family, a single consciousness."[1]

In some ways, McLuhan was right. Today's informed citizen daily consumes news of student demonstrations for democracy in China and Burma, of oil production in the Middle East, and of natural disasters in Asia. In no other age have we been so preoccupied with what is happening in other parts of the globe.

We know now that much of McLuhan's zany brand of media metaphysics was hopelessly idealistic. To be sure, there is a growing web of information and communication networks throughout the globe that connects far-flung places in a way unheard of even in McLuhan's time. But huge stretches of territory are not interconnected, and many of those information and communication networks carry content that is a far cry from the enlightened messages that would lead to the general "cosmic consciousness" McLuhan predicted.

Nor does the "global village" resemble a true neighborhood. Eurich goes so far as to say that most international communication is "theoretical chance or more or less anonymous, momentary contacts by telephone or by television; ignoring altogether those factors which impede communication, personal contact and community."[2]

Nor did McLuhan predict the tremendous growth in influence of so-called non-Western cultures. As the United Nations' membership increased, so too did the diversity of national cultures acting on the world scene. This "multicultural reality" has an important impact on global communication.

Some authors believe the world is far from a single human consciousness. Instead, a battle of opposing belief systems continues. The advent of *glasnost* and *perestroika* in Eastern Europe foretells extensive changes in those countries that formerly espoused Marxism–Leninism. But the fall of the Stalinist variety of socialism does not mean the triumph of capitalism. Capitalism and socialism will continue to wrangle for years to come. Nor is this competition limited only to the world's most widespread ideologies, capitalism and communism. Proponents of numerous insurgent "isms," from Islamic fundamentalism to Nicaraguan sandinism, will continue to fight in the pages of newspapers, on the airwaves, and through global propaganda media for the hearts and minds of attentive world publics.[3]

Some writers dispute this "war of ideas" thesis. In 1989 Francis Fukuyama argued that history had reached its ideological end. He believed that the changes in the former Soviet Union and Eastern Europe meant not "just the passing of a particular period of postwar history, but the end point of mankind's ideological evolution and the emergence of Western liberal democracy as the final form of human government."[4] According to Fukuyama, only two competing "isms" still confront democratic liberalism: religionism and nationalism.

Thirty years before Fukuyama, Daniel Bell predicted in his famous book, *The End of Ideology,* "the exhaustion of political ideas" and the final triumph of democratic liberalism.[5] How ironic that his book appeared just as the politics of ideology exploded around the world! The death of Stalinist socialism may well mean the birth of a new social system—a new beginning, not the end of history.

Nor is this clash of ideas new. As Krasner argues, "the international transfer of ideas, trade, and capital has been going on for 400 to 500 years."[6] So it may be an illusion that the world is just now uniting into a global village—an illusion fueled by the communications revolution.

COMMUNICATION AND NATIONAL SOVEREIGNTY

After the Second World War, the dominant worldview held that the free flow of information was a means of promoting peace, understanding, and development. But during the period of decolonization, when dozens of nations emerged to full independence, communication and information were seen increasingly as economic resources that should not be squandered or turned over to foreign interests. Some countries even viewed the free and unrestricted flow of information as a pretext by the dominant media countries to influence—even to undermine—local development in the former colonies. This debate is often expressed in terms of national sovereignty. In this section the sovereignty debate is examined in the context of three examples: transborder data, direct-broadcast satellites, and remote-sensing satellites.

International law guarantees the right of peoples and nations to permanent sovereignty over their natural wealth and resources. As a natural resource, the world's radiomagnetic spectrum is more valuable than oil and is subject, as are all finite resources, to pollution, congestion, and overuse. But the radiomagnetic spectrum is different from other natural resources because it can never be diminished, replenished, or depleted.[7]

Sovereignty traditionally refers to a country's right to protect its borders from military aggression; to preserve its natural wealth and resources; and to choose its political, social, economic, and cultural systems without interference by another state. The principle of "information sovereignty"—that nations enjoy the full rights of sovereignty and territorial integrity in the areas of communication and information— derives from this concept.

As Nordenstreng and Schiller wrote, communication and national sovereignty are closely related.[8] The French Commission on Data Processing and Liberties declared:

> Information is power and economic information is economic power. Information has an economic value and the ability to store and process certain types of data may well give one country political and technological advantage over other countries. This in turn leads to a loss of national sovereignty through transnational data flows.[9]

New communications technologies pose several problems for the concept of sovereignty. The technologies of message production, dissemination, and reception do not respect national boundaries. Electronic messages are generated on one side of a border. They are switched and directed on the other side. They pass through other countries and are processed and stored in still other countries. One "info-transaction" may involve many national jurisdictions, whose varying laws are difficult to reconcile.

Data sovereignty is usually measured by the extent to which a nation controls the collection, storage, analysis, manipulation, and transmission of its data. Nations around the world, both developed and developing, worry that they may lose control over information about their own internal functions and that this loss might leave them vulnerable to disruptions, technical failures, even catastrophes.

There is a potential for nations to disrupt, control, or destroy electronic communication flows in time of war or emergency. Concern about this eventuality arose repeatedly in the 1980s, when U.S. computer controllers froze Iranian, Philippine, Argentine, and Panamanian banking assets. During the 1979–1980 hostage crisis in Iran, the Carter administration even considered, but rejected, the idea of interrupting Iran's INTELSAT transmissions.[10] In 1982, as a sanction against the Soviet invasion of Afghanistan, the Reagan administration sought to enforce a prohibition on American companies communicating with their foreign subsidiaries that were working with the Soviet Union.[11]

Historically, governments created two mutually contradictory regulatory regimes to govern sovereignty: (1) the law of the sea, which *opened* maritime territories to all users; and (2) the law of land masses and airspace, which *closed* territories to foreigners. When many decades ago physical communications such as books, newspapers, and periodicals dominated the global flow of information, international law unambiguously regulated their transport. In today's electronic age, when signals freely traverse the atmosphere between satellites and earth stations, the situation is more complicated.

The transborder data flow (TDF) issue is closely related to the concept of information sovereignty. Unlike most products, which are sold, used, and consumed, information products can be resold and reused. New computer communications technologies make it possible to sell and use these data across national frontiers. Increasingly, Third World nations, as well as some Western European nations and Canada, complain that transborder information flows violate national security and personal privacy.

Transborder data flow has been virtually without internationally recognized regimes to regulate and enforce the flow. Desiring to protect their growing telematics industries, some European countries sought to change the free flow of TDF. A substantial amount of European data processing is done by American firms, who receive via cable or satellite personal banking, insurance, and credit information on Europeans. Sweden and other countries have expressed concern over their inability to protect the privacy of their citizens with respect to the information stored in U.S. data banks.

In 1973 Sweden passed its first Data Act, which made it illegal to set up computer files or data records without government authorization. Other countries, such as Japan, Canada, and France, erected protectionist provisions to reserve their markets for local computer and information processing and servicing industries. Many nations now have privacy laws or other "data protection" laws either on the books or in the making. Other nations have in force or under consideration similar laws dealing with security, confidentiality, and data protection.

The same concerns have arisen in regard to satellites. From their invention, direct-broadcast satellites (DBSs) have raised the issue of national sovereignty.[12] Satellite signals are especially susceptible to spillover because a satellite "footprint" (the geographical area covered by the signal) can never be shaped exactly to fit the intended coverage area. Of course, the problem of broadcast spillover is not new. Terrestrial radio and television stations located near a national border, even if equipped with a directional antenna, inadvertently spill some of their signals into the neighboring country.

Some argue that a country should be protected from unwanted signals. Direct television broadcasting by satellite from one country to another without the prior consent of the receiving state is a violation of national sovereignty, a threat to national economies and national cultures. The opposing argument, strongly advocated by the United States, has been to oppose any DBS regulation.[13]

Airspace law allows a state to exercise sovereignty over its airspace, whereas prevailing space law doctrines allow countries to explore and use outer space, the moon, and other celestial bodies on a basis of equality without national appropriation by claim of sovereignty. Outer space law and airspace law are thus diametrically opposed both in principle and practice. The questions arises, then, where does airspace end and outer space begin? The threshold between airspace and outer space is widely held to be the *Van Karman line*—the point to which states traditionally may claim sovereignty over the air above their territory. Beyond the Van Karman line, according to this view, state sovereignty ends.

This definition has not been without controversy. In 1976, nine equatorial countries[14] adopted the *Bogotá Declaration,* which states that the geostationary orbit (GSO) is a natural resource of the equatorial states and is thereby subject to their sovereignty.[15] These countries insisted that no object could be placed in the GSO without their approval:

> The geostationary orbit is a scarce natural resource, whose importance and value increase rapidly together with the development of space technology and with the growing need for communication; therefore, the Equatorial countries meeting in Bogota have decided to proclaim and defend on behalf of their peoples, the existence of their sovereignty over this natural resource.[16]

The United States and the former Soviet Union both disputed the Bogotá Declaration.[17]

There are four major positions on sovereignty over the geostationary orbit.[18] The first, advocated primarily by the United States, considers that the GSO should be allocated on a "first-come, first-served" basis. A second position, represented by the then Soviet Union, advocates the "Van Karman principle": There should be a clear demarcation point between outer space and aerospace, set at a specific altitude above sea level. Airspace below that boundary would be sovereign property. Above that limit it would be outer space to which all would have free access.

A third approach, defended mainly by the Third World countries, calls for global prior allocation of both orbital positions and frequencies. Advocates favor establishing an international regime to guarantee equal access. The fourth view, advocated by the equatorial nations, also supports the need for prior allocation; these nations claim to have preferential rights over the GSO.

Remote-sensing satellites also bring up questions of sovereignty. These satellites detect, measure, and analyze substances or objects on earth from orbit. There is little doubt that data gained in this way can increase the political and economic power of the "sensing" nation over the "sensed" nation. Knowledge of likely oil deposits, crop yields or failures, and mineral deposits can help governments and corporations make better judgments and more informed bids on the international market. At the same time, international law grants national governments absolute sovereignty over their natural resources. The issue here is whether a nation should have absolute sovereignty over *information* regarding those resources. To whom does the information belong when LANDSAT or another commercial satellite detects oil or rare metals in an African country? Typically that country is not aware of the existence of those resources or that information. Corporations may know more about the country than the nation does itself.[19]

Brazil and other developing countries have opposed the use of remote sensing systems or other advanced detection techniques without prior consent. Data obtained by these methods might provide foreign countries or companies with oil production data or with better information on potential deposits and distribution than is available to local authorities.[20] These countries' fears were not assuaged by a policy of unlimited availability of remote-sensing satellite data.

This debate resulted finally in the 1986 *Principles Relating to Remote Sensing of the Earth from Outer Space,* the first internationally recognized document guiding the conduct of remote-sensing satellites. According to this treaty, sensed nations have given up the demand for prior consent before data dissemination. But the Principles guarantee the sensed state's access to all data.[21]

Lately this debate has been enlivened by the technological prospect of NewsSats, news-gathering satellites operated by the international news agencies and commercial networks. U.S. television viewers saw LANDSAT pictures of the Chernobyl nuclear accident days before the Soviets acknowledged that the accident had even occurred. In 1984 *Aviation Week & Space Technology* published images of a Soviet submarine engaged in a test to launch nuclear missiles from beneath the Arctic ice pack. ABC news used LANDSAT pictures to reveal that Iran had deployed Chinese-made "silkworm" missiles. In 1987 ABC used images from the French SPOT remote-sensing satellite to reveal what it claimed was proof of Soviet violations of the Anti-Ballistic Missile Treaty. Said correspondent Rich Inderfurth:

> And now for the first time, commercial satellites will allow the public and the press to monitor what the Soviets decided to do about [the missiles], something in the past only governments with their highly classified spy satellites were able to do.[22]

A U.S. Congressional study predicts a rising conflict between the federal government and journalists seeking to use remote-sensing pictures to report on military movements, nuclear missile installations, and disasters. Already many news organizations obtain images from two commercial firms: EOSAT, formerly known as LANDSAT, now run as a joint venture between RCA Corporation and Hughes Aircraft Company; and SPOT of France. This issue is a thorny one. Would the U.S. government have the right to block the distribution of photos showing American forces preparing to invade Grenada or to delay news of Soviet missile buildup, as happened in Cuba in 1962?[23]

INCREASING CONCENTRATION AND TRANSNATIONALIZATION

A handful of huge conglomerates have begun to dominate the world's flow of information and communication. By mid-decade, five to ten corporate giants will control most of the world's important newspapers, magazines, books, radio and television outlets, cinema, recording industries, and videocassettes. Such financial concentration dwarfs the total combined gross domestic products of Jordan, Bolivia, Nicaragua, Albania, Laos, Liberia, and Mali.[24] This may be a new global village, but it is not as McLuhan foresaw. Today's "lords of the global village" are huge corporations. As Bagdikian remarked, they

> exert a homogenizing power over ideas, culture and commerce that affects populations larger than any in history. Neither Caesar nor Hitler, Franklin Roosevelt nor any Pope, has commanded as much power to shape the information on

which so many people depend to make decisions about everything from whom to vote for to what to eat.[25]

The information and communication industries control about 10 percent of the world's total gross product. Two-thirds of this is controlled by a network of eighty-six corporations. The network is strongly interlocked among corporations in the same geographical region. Sixty percent of these eighty-six corporations are headquartered in the United States. Forty-four of the foreign subsidiaries are located in North America and Western Europe. The strongest interlocks are found between the data processing sector and the telecommunication sector (see Table 5-1). Most of the trade in information goods and services is between North America and Western Europe. The markets in the different sectors of the industry show a strong degree of oligopolization.

The United States has been particularly susceptible to this trend toward concentration (see Table 5-2). In 1982 Bagdikian reported that fifty corporations owned or controlled half of American media. The second edition of Bagdikian's book revealed this figure to be only twenty-nine.[26] In 1990, Bagdikian reported, only twenty-three firms controlled the bulk of U.S. media channels.[27] But another trend is equally apparent. Between 1986 and 1989 Western European and Japanese companies invested more than $12 billion in American mass media. Although by law foreign investment in broadcasting may not exceed 20 percent, print media do not come under these restrictions and have been bought widely by foreign investors.[28]

In effect, new technological developments and increasing concentration have made national boundaries meaningless. *Encyclopedia Americana* is published by the French. The New American Library is published by a British firm. *Encyclopedia Britannica* is published by Americans. National media monopolies, especially in the European Community, are giving way to deregulatory pressures and are allowing commercial firms to enter the market, pushing products to larger and larger population segments.[29]

Why is this happening? The most fundamental reason is that fully integrated corporate control of media production and dissemination reaps vast profits and creates huge corporate empires. Present international law does not deal adequately with media concentration. A 1980 UNESCO resolution called for the "elimination of the negative effects of certain monopolies, public or private, and excessive concentrations."[30] Bagdikian called for global antitrust negotiations in the field of communication and information to take place in an appropriate forum, such as the General Agreement on Tariffs and Trade, the United Nations Commission on Transnational Corporations, or the United Nations Conference on Trade and Development.

At the same time, propelled by this increasing concentration, numerous alternative media outlets are trying to make an "end-run" around the information monopolies using a worldwide metanetwork of highly decentralized technologies—computer networks, fax machines, amateur radio, packet data satellites, VCRs, video cameras, and the like. For example, the Association for Progressive Communications (APC) carries a number of important alternative news sources serving nongovernmental organizations. These include Inter Press Service (the Third World's largest news agency), Environmental News Service (Vancouver), the United Nations Information Centre news service, Agencia Latinoamericana de Información, (Ecuador), and Alternet (Washington, DC).

TABLE 5-1
Top Ten Information and Communication Enterprises, 1988
(in billions of dollars)

Enterprise	Country	Total sales
IBM	USA	54
NTT	Japan	41
AT & T	USA	37
Matsushita	Japan	25
Deutsche Bundespost	Fed. Rep. Germany	20
NEC	Japan	20
Phillips	Netherlands	19
British Telecom	United Kingdom	17
France Telecom	France	17
Toshiba	Japan	16

SOURCE: Annual reports and other document supplied by firms; *Advertising Age* and selected national or sector-based classifications; compilations and estimates from the Institut pour le Developpement de l'Audiovisuel et des Telecommunications en Europe; UNESCO, *World Communication Report* (Paris: UNESCO, 1989), pp. 99–103.

TABLE 5-2
Top Ten Media Enterprises, 1988
(in billions of dollars)

Enterprise	Country	Media sales
Capital Cities/ABC	USA	4.4
Time	USA	4.2
Bertelsman	Fed. Rep. Germany	3.7
News Corp (Maxwell)	Australia	3.5
Warner Communications	USA	3.4
General Electric	USA	3.2
Gannett	USA	3.1
Times Mirror	USA	3.0
Gulf and Western	USA	2.9
Yomiuri Group	Japan	2.8

SOURCE: Annual reports and other document supplied by firms; *Advertising Age* and selected national or sector-based classifications; compilations and estimates from the Institut pour le Developpement de l'Audiovisuel et des Telecommunications en Europe; UNESCO, *World Communication Report* (Paris: UNESCO, 1989), pp. 104–105.

DEREGULATION AND PRIVATIZATION

Deregulation is a product of classical (liberal) economic theory. Like "laissez faire" capitalism, deregulation is based on a faith in the workings of the "invisible hand" of the marketplace. Liberalism calls for privatization and deregulation in areas that were previously the preserve of the state or quasi-state enterprises, of which communications and telecommunications are significant.[31]

Although it is becoming a worldwide phenomenon today, deregulation of telecommunications began in the United States. In 1986 the Federal Communications

Commission (FCC) relaxed restrictions on terminal equipment and adopted an "open skies" policy calling for competitive development of domestic communications satellites. By 1977 the courts had struck down limits on domestic interstate long-distance service competition. In 1982 the Justice Department split the world's largest corporation, AT & T, from its 22 local operating companies, which were grouped into seven comparably-sized Regional Bell Operating Companies (RBOCs). The settlement—called the Modified Final Judgment—went into effect on January 1, 1984. It prohibited the RBOCs from manufacturing their own equipment and from providing long-distance service. AT & T was allowed to keep the long-distance service and to enter the computer business.

The results of deregulation in the United States were astounding. Over one million new telephones were installed, raising the proportion of U.S. families with telephones to 93 percent. Long-distance rates fell by 30 percent, and long-distance use almost doubled. Local rates increased 40 percent, but combined local and long-distance rates have climbed at a slower rate than inflation.[32]

In most of the world deregulation is relatively new, but the precursors of this trend began in Great Britain and other European countries.[33] In Great Britain private TV began in 1951, and from 1954 the British have had both the public British Broadcasting Corporation (BBC) and the private Independent Television (ITV). The first step toward commercialism on the European continent took place in Italy in 1976. Italy's most aggressive broadcasting entrepreneur was Silvio Berlusconi, who by the beginning of the 1980s had won half the Italian television public.[34] But the real boom in European private broadcasting began only in the mid-1980s. In France, Canal Plus started operations in 1984. In 1986 La Cinq and TV6 went on the air. Then in 1987 the premiere French network, Television Française 1 (TF1), was privatized. In the Federal Republic of Germany, the individual *Länder* (states or provinces) gave the green light to private stations such as SAT and RTL Plus.

Other countries are joining these pioneers. In Spain Parliament created commercial television stations, and Canal 10 is broadcasting by satellite.[35] In the Netherlands a 1988 law allows private organizations to transmit, and TV viewers can already receive foreign stations. Private television began in Belgium in 1986. Denmark has allowed private broadcasting, but for the most part the Scandinavian countries are resisting this trend. Even Hungarian broadcasting has undergone privatization.[36]

THE "FLOW" CONTROVERSY

In the early nineteenth century, German author Johann Wolfgang von Goethe, the visionary as always, recognized that times had changed. He saw increases in the global flow of information and hoped these increases would "make a powerful contribution to that hoped-for common world literature." They would help us "perceive and understand one another. And even if there is no shared affection, at least [we] will learn to tolerate one another."[37]

But by the end of the twentieth century, former Finnish President Urho Kekkonen presented another interpretation:

The flow of information between states—not least the material pumped out by television—is to a very great extent a one-way unbalanced traffic, and in no way possesses the depth and range which the principle of freedom of speech requires.[38]

Kekkonen's countryman, Finnish communication researcher Kaarle Nordenstreng, concurs:

> Quantitatively it may be estimated that the total flow of communication taking place between the industrialized part of the world (inhabited by some one-third of mankind) and the Third World (comprising about two-thirds) takes place at least a hundred times more in the direction from the industrialized to developing countries than vice versa.[39]

Perhaps no area of global information relations has been so well investigated or has caused so much controversy.[40] But the term *flow* is somewhat illusive because it suggests a more or less orderly stream.[41] In practice, the "global flow of information" includes many elements: TV, film, and record products; news stories or news pictures; cultural exchanges; foreign correspondents; foreign media consumption; telephone conversations; transborder data flow; letter and parcel post; even airline traffic (see Figure 5-1). Rather than being an orderly flow, these elements are more like spurts and surges of physical and electronic message traffic.

One of the most persistent criticisms of news flows has been that the leading four transnational news agencies—Associated Press (AP), United Press International (UPI), Agence France Presse (AFP), and Reuters—control the bulk of the world's news flow. The Moscow-based news agency TASS ranks fifth in terms of words per day. Statistics show that these five wire services provided 37.5 million words daily. The next five leading news agencies accounted for only 1.09 million words daily, or about 3 percent of the "big five" total.[42] (See Table 5-3.)

A similar situation exists in the field of television programming. In their landmark 1974 study, Nordenstreng and Varis found two trends in the international flow of television programs: a one-way flow from the big exporting countries to the rest of the world, and domination of this flow by entertainment programming. These two aspects constituted a tendency toward concentration, they stated.[43]

Ten years later, in a follow-up study, Varis found one thing held constant: In most countries one-third or more of total TV programming is imported. But there was a notable increase in regional program exchanges, particularly in the Arab states and Latin America. About one-third of imported programs in the Arab world originated in the region itself. In Latin America that figure is about 10 percent. This finding adds an important dimension to the world television flow map.[44]

It is easy and somewhat misleading to divide the flow controversy into three opposing camps. First, there are the "free flow" advocates, whose position is based on the Universal Declaration of Human Rights, the International Covenant on Civil and Political Rights, and other documents. The United States made the "free flow of information" one of its primary post-World War II foreign policy goals.[45] As John Foster Dulles once said: "If I were to be granted one point of foreign policy and no other, I would make it the free flow of information."[46] At the drafting sessions in San Francisco in 1945, the United States tried to get an article on press freedom into the United Nations Charter. Although unsuccessful, the United States did succeed that year in getting the notion of free flow of information into the UNESCO Constitution:

Technological Orientation

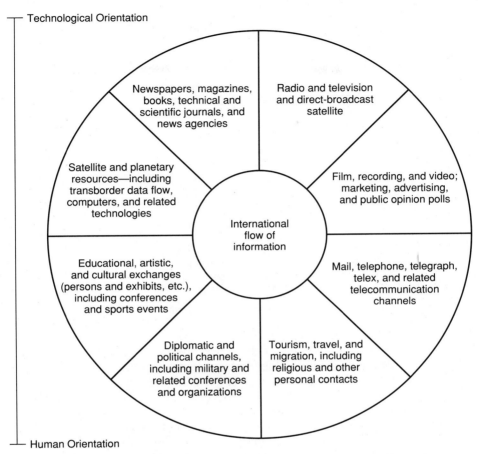

Newspapers, magazines, books, technical and scientific journals, and news agencies

Radio and television and direct-broadcast satellite

Satellite and planetary resources—including transborder data flow, computers, and related technologies

Film, recording, and video; marketing, advertising, and public opinion polls

International flow of information

Educational, artistic, and cultural exchanges (persons and exhibits, etc.), including conferences and sports events

Mail, telephone, telegraph, telex, and related telecommunication channels

Diplomatic and political channels, including military and related conferences and organizations

Tourism, travel, and migration, including religious and other personal contacts

Human Orientation

FIGURE 5-1 Channels and Types of International Information Flow. The techno-logical and human orientations should be thought of as being complementary, interrelated, and adaptive.

SOURCE: From *Global Information and World Communication: New Frontiers in International Relations,* by Hamid Mowlana, p. 2. Copyright © 1986 by Longman Publishing Group. Reprinted with permission from Longman Publishing Group.

To realize [its purposes] the Organization will:
Collaborate in the work of advancing the mutual knowledge and understanding of peoples, through all means of mass communication and to that end recommend such international agreements as may be necessary to promote the free flow of ideas by word and image.[47]

The second position is found among those who call for a "balanced flow" of information. These writers have pointed out that the free and uninhibited flow of information has led to a situation of dominance by the few. Put forward in 1976 most succinctly by the Non-Aligned Movement, here are some of the key arguments from the New Delhi Declaration on Decolonization of Information:

TABLE 5-3
Words Per Day of Major News Agencies, 1986–1987

Words per day (millions)	News Agency
17.000	Associated Press (AP)
14.000	United Press International (UPI)
4.000	TASS
1.500	Reuters
1.000	Agence France Presse (AFP)
.500	EFE (Spain)
.300	Agenzia Nazionale Stampa Associata (Italy)
.115	Deutsche Presse Agentur (Fed. Rep. Germany)
.150	Inter Press Service
.100	Non-Aligned News Pool
.075	Telegrafska Agencija Nova Jugoslavía (TANJUG)
.025	Caribbean News Agency
.020	Pan African News Agency
.018	Gulf News Agency

SOURCE: UNESCO, *World Communication Report* (Paris: UNESCO, 1989), pp. 136–141; UNESCO, *Draft World Communication Report* (Paris: UNESCO, 1988), p. 1.54.

1. The present global information flows are marked by serious inadequacy and imbalance. The means of communicating information are concentrated in a few countries. The great majority of countries are reduced to being passive recipients of information which is disseminated from a few centres.

2. This situation perpetuates the colonial era of dependence and domination. It confines judgments and decisions on what should be known, and how it should be made known, into the hands of a few.

3. The dissemination of information rests at present in the hands of a few agencies located in a few developed countries, and the rest of the peoples of the world are forced to see each other, and even themselves, through the medium of these agencies.

4. Just as political and economic dependence are legacies of the era of colonialism, so is the case of dependence in the field of information which in turn retards the achievement of political and economic growth.

5. In a situation where the means of information are dominated and monopolized by the few, freedom of information really comes to mean the freedom of the few to propagate information in the manner of their choosing and the virtual denial to the rest of the right to inform and be informed objectively and accurately.[48]

The third position begins with the premise that it is unreasonable to demand absolute balance in information flow. It makes no sense to demand that the United

States carry as much content in percentage terms about Canada as Canada carries about the United States. Balance must somehow take into account some notion of relative importance in terms of economic trade, political relations, cultural proximity, physical distance, and many other factors. So a third formulation has arisen, calling for a "free and balanced flow"; in other words, reversing the imbalance without impeding free flow.

THE "NEWS VALUES" CONTROVERSY

Closely related to the "flow of information" discussion, one of the most enduring controversies in global information relations has concerned the flow of news. Typical of the criticism, one Jamaican reggae song of the late 1970's excoriated the international media for not reporting the island's progress: "A little shanty town and a woman in a ratty dress, Bet yo life it makin' headlines in the foreign press."[49]

The issue of news values is critical because news constitutes the database on which most informed citizens make their decisions. Lippman once remarked: "The press . . . is like a beam of searchlight that moves restlessly about, bringing one episode and then another out of the darkness and into vision."[50] The problem is, as Gerbner has said, that "all news are views . . ."[51] News—biased and not— becomes part of the knowledge base upon which perceptions, judgments, and decisions are made.

Differing news values are sometimes explicit: Vietnam "fell to," but Afghanistan was "liberated from," the communists. Ronald Reagan called Nicaraguan contras "freedom fighters," whereas the Sandinistas referred to them as "mercenaries." Palestinians are "terrorists," whereas Israelis carry out "retaliation raids."

News values are always apparent in hindsight. For example, if we examine how the New York Times covered the Russian Revolution, we find that Lenin died twice, was ill three times, was missing twice, fled six times, and was in prison twice. For these errors, the Times published only two retractions.[52] A study of Time magazine's coverage of Germany and the USSR during the 1940s showed how these two countries switched from being our "friends" to being our "enemies" and from being described with "God terms" to being described with "devil terms."[53]

Rosenblum has classified the news values controversy in two basic complaints:

> The Western press gives inadequate and superficial attention to the realities of developing countries, often infusing coverage with cultural bias. The traditional emphasis on the dramatic, the emotional and the amusing—the "coups and earthquakes" syndrome—is seen not only as unbalanced but also as detrimental to the development process.
> The Western monopoly on the distribution of news—whereby even stories written about one Third World country for distribution in others are reported and transmitted by international news agencies based in New York, London and Paris—amounts to neocolonialism and cultural domination.[54]

In other words, news coverage is influenced by both qualitative and structural factors.

Regarding the structural factors, research has shown that much global news flows through metropolitan centers. This is an understandable legacy of colonial ties. African countries receive news of other African countries through London or Paris. Latin American countries learn of one another through New York. Mexican national dailies carry as much as two-thirds of all international news from the four transnational news agencies, and when other Western sources are included, that total comes to 90 percent.[55]

The second, more qualitative complaint reflects the dynamics of the typical newsroom. Because of bureaucratic constraints, space and time limitations, and other factors, journalists can never report all world events. In fact, they are seldom able to report even the events they gather or to which they otherwise have access. Journalists must select, and research has shown they have certain priorities.[56] One American critic sardonically summed this prioritizing process: "10,000 deaths in Nepal equals 100 deaths in Wales equals 10 deaths in West Virginia equals one death next door."[57] This may sound simplistic, but such "triaging" is a daily fact of life in the newsroom.

Journalism researchers for years have sought ways of identifying illusive news values. In one early pioneering study, Galtung and Ruge outlined some important factors. For news to be covered from "culturally distant nations that are low in international rank" (that is, from Third World countries):

> News will have to refer to people, preferably to top élite, and be preferably negative and unexpected but nevertheless according to a pattern that is consonant with the "mental pre-image" . . . . This will, in turn, facilitate an image of these countries as dangerous, ruled by capricious élites, as unchanging in their basic characteristics, as existing for the benefit of the topdog nations. Events occur, they are sudden, like flashes of lightning, with no build-up and with no let-down after their occurrence—they just occur and more often than not as part of the machinations of the ruling or opposition élites.[58]

Gerbner and Marvanyi devised a novel way to look at the biases in international news coverage. They showed that the picture of the world as reflected in sixty daily newspapers is not a reflection of the "real" geographical world. The authors drew maps to compare with actual physical land distributions. All deviated from the "true world" (see Figure 5-2). For example, more than two-thirds of the foreign coverage in American papers was of Western Europe (28 percent), South Asia and the Far East (18 percent), North America (10 percent), and the Middle East (7 percent). Latin America was conspicuously underreported. British and West German papers paid special attention to other Western European countries (36 percent), North America (12 percent), and Latin America (15 percent).[59]

One of the most rigorous analyses of international news was the *Foreign News in the Media* study undertaken by the International Association for Mass Communication Research (IAMCR) for UNESCO in the late 1970s and early 1980s. This massive study of twenty-nine countries stated six major conclusions:

1. Selection criteria in international news reporting have become almost universal.
2. All national media systems emphasize regional events and actors.
3. The United States and Western Europe are consistently newsmakers in all regions.
4. After the United States and Western Europe come the "hot-spot" stories.

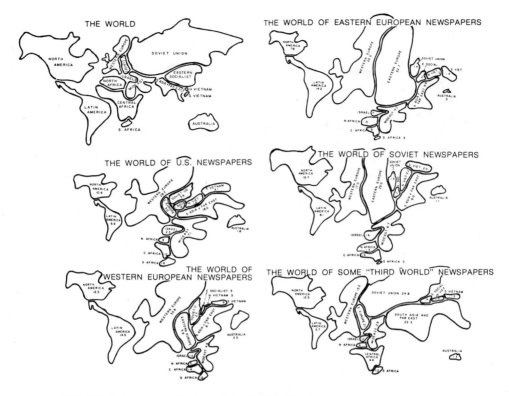

FIGURE 5-2   The Many Worlds of the World's Press.
SOURCE: From *World Communications: A Handbook,* by George Gerbner and Marsha Siefert. Copyright © 1984 by Longman Publishing Group. Reprinted with permission from Longman Publishing Group.

5. Third World countries not covered as "hot spots," together with the socialist countries, remain the least covered areas in international news reporting.
6. The national news agency, or the "own correspondent," is the most important source for international news, followed by the major international news agencies.

National media systems are thus exercising important secondary gatekeeping functions in selecting, interpreting, and processing news from external sources.[60]

Using these same IAMCR data, some writers have disputed the twin complaints that Rosenblum cited. Stevenson asserted that Western agencies do not ignore the Third World. "It is the second world of European socialism, not the Third World, which is invisible . . . " Nor did he find evidence that the Third World is singled out for any special negative coverage.[61]

Nor did Wilhoit and Weaver find any particular suppression of news about the developing countries. International news agencies provided their customers with many items about the Third World. One naturally tends to be interested in the foreign affairs of one's own country or region, so it is not fair to blame Western media alone for inadequate coverage of the Third World. African editors simply are not interested in Latin America, for example. Third World countries themselves participate in under-reportage.[62] In 1981 Wilhoit and Weaver found, however, that news about Third World countries tends to focus "more on conflicts and crises than does news about more developed countries."[63] Kirat and Weaver later found that by 1983 Third World news showed a decline in conflict or crisis coverage, "suggesting that criticisms of advocates . . . and previous research may have had some impact . . . "[64]

Another approach to the news values controversy is to analyze the so-called alternative news agencies to see if their coverage is any different. Stevenson and Marjanovic looked at Deutsche Presse Agentur, Kyodo, News Agency of Nigeria, Xinhua New China News Agency, TANJUG, Shihata News Agency of Tanzania, Non-Aligned News Agencies Pool, and Inter Press Service. On the whole, these agencies are similar to one another and different from major Western agencies. This goes a long way in validating that the aforementioned news values seem to be universal.[65]

One result of this debate was that some supporters of the "new information order" argued that the role of journalism and the style of reporting must be different in the Third World because of the difference in the level of development and the dissimilar social and historical conditions. They called for "development journalism," which would highlight development rather than sensationalism and would give needed information rather than exposés. Development journalism did not mean government-controlled news, as some critics maintained. Its goal was to harness communication and information to the needs of economic and social development.[66]

MEDIA IMPERIALISM

Like God, advertising and advertisements are everywhere. They literally grow on trees, they light up the sky, they line the streets, they decorate the buildings . . . And what more susceptible audiences, more sweetly credulous viewers are there than the mass consumer markets? They lap up every word, devour every picture and comic strip, absorb every musical note, ready to believe every extravagant claim made in advertisements.

Imelda Marcos[67]

Madame Marcos touches off another explosive issue in global information relations, the whole complex of questions subsumed under the label "media imperialism."

Only one century ago, at the height of European colonial expansion through Asia, Africa, and Latin America, the term *imperialism* referred to annexing foreign territory and exploiting raw resources. The means of exercising domination may have changed in our era, but the desire to dominate remains very much the same.[68]

The term *imperialism* is most commonly identified with the nineteenth-century European process of carving up the planet into "spheres of influence," but imperialism has existed in every age. One need only look at dynasties in ancient China and India, Athenian domination over the Greek city–states, Imperial Rome, the Ottoman (Turkish) Empire, and the Holy Roman Empire. Beginning in the sixteenth century, mercantilism, sea power, and the establishment of powerful national armies in Europe provided the stimulus for a new era of imperialism. Colonies supplied cheap labor, raw materials, and ready markets for European manufacturing, which was spurred on by the Industrial Revolution. Imperialism was also linked to racial and moral supremacy and was rationalized as "the white man's burden"—the so-called duty of the white race to bring civilization to backward peoples.

Since World War II, imperialism has taken on a new outline. Former colonies have gained independence. Direct military intervention is usually a last resort. (The American intervention in Vietnam and the Soviet invasion of Afghanistan may be exceptions.) Today nations use economic and cultural methods to control the destinies of people in foreign countries. Third World nations decry modern economic imperialism (called *neo-imperialism*), asserting that it seriously hampers their efforts toward economic growth and independence. Former colonies are increasingly complaining that media imperialism continues to dominate them. Schiller writes:

> It has been recognized for some time that familiar cultural products and services—films, TV programs, books, news records, etc.—besides offering entertainment, are ideological items embodying social values and messages, and consequently influence the organization of the entire social enterprise.[69]

Even France, Canada, and the European Community have expressed concern about the penetration of their cultures by foreign books, magazines, films, television programs, and other cultural products. These governments have adopted policies to reduce foreign cultural intrusion and to limit access of foreign advertising.

Araby defines media imperialism as "the imbalance and inequality in flow of mass media materials between developed and developing countries, and its subsequent effect on the developing country's society and culture."[70] Boyd-Barrett describes it as the "process whereby the ownership, structure, distribution or content of the media in any one country are singly or together subject to substantial external pressures from the media interests of any other country or countries without proportionate reciprocation of influence by the country so affected."[71]

Chin-Chuan Lee sees four levels of media imperialism:

1. television program exportation to foreign countries;
2. foreign ownership and control of media outlets;
3. transfer of the "metropolitan" broadcasting norms and institutionalization of media commercialism at the expense of "public interest"; and
4. invasion of capitalistic world views and infringement upon the indigenous way of life in the recipient nations.[72]

Some writers have cautioned us not to view media imperialism too simplistically. Boyd says critics "either de-emphasize or ignore the artistic, production, or financial limitations of many developing countries." The reasons Third World countries import Western programs are complex. We should also take into account other media channels in those countries, availability of home videocassette recorders, lack of production space and equipment, lack of engineering and artistic talent, lack of funds for local production, and pro-Western orientation of programmers due to their academic training in the West.[73]

What is it about Western (and particularly American) media products that has such a widespread influence over the world's peoples? Western culture seems to exploit essential human values, appeal to basic human emotions, and use universal modes of expression. Perhaps film critic Richard Reeves captures it best:

Film and television series of Hollywood and the Holiday Inns . . . the Nashville sound, and the sounds of the English language, Coca-Cola, blue jeans, sweat-shirts, shaking hands, majority rule and freedom of the press seem to appeal to something essential in men and women.[74]

The "media imperialism" controversy has found its way into every global communication channel. Let's explore two media—advertising and television.

Modernization theorists saw advertising as a beneficial factor in national development. It benefited the economy by encouraging competition, product innovation, efficient production, and lower consumer prices. Through its revenues, advertising also subsidized programming and technology. Finally, advertising could inform consumers about the quality, location, and price of goods.[75]

Many critics have written that advertising fostered commercialism; it made people want goods they did not need by creating artificial demands. It created and reinforced stereotypes that demeaned certain groups and limited their participation in society. In the Third World, many wrote, advertising cultivated a "false consciousness" and distracted people from the challenges of authentic development. It promoted consumerism and a taste for goods inappropriate for the local level of development and created rising frustration when poor people could not acquire the goods they saw.[76] As Indira Gandhi has said, "the media dazzle eyes and fill ears with images and reports of affluence. Even the modest expectations of our peoples are far beyond our present means."[77] Throughout the world attempts have been made to control the worst aspects of mass advertising.[78]

An illustration of the potential for media imperialism is the penetration of foreign television in the Caribbean region. One study showed that 79 to 88 percent of all television programs in the region are imported. United States entertainment programs constitute the largest portion. At an estimated cost of $400 per hour purchased, Caribbean television stations spend more than $11 million annually on importing these foreign programs.[79] Some countries can rent a one-hour program for $200, an amount too small to cover costs of five minutes of live domestic programming. This "dumping" by syndicators can undermine local, indigenous television.

Nor is this just a Third World question. Even rich nations, such as Canada, have had reason to complain about media imperialism. The influence of American programming on Canadian broadcasting is reflected in the following statistics. Of the 52,000 hours of English-language television programming available to the average Canadian each year, barely 370 hours are Canadian drama (including sitcoms, movies, and miniseries). Of the 27,000 hours of French-language television available to the average francophone viewer annually, barely 630 hours are Canadian drama. Ninety-eight percent of all drama on English-language television is foreign, whereas ninety percent of all drama on French-language television is foreign. Only 28 percent of all programming available on English-language television is Canadian; of the total time Canadians spend watching English-language television, less than one-third is devoted to Canadian programming. Francophone teenagers spend more than half their viewing time watching foreign programs; anglophone teenagers spend 80 percent of their viewing time watching foreign programs.[80]

How does media imperialism manifest itself? In his review of Latin American television content, Beltran found twelve values that pervade the medium: individualism, elitism, racism, materialism, adventurism, conservatism, conformism, self-defeatism, providentialism, authoritarianism, romanticism, and aggressiveness. These televised images come largely from United States television and film studios.[81]

A considerable effort has been made to change this dominance. Leading the resistance to cultural invasion is Minister of French Culture Jack Lang, who has proclaimed, "Our destiny is not to become the vassals of an immense empire of profit."[82] Caribbean nations are trying to set up a regional television production center called CaribVision.[83] The Caribbean Council of Churches and the Caribbean Association of Media Workers have launched self-reliance campaigns.[84] Some Latin American nations (particularly Mexico, Brazil, Venezuela, Peru, and Colombia) are emerging as important exporters of television products. There is increasing exchange within the region and increasing distribution to the Spanish-speaking audience in the United States.[85]

The debate over media imperialism is basically a critique of modernization theory, which proposed that media were positive forces for social change. There are three different schools of thought on the topic.

Adherents of the classical (liberal) perspective, such as Ithiel de Sola Pool and Wilson Dizard, acknowledge that an imbalance exists, but they insist that market forces will eventually redress the inequity. New technologies will allow disadvantaged societies to catch up. The United States, the argument continues, has a temporary market advantage and will continue to benefit until other societies find their particular competitive market niches. The imbalances even have positive consequences because cultures need competition to grow, and imbalances force cultures to strengthen themselves or perish.[86]

Centrists such as Elihu Katz, George Wedell, Jeremy Tunstall, and C. C. Lee approach the problem pragmatically. They recognize that countries such as the United States have an advantage in the economics of scale, but they maintain that each country, within limits, can mobilize sufficient internal strength to offset foreign media pressure. They argue further that the free flow of international communication, balanced or not, can have good as well as bad outcomes on foreign cultures.[87] Centrists would allow minimal state intervention to correct the imbalances, but they deny any structural inequity that states cannot surmount.

Other writers view media imperialism as institutionally determined. Injured parties can do little to correct the situation. Some view the inequitable flow as part of a large problem, namely cultural imperialism. Finnish researchers Kaarle Nordenstreng and Tapio Varis asserted that local oligarchies in the Third World allied themselves with the transnational media elite against the interests of the majority of the population. Flow imbalances, in their view, were just another manifestation of how ruling interests collaborated to oppress the poor and the disenfranchised.[88] Schiller concurred; in his book *Communication and Cultural Domination,* he described cultural imperialism as

> the sum of the processes by which a society is brought into the modern world system and how its dominating stratum is attracted, pressured, forced into shaping social institutions to correspond to, or even to promote, the values and structures of the dominant center of the system.[89]

Dependency theorists saw media as another way the metropolitan centers perpetuate their domination on "dependent" societies. This dependency was brought about through "alienation" or penetration of foreign cultural values, such as crass consumerism, or through the inherent "antidemocratic" nature of the media themselves.[90]

Empirical studies have tended to substantiate the media imperialism hypothesis. One early influential study by Nordenstreng and Varis showed that there was indeed a one-way flow of television from a few exporting nations to the rest of the world.[91] Others have replicated these findings.[92] Varis even duplicated his 1973 study ten years later and found no overall change.[93]

COMMUNICATION POLICIES

Some countries have tried to establish policies that affect the flow of information and communication within and between them. But the mere existence of communication policies has led to considerable dispute in such international fora as UNESCO.

UNESCO has defined communication policy as "sets of principles and norms established to guide the behaviour of communication systems."[94] Mowlana and Wilson define communication policy as "systematic, institutionalized principles, norms, and behaviour that are designed through legal and regulatory procedures and/or perceived through historical understanding to guide formation, distribution, and control of the system in both its human and technological dimensions."[95]

What would a national communication policy contain? The International Telecommunication Union suggests the following questions as the basis for national communication policy:

> What is the structure of the market? Which sectors are reserved for a monopoly operator and which opened to competitors? What is the mix of government, mixed and private ownership? What are the conditions and rules of entry to the market? What is the allowable rate of return? Where is the locus of authority? What is the process of establishing new policies? How is compliance monitored and enforced?[96]

It might seem unremarkable for a country to establish a policy to supervise the communication and information sector. After all, some Third World leaders have seen "national communications policies as being necessary to each country's economic and social development and of a nature to motivate its citizens on behalf of such development."[97] A 1989 ITU report maintained that "an effective policy and regulatory process will help bring about greater specification of national policy objectives and ongoing accountability for performance. . . . [and] should establish targets for telecommunication development."[98]

However, with the exception of a few nations such as Brazil, India, and the People's Republic of China, nations have little cohesive communication policy. Some countries have claimed that such policies would take the form of government censorship and would restrict or stop the international flow of information.[99]

For example, when in the mid-1970s UNESCO held intergovernmental conferences on communication policies in Latin America, critics charged that UNESCO was promoting "government control" of the media and telecommunication. The 1976 UNESCO Intergovernmental Conference on Communication Policies in Latin

America and the Caribbean in San Jose, Costa Rica, recommended that Latin American states "define and implement policies, plans and laws that will make possible the advent of more balanced communication relations at both the national and international levels."[100] Such groups as the United States-based Inter-American Press Association attacked the experts and their recommendations and organized an international campaign to boycott the conference.

What possible interest might some countries have in preventing others from establishing national communication policies? The case of Brazil might prove illustrative.[101]

After the 1964 coup, the military government invited multinational corporations to invest heavily in Brazil in order to speed up the country's industrialization. National industries suffered terribly, but the overall results were spectacular. By 1975 more than half of Brazil's revenues were generated by multinational corporations and about a quarter each by the Brazilian government and private Brazilian firms. (Corporations from Canada and the United States accounted for nearly three-fourths of foreign investment.)

In 1978 the Figueiredo administration began to establish clear policies in many sectors, including the informatics industry, to redress the balance. The concept of "reserving the market"—in this case, for Brazilian-made computers—arose. The policy of "assertive industrialization" was put into effect in 1984 in the "National Informatics Law." Covering all computers, scientific instruments, terminals, peripherals, and software, this law had far-reaching effects.

Protected from large firms such as IBM, many Brazilian entrepreneurs went into the computer business. The largest Brazilian microcomputer manufacturer, Microtec, was started in 1982 in a basement by a U.S.-educated Syrian emigré. By 1985 there were 274 Brazilian computer firms, and their revenues had surpassed those of foreign computer firms. In protecting this industry, the government gave it time to develop and compete. The idea that Brazil could control its informatics destiny captured the imagination of nationalists.

When Brazil closed its microcomputer industry to foreign capital, the Reagan administration and United States corporations were enraged. The president ordered preparations for economic sanctions against Brazil, including cutting imports from Brazil of shoes, aircraft, autos, and orange juice, supposedly accounting for the same amount lost in microcomputers. For more than two years, until the United States stopped threatening retaliation in March 1988, this was a source of tension between the two countries.

TRADE IN SERVICES

International trade negotiations may seem far removed from global information relations, but discussions on trade in services under way in the General Agreement on Tariffs and Trade (GATT) are extremely important for the future of global communication.[102]

What are services? Adam Smith once said that services were "unproductive of any value and do not fix or realize any permanent subject or vendable commodity which endures after the labor is performed." Services "like the proclamations of the orator or the tunes of the musician . . . perish in the very instance of their production.''[103]

One broad definition of services is "any exchanged product of economic activity that is not a good." But as Braman points out, the difference between goods and services is increasingly difficult to determine.[104] As information technologies increasingly design and produce goods, the physical form of that good constitutes an ever smaller portion of its total value.

The production and consumption of services traditionally had to take place in the same time and the same place. But new technologies collapse time and space and permit service transactions to take place at the same time in different parts of the world.[105] Such service sectors as accounting, telecommunications, banking, insurance, franchising, aviation, travel services, legal services, and maritime communication are wholly or partially dependent on new global information and communication technologies.

Service industries have become leading growth engines in the economy. They account for at least one-fourth of the value of all global trade, and trade in services is growing much faster than trade in goods. Many countries in industrial decline see the predicted growth in services as a possible source of economic salvation. To protect that potential, dozens of countries have established protectionist measures on transborder data flow.[106]

The call for global negotiations on trade in services is a reaction to the present situation, in which diverse national jurisdictions have created a patchwork of regulatory instruments that impede the free flow of information. There are four kinds of existing national regulations on the service sector:

1. Regulation of international data flows. These policy measures prohibit the inflow or outflow of certain categories of information or raise the cost of transmission so high that it is unprofitable.
2. Competition with communication monopolies. Obstacles often arise when a government allows foreign providers of data services or value-added communication services into a country but maintains the government-owned Post, Telephone and Telegraph (PTT) monopoly in a privileged position. Governments often choose a policy that limits the number of foreign providers and restricts the scope of their services.
3. Discriminatory standards. National policies sometimes establish discriminatory technical standards that impose obstacles to foreign companies.
4. Restrictions on the use of foreign data processing facilities. A number of countries restrict the use of computer facilities located in other countries. The economies of scale dictate that foreign concerns centralize data processing and retrieval centers.[107]

To untangle this mess, the United States has promoted GATT, the General Agreement on Trade and Tariffs. Many OECD nations resisted the idea at first, and the Group of 77, a coalition of Third World nations led by India and Brazil, resisted the idea so vigorously that eventually it was decided to split GATT negotiations in two: one set of negotiations for services and another for goods. Why did the United States want GATT to be the forum for international negotiations on trade in services?

GATT has enjoyed considerable success as a negotiating system in the past. It has a broad range of developed and developing countries as members, and its agreements are binding. The United States sees GATT as perhaps the only way to untangle the morass of different national laws that today regulate transborder data flow and impede the free flow of information.

But developing countries wanted another forum, one with a longer history of sympathy for Third World concerns. They saw their views best upheld in UNESCO, the United Nations Conference on Trade and Development (UNCTAD), or the Intergovernmental Bureau on Informatics (IBI). Braman points out that the debate over trade in services involved three groups of countries. The United States, joined now by most other OECD nations, wanted to treat services as it would any good. Another group of newly industrialized nations, such as South Korea, wanted to see their own services export sectors grow and were willing to see some relaxation in protectionism. Brazil, India, and Singapore joined other Third World countries in completely opposing this idea.

What are the arguments for and against global negotiations on trade in services? The United States and other pronegotiations countries believe negotiations on trade in services express the current state of the global economy. These negotiations could help create jobs already lost in the manufacturing sector. An agreement on trade in services would reduce protectionism in the services sector and stimulate economic growth in general. However, critics see the move by the United States and the other OECD countries as an attempt to increase dependency of developing nations on the informatics industries. A international agreement on trade in services would obstruct or even prevent developing nations from developing their own services industries. Worse yet, such a development would weaken national sovereignty and lead to greater commoditization.

PROTECTION AND LICENSING OF JOURNALISTS

The issue of protection and licensing of journalists has enraged professional journalists. No one disagrees that there is a problem, but efforts to address it have been rancorous.

It is impossible to collect comprehensive statistics, but one thing is sure: The situation is grave, however it is measured. Eighty-four journalists were killed in twenty-three countries in 1991, the worst year on record for murder and violence against journalists.[108] (See Figure 5-3.)

Protection of journalists has been one of the most widely publicized and hotly contested issues in international information relations. One cause of the problem has been the different ways nations have defined protection. For some, protection means guaranteeing the physical safety of journalists who are covering armed conflicts or who are operating in unstable or violent areas. In some countries it also means protection of journalists' rights to carry out their duties. This latter interpretation has led to the charge that some countries merely want to limit the ability of journalists to report or to force journalists to have a more "balanced" perspective.

Many objections have been made to various plans to protect journalists. Journalists have not asked for special privileges, and it has been argued that the guarantee of human rights for each individual should be the best insurance for freedom of news

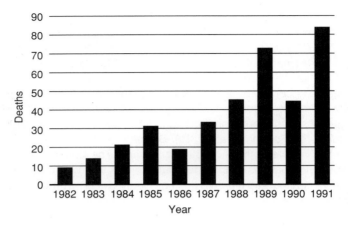

FIGURE 5-3   **Deaths of Professional Journalists Worldwide, 1982–1991. Journalists'
human and civil rights are in jeopardy as violence against the world's press corps
accelerates.**

SOURCE: Freedom House and International Federation of Journalists.

gatherers. Special protection measures would mean that journalists would constantly be under the supervision of authorities and that their work would be more difficult. Protection linked to the issuance of a license would allow authorities to decide who is and who is not a journalist.

Merrill found considerable support around the world for licensing of journalists if it were done by *national* journalists' associations (guilds, unions, societies, *colegios*, and the like). More than twice as many countries favored in-country licensing as did not. Opinion was more divided on the question of *international* licensing of journalists.[109]

Despite the present impasse, for years there have been efforts to address this issue.[110] Article 19 of the 1948 Universal Declaration of Human Rights guaranteed to all persons the right "to seek, receive, and impart information." This presumably included the right of media workers freely to gather this information. However, this was not binding international law. The UN General Assembly's Economic and Social Council (ECOSOC) sponsored the 1948 Conference on Freedom of Information, which proposed a *Draft Convention on Gathering and International Transmission of News.* Delegates to the conference defined important goals. The Draft Convention, which never became law, called for the freest possible movement of journalists and for the broadest access of foreign correspondents to their sources. It specified that journalists could not be expelled from a country because they lawfully exercised their right to seek, receive, or impart information or opinion.[111]

The 1949 Geneva Conventions did not specifically address the treatment of journalists.[112] But the 1970 UN Declaration on *Protection of Journalists Engaged in Dangerous Missions in Areas of Armed Conflict* reminded members that the United Nations relies heavily on journalists' reports of armed conflict and called on all states to protect war correspondents under existing Geneva Conventions.[113] In 1971 a *Preliminary Draft International Convention on the Protection of Journalists Engaged in Dangerous Missions* intended to go beyond the Geneva Conventions and set up an

International Professional Committee for the Protection of Journalists, which would issue safe-conduct cards.[114] Finally, a 1977 Additional Protocol to the Geneva Conventions defined a journalist carrying out his or her profession in areas of armed conflict as a civilian, with all the protection due thereto. This is the only binding international provision protecting journalists.[115]

In 1978 the nations of UNESCO unanimously passed the nonbinding Mass Media Declaration, which insisted that journalists "be assured of protection guaranteeing them the best conditions for the exercise of their profession."[116] The 1980 MacBride Report recommended better protection of journalists in dangerous situations, regardless of whether the situation is an international armed conflict. But the MacBride Commission did not propose special considerations to protect journalists. It stated, "To propose additional measures would invite the dangers entailed in a licensing system . . . " Commission Chair Sean MacBride dissented and called for "special status and protection."[117]

One event in particular incensed Western journalists and press managers. In 1981, UNESCO held a meeting of international and regional journalists' organizations that sparked a huge wave of protest. French political scientist Pierre Gaborit, in his UNESCO-sponsored paper, called for an international commission on the protection of journalists, comprised entirely of representatives of journalists' organizations, which would issue identity cards. Gaborit also sought to ensure that such correspondents "conform to generally accepted rules for professional ethics."[118]

The U.S. State Department learned of this meeting and demanded that four private press groups (International Federation of Newspaper Publishers, International Press Institute, Inter-American Press Association, and World Press Freedom Committee) be invited. They branded the Gaborit paper as an "attempt to license journalists working abroad and yet another UNESCO ploy to control press freedom by restricting reporters' access."[119] Western reporters seized on the notion that UNESCO was calling for the licensing of journalists. They overlooked the fact that UNESCO had taken no position on the issue and that the meeting was a continuation of a discussion that had been going on for decades. Three months later, Western media representatives issued the well-known Talloires Declaration, which among other things described itself as "an avowed response to seven years of debate at UNESCO over proposed curbs on press freedom."

In 1986 the International Committee of the Red Cross in Geneva established a "hotline" to monitor journalists' rights. This coincided with the period in which the number of acts of violence against journalists rose to an all-time high.

CODES OF ETHICS FOR MEDIA PRACTICE

Closely related to the aforementioned controversy are many nonbinding statements that have dealt with codes of ethics for the press. This issue has also elicited its fair share of attention in the worldwide information debates. Most journalists and press associations fervently oppose *mandatory* codes of ethics, be they national or international.

Before the ideological splits in journalism associations in the post–World War II period, the 1936 *Principles Adopted by the Congress of the International Union of Press Associations* stated the following:

A journalist worthy of the name is bound:

- To check conscientiously the truthfulness and authenticity of every news item, particularly such as may be likely to provoke prejudice, mistrust, hatred or contempt for other nations . . .
- To abstain from all praise of violence or incitement to the use of violence for the settlement of domestic disputes in other States . . .
- To insist on his own right and recognize the right of others to carry on propaganda in favor of full preparedness for defense against a possible attack from abroad . . .
- To abstain from anything that might be regarded as inculcating the spirit of violence or as giving preference to brutal force over justice and equity or as preparation for attack on another state.
- To fight everywhere against the mistaken idea that there are disputes in the world incapable of solution otherwise than by war and hence that war is inevitable . . . [120]

Another outcome of the 1948 Conference on Freedom of Information was an attempt to establish a *binding* code of ethics for journalists. A 1952 *Draft Code of Ethics* was approved by ECOSOC but subsequently failed to receive General Assembly approval. The draft code insisted that "freedom of information and of the press is a fundamental human right" and that a journalist had a "moral obligation to be truthful . . . [and] factually accurate." It even specified that journalists writing about a foreign country should "acquire the necessary knowledge of such country which will enable them to report and comment accurately and fairly thereon."[121]

Contrasting ethical statements arose in the heat of debate about the "New World Information and Communication Order." In 1979 the Latin American Federation of Journalists, aligned with the International Organization of Journalists and with Third World interests, drafted the *Latin American Code of Journalist Ethics,* which stated:

Journalism must be a service of collective interest [and] must contribute to strengthening peace, peaceful coexistence, self-determination of peoples, disarmament, international détente and mutual understanding . . .

[The journalist must] promote the conditions for the establishment of a free and balanced flow of news . . . fight for a new information order . . . endeavor to democratize information . . . and reject propaganda on the inevitability of war.[122]

Quite a different tone was struck by the 1981 *Declaration of Talloires* of the "Voices of Freedom" Conference, agreed upon by the leading Western press and broadcasting institutions:

We believe that the free flow of information and ideas is essential for mutual understanding and world peace. . . . We support the universal human right to be fully informed, which right requires the free circulation of news and opinion. . . . Denying freedom of the press denies all freedom of the individual.

We believe in any society that public interest is best served by a variety of independent news media. . . . We acknowledge the importance of advertising as a consumer service.

> *There can be no international code of journalistic ethics;* the plurality of views makes this impossible. . . . Members of the press should enjoy the full protection of national and international law. We seek no special protection or any special status and oppose any proposals that would control journalists in the name of protecting them. . . . Licensing of journalists by national or international bodies should not be sanctioned. . . . All journalistic freedoms should apply equally to the print and broadcast media.[123] [Emphasis added]

Journalists from socialist and Third World countries continued to press for an international code of ethics. Eight journalists' associations in 1983 agreed on the *International Principles of Professional Ethics in Journalism,* the thrust of which is evident in ten fundamental ethical standards:

> The People's Right to True Information; The Journalist's Dedication to Objective Reality; The Journalist's Social Responsibility; The Journalist's Professional Integrity; Public Access and Participation; Respect for Privacy and Human Dignity; Respect for Public Interest; Respect for Universal Values and Diversity of Cultures; Elimination of War and Other Evils Confronting Humanity; Promotion of a New World Information and Communication Order.[124]

Merrill's research has found little opposition in most nations to in-country codes of ethics. However, the United States, Great Britain, and Germany see no need for ethical codes because such codes would impose restrictions on independent journalism. Merrill also found that twice as many countries favored an international code of ethics as opposed it.[125]

A 1989 survey by the International Journalism Institute found that the following parties to the *Conference on Security and Cooperation in Europe (CSCE)* had professional codes of ethics of varying degrees of applicability: Austria, Belgium, Czechoslovakia, Denmark, the Federal Republic of Germany, Finland, France, Hungary, Italy, the Netherlands, Norway, Poland, Portugal, Sweden, Switzerland, Turkey, the USSR, the United Kingdom and Ireland, the United States, and Yugoslavia. In some countries the code amounts to a declaration of principles. In other countries the code lays down domestic rules for exercising professional journalism, with ethical principles included in professional journalists' organizations.[126]

THE STATUS OF WOMEN IN INTERNATIONAL COMMUNICATION

The socioeconomic status of women in society is shocking. The World Conference on the UN Decade for Women summed it up this way:

> While they represent 50 percent of the world adult population and one-third of the official labor force, [women] perform for nearly two-thirds of all working hours, receive only one-tenth of the world income, and own less than 1 percent of world property.[127]

There has been increasing recognition of the status of women in the information and communication sector.[128] The 1979 *Convention on the Elimination of All Forms of Discrimination Against Women* commits its signatories to "modify or abolish existing laws, regulations, customs and practices which constitute discrimination against women." The 1985 Nairobi World Conference to Review and Appraise the Achievements of the United Nations Decade for Women called for greater participation of women in the media, elimination of negative stereotypes, and improvement of women's access to communication. The MacBride Report stated:

> Attention should be paid to the communication needs of women. They should be assured adequate access to communication means and that images of them and of their activities are not distorted by the media or in advertising.[129]

Data are sketchy, but one thing is clear: Women around the world are among the poorest of the info-poor. Of the 840 million illiterates in the world, 60 percent are women. Few "hard-news" journalists are women. Very few film directors, cable managers, or broadcasters are women. In few countries is the percentage of women workers in the media greater than 25 percent (see Figure 5-4). Women rarely break into top management.[130] They do appear on the screen and work widely in educational and children's programming, but this reflects "a kind of sex-stereotyped segregation."[131] On the technical side, the story is mixed. Broadcasting engineering jobs are almost exclusively the domain of men, but in the electronics industry women account for almost 90 percent of the poorly paid work force.[132]

The recent intensive changes in communication technologies such as satellites, computerization, and digitalization have specific implications for women.[133] On the one hand, they widen the gap between men and women. On the other hand, these technologies are changing the traditional roles women have had in the communication media. For example, women were extensively employed in the telephone industry throughout its history. A study at American Telephone & Telegraph (AT & T) in the United States revealed that in the late 1970s, while 13,000 new jobs were filled by men as a result of the revolutionary changes in technology, the jobs of 22,000 women were made redundant.[134] Some argue that one possible benefit for women of these technological changes is that many women can now work at home in their "electronic cottages," but these jobs have little security and are poorly paid.

The portrayal of women in media content is also disturbing. A global review by UNESCO of the portrayal and participation of women in the media revealed that at best, media presentation of women is narrow; at worst, it is demeaning and unrealistic. Media portrayal of women confines them to the home; characterizes them as romantic, irrational, and unnewsworthy; and exploits them as advertising "bait."[135] Mainstream media pay little attention to the women's movement or to the social contributions made by independent and gifted women. Nor does an increase in women employed in the media necessarily lead to a change in media content.[136]

Given this situation, women around the world have organized a growing independent network of alternative media channels in the last fifteen years. Some women's alternative magazines, such as *Ms.* in the United States and *Emma* in Germany, have had circulations that rival those of the traditional women's magazines. There has been a sharp increase in women's alternative magazines in Latin America, Asia, and Africa, but the overall number remains low. Illegal women's radio stations have appeared in France (Les Nanas Radioteuses), Italy (Radio Donna), and the Netherlands (Vrouwenradio). Independent radio stations in Europe and North America broadcast programming produced by women (more than forty regular programs in the United States and Canada in 1986). Latin American community radio has also broadcast many programs for and by women.

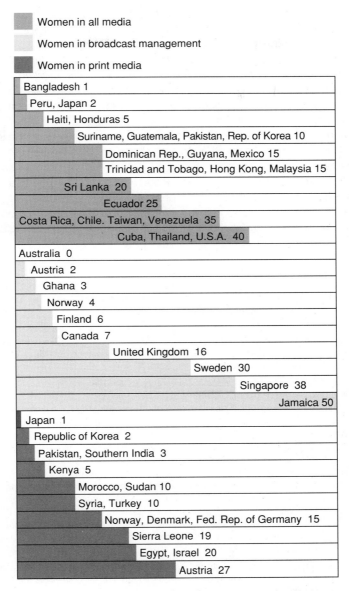

□ Women in all media

□ Women in broadcast management

□ Women in print media

Bangladesh 1	
Peru, Japan 2	
Haiti, Honduras 5	
Suriname, Guatemala, Pakistan, Rep. of Korea 10	
Dominican Rep., Guyana, Mexico 15	
Trinidad and Tobago, Hong Kong, Malaysia 15	
Sri Lanka 20	
Ecuador 25	
Costa Rica, Chile. Taiwan, Venezuela 35	
Cuba, Thailand, U.S.A. 40	
Australia 0	
Austria 2	
Ghana 3	
Norway 4	
Finland 6	
Canada 7	
United Kingdom 16	
Sweden 30	
Singapore 38	
Jamaica 50	
Japan 1	
Republic of Korea 2	
Pakistan, Southern India 3	
Kenya 5	
Morocco, Sudan 10	
Syria, Turkey 10	
Norway, Denmark, Fed. Rep. of Germany 15	
Sierra Leone 19	
Egypt, Israel 20	
Austria 27	

FIGURE 5-4   Women in the Media. Female populations are part of the world's info-poor. Here we see women as a proportion of media workers (most recent year available since 1970).

SOURCE: J. Seager and A. Olsen, "Women in the World: An International Atlas," in *World Communication Report* (Paris: UNESCO, 1989), p. 210.

In the area of news, the Women's Features Service, begun with the assistance of UNESCO and the UN Fund for Population Activities and for many years operated by Inter Press Service, has been a success. WFS puts out two features from women journalists per day on the IPS wire. ISIS International in Rome and the International Women's Tribune Center in New York operate international women's information networks and data bases.

The 1991 International Conference on Women, Media, and Advertising called on media to include major coverage of women in the public sphere, called on women to examine existing codes of media ethics and to ensure that these codes evolve and respond positively to women's issues and rights, and called on consumers to take issue against sexist advertisements.[137]

As Roach has pointed out, women have been largely ignored in the information debates. The Mass Media Declaration does not even mention women. The MacBride Report devotes only two pages and one of its eighty-two recommendations to women. Why have women been ignored? Roach believes "the unequal relations of power between men and women in societies at large are reflected in the field of communications."[138] As this chapter has demonstrated, it is not only women, but all segments of society that suffer these "unequal relations," who are "info-poor."

NOTES

1. Marshall McLuhan, *Understanding Media: The Extensions of Man* (New York: New American Library, 1964), p. 67. See also Marshall McLuhan and Quentin Fiore, *War and Peace in the Global Village* (New York: Bantam Books, 1968).

2. Claus Eurich, "Communications Polluting Speech," *Development: Seeds of Change* 1 (1985): 75, cited by John A. Lent, "New Information Technology: Myths, Questions, Alternatives." Paper presented at Conference of the International Association for Mass Communication Research, New Delhi, August 1986.

3. See Georgi Arbatov, *The War of Ideas in Contemporary International Relations* (Moscow: Progress, 1973); Howard H. Frederick, *Cuban-American Radio Wars: Ideology in International Telecommunication* (Norwood, NJ: Ablex, 1986); Cees Hamelink, *The Corporate Village: The Role of Transnational Corporations in International Communications* (Rome: IDOC International, 1977); William A. Hatchen in collaboration with Marva Hatchen, *The World News Prism: Changing Media, Clashing Ideologies* (Ames, IA: Iowa State University Press, 1981); Harold D. Lasswell, Daniel Lerner, and Hans Speier, *Propaganda and Communication in World History*, 3 vols. (Honolulu, HI: University Press of Hawaii, 1979 and 1980); Armand Mattelart, *Multinational Corporations and the Control of Culture: The Ideological Apparatuses of Imperialism* (Atlantic Highlands, NJ: Humanities Press, 1979); Thomas McPhail, *Electronic Colonialism: The Future of International Broadcasting and Communication* (Beverly Hills, CA: Sage, 1981); Herbert I. Schiller, *Mass Communication and the American Empire* (Boston: Beacon Press, 1971); and Anthony Smith, *The Geopolitics of Information: How Western Culture Dominates the World* (New York: Oxford University Press, 1980).

4. Francis Fukuyama, "The End of History," *The National Interest*, Summer 1989, pp. 3–18. See also Torbjørn L. Knutson, "Answered Prayers: Fukuyama, Liberalism, and the End-of-History Debate," *Bulletin of Peace Proposals* 22 (1, 1991): 77–85.

5. Daniel Bell, *The End of Ideology: On the Exhaustion of Political Ideas in the Fifties* (Glencoe, IL: Free Press, 1960).

6. Stephen Krasner quoted in Susan Wels, "Global Integration: The Apparent and the Real," *Stanford Magazine,* September 1990, p. 48.

7. See William Read, "Information as a National Resource," *Journal of Communication* 29 (1, 1979): 172–178; and Martin A. Rothblatt, "The Space WARC: International Accommodations for Satellite Communications," in *Regulation of Transnational Communications: Michigan Yearbook of International Legal Studies, 1984,* ed. Leslie J. Anderson (New York: Clark Boardman, 1984), pp. 43–44.

8. See Kaarle Nordenstreng and Herbert I. Schiller, *National Sovereignty and International Communication* (Norwood, NJ: Ablex, 1979).

9. Louis Jionet, Secretary-General of the French Commission on Data Processing and Liberties, quoted in House Committee on Government Operations, *International Information Flow: Forging a New Framework,* 1980 H.R. Rept. No. 1525, 96th Congress, 2nd session, p. 20, note 49, cited in Sol Glasner, "Multinational Corporations and National Sovereignty," in *Toward a Law of Global Communications Networks,* ed. Anne W. Branscomb (New York: Longman, 1986), p. 336.

10. William J. Broad, "No Go for Satellite Sanctions Against Iran," *Science,* May 16, 1980, pp. 685–686.

11. David E. Sanger, "Waging a Trade War over Data," *New York Times,* March 13, 1983, p. f1+.

12. Hemant Shah, "International Regulation of Direct Broadcast Satellites: The Roles of UNESCO, ITU, and the UN," n.p.

13. Rolf T. Wigand, "Direct Satellite Broadcasting: Definitions and Prospects," in *World Communications: A Handbook,* ed. George Gerbner and Marsha Siefert (New York: Longman, 1984), pp. 229–235; Joseph N. Pelton, "The Communication Satellite: Revolutionary Change Agent," *Columbia Journal of World Business* 18 (Spring 1983): 77–84; John Pike, "Space is Big Business," *Multinational Monitor* 4 (September 1983): 16–20; Lawrence Schnapf, "Explorations in Space Law: An Examination of the Legal Issues Raised by Geostationary, Remote Sensing, and Direct Broadcasting Satellites," *New York Law School Law Review* 29 (1985): 687–748; and U. S. International Communication Agency, *The United States and the Debate on the World "Information Order"* (Washington, DC: Academy for Educational Development, 1979).

14. The countries were Brazil, Colombia, the Congo, Ecuador, Gabon, Indonesia, Kenya, Somalia, Uganda, and Zaire.

15. This is similar to the American law by which the owner of "lakefront" property "owns" the lake bed out to the middle of the lake. Such ownership coexists with the passage and anchoring of boats, swimming, and so forth. See Harry Levin, "Political Economy of Orbit Spectrum Leasing," in Rothblatt, "The Space WARC," in *Regulation of Transnational Communications, International Legal Studies, 1984,* note 6, p. 64.

16. "The Bogotá Declaration of 1976," reprinted in Nicolas Mateesco Matte, *Aerospace Law: Telecommunications Satellites* (Toronto: Butterworth, 1982), p. 341.

17. The argument made by the United States and the USSR was that the satellite's path through space is not determined by any single factor; rather, it is affected by a combination of factors, including at least the energy imparted by the launched vehicle; the mass of the spacecraft; the altitude at which it moves above the Earth; the forces of gravity of the Earth, the Moon, and the Sun; and the radiation pressure of the Sun. See Carl Q. Christon, *The Modern International Law of Outer Space* (New York: Pergamon Press, 1982), pp. 455–456; and Boris Belitzky, trans., *International Space Law* (New York: Praeger, 1984), p. 157; both cited by Leonardo Ferreira, "The Geostationary Orbit and the Equatorial Countries' Claim of Sovereignty: Historical Overview and Update." Paper presented at Conference of the International Communication Association, New Orleans, 1988, p. 33.

18. Ferreira, "The Geostationary Orbit," pp. 69–72.

19. Marcel Barang, "Remote Sensing: Short Cut to the Long View," *South,* May 1987, pp. 64–65.

20. Geza Feketekuty and Jonathan David Aronson, "Restrictions on Trade in Communication and Information Services," in *Regulation of Transnational Communications,* p. 151.

21. *Principles Relating to Remote Sensing of the Earth from Outer Space,* United Nations General Assembly, December 3, 1986. See Charles E. Knox, "Remote-Sensing 'Principles' Prescribes Cooperation within Framework of Economic Cooperation," University of Washington, School of Communications, n.d.

22. "ABC World News," April 2, 1987.

23. David E. Sanger, "Conflict Seen as Likely in News Media Use of Satellite Images," *New York Times,* May 28, 1987, p. A6; U.S. Congress, Office of Technology Assessment, *Commercial Newsgathering from Space: A Technical Memorandum* (Washington, DC: Government Printing Office, May 1987); William E. Smith, "Spacecam: Legal Issues in the Use of Remote-Sensing Satellites for News Gathering." Paper presented at the Conference of the Association for Education in Journalism and Mass Communication, Norman, Oklahoma, 1986; and Robert J. Aamoth, Esq., "From Landsat to Mediasat: The Development of Remote Sensing Technology and the First Amendment Right of the Press to Use that Technology for News Reporting," in *American Enterprise, The Law and the Commercial Use of Space,* vol. 2, ed. National Legal Center for the Public Interest, 1986, pp. 1–24.

24. Peter Muzik, *Die Medien Multis* (Vienna: Verlag Orac, 1989).

25. Ben H. Bagdikian, "The Lords of the Global Village," *The Nation,* June 12, 1989, p. 807.

26. Ben H. Bagdikian, *The Media Monopoly* (Boston: Beacon Press, 1st ed. 1982; 2nd ed. 1987).

27. Ben H. Bagdikian, Speech, University of Southern California, Los Angeles, March 15, 1990.

28. Bertelsmann paid over $800 million for Doubleday and RCA. Sony owns CBS Records and Columbia Pictures. Hachette paid $1.1 billion for Grolier and Diamandis Communications. Four of the seven major Hollywood motion pictures studios are foreign-owned. Three-fourths of U.S. record companies are foreign-owned. See Thomas B. Rosenstiel, "The Selling of the U.S. Media: Have Foreign Buys Gone Too Far?" *Los Angeles Times,* November 4, 1990, p. D10.

29. Muzik, *Die Medien Multis.*

30. UNESCO Resolution 4/19 on the International Commission for the Study of Communication Problems, October 1980, Para. 14, a.ii., in Kaarle Nordenstreng, Enrique Gonzales Manet, and Wolfgang Kleinwächter, *New International Information and Communication Order: A Sourcebook* (Prague: International Organization of Journalists, 1986), p. 249.

31. John Armstrong, "Deregulating the International Telecommunications Satellite System: The Implications for INTELSAT and the Shape of International Telecommunications." Paper presented at the Conference of the International Communication Association, New Orleans, 1988.

32. Richard C. Beiard, "Telecommunications as an Engine of Economic Growth," Washington, DC: U. S. Department of State, 1989.

33. Michael Palmer and Jeremy Tunstall, "Deregulation and Competition in European Telecommunications," *Journal of Communication* 38 (1, 1988): 60–69.

34. The most immediate results of the Italian court's 1976 decision to permit commercial television was a huge increase in U.S. films on Italian television. Italian viewers flocked to this type of programming, and the well-respected RAI broadcasting suffered tremendously. David Waterman, "World Television Trade," *Telecommunications Policy,* June 1988, p. 141.

35. The Spanish government awarded licenses in 1989 for Spain's first three private television channels to companies headed by Canal Plus of France, Antena 3 of Spain, and Berlusconi. "Spain Awards TV Licenses," *International Herald Tribune,* August 26–27, 1989, p. 11.

36. "Balaton Channel, Première Television Priveé de Hongrie," *Le Monde,* June 24, 1989, p. 20.

37. Johann Wolfgang von Goethe, "Äusserungen über 'Weltliteratur,'" *Goethes Werke,* vol. 12 (Hamburg, FRG: Christian Wegner Verlag, 1953), pp. 362–363.

38. Quoted in James Stover, *Information Technology in the Third World: Can I.T. Lead to Humane National Development?* (Boulder, CO: Westview Press, 1984), p. 31.

39. Kaarle Nordenstreng, "Three Theses on the Imbalance Debate," *Politics of News: Third World Perspectives,* ed. J. S. Yadava (New Delhi: Concept, 1984).

40. See "International News Flows," special issue of *Communication Research Trends* 10 (4, 1989); Al Hester, "The Collection and Flow of World News," in *Global Journalism: Survey of International Communication,* ed. John C. Merrill, 2nd ed. (New York: Longman, 1991), pp. 29–50; K. Kyoon Hur, "A Critical Analysis of International News Flow Research," *Critical Studies in Mass Communication* 1 (4, 1984): 365–378; Hamid Mowlana, *Global Information and World Communication: New Frontiers in International Relations* (New York: Longman, 1986);

Jim Richstad and Michael Anderson, eds., *Crisis in International News: Policies and Prospects* (New York: Columbia University Press, 1981); and Robert L. Stevenson, *Communication, Development, and the Third World: The Global Politics of Information* (New York: Longman, 1988).

41. Denis McQuail, "International Information Flows: Evidence of Content Analysis," in *Approaches to International Communication,* eds. Ullamaija Kivikuru and Tapio Varis (Helsinki: Finnish National Commission for UNESCO, 1986), p. 131.

42. Mowlana, *Global Information,* p. 28; International Journalism Institute, *The Mass Media in the World, 1987,* p. 40, citing UNESCO, *World Communication Report* (draft) (Paris: UNESCO, 1988), p. 1.54; and UNESCO, *World Communication Report* (Paris: UNESCO, 1989), pp. 136–137.

43. Kaarle Nordenstreng and Tapio Varis, *Television Traffic—A One-Way Street?* Reports and Papers on Mass Communication, no. 70 (Paris: UNESCO, 1974).

44. Tapio Varis, "International Flow of Television Programs," *Journal of Communication* (Winter 1984): 143–152; and Tapio Varis, "International Flow of Television Programs," in *Current Issues in International Communication,* eds. L. John Martin and Ray Eldon Hiebert (New York: Longman, 1990), pp. 26–34.

45. See Margaret A. Blanchard, *Exporting the First Amendment: The Press–Government Crusade of 1945–1952* (New York: Longman, 1986).

46. Cited in Herbert I. Schiller, *Communication and Cultural Domination* (White Plains, NY: Sharpe, 1976), p. 24.

47. "Constitution of UNESCO," in Nordenstreng, Gonzales Manet, and Kleinwächter, *New International Information,* p. 211.

48. "Declaration of the Ministerial Conference of Non-Aligned Countries on Decolonization of Information, July 13, 1976, New Delhi," in Nordenstreng, Gonzales Manet, and Kleinwächter, *New International Information,* p. 285.

49. Lyrics from reggae tune "The Foreign Press," by Bob Marley, circa 1978.

50. Walter Lippman, *Public Opinion* (New York: MacMillan, 1922; 16th printing, 1961), p. 364.

51. George Gerbner, "Ideological Perspectives and Political Tendencies in News Reporting," *Journalism Quarterly* 41 (1964): 495.

52. *Extra!* December 1987, p. 16.

53. Shirley M. Keddie, "Naming and Renaming: *Time* Magazine's Coverage of Germany and the Soviet Union during the 1940s" (Ph.D. diss. University of Massachusetts, 1985).

54. Mort Rosenblum, "Reporting from the Third World," *Foreign Affairs,* July 1977, p. 816.

55. Josep Rota and Gilda S. Rota, "A Content Analysis of International News Published by the Leading Newspapers in Mexico City." Paper presented at the Conference of the Latin American Studies Association, Albuquerque, 1985.

56. See David Manning White, "The 'Gate Keeper': A Case Study in the Selection of News," *Journalism Quarterly* 27 (1950): 386; and Frederick, *Cuban-American Radio Wars,* pp. 68–70.

57. Edwin Diamond, *The Tin Kazoo: Television, Politics and the News* (Cambridge, MA: MIT Press, 1975), p. 94.

58. Johan Galtung and Mari Holmboe Ruge, "The Structure of Foreign News: The Presentation of the Congo, Cuba, and Cyprus Crises in Four Foreign Newspapers," in *Media Sociology: A Reader,* ed. Jeremy Tunstall (Urbana, IL: University of Illinois Press, 1970), p. 291. This article appeared originally in *Journal of International Peace Research* 1 (1965): 64–90. Similar studies are found in Herbert G. Kariel and Lynn A. Rosenvall, "Factors Influencing International News Flows," *Journalism Quarterly* 61 (Autumn 1984): 509–516; and Sophia Peterson, "Foreign News Coverage and Criteria of Newsworthiness," *Journalism Quarterly* 56 (1, Spring 1979): 116–125.

59. George Gerbner and G. Marvanyi, "The Many Worlds of the World's Press," *Journal of Communication* 27 (1, 1977): 52–66. Reprinted in *World Communications: A Handbook,* pp. 92–102.

60. Adapted from UNESCO, "Content and Sources of News," in UNESCO, *World Communication Report,* pp. 141–142. See the original study: UNESCO, *Foreign News in the Media: International Reporting in 29 Countries,* Reports and Papers on Mass Communication, no. 93 (Paris: UNESCO, 1982). See also Annabelle Sreberny-Mohammadi, "The 'World of the News' Study: Results of International Cooperation," *Journal of Communication* 34 (1, 1984): 121–133; Annabelle Sreberny-Mohammadi, "The 'World of the News,' " in *Current Issues in International Communication,* pp. 8–17; Robert L. Stevenson, "The 'World of the News' Study: Pseudo Debate," *Journal of Communication* 34 (1, 1984): 134–137; and Kaarle Nordenstreng, "The 'World of the News' Study: Bitter Lessons," *Journal of Communication* 34 (1, 1984): 138–142.

61. Robert L. Stevenson, "The Western News Agencies Do Not Ignore the Third World," *Editor & Publisher,* July 5, 1980, pp. 11+.

62. G. Cleveland Wilhoit and David H. Weaver, "Foreign News Coverage in Two U.S. Wire Services: An Update," *Journal of Communication* 33 (2, 1983): 132–148.

63. David H. Weaver and G. Cleveland Wilhoit, "Foreign News Coverage in Two U.S. Wire Services," *Journal of Communication* 31 (Spring 1981): 55–63.

64. Mohamed Kirat and David Weaver, "Foreign News Coverage in Three Wire Services: A Study of AP, UPI, and the Nonaligned News Agencies Pool," *Gazette* 35 (1, 1985): 45.

65. Robert L. Stevenson and Stevan Marjanovic, "A Look at Alternative News Sources." Paper presented at the Conference of the International Association for Mass Communication Research, Prague, 1984.

66. Narinder Aggarwala, "News with Third World Perspectives," in *The Third World and Press Freedom,* ed. Philip Coltorton (New York: Praeger, 1978), pp. 197–209; Narinder Aggarwala, "A Third World Perspective on the News," *Freedom at Issue,* (May–June 1978), pp. 13–20; and *Current Issues in International Communication,* pp. 355–362; Alan B. Chalkley, *A Manual of Development Journalism* (New Delhi: Vikas, 1970); Narinder Aggarwala, "News: A Matter of People [Development Journalism]," *Studies in Third World Societies* (9, 1979): 45–56; and Al Hester, "Revolutionary and Development Journalism," in *Handbook for Third World Journalists,* ed. Albert L. Hester and Wai Lan J. To (Athens, GA: Center for International Mass Communication Training and Research, 1987), pp. 57–67.

67. Imelda Marcos, 1978, cited in John J. Kochevar, "The Effects of Advertising in the Developing Nations." Paper presented at the Conference of the International Communication Association, Acapulco, Mexico, 1980, p. 10.

68. For basic works on colonialism and imperialism, see Kenneth Boulding and Tapan Mukerjee, eds., *Economic Imperialism* (Ann Arbor, MI: University of Michigan Press, 1972); David K. Fieldhouse, *The Colonial Empires: A Comparative Survey from the Eighteenth Century* (New York: Delacorte Press, 1966); Louis A. Hartz, ed., *The Founding of New Societies* (New York: Harcourt, Brace & World, 1964); J. A. Hobson, *Imperialism,* 3rd ed. (London: Unwin Hyman, 1988); George Lichtheim, *Imperialism* (New York: Praeger, 1971); Albert Memmi, *The Colonizer and the Colonized* (Boston: Beacon Press, 1967); John H. Parry, ed., *Trade and Dominion: The European Overseas Empires in the Eighteenth Century* (New York: Praeger, 1971); Joseph Schumpeter, *Imperialism and Social Classes* (New York: Meridian Books, 1955); Tony Smith, ed., *The End of European Empire: Decolonization after World War II* (Lexington, MA: Heath, 1975); Charles Verlinden, *The Beginnings of Modern Colonization* (Ithaca, NY: Cornell University Press, 1970); Robin Winks, ed., *Age of Imperialism* (Englewood Cliffs, NJ: Prentice-Hall, 1969); and Harrison M. Wright, ed., *The "New Imperialism": Analysis of Late Nineteenth-Century Expansion,* 2nd ed. (Boston: Heath, 1976).

69. Herbert I. Schiller, *Who Knows: Information in the Age of the Fortune 500* (Norwood, NJ: Ablex, 1981), p. 5. See also S. S. Gill, "North Uses Information Technology to Control South," *Third World Resurgence* (3, 1991): 33–34.

70. Osman Araby, "Media Imperialism: Theoretical Considerations." Paper presented at the Conference of the International Communication Association, Montreal, Canada, 1987, p. 3.

71. Oliver Boyd-Barrett, "Media Imperialism: Toward an International Framework for the Analysis of Media Systems," in *Mass Communication and Society,* ed. J. Curran, M. Gurevich, and J. Woolacoot (Beverly Hills, CA: Sage, 1979), p. 117.

72. C. C. Lee, *Media Imperialism Reconsidered* (Beverly Hills, CA: Sage, 1980), p. 68.

73. Douglas A. Boyd, "The Janus Effect? Imported Television Entertainment Programming in Developing Countries," *Critical Studies in Mass Communication* 1 (1984): 389. See also John Sinclair, "From 'Modernization' to Cultural Dependence: Mass Communication Studies and the Third World," *Media Information Australia* 23 (February 1982): 12–18, and in *Current Issues in International Communication,* pp. 286–293.

74. Richard Reeves, *American Journey: Traveling with Tocqueville in Search of Democracy in America* (New York: Simon & Schuster, 1982), p. 81, cited in Sydney Head, *World Broadcasting Systems: A Comparative Analysis* (Belmont, CA: Wadsworth, 1985), p. 229. See also Carl Bernstein, "The Leisure Empire," *Time,* December 24, 1990, pp. 56–59.

75. C. P. Kindleberger, *Economic Development* (New York: McGraw-Hill, 1958); W. W. Rostow, *The Stages of Economic Growth* (New York: Cambridge University Press, 1960); J. Backman, *Advertising and Competition* (New York: New York University Press, 1967); F. X. Callahan, "Does Advertising Subsidize Information?" *Journal of Advertising Research* 18 (1978): 19–22; J. M. Ferguson, *Advertising and Competition: Theory Measurement and Fact* (Cambridge, MA: Ballinger, 1974); and J. S. Wright et al., *Advertising* (New York: McGraw-Hill, 1971).

76. See Richard Barnet and R. Muller, *Global Reach: The Power of the Multinational Corporations* (New York: Simon & Schuster, 1974); Luis R. Beltran and Elizabeth Fox de Cardona, "Latin America and the United States: Flaws in the Free Flow of Information," in *National Sovereignty and International Communication,* pp. 33–64; Elizabeth de Cardona, "Multinational Television," *Journal of Communication* 25 (1975): 122–128; Nicholas Kaldor, "The Economic Aspects of Advertising," *Review of Economic Studies* 18 (1950): 1–27; Noreene Janus, "Advertising and Global Culture," *Cultural Survival Quarterly* 7 (2, 1983): 28–34; Hidetashi Kato, "Global Instantaneousness and Instant Globalism—The Significance of Popular Cultures in Developing Countries," in *Communication and Change: The Last Ten Years—and the Next,* ed. Wilbur Schramm and Daniel Lerner (Honolulu, HI: University Press of Hawaii, 1978); Lucy Komisar, "The Image of Women in Advertising," in *Women in Sexist Society: Studies in Power and Powerlessness,* ed. Vivian Gornick and Barbara K. Moran (New York: New American Library, 1972); Karl P. Sauvant, "Multinational Enterprises and the Transmission of Culture: The International Supply of Advertising Services and Business Education," *Journal of Peace Research* 13 (1976): 49–65; Schiller, *Communication and Cultural Domination;* Alan Wells, *Picture Tube Imperialism: The Impact of U.S. Television on Latin America* (Maryknoll, NY: Orbis Books, 1972).

77. Indira Gandhi, "Speech to the United Nations General Assembly," *New York Times,* September 29, 1983, p. A8.

78. J. J. Boddewyn, "The Global Spread of Advertising Regulation," *MSU Business Topics* 24 (2, Spring 1981): 5–13, and in *Current Issues in International Communication,* pp. 82–90.

79. "Western Satellite TV Invasion in the Caribbean," *Democratic Journalist,* March 1989, p. 19. See also Maria C. Wert and Robert L. Stevenson, "Global Television Flow to Latin American Countries," *Journalism Quarterly* 65 (1, Spring 1988): 182–185, and in *Current Issues in International Communication,* pp. 42–46.

80. Stanford Garikayi Mukasa, *The Epistemology of the New World Information/Communication Order* (Montreal: McGill University, Center for Developing Area Studies, 1987), p. 7.

81. Luis Ramiro Beltran S., "TV Etchings in the Minds of Latin Americans: Conservatism, Materialism, and Conformism," *Gazette* 24 (1978): 61–85.

82. Carl Bernstein, "The Leisure Empire," p. 58.

83. *Intermedia,* (3, 1988): 39–41, cited in *Mass Communication Media in the World* 5 (8, 1988): 15.

84. Howard H. Frederick, "Caribbean Media Workers Combat Information Colonialism," *Extra!,* January/February 1988, p. 14.

85. Mexico's Televisa is the largest television enterprise in the region. Of its 7,000 hours' annual production, about 70 percent is destined for regional and international distribution. Together with its 400,000 hours of archives, Televisa exports about 20,000 hours yearly. In December 1988 Televisa launched Galavision, a twenty-four-hour satellite service of news, light entertainment, and soap operas, to Western Europe. Televisa is now one of Western Europe's five largest television suppliers. *Entwicklungstendenzen der Massenmedien,* December 1988, p. 20, cited in *Mass Communication Media in the World* 6 (3, 1989): 22.

86. Ithiel de Sola Pool, "The Changing Flow of Television," *Journal of Communication* 27 (2, 1977): 139; and Wilson P. Dizard, Jr., *The Coming Information Age: An Overview of Technology, Economics, and Politics,* 3rd ed. (New York: Longman, 1989), pp. 186–189.

87. C. C. Lee, *Media Imperialism Reconsidered,* p. 175; Jeremy Tunstall, *The Media Are American: Anglo-American Media in the World* (New York: Columbia University Press, 1977); and Elihu Katz and George Wedell, *Broadcasting in the Third World* (Cambridge, MA: Harvard University Press, 1977).

88. Nordenstreng and Varis, *Television Traffic,* p. 55.

89. Schiller, *Communication and Cultural Domination,* p. 9.

90. Evelino Dagnino, "Cultural and Ideological Dependence: Building a Theoretical Framework," in *Structures of Dependency,* ed. Frank Bonilla and Robert Girling (E. Palo Alto, CA: Nairobi Bookstore, 1973), pp. 129–148; Rita Cruise O'Brien, "Mass Communications: Social Mechanism of Incorporation and Dependence," in *Transnational Capitalism and National Development: New Perspectives on Dependence,* ed. Jose J. Villamil (Atlantic Highlands, NJ: Humanities Press, 1979), pp. 129–144; Antonio Pasquali, *Comunicación y Cultura de Masas,* 4th ed. (Caracas: Monte Avila, 1977); and Oswaldo Sunkel and E. F. Fuenzalida, "Transnationalization and Its National Consequences," in *Transnational Capitalism and National Development,* pp. 67–94.

91. Nordenstreng and Varis, *Television Traffic.*

92. Lee, *Media Imperialism Reconsidered,* p. 175; Joseph Straubhaar, "The Transformation of Cultural Dependence: The Decline of American Influence on the Brazilian Television Industry" (Ph.D. diss., Tufts University, 1981); Katz and Wedell, *Broadcasting in the Third World.*

93. Varis, "International Flow of Television Programs," p. 143.

94. UNESCO, "Reports of the Meeting of Experts on Communication Policies and Planning" (Paris: UNESCO, 1972), cited in Hamid Mowlana and Laurie J. Wilson, *Communication Technology and Development* (Paris: UNESCO, 1988), p. 16.

95. Mowlana and Wilson, *Communication Technology and Development,* p. 16.

96. Adapted from International Telecommunication Union, *The Changing Telecommunication Environment: Policy Considerations for the Members of the ITU* (Geneva: ITU, 1989), p. 37.

97. Mustafa Masmoudi, "The New World Information Order," *Journal of Communication* 29 (1979): 172. See also Robert A. White and James M. McDonnell, "Priorities for National Communication Policy in the Third World," *The Information Society Journal* 2 (1, 1983): 5–33.

98. International Telecommunication Union, *The Changing Telecommunication Environment,* p. 25.

99. Leonard J. Theberge, "UNESCO's 'New World Information Order': Colliding with First Amendment Values," *American Bar Association Journal* 67 (1981): 717–718.

100. UNESCO, *A Documentary History of a New World Information and Communication Order Seen as an Evolving and Continuous Process,* Documents on Communication and Society, no. 19 (Paris: UNESCO, n.d.), p. 7.

101. Carlos von Doellinger and Leonardo C. Cavalcanti, *Empresas Multinacionais na Industria Brasileira* (Rio de Janeiro: Instituto de Planejamento Economico e Social, 1975), p. 27; M. Margolis, "The United States and Brazil: Anatomy of a Trade Dispute," *Christian Science Monitor,* March 27, 1987, p. 17; U. S. Department of Commerce, *A Competitive Assessment of the U. S. Microcomputer Industry* (Washington, DC: International Trade Administration, August 1986); "Brazil Takes on a Protectionist Ring," *The Economist,* October 12, 1985, p. 86; Jean Michel Quadrepoint, "U. S. Offensive against Latin American Informatics: Avoiding the Conta-

gion of the 'Bad Example' of Brazil," *Le Monde Diplomatigue,* July 1986, p. 17; Norman Gall, "Does Anyone Really Believe in Free Trade?" *Forbes,* December 15, 1986, pp. 115–120; Linda Bower, "New Law Affects Brazil's Big 'Informatics' Market," *Business America,* December 10, 1984, p. 45; and Peter B. Evans, "Declining Hegemony and Assertive Industrialization: U.S.–Brazil Conflicts in the Computer Industry," *International Organization* 43 (2, Spring 1989): 207–238.

102. Christoph Dornbacher and Oliver Fischer, "Telecommunications in the Uruguay Round," *Intereconomics: Review of International Trade and Development* 25 (July/August 1990): 185–192.

103. Cited in Joseph N. Pelton, "Toward an Equitable Global Information Society," in *International Information Economy Handbook,* ed. G. Russell Pipe and Chris Brown (Springfield, VA: Transnational Data Reporting Service, 1985), p. 95.

104. Sandra Braman, "Trade and Information Policy," *Media, Culture & Society* 12 (3, July 1990): 364–367.

105. Karl P. Sauvant, "The International Politics of Data Services Trade," in *International Information Economy Handbook,* p. 101.

106. Braman, "Trade and Information Policy," pp. 374–375.

107. Geza Feketekuty and Jonathan David Aronson, "Restrictions on Trade in Communication," pp. 148ff.

108. See Leonard R. Sussman, "Censors Retreat—Except in the Gulf," *Freedom Review* (January–February 1992): 39–44; International Federation of Journalists SafeNet, Press Release, December 31, 1991, "Journalists Killed 1991: UPDATE;" and Jonathan Power, "The Bloody Contest of Pen and Sword," *Los Angeles Times,* March 26, 1990, p. B7.

109. John C. Merrill, "Governments and Press Control: Global Attitudes on Journalistic Matters," *Political Communication and Persuasion* 4 (1987): 223–262. During 1987 Merrill conducted interviews with more than sixty information/press officers at UN missions in New York City and embassy press attaches in Washington, DC.

110. For a complete history of these proposals, see Susan Holmberg, "The Protection and Licensing of Journalists: A Global Debate," *International Communication Bulletin* 22 (Spring 1987): 21–29.

111. *Draft Convention on the Gathering and International Transmission of News,* Economic and Social Council, 1948, in Edward W. Ploman, ed., *International Law Governing Communications and Information: A Collection of Basic Documents* (Westport, CT: Greenwood Press, 1982), p. 133.

112. *Conventions for the Protection of War Victims Concerning I. Amelioration of the Condition of Wounded and Sick in Armed Forces in Field; II. Amelioration of the Condition of the Wounded, Sick, and Shipwrecked Members of the Armed Forces at Sea; III. Treatment of Prisoners of War; IV. Protection of Civilian Persons in the Time of War,* Geneva, August 12, 1949. Entered into force October 21, 1950; for the United States, August 2, 1955. M. J. Bowman and D. J. Harris, *Multilateral Treaties: Index and Current Status* (London: Butterworth, 1984) and *Fifth Cumulative Supplement* (Nottingham: University of Nottingham Treaty Centre, 1988), pp. T238–241.

113. *Protection of Journalists Engaged in Dangerous Missions in Areas of Armed Conflict,* UN General Assembly Resolution 2673 (XXV), 1970, in Ploman, *International Law Governing Communications,* p. 178.

114. "Preliminary Draft International Convention on the Protection of Journalists Engaged in Dangerous Missions," transmitted to the UN General Assembly by the Economic and Social Council Resolution 1597 (I), 1971, in Ploman, *International Law Governing Communications,* p. 179.

115. Article 79.1, *Protocols Additional to the 1949 Geneva Conventions and Relating to the Protection of I. Victims of International Armed Conflict; II. The Protection of Victims of Non-International Armed Conflicts,* Geneva, June 8, 1977. The 1949 Conventions had not applied to civil wars at all. Protocol I defines conflict so as to include wars of self-determination and to protect guerrilla forces fighting them.

116. *Declaration on the Fundamental Principles Concerning the Contribution of the Mass Media to Strengthening Peace and International Understanding; to the Promotion of Human Rights; and to Countering Racialism, Apartheid, and Incitement to War* (Mass Media Declaration), UNESCO General Conference, Resolution 4/9.3/2, November 28, 1978, Article II, para. 4. See Nordenstreng, Gonzales Manet, and Kleinwächter, *New International Information,* p. 225; and Ploman, *International Law Governing Communications,* p. 172.

117. International Commission for the Study of Communication Problems, *Many Voices, One World* (Paris: UNESCO, 1980), p. 264.

118. Pierre Gaborit, "Project for the Establishment of an International Commission and a Periodical International Conference for the Protection of Journalists." Paper presented at the Consultative Meeting on the Protection of Journalists, February 16–17, 1981, Doc. CC-80/WS/53 (Paris: UNESCO, 1980). Page 1 contains an important note: "The point of view adopted in this document, the choice of facts presented in it and the opinions expressed with regard to the facts are the responsibility of the author and do not necessarily reflect the views of UNESCO."

119. William G. Harley to United States National Commission for UNESCO, April 15, 1981, p. 3.

120. *Principles Adopted by the Congress of the International Union of Press Associations,* Prague, 1936, in Nordenstreng, Gonzales Manet, and Kleinwächter, *New International Information,* p. 361.

121. *Draft Code of Ethics,* UN Economic and Social Council Resolution 442B (XIV), 1952, in Ploman, *International Law Governing Communications,* p. 181.

122. "Latin American Code of Journalist Ethics," Caracas, July 7, 1979, in Nordenstreng, Gonzales Manet, and Kleinwächter, *New International Information,* p. 362.

123. *The Declaration of Talloires of the "Voices of Freedom" Conference,* May 17, 1981, in Nordenstreng, Gonzales Manet, and Kleinwächter, *New International Information,* p. 368.

124. "International Principles of Professional Ethics in Journalism," Paris, November 20, 1983, in Nordenstreng, Gonzales Manet, and Kleinwächter, *New International Information,* p. 371. The associations, representing more than 400,000 working journalists, included: International Organization of Journalists (IOJ), International Federation of Journalists (FIJ), International Catholic Union of the Press (UCIP), Latin American Federation of Journalists (FELAP), Latin American Federation of Press Workers (FELATRAP), Federation of Arab Journalists (FAJ), Union of African Journalists (UJA), and Confederation of ASEAN Journalists (CAJ).

125. Merrill, "Governments and Press Control," pp. 223–262.

126. International Journalism Institute, *Professional Codes of Ethics in Journalism from CSCE Countries,* ed. Jiri Hosek and Zuzana Zrustova (Prague: International Journalism Institute, 1989).

127. World Conference on the UN Decade for Women, *Program of Action for Second Half of the UN Decade for Women: Equality, Development, and Peace,* Doc. A/CONF. 93/34 (New York: United Nations, 1980), cited in Margaret Gallagher, "Women and NWICO," in *Communication for All: New World Information and Communication Order,* ed. Philip Lee (Maryknoll, NY: Orbis, 1985), p. 34.

128. This section owes a debt of thanks to the pioneering work of Jane Cottingham of ISIS (Switzerland) and Margaret Gallagher of the City University (United Kingdom) for their important contribution, "Women in Communication," in UNESCO, *World Communication Report,* pp. 208–229; and to Colleen Roach, particularly for her section, "Women and the NWICO," in "The Movement for a New World Information and Communication Order: A Second Wave?" *Media, Culture & Society* 12 (3, July 1990): 298–301.

129. International Commission for the Study of Communication Problems, *Many Voices, One World,* p. 267.

130. UNESCO, *Women and Media Decision-Making: The Invisible Barriers* (Paris: UNESCO, 1987).

131. Cottingham and Gallagher, "Women in Communication," p. 210; International Commission for the Study of Communication Problems, *Many Voices, One World,* p. 190.

132. World Conference on the UN Decade for Women, *Technological Change and Women Workers: The Development of Microelectronics,* Doc. A/CONF. 94/26 (New York: United Nations, 1980), cited in Margaret Gallagher, "Women and NWICO," p. 41.

133. See Ramona R. Rush and Donna Allen, eds., *Communications at the Crossroads: The Gender Gap Connections* (Norwood, NJ: Ablex, 1989). See also the special issue on women in *Development Communication Report* (3, 1990).

134. Cottingham and Gallagher, "Women in Communication," p. 212.

135. Quoted in Cottingham and Gallagher, "Women in Communication," p. 209.

136. What kind of news is news on women's terms? See Irma Kaarina Halonen, "Women and the Public Sphere," *Nordicom Review* (1, 1991): 9–14.

137. International Conference on Women, Media, and Advertising, Manila. For further information, contact: WOMANWATCH, Women's Media Circle Foundation, Inc., 90 Maningning St., Teachers Village, Quezon City, Philippines. FAX: 921–0955; and Radio for Peace International, Debra Latham, General Manager, PO Box 88, Santa Ana, Costa Rica. FAX: 506–49-1929. Email: rfpicr@huracan.cr

138. Colleen Roach, "The Movement for a New World Information and Communication Order: A Second Wave?" *Media, Culture & Society* 12 (3, July 1990): 301.

6

Communication, Information, and "New World Orders"

In the last century the North Atlantic news agencies divided the world into spheres of influence. Roads, ocean routes, transoceanic cables, telegraph, and radio frequencies followed colonial routes. Even today, with satellites, television, fiber optics, and computer communications, much of the information continues to flow along the North Atlantic axis.

The difference is that after World War II national liberation movements in Asia, Africa, and Latin America transformed the way the world was organized at the political level. But the old structures of economic and information dependence still persisted.

That was challenged in 1973 when nations representing two-thirds of humanity, gathered for the fourth Non-Aligned Summit Conference in Algiers, proclaimed:

> Developing countries should take concerted action [toward the] reorganization of existing communication channels, which are a legacy of the colonial past and which have hampered free, direct and fast communication between them.[1]

This led to a decade of intense debate and controversy about the "New World Information and Communication Order."[2] The debate ended in bitterness and with the withdrawal of the United States from UNESCO. This debate is important not only as a context for today's global communications controversies, but also because it illustrates how the mercurial process works within international organizations.

PRELIMINARY CONCEPTS

That the debate had been politicized was apparent in its very name. The Non-Aligned Movement issued declarations calling for a "New *International* Information and Communication Order" (NIICO), but UNESCO and the UN primarily called it a "New *World* Information and Communication Order" (NWICO—pronounced "new-ee-ko"). To some, speaking of a "*world* order" implied an "interdependent world" that incorporated diverse, sovereign cultures and communities into one world, or a "global village." "*International* order" connoted a respect for relations between sovereign nations (as well as cultures and peoples).

From the beginning one of the "fathers" of the debate, Tunisian statesman Moustafa Masmoudi, has used "New *World* Information and Communication Order." This, he maintains, takes the debate away from governments and puts it in the spectrum of nongovernmental organizations. As *Media Culture & Society* editorialized:

> A new *international* order implies a struggle and a re-negotiation between different national states and thus ruling classes. In that framework the masses are at best a stage army. . . . A new *world* order, on the other hand, suggests at least the possibility that the founding principles might be based not only on the genuine needs but also on the self-activity of the masses themselves.[3] [Emphasis added]

The term "order" acquired still another connotation when U.S. President Bush proclaimed the "new world order." So the information-order debate is caught in the semantics of what constitutes a "new order," with all its attendant political baggage. For the sake of consistency, this author chooses to use the term the "MacBride Movement" (after Seán MacBride, the leader of the MacBride Commission; see the discussion later in this chapter) to describe proponents of the new information order.

HISTORICAL PRECEDENTS

Little in this debate was truly new because the debate itself was the outgrowth of the well-established process of decolonization.[4] Virtually all the debate's points had been made earlier—often decades earlier—in political, professional, and academic writings. The news-values controversy harks back at least to the early 1950s. Concern over underdevelopment of national communication and information infrastructures was apparent in 1960 at the beginning of the United Nations' First Development Decade. The controversy over direct-broadcast satellites arose in the United Nations soon after the launching of the first satellite.

The present-day Non-Aligned Movement had its intellectual beginnings in the 1927 Congress of Oppressed Nationalities held in Brussels. This extraordinary meeting was organized by the Association of Oppressed Peoples, also known as the "Anti-Imperialist League," in Moscow in 1924. Intellectuals such as W. E. B. Du Bois, Ho Chi Minh, Kwame Nkrumah, and Jawaharlal Nehru came together to discuss common problems, one of which was culture.

At the 1955 Asian–African Conference in Bandung, Indonesia, where the Non-Aligned Movement was launched, representatives condemned colonialism's devastating impact on culture:

> [The] existence of colonialism in many parts of Asia and Africa, in whatever form it may be, not only prevents cultural co-operation but also suppresses the national cultures of the peoples. . . . Some colonial powers have denied their dependent peoples basic rights in the sphere of education and culture. [These policies amount to a denial of the fundamental rights of man.][5]

The debate gained momentum in the 1970s with an enhanced political will to grapple with questions of information and communication. The debate arose not because of new information or ideas—the facts had long been known—but "because a sufficiently strong coalition of social forces had accumulated to enforce a new order."[6]

Ironically, the debate was new only because different countries were expressing an old sentiment. At the turn of the century, Americans complained of being misreported by the British press. For many years, British overseas cable networks dominated world information flows and held the Crown's far-flung colonial empire together—to the disadvantage of the United States. The United States complained that the European news services—British Reuters, French Havas, and German Wolff—"collectively and individually exercised a dictatorship over their weaker colleagues in the smaller countries."[7] Led by Kent Cooper, for more than twenty-five years General Manager of Associated Press, the refrain sounded similar to what some Third World countries were criticizing in the 1970s:

> International attitudes [about the United States] have developed from impressions and prejudices aroused by what the [European] news agencies reported. The mighty foreign propaganda carried out through these channels in the last 100 years has been one of the causes of wars. [Of America], these agencies told the world about Indians on the warpath in the West, lynching in the South, and bizarre crimes in the North. For decades, nothing credible to America was ever sent.[8]

Although the information-order debate totally transformed UNESCO and for years was the subject of bitter editorials in newspapers, most Americans have never heard of it.[9] The National News Council, an independent monitoring agency supported by U.S. media, asserted that American news coverage "provided an inadequate foundation for independent judgment by Americans of the correctness of the editorial positions their newspapers were taking on the UNESCO communications issue."[10] A University of Washington study found that "Americans who had no source of information other than their local media were not, for the most part, exposed to sufficient factual material or opposing viewpoints to make informed judgments."[11] Worse, more than a fifth of the editors of small and mid-size American newspapers surveyed admitted a total lack of knowledge about the issue.[12]

One of the primary figures in the debate, Nobel and Lenin Peace Prize laureate Seán MacBride, once commented: "What created this distortion was not editorialization in the writing but the selective process in which news reports were used."[13] This selective process led Giffard to assert: "One of the complaints from proponents of a New International Information Order is that issues of importance to them are treated unsympathetically in the Western media. [My analysis of Western press coverage of the debate is] a case study of the validity of their criticisms."[14]

THE GATHERING OF FORCES

As early as 1952, the United Nations General Assembly expressed its concern as follows:

> It is essential for a proper development of public opinion in underdeveloped countries that independent domestic information enterprises should be given facilities and assistance in order that they may be enabled to contribute to the spread of information, to the development of national culture and to international

understanding . . . the time has arrived for the elaboration of a concrete programme and plan of action in this respect."[15]

From its beginnings UNESCO focused on the development of communication
infrastructures in member states. By 1960 the Economic and Social Council
(ECOSOC) had asked UNESCO to survey press, radio, film, and television development worldwide. The resulting reports "raised questions of control of information by
world news agencies, news distorted to respond to interests of Western clients, and
lack of news flows between Asian countries."[16] UNESCO gathered sufficient data to
report that most of the earth's population did not have adequate access to information. As a result of UNESCO's work, the United Nations General Assembly could say
in 1962: "Seventy percent of the population of the world lack adequate information
facilities and are thus denied effective enjoyment of the right to information."[17]

The first articulation of the need for a new information order came in Montreal,
Canada. In 1969 a UNESCO meeting of experts on mass communication and society
for the first time used the expression "new world information and communication
order." The report of the meeting said that disparities between nations of the developed and developing world made free circulation of news and information a one-way
flow rather than a real exchange. The report stressed the need to safeguard the
cultural integrity of developing countries from the destructive onslaught of programs
carrying alien values.[18]

THE ROLE OF THE NON-ALIGNED MOVEMENT

The Non-Aligned Movement (NAM) today consists of nations and liberation movements in Asia, Africa, and Latin America and represents two-thirds of humanity. Its
twin goals of decolonization and democratization have suffused the "MacBride
Movement" from the very beginning.[19]

The period between NAM's 1973 Summit Meeting in Algiers and its 1976 Summit Meeting in Colombo is crucial for understanding the development of the information-order debate. This was the period in which the Non-Aligned Movement
developed the concept of the New International Economic Order (NIEO). Indeed, the
demands for a New World Information and Communication Order must be seen as
an outgrowth of the values inherent in the NIEO debate.[20] The rationale was that the
old economic order was too capital- and technology-intensive and was based on
disharmony with the environment and little respect for basic human needs.

The *new* economic order was to be dramatically different. Its values were to be
equity, interdependence, orientation toward people rather than toward capital and
technology, harmony with the environment, respect for human rights, and satisfaction of basic human needs. Arising from the Non-Aligned Movement, the NIEO issue
was debated in the United Nations, which in 1974 passed the *Declaration on the
Establishment of a New International Economic Order*.[21] NIEO did not directly challenge capitalism. Rather, it demanded better terms of trade with the industrialized
nations and more local control over productive assets such as capital, labor, and
technology. It also called for greater trade among Third World nations, greater investment by the rich countries, and greater Third World control over world economic
institutions.

Within this context arose the debate over the new information order. One order was insufficient without the other, many delegates argued. Communication was an antecedent and engine to economic activity. Information was a *sine qua non* for producing, exchanging, and consuming any other economic good. It was a "merit good" (like education and health care), one whose availability is so highly valued that its provision to all should not be left to market forces. The new information order would alter the "communication terms of trade" by increasing two-way flow of information; promoting Third World control over its own communication assets; transmitting more news about other Third World countries throughout the world; facilitating more Third World control over First World production; and giving the Third World more control over world communication institutions.[22]

At its 1973 Algiers summit the Non-Aligned Movement had called for the "reorganization of existing communication channels, which are a legacy of the colonial past and which have hampered free, direct and fast communication between [developing countries]."[23] It also stated that "the activities of imperialism are not confined solely to the economic or political fields but also cover cultural and social fields, thus imposing an alien ideological domination over the peoples of the developing world."[24]

During this period numerous meetings were held to develop the "new information order" concept. In March 1976 the Non-Aligned Movement held its pivotal Tunis Symposium on Information. Its final report summarized the Non-Aligned Movement's thinking:

> [N]on-aligned countries are at the moment suffering from the domination of their mass communication media by the developed countries which have the monopoly over most of the world's communication media, through which much of the news is transmitted and the activities of the non-aligned countries made public. The information media thus monopolised tend to distort news from the non-aligned countries, either by falsifying it or by remaining totally silent in the many cases of success achieved in the different fields by peoples of the non-aligned countries.
>
> Domination in information has many subtle and varied forms, in the manipulation and control of the biggest part of information by the powerful transnationals such as the big International Press Agencies, and in the technological control of the information media at the hands of the most powerful nations.
>
> Since information in the world shows a disequilibrium favoring some and ignoring others, it is the duty of the non-aligned countries and other developing countries to change this situation and obtain the decolonization of information and initiate a new international order of information.[25]

Leading up to the Colombo summit, at the Conference of Ministerial Level Government Representatives and Heads of News Agencies of Non-Aligned Countries in New Delhi, representatives of fifty-nine countries met to consider the persistent and serious imbalance in the global information situation. The New Delhi Declaration on Decolonization of Information "reaffirmed the determination of the non-aligned countries not to continue to suffer individually or collectively because of the present inequitable global situation." It stressed that "the decolonization of information is essential for these purposes and that the establishment of a New International Order for Information is as necessary as the New International Economic Order."[26]

Not content simply with critique, the Non-Aligned Movement also launched two concrete efforts aimed at redressing the imbalances in the world's information flows. In 1975 the Yugoslav news agency TANJUG initiated the Non-Aligned News

Agencies Pool (NANAP) to provide news and information not usually found in Western wire services. In 1977 NAM organized the Broadcasting Organizations of the Non-Aligned Countries (BONAC) to ensure dissemination of broadcast information in and from non-aligned countries.

The 1976 Non-Aligned Summit Meeting in Colombo stated unequivocally for the first time that "a new international order in the fields of information and mass communication is as vital as a new international economic order."[27] This was the threshold for the "Great Information Debate's" emergence onto the world stage. The Colombo meeting gave Tunisia the mandate to raise the issue at the upcoming UNESCO General Conference in Nairobi.[28]

GROWING CONTROVERSY IN UNESCO

By this time there were three different schools of thought in UNESCO. UNESCO'S longtime focus on the *free flow of information* had been promoted by the victorious Allies of World War II. Later, when the Soviet Union joined in 1954, UNESCO also became concerned with the *content* of information, especially with putting it at the service of peace and world understanding. When Third World countries entered UNESCO (three-fourths of the membership by 1980), questions of free flow and content encountered equivalent concerns for the *development of the mass media.*

The crucial decade opened at the 1970 General Conference, which debated UNESCO's contributions to peace and to eliminating colonialism. Delegates called on the Director-General to carry out research on how mass media might assist in these goals. Throughout the early 1970s UNESCO's work complemented that of the Non-Aligned Movement, with numerous meetings and consultations, culminating in the 1976 Conference on Communication Policies in Latin America and the Caribbean, held in San José, Costa Rica. In a burning atmosphere of controversy, the "San José Declaration" "recognize[d] that a more balanced international circulation of information and communication is a just and necessary demand." It recommended that Latin American states "define and implement policies, plans and laws that will make possible the advent of more balanced communication relations at both the national and international levels."[29] The San José conference advocated a balanced flow of information, recommended the creation of national and regional news agencies, and proposed the establishment of national communication planning councils.

By this time declarations were flowing in from all directions. At the 1976 UNESCO General Conference in Nairobi, discussion on a definitive "Mass Media Declaration" resulted in an acrimonious and divisive debate. A vote on the Mass Media Declaration was postponed until 1978, and the Director-General was invited to create a commission to review the status of global communication and information. This commission was chaired by Seán MacBride and was named after him.

These two watershed events—the Mass Media Declaration and the MacBride Commission—must be seen in the context of one other actor, the United Nations General Assembly itself.

ACTIVITIES OF THE UNITED NATIONS GENERAL ASSEMBLY

The first General Assembly in London in 1946 recommended that ECOSOC establish a Commission on Human Rights (CHR), which was to address the information and communication issue.[30] CHR at its first session set up a Sub-Commission on Freedom of Information and the Press, which ultimately produced Article 19 of the Universal Declaration of Human Rights.

During this early period there was still a remarkable consensus in the General Assembly, dominated by the United States, France, Britain, and the Soviet Union. The Assembly passed three important communication and information resolutions. Resolution 59(I) called freedom of information a "fundamental human right." Resolution 110(II) condemned "all forms of propaganda . . . designed or likely to provoke or encourage any threat to the peace, breach of the peace or act of aggression." Resolution 127(II) called it "essential to facilitate and increase the diffusion in all countries of information calculated to strengthen mutual understanding [and] to combat . . . the publication of false or distorted reports."'[31]

Within this spirit of consensus, the United Nations made a valiant but mostly unsuccessful attempt to reach binding accord on international norms of freedom of expression. ECOSOC sponsored the 1948 *Conference on Freedom of Information* in Geneva, in which fifty-seven states took part.[32] Recalling that freedom of expression and information was gravely violated during World War II, the Conference's mission was to study

> measures for counteracting the persistent spreading of demonstrably false or tendentious reports which confuse peoples of the world, aggravate relations between nations, or otherwise interfere with the growth of international understanding, peace and security against a recurrence of Nazi, Fascist or Japanese aggression.[33]

The Conference on Freedom of Information labored mightily and drafted many important declarations and conventions. The whole package of three draft conventions, forty-two resolutions, and the draft articles for the Human Rights Declaration was sent to the General Assembly.[34] But by then the Cold War was intensifying, and the consensus among the victors was breaking down. In the end, they agreed only on the language for the Universal Declaration on Human Rights, which was not a binding document. Despite the Conference's failure, the discussion of the draft conventions went on for years in the Economic and Social Council and the General Assembly.[35]

Only one convention eventually became binding international law. In 1952 nine states (by 1988, twelve) agreed to the *Convention on the International Right of Correction,* which requires news correspondents and agencies

> [t]o report facts without discrimination and in their proper context and thereby to promote respect for human rights and fundamental freedoms, to further international understanding and cooperation and to contribute to the maintenance of international peace and security . . . .
>
> In cases where a Contracting State contends that a news dispatch capable of injuring its relations with other States or its national prestige or dignity . . . is false or distorted, it may submit its version of the facts . . . to correct the news dispatch in question.[36]

All told, from 1945 to 1980, more than forty-four instruments of international law contributed to the information debate. Twenty-seven dealt with peace and freedom; eighteen with war propaganda; thirty-one with understanding among peoples; eigh-

teen with news objectivity; sixteen with racial equality; nineteen with other obligations; and twenty-five with the free flow of information.[37]

THE THRESHOLD EVENT: THE MASS MEDIA DECLARATION

The threshold event—one that contributed to U.S. withdrawal from UNESCO—was
the 1978 *Mass Media Declaration.* The Declaration's history goes back to 1970,
when Byelorussia submitted a draft resolution to forbid "using information media for
propaganda on behalf of war, racialism and hatred among nations."[38] This raised the
hackles of those delegations concerned that UNESCO not enact content regulations
that governments would have to enforce. Instead, a two-part compromise turned the
original *proscriptive* formulation into a *prescriptive* norm ("encourag[ing] the use of
information media against propaganda on behalf of war, racialism and hated among
nations . . . ") and asked the Director-General to prepare a report collecting information about possible laws and appropriate measures to implement this principle.[39]

The Secretary General presented this report to the 1972 General Conference,
during which Byelorussia brought the issue to a head by presenting a "Draft Declaration on Fundamental Principles Concerning the Contribution of the Mass Media to
Strengthening Peace and International Understanding, to the Promotion of Human
Rights and to Countering Racialism, Apartheid and Incitement to War," also known
as the "Mass Media Declaration." The first draft contained language that would have
required the mass media to serve the cause of peace and international understanding. To many delegates this represented a direct threat to press freedom, so the
General Conference directed the Director-General to rework the draft.

A meeting of experts took place in Paris in December 1975 to work out a final
draft to submit to the UNESCO General Conference in 1976. Yugoslavia proposed
that the preamble to the Mass Media Declaration refer to the UN General Assembly
resolution equating Zionism with racism. The United States and twelve other delegations left the building in protest. The remaining delegations continued their work and
submitted a draft declaration to the Nairobi General Conference in 1976. One article
contained a formulation obliging states to be responsible for mass media under their
jurisdiction. At this point U.S. Secretary of State Henry Kissinger threatened that if
UNESCO adopted this declaration, the United States would be compelled to
withdraw.

Kissinger's threat reflected deep concern about the Non-Aligned Movement's
call in Colombo that "a new international order in the fields of information and mass
communications is as vital as a new international economic order." This declaration
had been carried to Nairobi by an increasingly powerful bloc of non-aligned countries,
with the support of the socialist countries. The new Director-General, Amadou-
Mahtar M'Bow of Senegal, was eager to have the first General Conference to take
place on African soil end harmoniously, so the confrontation ended with a compromise. A resolution was passed calling on UNESCO to create a study commission (the
MacBride Commission), and the vote on the Mass Media Declaration was postponed
until 1978.

Compromise was in the air. By 1978 in Paris, Western countries had succeeded
in removing language they found offensive. There no longer were any references to
state control of the media. While the declaration did call for a "free flow and a wider

and more balanced flow of information," no concrete measures were proposed to implement this. The final text insisted that "journalists must have freedom to report and the fullest possible facilities of access to information." Instead of calling for an international code of ethics (a red flag for the Western press), the final version merely called on professional organizations and media professionals to "attach special importance" to the declaration's principles when drawing up codes of ethics.

Throughout the debates on the Mass Media Declaration, there were two opposing camps. Many Western delegates believed the mass media should be independent of state control and should ensure that *each individual citizen* received the information needed in a democracy. These delegates' counterparts in developing and socialist countries held that the mass media should serve the interests of the state and guarantee the *people as a whole* that the media remain free of particular interests and serve the interests of peace and national development.

At the twentieth General Conference in Nairobi in 1978, the declaration was passed unanimously, setting forth fundamental norms for the mass media. The declaration addressed protection of journalists, freedom of information, access and democracy, racism and colonialism, professional training, and dozens of other important components of the then-developing New World Information and Communication Order. Characteristic of the declaration is this passage:

> With a view to strengthening peace and international understanding, to promoting human rights and to countering racism, apartheid and incitement to war, the mass media throughout the world, by reason of their role, contribute to promoting human rights, in particular by giving expression to oppressed peoples who struggle against colonialism, neo-colonialism, foreign occupation and all forms of racial discrimination and oppression and who are unable to make their voices heard within their own territories.[40]

What has been the impact of the Mass Media Declaration? Among media professionals, there is a low level of awareness about the declaration's institutional history and the unanimity of support among UNESCO member states who adopted it consensually. Some fora have debated components of the declaration, especially the questions of freedom of opinion, access by the public to information, the media's role in international relations, peace and human rights, and the free and balanced dissemination of information. However, the declaration has not received great attention in the academic research community.[41]

POST–MASS MEDIA DECLARATION

Within less than five years—from 1973 in Algiers to 1978 in Paris—the Non-Aligned Movement had achieved many of its political aims. The "new information order" was on the agenda of UNESCO. Basic norms and principles of the role and performance of the mass media had been adopted. Political decisions had been made; the basis for action had been laid. But the will to implement was very weak.

Until 1978 most actions were taken consensually; even the United States voted in favor of the Mass Media Declaration. But that consensus was fragile and began to unravel, particularly as the Western press and media lobbies became more active. As long as all the decisions remained mere recommendations, not much practical action could be expected. So various organizations began to look more toward concrete efforts to implement these principles.

The Non-Aligned Movement set the pace. The Intergovernmental Council for Cooperation of Information among Non-Aligned Countries, held in 1979 in Lomé, Togo, re-articulated the movement's fundamental principles:

- The independence, sovereignty, and territorial integrity of all countries and the principle of noninterference in internal affairs of others;
- The right of each country to develop its information system as well as its economic and social systems and to combat the monopolizing of information;
- The right of each country to use its information media in order to make known its interests, aspirations, and its political, moral and cultural values;
- The right of each nation to be informed in a rapid, objective and complete manner;
- The exchange of information among all countries under conditions of equality;
- The responsibility of different subjects in the process of information [that is, journalists] for its authenticity, objectivity and background;
- The right of each state to combat, within constitutional limits, the dissemination of false or distorted news which can be to the prejudice of its interests or harmful to good relations between states;
- The search for substantive information conducive to international cooperation on the basis of equality, understanding among peoples, peace, security, progress and democratic relations among countries and peoples;
- Guarantees for and the necessary protection of journalists and other factors of information in the performance of their mission, and the responsibility of journalists in the performance of this mission;
- The imperative of a more equitable distribution of information media;
- Development of cooperation in all sectors of information on an equal footing and at all levels.[42]

A flurry of activity followed. The 1979 Non-Aligned Summit in Havana "took note with gratification of the fact that non-aligned and other developing countries have made notable progress along the path of emancipation and development of national information media."[43] Non-aligned countries agreed "to promote the horizontal flow of authentic information" in the 1979 Statute of the News Agencies Pool.[44] The 1980 "Baghdad Resolution" stated that a new information order should be based on international law, national sovereignty, and cultural identity, in particular, by regulating the transnational corporations."[45] The 1983 New Delhi Summit Conference Political Declaration proclaimed the "need to establish a new equilibrium and greater reciprocity in the flow of information to and from developing countries and also between these countries by strengthening and expanding the mass media and information infrastructures in developing countries."[46] The "Jakarta Declaration" stressed that "the right to communicate is a fundamental human right and that information is a vital resource."[47] Numerous other declarations up to the present continue to promote the "five Ds:" decolonization, development, democratization, demonopolization, and disarmament.[48]

The United Nations General Assembly continued to support the concept of a new information order. It routinely approved resolutions submitted by its Committee on Information. Its 1978 Resolution 33/115 "affirm[ed] the need to establish a new, more just and more effective world information and communication order, intended to strengthen international peace and understanding and based on the free circulation and wider and better-balanced dissemination of information."[49] Its 1980 Resolution 35/201 expressed the General Assembly's satisfaction with UNESCO. A 1983 resolution was "conscious of the need for all countries, the United Nations system as a whole and all others concerned to collaborate in the establishment of a new world information and communication order."[50]

THE WORK OF THE MACBRIDE COMMISSION

Back to 1976 in UNESCO: Realizing that many questions regarding global communication and information were inadequately answered, the 1976 General Conference established an *International Commission for the Study of Communication Problems,* chaired by Seán MacBride.[51] The commission's report, *Many Voices, One World,* was presented at the 1980 General Conference.[52] The MacBride Commission strongly advocated the establishment of a New World Information and Communication Order and especially focused on the democratization of communication.

The MacBride Commission's work must be seen in the context of debate on the Mass Media Declaration. By the time of the 1976 General Conference in Nairobi, polarization over the declaration was severe. Member states failed to reach a consensus on a draft declaration. Western governments and independent news media mounted a strong campaign that won a two-year delay in voting on it. To save face for supporters of the declaration, Western opponents agreed to a compromise that created the MacBride Commission. The commission's goals were to study the problems of communications in a global context, to make recommendations for practical action, to examine problems surrounding a free and balanced flow of information, and to study how a new information order might be established and how media might become vehicles for enhancing public opinion about world problems.

From December 1977 to November 1979 the commission continued its work. In addition to MacBride, its membership included fifteen distinguished communication scholars and practitioners from around the world.[53] Some critics expressed surprise that there was no representative from Great Britain, but the composition of the commission signified a shift of power toward the Third World and Great Britain's shrinking influence in UNESCO. The West generally regarded the commission as another document-writing exercise, with the final controversy and decision to accept or reject the recommendations to be left up to the UNESCO General Conference in 1980.

The MacBride Commission contracted one hundred individual studies and background papers that greatly elevated the debate.[54] The final report cannot claim to be a scientific analysis, but it did present a series of condition reports which led to the eighty-two recommendations. The commission vehemently condemned censorship. The right of access, the MacBride Report said, was applicable to all sectors of information, public and private. Journalists did not need special protection, but their rights were secured as all rights of citizens are guaranteed. The commission rejected the licensing of journalists, contending that this would require a higher body or authority to establish standards. Finally, the commission condemned the use of journalists for gathering national security intelligence.

The commission's conclusions and recommendations were consistent with earlier UNESCO resolutions and activities. The MacBride Report made a strong case for treating communications as a vital social resource and for incorporating it into overall development policymaking and planning. National planning, the report said, should pay more attention to formulating communication policies and allocating scarce resources. In one controversial statement, the commission called for reducing commercialism in communications and emphasized the media's role in aiding oppressed peoples to gain greater freedom, independence, access to information, and right to expression. The commission also envisioned an expanded role for UNESCO in implementing these recommendations. To pay for these projects, the report discussed such revenue possibilities as taxing surplus profits on raw materials, an international duty on the use of the radio spectrum and the geostationary orbit, and an international tax on the profits of transnational communication enterprises. Critics attacked the MacBride Report for being too descriptive (radical advocates) or too prescriptive (Western opponents). Partly due to the diverse backgrounds of the commission, the document was eclectic. The disparities lent themselves to both approval and criticism from all perspectives.

Aside from the MacBride Commission, perhaps the most significant long-term project of UNESCO was the founding of the *International Programme for the Development of Communication (IPDC)*. Recognizing that the minimum communication and information goals set by the First Development Decade had not been reached even by the end of the 1970s, UNESCO began to strengthen its practical efforts to help developing countries build effective national communication systems. The 1980 General Conference meeting in Belgrade established IPDC with a 35-nation council.

When the MacBride Report was presented in Belgrade in 1980, UNESCO's General Conference passed a resolution "On the International Commission for the Study of Communication Problems" that summed up the "state of the art" to that point:

This new world information and communication order could be based, among other considerations, on:

1. elimination of the imbalances and inequalities which characterize the present situation;
2. elimination of the negative effects of certain monopolies, public or private and excessive concentration;
3. removal of the internal and external obstacles to a free flow and wider and better balanced dissemination of information and ideas;
4. plurality of sources and channels of information;
5. freedom of the press and information;
6. the freedom of journalists and all professionals in the communication media, a freedom inseparable from responsibility;
7. the capacity of developing countries to achieve improvement of their own situations, notably by providing their own equipment, by training their personnel, by improving their infrastructures and by making their information and communication media suitable to their needs and aspirations;

8. the sincere will of developed countries to help them attain these objectives;
9. respect for each people's cultural identity and for the right of each nation to inform the world public about its interests, its aspirations and its social and cultural values;
10. respect for the right of all peoples to participate in international exchanges of information on the basis of equality, justice and mutual benefit;
11. respect for the right of the public, of ethnic and social groups and of individuals to have access to information sources and to participate actively in the communication process.

This new world information and communication order should be based on the fundamental principles of international law, as laid down in the Charter of the United Nations.

Diverse solutions to information and communication problems are required because social, political, cultural and economic problems differ from one country to another, and, within a given country, from one group to another.[55]

The last General Conference in which the United States participated took place in 1982 in Paris. This meeting was characterized by efforts toward consensus, but no concrete decision was made to implement the new information order; the framework remained empty. For the first time, a compromise formula appeared that seemed to satisfy Western delegates:

[The General Conference] invites the Director–General to continue to study and make known the most effective means of remedying the imbalance affecting regional and interregional exchanges of information with a view to strengthening the bases upon which a new world information and communication order—*seen as an evolving and continuous process*—conductive to a free flow and wider and better balanced dissemination of information might be established.[56] [Emphasis added]

The significant new words were "evolving and continuous process." This formulation was meant to reassure the Western countries that a New Order was not a set of measures that could be adopted by UNESCO through a majority vote of socialist and developing countries.

CONSENSUS BEGINS TO UNRAVEL

In the early 1980s efforts to maintain the equilibrium at UNESCO began to falter. The resulting events greatly upset UNESCO; indeed, they disturbed all those working for internationalism. The story begins with the role of the Western press lobbies and the United States press.

Debates in UNESCO take place as much among national interest groups as they do among governments. Governments represent the particular viewpoints and perspectives of persuasive constituents. Nongovernmental and private interest groups often formulate policy ideas that are passed to governmental channels and receive official approval. Sometimes this is formalized, such as in the many national

UNESCO commissions. In other cases, it is the result of lobbying efforts by certain sectors in alliance with the government. These nongovernmental and private organizations had a great impact on the course of the debate.

In the late 1970s Western press and publishing interests formed influential lobbying groups opposed to the new information order on the premise that it would lead to government control.[57] The World Press Freedom Committee emerged prior to the 1976 Nairobi General Conference to unify the defenders of the free press. As a watchdog for the "free world" media, WPFC's first goal was to derail or alter the Mass Media Declaration. WPFC objected particularly to the article stating that "States are responsible for the activities in the international sphere of all mass media under their jurisdiction." Through WPFC's efforts, this provision was eventually deleted.

The Inter-American Press Association (IAPA), made up of the major owners of the commercial press in the Western Hemisphere, convened its own meeting at the same time as the 1976 UNESCO-sponsored Conference on Communication Policies in Latin America and the Caribbean in San José, Costa Rica. IAPA attacked the experts and their recommendations and organized an international campaign to boycott the conference. In the months before the San José Conference, more than seven hundred articles opposing the meeting were published by dailies in Latin America that were affiliated with IAPA.[58] The campaign had some success: The site was changed several times, and the meeting was postponed.

The most significant opposition meeting was the 1981 "Voices of Freedom" Conference in Talloires, France. Held during U.S. Congressional hearings on U.S. withdrawal from UNESCO, and possibly held in an attempt to sway their course, the World Press Freedom Committee, with the Fletcher School of Law and Diplomacy at Tufts University, arranged a conference that allowed the Western media and press interests to vent their anger against the developments in UNESCO. More than sixty representatives of "Western and other free newspapers, magazines and broadcasters" and lobbying interests attended. The resulting *Talloires Declaration* "took a unified stand against the campaign by the Soviet bloc and some Third World countries to give UNESCO the authority to chart the media's future course." The declaration put into concrete form the serious concerns of the opponents:

> We believe that the free flow of information and ideas is essential for mutual understanding and world peace. We consider restraints on the movement of news and information to be contrary to the interests of international understanding, in violation of the Universal Declaration of Human Rights, the Constitution of UNESCO, and the Final Act of the Conference on Security and Cooperation in Europe, and inconsistent with the Charter of the United Nations.
>
> We support the universal human right to be fully informed, which right requires the free circulation of news and opinions. We vigorously oppose any interference with this fundamental right.
>
> . . . We believe the debate on news and information in modern society that has taken place in UNESCO and other international bodies should now be put to constructive purposes. . . . We pledge cooperation in all genuine efforts to expand the free flow of information worldwide. We believe that time has come within UNESCO and other intergovernmental bodies to abandon attempts at regulating news content and formulating rules for the press.[59]

The bottom line was that Western free-press advocates had lost their patience.

The price being paid for consensus on the information-order debate was too high. "The debate itself was harmful to fundamental principles of freedom of the press and freedom of speech."[60] President Reagan welcomed the Talloires Declaration. With his endorsement, this declaration became the centerpiece for the counterstrategy.

Opponents enjoyed the near-unanimous support of the opinion molders on the editorial pages and in the boardrooms of the large newspapers. *Newsweek* magazine represented the debate to its readers as attempts by Third World nations "to replace Western coverage of their affairs with a collective, government-managed conduit of information."[61] The *New York Times* pulled no punches: "American journalism values its freedom from official scrutiny and control more than it values UNESCO, or even the United Nations."[62] The *Times* opened the policy road for eventual U.S. departure from UNESCO: "A United States withdrawal would not harm any democratic cause of global understanding."[63] As one "high-level" U.S. official told a *Times* columnist: "When that editorial appeared, we had a free pass. Nobody in the Reagan Administration wanted The Times to get to the right of us."[64]

They also benefited from the increasing consternation of the U.S. government. In 1976 the Carter administration had hoped to forestall a collapse of the U.S. position by adopting a "flexible strategy" to assist the Third World in its communication development if these countries refused attempts to politicize the debate. This was the era when the United States Information Agency (USIA) changed its name to the International Communication Agency (ICA) to show that the new administration was ready not merely to provide information, but to communicate with the peoples of the world. A U.S. Senate study at the time said "that the [United States] need not be a loser [in the information debate] if appropriate actions are taken."[65]

In 1978 Carter sent ICA Director John Reinhardt to the UNESCO General Conference prepared to bargain. The United States would provide millions of dollars in technical assistance and new communications technology if the debate could be depoliticized.[66] To show its willingness to compromise, the United States even voted *for* the Mass Media Declaration, which by then had eliminated references to the duties of states in implementing the declaration. The wording of a "free flow and wider and more balanced dissemination of information" had attracted adherents even among the United States and its allies.

This two-pronged initiative seemed to work. A meeting of experts was convened in Washington to prepare for a UNESCO conference on development aid in the area of information. The Carter administration proposed what it hoped would be a *coup de grace* to the new information-order debate: a proposal that UNESCO, the World Bank, and the United Nations Development Programme set up a so-called "clearinghouse" to promote communication development. This led eventually to the *International Program for the Development of Communication (IPDC),* albeit without the participation of the World Bank and multinational corporations and with a democratic council of member states.

Despite this accommodation, hard-liners were preparing other strategies in advance of the expected victory of Ronald Reagan. In fact, the decision to withdraw from UNESCO and to obstruct the NWICO may have been made not in the government at all but in the Heritage Foundation, which claimed that the pullout was a "direct result" of its efforts.[67] The Foundation saw UNESCO as a thoroughly politicized institution dedicated to attacking fundamental Western values, interests, and institutions. UNESCO had attacked and sought to circumscribe the free Western press. It had characterized Western culture as an "imperialist" threat to the identity of other peoples, attacked the free-market economy and multinational corporations, and sought to downgrade individual human rights in favor of nebulous and proliferating "rights of peoples."[68]

When the Reagan administration came to power, it was clear that Carter's flexible policy had not stopped the perceived tilt against U.S. interests. Even the U.S. delegate to the MacBride Commission, Elie Abel, could not separate himself from this consensus.[69] Reflecting on this more than a decade later, the State Department asserted: "The more harmful elements—a balanced flow, the contribution and role of the media, a right of reply for those who feel unfairly treated by the media—were seen by the Carter Administration as a necessary price to pay for the reaffirmation of fundamental freedoms."[70]

In the eyes of the Heritage Foundation and the Reagan administration, the United States had acquiesced to avoid a worse outcome. The one positive outcome, the IPDC, did not satisfy the United States. Everyone agreed on the necessity of technical assistance; what irritated the United States was that the private sector was limited in its influence and participation in the program. But the U.S. had invested so much effort into the concept that it could not withhold its support.

Ronald Reagan came into office just eight weeks after the UNESCO General Conference in Belgrade. Reagan's foreign policy, designed to recapture lost American power, focused first on stationing medium-range nuclear missiles in Western Europe, then sent an invasionary force into Grenada. Reagan's policy began to attack the United Nations system itself. One former U.S. government official put it this way: "They found the smallest, weakest international organization to attack. UNESCO is the Grenada of the U.N."[71]

Just two days after the Talloires meeting, the House of Representatives passed a resolution "[e]xpressing the sense of the House of Representatives that [UNESCO] should cease efforts to attempt to regulate the flow of news and information around the world."[72] Assistant Secretary of State for International Organization Affairs, Elliott Abrams, alluded to the inevitable:

> The mistrust of UNESCO has gone very far. . . . Important constituencies within the U.S. are calling for the reduction of U.S. participation or outright withdrawal. . . . This is a war UNESCO cannot win, for we in the Administration will never accept defeat or even compromise. I would say it is not the future of press freedom which is at stake, but the future of UNESCO.[73]

In March 1981 the House of Representatives Committee on Foreign Affairs began its "Review of U.S. Participation in UNESCO." While boasting that the Mac-Bride Report had for the time been "neutralized," the State Department's Sarah Powers nevertheless added forebodingly:

> There is no way to reconcile the U.S. first amendment values with those of totalitarian societies. On this point we will not compromise. . . . We cannot ignore the challenge of our interests in the information and communication field.[74]

Thus began the unraveling of U.S. participation in UNESCO. Materials appeared claiming that a Soviet threat hung over the future operations of UNESCO and that the IPDC endangered press freedom.[75] The Tunisian Information Minister and Mac-Bride Commission member Moustafa Masmoudi was accused of being a communist because he had written that information should be viewed as a social good, not as a commodity.[76] Seán MacBride himself was portrayed as a close ally of Moscow. UNESCO Director-General M'Bow was depicted as a former radical leader of the Black African student movement in France.[77]

Actually things did not go badly for the United States at the 1982 UNESCO General Conference in Paris. The conference avoided bitter ideological clashes over press freedom. It approved unanimously a communication research program to study the "watchdog" role of the press, to examine governmental censorship, and to treat the movement toward a new information order as an "evolving process" rather than as a series of regulations.[78] The "right to communicate" no longer appeared in the program. Even longtime foes were pleased. Leonard Sussman of Freedom House saw this program as "a gain for free-press supporters."[79] Dana Bullen of the World Press Freedom Committee stated: "If anyone is looking for an assault on the media at this conference serious enough to justify United States withdrawal, they won't find it."[80]

But the Heritage Foundation stepped up its pressure. It said the 1982 General Conference had changed nothing. America's problems lay not in the rules of the game, but in the very nature of the game itself.[81] This fed the flame already burning in the State Department's Office for International Organization Affairs, whose director, Gregory J. Newell, was the major agitator in the Reagan administration for U.S. withdrawal. Newell informed Secretary of State George Schulz that the $50 million annual cost of supporting UNESCO was not yielding corresponding benefits. He recommended withdrawal to Reagan and Schulz.

In December 1983 the United States announced its intent to withdraw from UNESCO at the end of 1984.[82] The reasons given included the following:

> [UNESCO] has taken on an anti-Western tone and become unwilling to defend the ideals of free thought and free expression upon which it was founded.
>
> It has become a comfortable home for statist, collectivist solutions to world problems and for ideological polemics.
>
> It has generally been unresponsive to U.S. efforts over recent years to change this orientation.
>
> It rejects sound management principles in favor of self-serving and self-promoting procedures.
>
> It continues to press for a so-called New World Information and Communications Order, which embodies elements threatening to a free press and a free market. In particular, it is a way for governments to define "responsible" reporting and control what is written about their nations and in their nations.[83]

Throughout 1984 there was a heated debate over whether to follow through with the threat. Scientists warned of the losses to U.S. science efforts after the planned withdrawal. The U.S. Commission for UNESCO voted overwhelmingly for continued U.S. membership, but Newell told the commission that the Reagan administration was concerned that UNESCO "had gone so far adrift that it can't be brought back to the course."[84] Members of the commission charged that the Reagan administration had used "misleading tactics" and spread "distorted information" to support its decision to withdraw. Leonard Sussman went so far as to say: " . . . the relevant evidence [has been] buried and ideological dogma substituted for honest debate."[83] Toward the end of 1984 Sussman stated that there had been a "significant shift" in UNESCO away from the issue of licensing journalists.[86] On December 31, 1984, U.S. membership ceased. Great Britain announced its intent to withdraw in one year.

POST–U.S. WITHDRAWAL TO TODAY

What has been the impact of U.S. withdrawal? For almost forty years the United States had benefited greatly from membership in UNESCO. After all, only a small portion of UNESCO's budget was spent on communication.[87] The Navy depended on UNESCO oceanographic science. Many governmental departments participated in the Man in the Biosphere project. All Americans benefited from UNESCO's work on copyright enforcement. There were numerous "positive aspects of the organization's activities that could have been, but usually were not, included in the U.S. press coverage of the withdrawal."[88] Freedom House's Leonard Sussman, a thoughtful opponent of NWICO, has said:

> In all the years of acrimonious debates at UNESCO, I believe, there was never a resolution or an official action that assaulted a basic American interest. Indeed, the greatest loss to American interests and credibility were incurred by the policy of withdrawal and by the withdrawal itself."[89]

One of the main reasons the United States gave for leaving UNESCO was "extraneous politicization." UNESCO is composed of more than 160 governments with diverse policies and viewpoints; therefore, calling it politicized is stating the obvious. Another reason for this precipitous action was the perceived threats to freedom. Despite press reports, UNESCO never called for licensing journalists, government control of the press, controlling the distribution of news, limiting individual liberties, or journalists' codes of conduct. UNESCO did not and could not establish a New World Information and Communication Order. It has never approved of censorship. As a U.S. Congressional document said:

> [UNESCO] is not, at this time, implementing any policy or procedure the effect of which is to license journalists or their publications, to censor or otherwise restrict the free flow of information within or among countries, to impose mandatory codes of journalistic practice or ethics.[90]

Even the Department of State has stated that "UNESCO had never adopted proposals for the licensing of journalists."[91]

At UNESCO, the U.S. withdrawal resulted in the information and communication issue being shifted to the "back burner." Despite some sparks of activity, the information debate was largely quashed by the U.S. action.

Mindful that the crisis was caused largely by the information-order debate, in 1985 UNESCO's Executive Board began the process of trying to convince the West that UNESCO was moving away from confrontation. The Communication Programme was changed to place greater emphasis on practical approaches and to emphasize that nothing could happen quickly. The 1985 Sofia UNESCO General Conference reaffirmed that it was "essential *gradually* to eliminate existing imbalances . . . with a view to the establishment of a new world information and communication order, *seen as an evolving and continuous process.*"[92] Nevertheless, support for restructuring communication and information was still considerable in UNESCO: "All delegates without exception had taken the concept of a new world information and communication order as the central reference."[93] But nothing was done on a practical level to implement this program. In fact, seminars of experts were canceled, publications were stopped, and studies were reduced and their distribution limited.

The 1987 UNESCO General Conference in Paris elected a new Director-General, Spanish biochemist and politician Federico Mayor Zaragoza. Mayor announced UNESCO's return to its original purposes of education, science, and culture and pledged to revamp the organization's programs so the United States and Britain would return to the world body. "UNESCO must guarantee the free flow of information full stop," he said. He said plans for a new information order "no longer exist" at UNESCO.[94] He "rejected the concept of a 'new world information order' promoted by Third World and Soviet bloc nations."[95]

In its "new" strategy contained in its 1990–1995 plan, UNESCO seems to be returning to its historical mandate: investment in infrastructure and modernization of developing countries' network; training of human resources; research on the impact of communication and news technologies on society and culture; and development of programs to educate media users so they can critically choose among available messages, defend against media manipulation, and safeguard their rights as citizens. The plan mentions NWICO only in its introduction, not in the operational sections, and does not mention such important NWICO issues as global news flows, the right to communicate, or national communication policies.[96]

Meanwhile, one organization has begun to play an increasing role in the information debate. The *Conference on Security and Cooperation Europe (CSCE),* also known as the "Helsinki Process," is composed of more than forty European countries, the United States, and Canada.[97] Meeting for the first time in Helsinki, Finland, in 1975, its Final Act contained a substantial section on communication and information.[98] The signatories agreed to facilitate wider and freer dissemination of information, to encourage cooperation in the field of information and exchange of information with other countries, and to improve the working conditions of journalists.[99] The CSCE called a special meeting, the so-called London Information Forum, in 1989 to discuss questions of information and communication in more detail. Especially important was the changing nature of Europe, the Russian policy of *glasnost,* democratization, and restructuring in the Eastern European countries.[100] Yet two themes emerged clearly: Human rights are fundamentally important in the all–European process; and information issues are fundamentally important for expanding relations and cooperation among nations.

The International Telecommunication Union also joined the political fracas.[101] Just as the United States was leaving UNESCO, ITU produced the "Maitland Report," also known as *The Missing Link.* Stating that "our task was essentially political in character," the Maitland Report declared that the Third World must be prepared for the "wholly digital" revolution in electronics. Telecommunications was essential in development:

Where information flows so does commerce. More world trade and other contacts will increase understanding. An expanded telecommunications network
will make the world a better and safer place. . . . But there is a wide disparity in
the extent and quality of service as between industrialized and developing countries, and within the developing countries between urban and remote areas.[102]

The Maitland Report identified growing disparities in telecommunications
between the developed and the developing countries and highlighted the obstacles in
the way of telecommunications development. It listed ways in which the right conditions for development of telecommunications could be created and how existing
services could be improved. Thus, the Maitland Commission radically altered the
traditional role of ITU. ITU was no longer a purely technical and engineering group
but had become a more activist, pro-development organization. In so many words,
ITU was calling for the establishment of a New World Telecommunication Order. By
1989 ITU was even questioning the wisdom of its own past work:

Traditionally . . . ITU focused almost exclusively on the international telecommunication network between national gateways, leaving the national networks to
the sovereign states. . . . This state of affairs cannot continue if ITU is to be
responsive to the new telecommunication environment and to maintain its
supremacy as the forum for promoting and guiding global telecommunication
development.[103]

The United Nations Committee on Information (CoI) in 1990 forwarded a resolution to the General Assembly that for the first time did not support the new information order,[104] but the General Assembly passed this resolution that nonetheless
recognized "the call . . . for what in the United Nations and at various international
forums has been termed a 'new world information and communication order, seen as
an evolving and continuous process.' "[105]

The Non-Aligned Movement has continued to support the broad outlines of the
MacBride Movement. At the 1989 summit in Belgrade, the heads of state or government reaffirmed the need

to establish a new international information and communication order on the
basis of the free and balanced flow of information and speedily to remove disparities in communication capabilities within the era of rapid technological
advances that create new imbalances and place new and complex obstacles in
the way of the democratization of the global information and communication
process.[106]

Portending a new decade of struggle, Julius Nyerere's South Commission
asserted that to reduce dependency, a strong communication infrastructure
between countries in the South was needed. "The South has to act collectively so as
to minimize its dependence on Northern sources for data flows in critical areas," the
1990 report said.[107]

WHITHER THE NEW ORDER?

United States policy since withdrawing from UNESCO has been to work for reforms
based on three criteria: financial and budgetary discipline; management reform in the
UNESCO Secretariat; and "major programmatic changes, including the termination

of tendentious and politically motivated programs, the cessation of efforts to foster state control of the international press, and renewed concentration on UNESCO's original, non-political purposes."[108] In the U.S. view, UNESCO Director-General Mayor has "more easily articulated than achieved" these goals. He is a "well-intentioned but poor administrator."

Three contentious issues are most troublesome to the U.S. State Department. First, member states still call for the expulsion of Israel from UNESCO and submit "biased" resolutions based on "false" accusations. Second, UNESCO keeps advocating "rights of peoples" or "collective rights" that do nothing more than justify the denial of individual human rights, such as freedom of speech. Finally, UNESCO continues to promote the new information order, "a neat ideological framework in which the free press could be attacked as an 'imperialist tool.' "[109]

Mayor has in fact denied that the MacBride Movement is dead. He has referred to three important facts. First of all, despite many improvements in communications, there is a growing disparity between the North and South. Further, although some progress has been made in making developing countries' concerns heard, the current flow of information is more unbalanced today than it ever was before. Finally, although some transnational mass media have improved their coverage of the Third World, images of these countries are still distorted.[110] Nevertheless, in 1989 a panel of prominent U.S. citizens recommended that the United States rejoin UNESCO.[111]

In fact, in 1991 in Trinidad, Mayor said UNESCO is still committed to a new international communication and information order. "The media constitute the most important tool for peace in the world," he said. Nevertheless, "UNESCO intends to stick to its charter, which says that the organisation must guarantee the 'free flow of information.' "[112]

UNESCO's current vacillation contrasts with other signs of support and interest. In 1980 the MacBride Commission mandated that a series of roundtables should take place at the international level. However, that process was short-circuited by U.S. and British withdrawal from UNESCO. The first MacBride Roundtable was held in Zimbabwe in 1989 to assess the state of global communication ten years after the publication of the MacBride Report.[113]

One participant in the first MacBride Roundtable, Hamid Mowlana, noted ominously that a new information order *had* emerged, but not one advocated by the non-aligned nations: "It [was] the new order of the advanced industrialized nations."[114] The resulting "Harare Statement" articulated some important new points of departure. "Cultural ecology is now an indivisible and central part of the global communication debate," the Harare Statement said. The "operation of the mass media . . . should be determined primarily by professional media personnel, committed to the public interest, without undue government or commercial influence." Finally, the Harare Statement stressed that democratic participation "includes access to the media, people's right of reply, and their involvement in the decision-making process."[115] The Harare meeting firmly established the "grassroots line" of the Mac-Bride Movement. The Harare Statement repeated the words of Seán MacBride himself: "There has been a change in the center of the gravity of power in the world—from governments to public opinion, to the public sector."

The second MacBride Roundtable, held in Prague in 1990, discussed the Movement in light of the changes sweeping Eastern Europe. For the first time delegates were able to debate the issues outside of former ideological polarizations. The round-table noted that communications development "has bypassed many countries in the South." Important communication technologies are still unavailable or inaccessible. The meeting reaffirmed the MacBride Report's recommendations and the concept of the "right to communicate," which is, in the words of Seán MacBride, "the very foundation of other human rights."[116]

The third MacBride Roundtable, held after the 1991 Gulf War, in Istanbul, warned that the MacBride Report's principles had been thwarted by the "monopoly of global conglomerates" and by the "transnational industrial–media complex under its American military protectorate." The "symbolic and cultural environment . . . serves marketing strategies and government priorities that are increasingly beyond the reach of democratic policy making." The MacBride Movement must "build new peoples' coalitions and constituencies" and must "demilitarize cultural products and processes."[117]

One organization that has emerged as a leader in the movement for a New World Information and Communication Order is the World Association for Christian Communication (WACC).[118] Its 1989 "Manila Declaration on Communication and Community" stressed the importance of "media ecology," that intersection of nature and the human-made environment energized by communication. The human urge to exploit has contaminated both areas. "To change this, communication has a decisive role to play, not only in challenging the exploitation of the natural environment, but also in giving voice to the human victims of that same exploitation."[119]

The reasoning behind the preceding statement is that the cultural environment, like the physical environment, is threatened with degradation. As Gerbner has noted, for the first time in human history, a child is born into an alien cultural environment, largely independent of home, school, church, and community, the local culture, even the native country. Most of the time, most of the stories are brought to most children not by parents, teachers, clergy, or community with their own stories to tell but by distant conglomerates with something to sell. This astounding development frames what we know, think, and do in common. It cultivates conceptions of reality according to its own image.

In the 1990s the MacBride Movement is merging with the Cultural Environmental Movement. Both are trying to salvage a culture from massive industrialization and rampant mercantilism. They are also trying to reinvent democracy by moving away from Newtonian democracy, based on a mechanistic understanding of science and culture, and away from a democracy that can be manipulated by crass means from the top. This movement of the 1990s is trying to create a democracy based on systems theory—interaction and flexible feedback with no fixed flow of information and power from top to bottom.

Perhaps it all comes down to semantics. Everyone uses the same words, but their meanings are as different as totalitarianism and democracy. What is a "responsible" press? Who decides what is "responsible" coverage? What some call the "right to acquire adequate information," others interpret as attempts to regulate the mass media. What is "balance" in the media? Achieving "balance" can justify editing and selection of the news. "Protection of journalists" can mean shackling the labors of a free press. Clearly the MacBride Movement is not dead. It is apparent that the critical arguments and visible disparities that propelled it into prominence are still present.

NOTES

1. "Action Programme for Economic Cooperation of the Fourth Summit Conference of the Non-Aligned Countries, August 1973, Algiers," in Kaarle Nordenstreng, Enrique Gonzales Manet, and Wolfgang Kleinwächter, *New International Information and Communication Orders: Sourcebook,* foreword by Seán MacBride (Prague: International Organization of Journalists, 1986).

2. Works on the New World Information and Communication Order not cited elsewhere in this chapter (with thanks to Colleen Roach): Margaret A. Blanchard, *Exporting the First Amendment* (New York: Longman, 1988); R. A. Coates, *Unilateralism, Ideology, and U.S. Foreign Policy: The United States In and Out of UNESCO* (Boulder, CO: Lynne Rienner, 1988); Johan Galtung and Richard C. Vincent, *Global Glasnost: Towards a New World Information and Communication Order* (Norwood, NJ: Ablex, forthcoming); Peter Golding, Philip Harris and N. Jayaweera, eds. *Beyond Cultural Imperialism: New Perspectives on the New World Information Order* (London: Sage, 1992); Cees J. Hamelink, *Cultural Autonomy in Global Communications: Planning National Information Policy* (New York: Longman, 1983); Hans Kochler, *The New International Information and Communication Order: Basis for Cultural Dialogue and Peaceful Coexistence Among Nations* (Vienna: Braumuller, 1985); Philip Lee, ed., *Communication for All: New World Information and Communication Order* (Maryknoll, NY: Orbis, 1986); Sara F. Luther, *The United States and the Direct Broadcast Satellite* (New York: Oxford University Press, 1988); Seán MacBride and Colleen Roach, "New International Information Order," *International Encyclopedia of Communication* (New York: Oxford University Press, 1989); Achal Mehra, *Free Flow of Information: A New Paradigm* (New York: Greenwood Press, 1986); Hamid Mowlana, ed., *International Flow of News: An Annotated Bibliography* (Paris: UNESCO, 1985); Hamid Mowlana, *Global Information and World Communication* (New York: Longman, 1986); Kaarle Nordenstreng, *The Mass Media Declaration of UNESCO* (Norwood, NJ: Ablex, 1984); Herbert I. Schiller, *Communication and Cultural Domination* (New York: International Arts and Sciences Press, 1976); Herbert I. Schiller, *Information and the Crisis Economy* (Norwood, NJ: Ablex, 1984); Herbert I. Schiller, *Culture Inc.: The Corporate Takeover of Public Expression* (New York: Oxford University Press, 1989); Govind Narain Srivastava, *NAM and the New International Information and Communication Order,* 1st ed. (New Delhi, India: Indian Institute for Non-Aligned Studies, 1989); Robert L. Stevenson, *Communication, Development and the Third World* (New York: Longman, 1988); Michael Traber, *The Myth of the Information Revolution: Social and Ethical Implications of Communication Technology* (London: Sage, 1986); Janet Wasko and Slavko Splichal, eds., *Communication and Democracy* (Norwood, NJ: Ablex, 1992).

3. "Editorial," *Media, Culture & Society* 12 (3, July 1990): 279.

4. See "Analysis of the Problems of the 'Old Order,' " *Communication Research Trends* 1 (2, 1980).

5. "Asian-African Conference: Final Communiqué, Bandung, April 18–24, 1955," *The Third World Without Superpowers: The Collected Documents of the Non-Aligned Countries,* vol. 1, ed. Odette Jankowitsch and Karl P. Sauvant (Dobbs Ferry, NY: Oceana Publications, 1978), p. lxi.

6. Kaarle Nordenstreng, "Defining the New International Information Order: Parameters, Principles, and Terminology with Regard to International Relations." Paper presented at the conference on World Communications: Decision for the Eighties, Philadelphia, 1980, p. 5.

7. Kent Cooper, *Barriers Down* (New York: Farrar & Rinehart, 1942), p. 36.

8. Ibid., p. 9. Cooper called for unrestricted freedom of movement for U.S. journalists throughout the world. *The Economist* (London) wrote of Cooper in 1948: "Like most business executives, [Cooper] experiences a peculiar moral glow in finding that his idea of freedom coincides with his commercial advantage . . . democracy does not necessarily mean making the world safer for AP." Quoted in Herbert Brucker, *Freedom of Information* (New York: Macmillan, 1951), p. 214.

9. The first American college textbook chapter on the debate is Robert G. Picard, "Global Communications Controversies," in *Global Journalism: Survey of International Communication,* 2nd ed., ed. John C. Merrill (New York: Longman, 1991), pp. 73–87.

10. National News Council, "Report on News Coverage of Belgrade UNESCO Conference," ed. A. H. Raskin (New York: National News Council, 1981), p. 10.

11. C. Anthony Giffard, *UNESCO and the Media* (New York: Longman, 1989), p. 277.

12. Michael B. Salwen and Bruce Garrison, "The Dimensions of the News Selection Process: What Makes News in Latin America and the United States." Unpublished paper, February 1989, pp. 17–18.

13. Seán MacBride, "Preface," in *Information Technology and the New Information Order,* ed. Jörg Becker (Lund, Sweden: Studentlitteratur & Chartwell-Bratt, 1984), p. 11.

14. Giffard, *UNESCO and the Media,* p. xviii.

15. UN Resolution 633, December 16, 1952, cited in Nordenstreng, "Defining the New International Information Order," p. 4. UN Resolution 1313, December 12, 1958, invites UNESCO "to formulate concrete proposals to assist in meeting the needs of less developed countries in building up adequate media of information."

16. Thomas McPhail, "The New International Information Order," *Communication Research Trends,* Summer 1980, p. 8. See the following reports: UNESCO, *Statistics on Radio and Television, 1950–1960* (Paris: UNESCO, 1963); UNESCO, *World Radio and Television* (Paris: UNESCO, 1963); UNESCO, *Statistics on Radio and Television, 1960–1970* (Paris: UNESCO, 1978); International Commission for the Study of Communication Problems [MacBride Commission], *Many Voices, One World* (Paris: UNESCO, 1980); UNESCO, *Latest Statistics on Radio and Television Broadcasting* (Paris: UNESCO, 1987); UNESCO, *World Communication Report* (Paris: UNESCO, 1989); and annual UNESCO *Statistical Yearbook.*

17. UN Resolution 1778, December 7, 1962, cited in Nordenstreng, "Defining the New International Information Order," p. 4.

18. Hamdy Kandil, "UNESCO and a New World Information and Communication Order: The Landmarks and the Issues," in *Towards a Canadian Perspective on International Communication Issues* (Ottawa: Canadian Commission for UNESCO, 1982), p. 1.

19. See A. Singham and S. Hune, *Non-Alignment in the Age of Alignment* (New York: Lawrence Hill, 1986).

20. Jan Pronk, "Some Remarks on the Relation Between the New International Information Order and the New International Economic Order," Document no. 35 prepared for the International Commission for the Study of Communication Problems (Paris: UNESCO, n.d.); Breda Pavlic and Cees J. Hamelink, *Interrelationship between the New International Economic Order and a New International/World Information–Communication Order* (Paris: UNESCO, 1984); and Shelton Gunaratne and Andrew Conteh, *Global Communication and Dependency: Links between the NIEO and the NWICO Demands and the Withdrawals from UNESCO* (Moorhead, MN: Moorhead State University Bookstore, 1990). One might also predict that both these orders might one day be subsumed under the growing concept of the New World Environmental Order. See Manuel Cifuentes Vargas, *Hacia Un Nuevo Orden Ecológico Mundial: Una Propuesta* (Mexico City: n.p., 1991), available from the author: Mirabosques No. 45, Secc. Cumbira Cuautitlan Izcalli, Estado de Mexico, C.P. 54740, Mexico.

21. "Declaration on the Establishment of a New International Economic Order," in Nordenstreng, Gonzales Manet, and Kleinwächter, *New International Information,* pp. 165–167.

22. Johan Galtung, "Social Communication and Global Problems," in *Communication for All: New World Information and Communication Order,* ed. Philip Lee (Maryknoll, NY: Orbis Books, 1985), pp. 10–14.

23. Nordenstreng, Gonzales Manet, and Kleinwächter, *New International Information,* p. 275.

24. Cited by Luis Ramiro Beltran S. and Elizabeth Fox de Cardona, "Mass Media and Cultural Domination," *Prospects* 10 (1, 1980): 79.

25. "The Emancipation of the Mass Media in the Non-Aligned Countries," in Nordenstreng, Gonzales Manet, and Kleinwächter, *New International Information,* pp. 276, 281, 282.

26. "New Delhi Declaration," in Nordenstreng, Gonzales Manet, and Kleinwächter, *New International Information,* p. 286.

27. "Political Declaration of the Fifth Summit Conference of Non-Aligned Countries," in Nordenstreng, Gonzales Manet, and Kleinwächter, *New International Information,* p. 288.

28. Giffard, *UNESCO and the Media,* p. 22.

29. Intergovernmental Conference on Communication Policies in Latin America and the Caribbean, San José, Costa Rica, "San José Declaration," in UNESCO, *A Documentary History of a New World Information and Communication Order Seen as an Evolving and Continuous Process,* Documents on Communication and Society, no. 19 (Paris: UNESCO, 1986), p. 7.

30. This chronology owes a great debt to Wolfgang Kleinwächter, "The Birth of Article 19—A UN Twin Concept," in *Human Rights, Communication, and Culture,* eds. Kaarle Nordenstreng and Wolfgang Kleinwächter (Tampere, Finland: Department of Journalism and Mass Communication, 1989).

31. See *Yearbook of the United Nations 1946–47* (New York: United Nations, 1948), pp. 526, 176.

32. "Calling of an International Conference on Freedom of Information," General Assembly Resolution 59 (I), 1946, in Edward W. Ploman, *International Law Governing Communications and Information: A Collection of Basic Documents* (Westport, CT: Greenwood Press, 1982), p. 132.

33. Cited in Elizabeth A. Downey, "A Historical Survey of the International Regulation of Propaganda," in *Regulation of Transnational Communications: Michigan Yearbook of International Legal Studies, 1984,* ed. Leslie J. Anderson (New York: Clark Boardman, 1984), p. 346.

34. "Final Act of the United Nations Conference on Freedom of Information," Geneva, April 21, 1948, in Nordenstreng, Gonzales Manet, and Kleinwächter, *New International Information,* p. 115.

35. Discussion of the draft conventions went on for years in the Economic and Social Council and in the General Assembly. In 1960 ECOSOC adopted a Draft Declaration on Freedom of Information, Economic and Social Council Resolution 756 (XXIX), 1960 (in Ploman, *International Law,* p. 138), which has never gained General Assembly approval. The draft convention on Freedom of Information has been the subject of debates for decades, but only a few articles have been adopted by the General Assembly. See "Freedom of Information: Interference with Radio Signals," General Assembly Resolution 424 (V), 1950, in Ploman, *International Law,* p. 137; and "Freedom of Information," General Assembly Resolution 2448 (XXIII), 1968, in Ploman, International Law, p. 139; and "Draft Convention on Freedom of Information," as Adopted by the Third Committee, 1973, in Ploman, *International Law,* p. 140. The Draft Declaration on Freedom of the Press finally disappeared from the agenda in the mid-1970s.

36. Convention on the International Right of Correction, December 16, 1952, New York, Article II. Entered into force August 1962. In 1987 Burkina Fasa became the twelfth party (and the first in twenty years) to join. The other eleven adherents include Cuba, Cyprus, Egypt, El Salvador, Ethiopia, France, Guatemala, Jamaica, Sierra Leone, Uruguay, and Yugoslavia.

37. Kaarle Nordenstreng, "Defining the New International Information Order."

38. Kaarle Nordenstreng with Lauri Hannikainen, *The Mass Media Declaration of UNESCO* (Norwood, NJ: Ablex, 1984), p. 80.

39. Brigitte Weyl, "The Long Road to Consensus," in *The Global Media Debate: Its Rise, Fall and Renewal,* ed. Kaarle Nordenstreng, Hamid Mowlana, and George Gerbner (Norwood, NJ: Ablex, forthcoming).

40. "Declaration on the Fundamental Principles Concerning the Contribution of the Mass Media to Strengthening Peace and International Understanding, to the Promotion of Human Rights, and to Countering Racialism, Apartheid and Incitement to War" (Mass Media Declaration, Article II, Section 3), UNESCO General Conference, Resolution 4/9.3/2, November 28, 1978, Article I., in Nordenstreng, Gonzales Manet, and Kleinwächter, *New International Information,* p. 227.

41. Hamid Mowlana and Howard H. Frederick, "Knowledge, Perception and Utilization of the Declaration," in Nordenstreng, Mowlana, and Gerbner, *The Global Media Debate,* (forth-

coming). Also appeared in "Völkerrechtliches Gewaltverbot und Humanitäre Zusammenarbeit," special issue of *Internationale Studien: Leipziger Hefte zur Friedensforschung* (3, 1989): 127–132.

42. "Resolution on Cooperation of Non-Aligned Countries in Information of the Third Meeting of the Intergovernmental Council [for] Coordination of Information among Non-Aligned Countries," Lomé, April 26, 1979, in Nordenstreng, Gonzales Manet, and Kleinwächter, *New International Information*, p. 290.

43. "Political Declaration of the Sixth Summit Conference of Non-Aligned Countries," in Nordenstreng, Gonzales Manet, and Kleinwächter, *New International Information*, p. 296.

44. "Statute of the News Agencies Pool of Non-Aligned Countries," in Nordenstreng, Manet Gonzales, and Kleinwächter, *New International Information, p. 297.*

45. "Resolution on the New International Information Order of the Fourth Meeting of the Intergovernmental Council for Coordination of Information among Non-Aligned Countries," Baghdad, Iraq, June 7, 1980, in Nordenstreng, Manet Gonzales, and Kleinwächter, *New International Information*, p. 303.

46. "Political Declaration of the Seventh Summit Conference of Non-Aligned Countries," New Delhi, March 1983, in Nordenstreng, Manet Gonzales, and Kleinwächter, *New International Information*, p. 306.

47. "Declaration and Resolutions of the Jakarta Conference of the Ministers of Information of Non-Aligned Countries," Jakarta, January 30, 1984, in Nordenstreng, Manet Gonzales, and Kleinwächter, *New International Information*, pp. 312–326.

48. International Organization of Journalists, *NAM & NIICO: Documents of the Non-Aligned Movement on the New International Information and Communication Order (1986–1987),* ed. Kaarle Nordenstreng (Prague: International Organization of Journalists, 1988), p. 9.

49. UNESCO, *Documentary History*, p. 43.

50. Noteworthy in the 1980s was the fact that the Committee on Information's "Questions Relating to Information" was no longer passed by consensus; in counted votes, the United States and other countries yearly voted against the resolution.

51. See "Seán MacBride: A Short Biography," *Few Voices, Many Worlds: Towards a Media Reform Movement,* ed. Michael Traber and Kaarle Nordenstreng (London: World Association for Christian Communication, 1992), pp. 18–23. Seán MacBride's writings on communication include the following: "Preface", International Commission for the Study of Communication Problems, *Many Voices, One World* ["The MacBride Report"] (Paris: UNESCO, 1980); "Preface," in Becker, *Information Technology;* "Foreword," in Nordenstreng, Gonzales Manet, and Kleinwächter, *New International Information;* "Foreword," *Papiertechnologie und Dritte Welt,* ed. Jörg Becker, in association with Lutz Meyer and Arthur W. Western (Braunschweig, Germany: Vieweg, 1988); and "Preface," in William Preston, Jr., Edward S. Herman, and Herbert I. Schiller, *Hope and Folly: The United States and UNESCO, 1945–1985* (Minneapolis, MN: University of Minnesota Press, 1989).

52. International Commission for the Study of Communication Problems [MacBride Commission], *Many Voices, One World.* The book is out of print at UNESCO but can be obtained from the World Association for Christian Communication, 357 Kennington Lane, London SE11 5QY, United Kingdom, Tel: 44-71-582-9139, Fax: 44-71-735-0340, Email address: wacc@gn.apc.org (Internet).

53. Elie Abel, United States; Hubert Beuve-Mery, France; Elebe Ma Ekonzo, Zaire; Sergei Losev, USSR; Gabriel García Márquez, Colombia; Mochtar Lubis, Indonesia; Mustapha Masmoudi, Tunisia; Betty Zimmerman, Canada; Michio Nagai, Japan; Fred Isaac Akporuaro Omu, Nigeria; Bogdan Osolnik, Yugoslavia; Gamal El Ateifi, Egypt; Johannes Pieter Pronk, Netherlands; Juan Somavia, Chile; Boobli George Verghese, India.

54. The most widely recognized papers were "The New World Information Order" by Tunisian Moustapha Masmoudi and "Communication for an Independent, Pluralistic World" by American Elie Abel.

55. "UNESCO Resolution 4/19—On the International Commission for the Study of Communication Problems," October 21, 1980, Belgrade, in Nordenstreng, Gonzales Manet, and Kleinwächter, *New International Information,* pp. 249–250.

56. UNESCO General Conference, Resolution 3.3, 1983, in UNESCO, *Documentary History,* p. 179.

57. Colleen Roach, "The Position of the Reagan Administration on the NWICO," *Media Development* 34 (4, 1987): 32–37.

58. Oswaldo Capriles, "Actions and Reaction to Communication Policies within the Framework of UNESCO: Analysis of the Costa Rica Conference." Paper presented to the Seminar on International Communication and Third World Participation: A Conceptual and Practical Framework, Amsterdam, 1977, as cited in Luis Ramiro Beltran S. and Elizabeth Fox de Cardona, "Mass Media and Cultural Domination," *Prospects* 10 (1, 1980): 83.

59. "Declaration of Talloires of the 'Voices of Freedom' Conference," in Nordenstreng, Gonzales Manet, and Kleinwächter, *New International Information,* pp. 369–370.

60. U.S. Department of State, *The Activities of UNESCO Since U.S. Withdrawal: A Report by the Secretary of State,* April 1990 (Washington, DC: Bureau of International Organization Affairs, 1990), p. 14.

61. "A Bow to Big Brother," *Newsweek,* September 6, 1976, pp. 69–70.

62. "UNESCO as Censor" (editorial), *New York Times,* October 24, 1980, p. A32.

63. "Little Education, Science, or Culture" (editorial), *New York Times,* December 16, 1983, p. A34.

64. William Safire, "The New Order Changeth," *New York Times,* December 25, 1983, p. D13.

65. U.S. Senate, Committee on Foreign Relations, *The New World Information Order,* ed. George Kroloff and Scott Cohen (Washington, DC: Committee on Foreign Relations, 1977), p. 1.

66. U.S. Department of State, "Goals for UNESCO," *News Release,* Speech by Ambassador John R. Reinhardt at the General Conference of UNESCO, Nairobi, November 1, 1976, p. 4.

67. "Foundation Seeks Cash to Back UNESCO Pullout," *Washington Post,* October 20, 1984, p. A15.

68. Owen Harries, "U.S., Quit UNESCO," *New York Times,* December 21, 1983, p. A27.

69. Abel's views are summarized in Elie Abel, "Global Information: The New Battleground," *Political Communication and Persuasion* 1 (4, 1982): 347–357; and in *Current Issues in International Communication,* ed. L. John Martin and Ray Eldon Hiebert (New York: Longman, 1990), pp. 68–73.

70. U.S. Department of State, *The Activities of UNESCO,* p. 13.

71. "Serving Notice to UNESCO," *Newsweek,* January 9, 1984, p. 32, cited in "World Forum: The U.S. Decision to Withdraw from UNESCO," *Journal of Communication* 34 (4, 1984): 100.

72. U.S. Congress, House of Representatives, *Review of U.S. Participation in UNESCO, Hearings and Markup before the Subcommittees on International Operations and on Human Rights and International Organizations of the Committee on Foreign Affairs, March 10, July 9 and 16, 1981* (Washington, DC: Government Printing Office, 1982), p. 199. Only one voice, that of Dr. Hamid Mowlana of American University, protested the torrent of criticism directed at UNESCO.

73. *Review of U.S. Participation in UNESCO,* pp. 79–80.

74. Ibid., p. 20.

75. "The IPDC: UNESCO vs. The Free Press," *Backgrounder,* March 10, 1983.

76. Michael Massing, "UNESCO Under Fire," *Atlantic Monthly,* July 1984, pp. 88–92.

77. Harries, "U.S., Quit UNESCO," p. A27.

78. MacBride Commission member Bogdan Osolnik believes this gutted the "MacBride Movement," for it "eliminates every basis for recrimination that a new order should be installed." Bogdan Osolnik, "A Reassessment of the MacBride Commission Report—Ten Years After," *Mass Media in the World* (4, 1990): 53.

79. Leonard Sussman, "Press Freedom Advocates Are Gaining, Not Losing, at UNESCO" (letter), *New York Times,* January 31, 1984, p. A22.

80. Paul Lewis, "UNESCO's Budget Hits $374 Million," *New York Times,* November 17, 1983, p. A17.

81. "The U.S. and UNESCO: Time for Decision," *Executive Memorandum,* no. 40 (Washington, DC: Heritage Foundation, December 5, 1983).

82. "Letter of Secretary of State George Schulz to Amadou-Mahtar M'Bow," in "World Forum," p. 82.

83. William G. Harley, "Department of State Memorandum, February 9, 1984," in "World Forum," p. 89.

84. David Shribman, "U.S. Insists on Big Changes in UNESCO," *New York Times,* December 17, 1983, p. A3.

85. Richard Bernstein, " 'Distortion' Laid to U.S. on UNESCO," *New York Times,* August 9, 1984, p. A9.

86. Alex S. Jones, "UNESCO Reported to Move Away from Issue of Licensing Reporters," *New York Times,* November 6, 1984, p. A16.

87. Giffard, *UNESCO and the Media,* p. 3.

88. Ibid., p. 4.

89. Leonard Sussman, "Foreword: Who Did In UNESCO?," in Giffard, *UNESCO and the Media,* p. xiii.

90. U.S. Government, *Report to Congress on UNESCO Policies and Procedures, with Respect to the Media Question in Section 109 of Public Law 97–241,* in "World Forum," p. 123.

91. U.S. Department of State, *The Activities of UNESCO,* p. 14.

92. UNESCO, "Draft Report of Commission IV," Document 23 C/COM.IV/2, Part I, November 4, 1985, p. 4.

93. UNESCO, *Report of Commission IV,* 23 C/COM.IV/2, Part I, p. 28, cited in Colleen Roach, "The Movement for a New World Information and Communication Order: A Second Wave?" *Media, Culture & Society* 12 (3, July 1990): 286.

94. Ethan Schwartz, "UNESCO Chief Vows Major Reforms: Director-General Seeks to Persuade U.S. to Rejoin the Agency," *Washington Post,* February 25, 1989, p. A19.

95. Associated Press, October 7, 1988, as cited by Roach, "Movement for a New World Information and Communication Order," p. 287.

96. "Communication in the Service of Humanity" (UNESCO Third Medium-Term Plan, 1990–1995), *Media Development* (3, 1990): 23–24.

97. Russia assumed the Soviet Union's CSCE seat. Byelorussia, Ukraine, Moldavia, Tadjikhistan, and Uzbekhistan signed the Helsinki Final Acts in 1992. Azerbaijan, Turkmenistan, Armenia, Kirgistan, and Kazakhstan have said they will sign in 1992. Georgia has given no indication of when it might be ready to become a signatory.

98. Norbert Ropers, "Information and Communication between East and West within the CSCE Process," in *Europe Speaks to Europe: International Information Flows between Eastern and Western Europe,* ed. Jörg Becker and Tamas Szecsko (Oxford: Pergamon Press, 1989), pp. 363–384.

99. See semiannual reviews, *inter alia* U.S. Department of State, *Implementation of Helsinki Final Act, October 1, 1988–March 31, 1989* (Washington, DC: Bureau of Public Affairs, 1989).

100. *London Information Forum: Summary, Documents* (Prague: International Journalism Institute, 1989); Leonard H. Marks, "The London Information Forum Public Report." Unpublished paper, 1989.

101. William M. Ellinghaus and Larry G. Forrester, "A U.S. Effort to Provide a Global Balance: The Maitland Commission Report," *Journal of Communication* 35 (2, 1985): 14–19.

102. "Final Report of the Independent Commission for World Wide Telecommunications Development," Geneva, January 22, 1985, in Nordenstreng, Gonzales Manet, and Kleinwächter, *New International Information,* p. 265. The original report was International Telecommunication Union, *The Missing Link: Report of the Independent Commission for World Wide Telecommunications Development* (Geneva: ITU, December 1984).

103. International Telecommunication Union, *The Changing Telecommunication Environment: Policy Considerations for the Members of the ITU* (Geneva: ITU, 1989), pp. iii, 30, 45.

104. United Nations General Assembly, "Committee on Information Draft Report," A/AC.198/1990/L.1/Add.2, April 30, 1990.

105. Hamid Mowlana and Colleen Roach, "New World Information and Communication Order since Prague: Overview of Developments and Activities." Paper presented at the Third MacBride Round Table on Communication, Istanbul, Turkey, June 21, 1991.

106. Ninth Conference of Heads of State or Government of Non-Aligned Countries, *Information and Communications,* NAC 9/PC/Doc. 26, Belgrade, Yugoslavia, September 7, 1989.

107. *The Challenge to the South: the South Commission under the Chairmanship of Julius Nyerere* (New York: Oxford University Press, 1990), cited in Hamid Mowlana and Colleen Roach, "New World Information and Communication Order: Overview of Developments and Activities," in *Few Voices, Many Worlds: Towards a Media Reform Movement,* ed. Michael Traber and Kaarle Nordenstreng (London: World Association for Christian Communication, 1992), p. 10.

108. U.S. Department of State, *The Activities of UNESCO,* p. 4.

109. U.S. Department of State, *The Activities of UNESCO,* p. 13.

110. Wolfgang Kleinwächter, "The Great Media Debate: NWICO and the UN System." Paper presented at the MacBride Round Table on Communication, Harare, Zimbabwe, October 27–29, 1989.

111. Mowlana and Roach, "New World Information and Communication Order since Harare."

112. Inter Press Service, "Information: Search for New Order Is Still On, UNESCO Chief Says," September 12, 1991.

113. Slavko Splichal, "NIICO—Dead or Alive? MacBride Round Table on Communication in Harare, October 27–29, 1989," *Media, Culture & Society* 12 (3, July 1990): 399–401.

114. Hamid Mowlana, "The Emerging Global Information and Communication Order and the Question of Cultural Ecology." Paper presented at the MacBride Round Table on Communication, Harare, Zimbabwe, October 27–30, 1989.

115. "Harare Statement of the MacBride Round Table on Communication," Harare, Zimbabwe, October 27–29, 1989; and in *Few Voices, Many Worlds,* pp. 24–26.

116. "Prague Statement of the MacBride Round Table on Communication," Prague, Czechoslovakia, September 21–22, 1990, in *Few Voices, Many Worlds,* pp. 27–30.

117. "Istanbul Statement of the MacBride Round Table on Communication 'Few Voices, Many Worlds,' " Istanbul, Turkey, June 21, 1991, in *Few Voices, Many Worlds,* pp. 31–32.

118. World Association for Christian Communication, 357 Kennington Lane, London SE11 5QY, United Kingdom, Voice: 44–71–582–9139; Fax: 44–71–735–0340; Email address: wacc@gn.apc.org (Internet).

119. World Association for Christian Communication, "Communication and Community: Manila Declaration," *Few Voices, Many Worlds,* pp. 33–36.

7

Contending Theories of
Global Communication

In this chapter, the various theories of global communication are examined. Communication and international relations have become so intertwined that "it is impossible to explain international political interaction without looking at the communication phenomena accompanying its many forms."[1]

THEORY, FACT, AND THE LEVEL OF ANALYSIS

As human beings, we know what we know through two kinds of input: theory and fact.[2] *A fact is an undeniable phenomenon* impinging on the senses as a physical observation. *A theory is a thought, idea, image, or symbolic representation* that stands at some level of abstraction above the world of facts. It is "a general explanation of certain selected phenomena set forth in a manner satisfactory to someone acquainted with the characteristics of the reality being studied."[3] A theory is not identical to a fact, but theories somehow correspond to facts (see Figure 7-1).

It is important to verify a theory in the real world. This process, called *empirical verification,* starts in the plane of facts with Fact 1 (F_1); proceeds by rules of correspondence to theoretical concepts, from concept to concept; and finally returns to the plane of facts at Fact 2 (F_2). When real-world facts are connected by a large number of such concepts, when this diagram is traversed by a great number of such circuits, a theory is said to be verified (or to be "true"), and the theoretical concepts are said to correspond to the facts, even to compose reality.[4]

A theory can *explain* an occurrence or event and gives us something to test. A theory can also *predict* what we might find in the real world. It is usually based upon an observed event and tells us what we are likely to find if the same conditions hold in the future. A theory can also tell us, by what it does not explain or predict, some of the things we don't yet know. We call this a theory's *heuristic value.* Finally, a theory can also deal with what *ought* to be rather than what is. These are called *normative theories.* They help to outline a better world and to suggest paths by which we might arrive there.

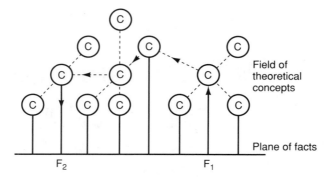

FIGURE 7-1   The Realm of Theory and the Plane of Facts. A circuit of verification begins in the plane of facts (F_1), proceeds from concept to concept using rules of correspondence (C), and returns to the plane of facts (F_2).

One of the main difficulties in global communication theory is the "level of analysis problem." The essential question here is, who are the actors? Global communication theory has roamed up and down the "ladder of abstraction" from nation–states and international organizations to interest groups, social classes, and the elite, down to individuals. Global communication is often carried out by *individuals* (journalists, politicians, and individual citizens), *institutions* (the Associated Press, the World Press Freedom Committee, the Non-Aligned Movement), *governments* (the U.S. State Department), and *transnational entities* (the United Nations and global corporations). To complicate matters further, sometimes our focus is on communication *technologies* (mass communication); other times, it is on *communication between individuals* (interpersonal communication).

One useful way to divide theories is along a "micro–macro spectrum." At one end we have the *micro-level* of analysis, the point of departure for psychologists, social psychologists, biologists, game theorists, and decision-making theorists. These scientists make inferences about higher levels of behavior from the behavior of individual human beings. At the other end of the spectrum, known as the *macro-level* of analysis, is the operating realm of political scientists, international relations analysts, and systems theorists. They are interested in the largest order of aggregations, such as nation–states, cultures, and the "international system." Somewhere in the middle we find the area of *mid-range* theories. This is the realm where sociologists, anthropologists, and geographers are interested in large social groups, communities, institutions, social classes, and political movements.

MICRO-LEVEL THEORIES OF GLOBAL COMMUNICATION

Micro-level theories look at the human mind; they begin with the presumption that the influence of individual human beings on social forces is "many times stronger than the influence of the social forces which play upon man."[5] Micro-level theory shifts our focus from huge systems to persons and groups; from organizational explanations to human explanations; from the study of observable behavior to hidden motivations and human needs, fears, and desires. True, human needs, fears, and desires are often no more observable than atomic particles. But the invisibility of atoms has not deterred physicists, nor has the invisibility of human motivations deterred psychologists and other social theorists, who have compiled an impressive body of micro-level explanations relevant to global communication.[6] Micro-level theorists believe war and conflict are traceable to human nature and behavior. These theorists' goal is to find out the motives, reasons, and causal forces that lead individuals and groups of individuals toward war and aggression even though they may not be aware of these factors.

Communication and Learning Theories

One oft-quoted micro-level aphorism is the preamble to the UNESCO Constitution: "Since wars begin in the minds of men, it is in the minds of men that defences of peace must be constructed." In communication terms, if only the right things are communicated to the right people at the right time, a change can be made in the attitudes of nations toward each other that will make peace possible. Advocates of this point of view assume that people can learn and that the necessary information can be communicated to them—the two essential components of learning theory.[7]

In this view, people process incoming messages in predictable ways.[8] Messages create images in the mind that guide decisions and simplify choices. Images are created by the educational system, culture, folklore, socialization, and the news media. Consisting of facts, attitudes, images, and past experience, these images serve as perceptual screens, filtering out some stimuli while allowing others to pass through.[9] Put another way, the brain has well-traveled roads laid down by past experience and is on the lookout for needed information before it arrives. The brain has a mental image of the object sought. This explains the phenomenon of "self–confirming reality;" why, for example, some Americans viewed events in Nicaragua as evidence of communism while others saw them as confirmation of liberation. Ideological preconceptions tend to be reinforced by experience because the mind has difficulty changing its pathways.

A variety of cognitive mechanisms influence our perception of mediated global events. One powerful mental device, *selective perception,* can hide a painful truth. For example, when media present the frightful effects of nuclear war, some people soften such "a looming anxiety [with] a twist of attention." Just as a person whose leg is mauled by a lion can run for miles without pain, psychological self-deception can lead our minds away from other forms of pain. Psychiatrists give the name "nuclear numbing" to the "widely observed inability of people to let themselves feel the fear, anger, and rebelliousness that fully grasping the human predicament— notably, the arms race—might bring them."[10] Some evidence indicates that people who read an unrepresentative news story about a foreign country make less accurate inferences about that country than people who read no story at all about that country. People make inaccurate judgments about people in other countries based on biased news and information.[11]

Another micro-level approach is frustration–aggression theory.[12] It begins with an assumption that political instability may be due to unrelieved social frustration. Part of this frustration may be media-related. Communication across borders and cultures has improved in quality and quantity. Through new technologies, once-isolated peoples are able to see how others live across vast distances. They sometimes become envious of what they see and frustrated by what they lack in comparison. Increased global communication can cause a "grass-is-greener" syndrome among those whose economic or political situation inhibits their material satisfaction. This frustration may lead to aggression; often it leads to a malaise about existing conditions and even a desire to emigrate.

Part of this theory is known as the *Dollard–Doob hypothesis.* Frustration occurs whenever a barrier is put between a person and his or her desired goal. A natural response is to strike out at the barrier, but barriers are sometimes only symbolic and are too strong or sacred, or are otherwise immune from attack. In this case, the aggression may be displaced onto someone or something not associated with the barrier.[13] The 1979 Iranian revolution can be interpreted as the result of frustrations created by the import of Western culture and media products in the face of Islamic tradition. Imported media, according to this theory, created intolerable frustration and contributed to the creation of the conditions for revolution.

How do people handle incoming media messages that contradict established attitudes? Cognitive dissonance theory argues that people strive for internal consistency between their beliefs (and actions) and incoming information. When "dissonance" occurs, people try to reduce it either by changing their beliefs or by exposing themselves selectively only to new information compatible with their beliefs.[14] Such "cognitive dissonance reduction" plays a role in international affairs. For years Americans believed that the Soviet Union was the antithesis of American values. But in the early 1980s President Reagan, much to the distress of his supporters, began to restructure his knowledge and belief patterns and abandoned his earlier insistence that the Soviet Union was the "evil empire." After Reagan "reduced his cognitive dissonance," American media began to flood the public with positive images of the Soviet Union.

One approach that applies psychological mechanisms to international affairs is known as *psychohistory.* Making this large leap of logic allows one to consider that entire nations have mental disorders and might be prone to suicide or homicide.[15]

Stereotypes and the Mirror Image Hypothesis

Stereotypes are "pictures in our heads" about a class of people.[16] They are a set of beliefs based upon simplified and often false assumptions held to be true.[17] We see stereotypes in one-line characterizations: Germans are scientifically minded and industrious. Italians are artistic and passionate. Americans are materialistic and ambitious. While the stereotype may be accurate for some members of the group, people tend to disregard the cases for which it is not true and to neglect variations that do exist. Stereotypes seem to fulfill certain needs in human nature. As Walter Lippman wrote, "stereotypes guarantee . . . our self-respect. . . . [T]hey are a fortress of our own tradition and behind its defenses we can continue to feel ourselves safe in the position we occupy."[18] In short, stereotypes simplify the world and make it more manageable; they help rationalize and justify our treatment of others.

Global media share responsibility for perpetuating stereotypes. Rather than providing accurate information that might promote understanding between peoples, media images sometimes fan feelings of fear and hostility, thereby entrenching prevalent stereotypes. Media can also help change stereotypes, which can "adapt themselves to the positive or negative relationship based on matters unrelated to images of the people concerned."[19] American stereotypes of the Soviet Union have always reflected the political conditions of the moment. As allies against Nazi Germany, Americans saw the Soviets as idealistic and stalwart opponents of fascism. During the Cold War, the Soviets became immoral, unjust, and unreasonable; its leaders, brutal and enigmatic. Under Gorbachev, they became builders of democracy.

During the Cold War, psychologist Uri Bronfenbrenner made a trip to the Soviet Union. His conclusion caused much controversy: *Americans and Soviets had the same stereotypes about one another.* "The Russian's distorted picture of us was curiously similar to our view of them—a mirror image. . . . They are the aggressors. . . . Their government deludes and exploits the people. . . . The masses are not really sympathetic. . . . They cannot be trusted. . . . Their policy verges on madness."[20]

Humans organize the world into artificial frames of reference, categorizing some nations as good and others as bad. We create the *diabolical enemy image:* "Each side believes the other to be bent on aggression and conquest, to be capable of great brutality and evil-doing, to be something less than human and therefore hardly deserving respect or consideration, to be insincere, and untrustworthy, etc."[21] This is coupled with the *morally innocent self-image:* "In judging its own behavior, a country is likely to regard that behavior as natural or even inevitable . . . The other is unchangeably evil."[22] These images are communicated to mass populations through the media.[23]

Decision-Making, Communication, and Crisis

What happens to the communication process in times of crisis? This is a crucial question because

> the effectiveness of bargaining depends in large part upon the exchange of sufficient credible information between the parties. When the information exchanged appears to be insufficient or distorted, bargainers have no real basis on which to assume good or equitable intentions on the part of the other. Nor is there sufficient basis for recognizing common interests. . . . Thus communication isolation, whether it results from physical or psychological conditions, imposes constraints on the development of cooperation and is likely to promote mistrust and suspicion.[24]

Conflict resolution is more likely if each opponent can communicate the intention to cooperate, the expectation that the other will cooperate, the intention to retaliate against noncooperation, and forgiveness of the opponent's previous uncooperative acts.[25]

Milburn examined the patterns of communication that led both to the outbreak of World War II and to the resolution of the Cuban missile crisis. Two important commonalities emerged. The first was overreliance on a single information channel. "The greater the dependency on one method or channel of information in a crisis, the greater the distortion in information available to the decision makers . . . " He recommended that decisionmakers "not rely on any *single* method or channel of information, nor upon a single point of observation. Use several techniques for evaluating the situation and conduct checks on the fidelity of information sources." The other common element was information overload. As crises reduce the number of channels, they also increase the volume of communication transmitted.[26]

Communication habits change in times of crisis: "The higher the stress in a crisis situation, the greater the tendency to rely upon extraordinary or improvised channels of communication."[27] During the Cuban missile crisis, normal communication channels between Moscow and Washington were poor, so Kennedy and Khrushchev resorted to extraordinary means of communicating with one another. Kennedy sent out an important message affirming the American desire to de–escalate unencrypted rather than in code. Khrushchev's acceptance of Kennedy's formula was broadcast by Radio Moscow rather than through normal channels, which might have taken hours.

Summarizing diplomatic communications leading to World War I, Zinnes and colleagues showed that the number and intensity of hostile messages increase during a crisis. What is worse, hostile messages led to even more hostile messages as nations vied to answer hostility with counterhostility.[28] Beer called these increasingly hostile exchanges *image races,* which take on a life of their own, no longer supporting the rational purposes of the actors, but impelling them to actions they might prefer to avoid.[29] During crises, enemy images in the media increasingly dehumanize the opponent and reach peaks in rapid, dense exchanges of blunt messages.[30]

Game Theory, Bargaining, and Gaming

Game theory analyzes the communication transactions and outcomes of actors involved in bargaining and conflict.[31] The channels of global communication provide the means by which widely separated actors on the international stage can (or cannot) exchange messages as the "game" progresses. Game theory is similar to playing poker or chess, buying a new car, or negotiating with a child. What unites these diverse situations are *players* (people, groups, or countries), *payoffs* (outcomes with values), and *communication* (strategies for maximizing profits or, at least, for minimizing damages). Chess is a typical "game of perfect information" because there are no hidden moves. Poker, by contrast, is a game of "imperfect information" because decisions must be made without knowing the identity of the concealed cards.

How do games relate to global communication? Let's look at an example. "Chicken," a well-known game among American teenagers, involves two youngsters driving automobiles. The drivers race at full speed toward one another. Whoever swerves first is the "chicken," or coward. There are four possible outcomes: If both drivers A and B swerve, both are "chicken," but neither loses face. If A swerves but B does not, then A is "chicken" and loses face, and B gains stature. If B swerves and A does not, then the payoffs are reversed. Finally, if neither swerves, they crash, and the payoff is death. Both drivers have "perfect information"; all the moves of one player are visible to the other.

The most probable outcome is that both drivers swerve. This is called the *mini-max strategy,* a damage-minimizing strategy that guarantees the best of the worst outcomes.[32] But what happens when the two actors are separated by thousands of miles and each has "imperfect information" about the other's moves, information

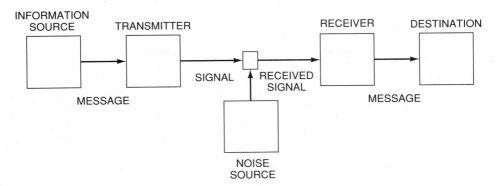

FIGURE 7-2   The Shannon–Weaver Model of the Communication Process.

SOURCE: From *The Mathematical Theory of Communication,* by Claude E. Shannon and Warren Weaver. Copyright © 1949 by the Board of Trustees of the University of Illinois. Reprinted by permission.

supplied by imperfect channels of communication? This is the case in another variation of "chicken," the nuclear confrontation. The decision to swerve or not to swerve is analogous to stepping back from the brink of nuclear war or proceeding with all-out nuclear destruction, as in the case of Kennedy and Khrushchev at the Cuban Missile Crisis. The most probable outcome would be that of both parties swerving, in which neither loses face. The next probable outcome is one party swerving, thus losing face but avoiding the nuclear holocaust—which is indeed what happened when, in the Kennedy–Khrushchev showdown, the Soviet leader blinked first and backed down.

Another aspect of game theory relevant to global communication is *tacit bargaining,* which illustrates the phenomenon of how communication can actually take place between parties who have no contact whatsoever. This involves complex forms of "signaling" in which the process of military escalation or limited war can be transmitted to an enemy without direct contact. One good example of tacit bargaining is the lack of gas warfare during World War II. All sides had experienced the horrors of this type of destruction during World War I, but when one side refrained from launching gas attacks in World War II, so did the others. When opponents reach such tacit accords without communicating directly, they rely on what game theorists call *prominent solutions,* solutions that stand out from the alternatives.[33]

MID-RANGE THEORIES OF GLOBAL COMMUNICATION

Mid-range theories relate social groups, communities, institutions, social classes, and political movements to the subject of war and peace.

Theories of Global Information Flow

Global communication connects a source and a receiver across international boundaries. Between the source and the receiver flow messages and signals. A *message* is the meaning with which the source wishes to affect the receiver. But a message cannot be transmitted directly. It must be encoded into *signals,* the physical form by which it is transmitted. The message might be "we support your struggle," but the signal might be a stream of digital bits and bytes. Information transfer always takes place within a *channel*, the physical means for carrying the signal from source to receiver.

The *Shannon–Weaver model* represented the essential components in the communication process: a *source* of information with a message to send; a *transmitter* with the capacity to *encode* the message into a signal; a *receiver* that *decodes* the signal to retrieve the message; a *receiver* for whom the message is intended; and a *noise source*, namely any interference added to the signal between source and destination (this can be both mechanical noise, such as radio static, or semantic noise, such as cross-cultural differences).[34] (See Figure 7-2.)

But global communication is a vastly more complicated process; the source (for instance, a news agency) might consist of dozens, if not hundreds, of people. So Cioffi-Revilla and Merritt added *gatekeepers* to the model. Most of the information we obtain about foreign countries is mediated by gatekeepers, including reporters and newscasters, lecturers, and recent visitors.[35] So a model of global communication must have at least two major additions to the Shannon–Weaver model. It must contain at least four actors (observer, network/organization, broadcaster, and audience), and it must be "noisy." Each of the four actors contains the various components already discussed.[36] The two endpoints are the universe of events and the audience's perception of those events. (See Figure 7-3.)

Mowlana distinguished between two stages in the global communication process: production and distribution. To the production–distribution axis he added a technology axis. Technology was divided into two poles: communication hardware and communication software.[37] (See Figure 7-4.)

How do people receive communication about other parts of the world? Gumpert and Cathcart's intercultural interaction model outlined one way. Two people (A and B) in one country have no direct contact with a group or individual in another country (O). A and B must rely on media reporting (M) of O, which may wittingly or unwittingly introduce stereotypes or other biases into A's and B's perceptions of O.[38] (See Figure 7-5.)

This intervening media variable is also found in the Westley–MacLean model. Again, A and B are located in different countries. The message that the communicator C transmits to B (X'') is composed out of A's reports of various events in his country (X_1 to X_∞) plus C's own impressions ($^>X$) of those events.[39]

Lazarsfeld called this the *two-step flow theory of communication*. Information moved first to relatively well-informed people who listened to or viewed the media. Then it moved through interpersonal channels to others with less exposure to the media.[40] International shortwave-radio listening is a case in point. The broadcasts are picked up by opinion leaders, who play an important role in shaping the opinions of those to whom they pass the information.

One interesting middle-range flow theory is the "small world" phenomenon, which occurs when two strangers discover they have a common acquaintance. The name comes from their comment: "It's a small world, isn't it?" The theory predicts that at most seven intermediaries, and more commonly two or three intermediaries (acquaintances of acquaintances), connect almost any two people in the world! The explanation for this is that humans communicate in nodal networks, much like computers.[41]

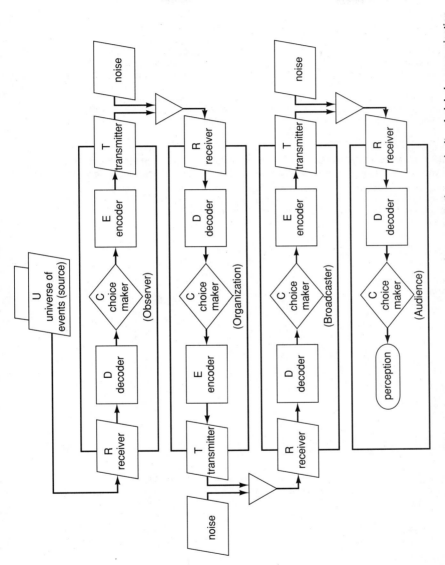

FIGURE 7-3 Cioffi-Revilla and Merritt elaborated Shannon's model to demonstrate the complexity of global communication.

SOURCE: Claudio Cioffi-Revilla and Richard L. Merritt, "Communication Research and the New World Information Order," *Journal of International Affairs* 35 (2, 1981/1982): 240. Published by permission of the Journal of International Affairs and the Trustees of Columbia University in the City of New York.

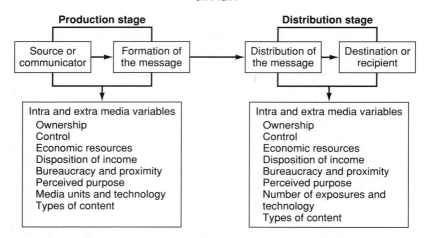

FIGURE 7-4   Mowlana's Two Stages of Information Flow. Control of distribution is the most important index of how power is distributed in a communication system.

SOURCE: From *Global Information and World Communication: New Frontiers in International Relations,* by Hamid Mowlana, p. 10. Copyright © 1986 by Longman Publishing Group. Reprinted with permission from Longman Publishing Group.

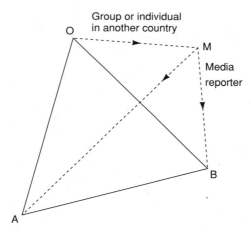

FIGURE 7-5   Gumpert and Cathcart's Intercultural Interaction Model of Communication. The model shows two people (A and B) in one country who have no direct contact with a person (O) in another country. Their perceptions of O must rely on media reporters (M).

SOURCE: From "Media Stereotyping: Images of the Foreigner," by G. Gumpert and R. Cathcart. In L. A. Samovar and R. E. Porter (eds.), *Intercultural Communication: A Reader,* p. 352. Copyright © 1984 by Wadsworth, Inc. Reprinted by permission of the publisher, Wadsworth Publishing Company, Belmont, CA.

Theories of International Communication Messages

Structuralism studies the patterns undergirding social behavior and culture.[42] One such approach, *semiology,* looks at the *form* of communication signs and symbols rather than at their *content.* Semiology identifies the symbolic structures of communication and interprets their meanings not from their inherent character, but rather from their relative positions to one another and within their cultural context. One proposition, known as the *Sapir–Whorf hypothesis,* stated that the world is experienced differently in different linguistic communities because each language embodies and perpetuates a different world view.[43] Thus, the precision of the German language would lead a German speaker to have a different worldview than, say, a French speaker, whose language might be more "romantic." These differences can often be seen in "untranslatable" concepts.[44]

Some writers have suggested that global messages are cast in recurrent structuring devices known as *frames,* which affect the message's content and form.[45] Kervin examined the formal codes (editing, camera distance, camera angle, and camera movement) in television news coverage of El Salvador. Her results showed that certain repeated and consistent formal devices reinforced the U.S. government's arguments about the conflict.[46] Anderson's study of photojournalism coverage of the same conflict found frames emphasizing law and order, hopelessness, and justification of war.[47]

Another way to look at global communication content is through its *discourse.* Discourse is more than the utterance of speakers; it is also the turn-taking interaction between communicators as well as the rules and conventions operating in a given context.[48] Discourse is the product of social, historical, and institutional circumstances. Discourse analysis arises from three premises: (1) Media producers do not simply select content but actually produce "the world" and construct meaning; (2) Audiences do not simply respond to "effects" but actually negotiate and reconstruct meaning on their own terms; (3) Media are produced by "industrially organized media" that have their own agendas.[49]

Discourse analysis at the global level proceeds from the assumption that growing economic concentration and cultural domination have a direct impact on media texts and their uses. Comparing media products across cultures allows us to see those themes, styles, and rhetoric that are imposed by dominant communication monopolies. Global communication channels transmit ideologies.[50] They justify nuclear weapons.[51] They even transmit the concrete ways that audiences are supposed to decode their media.[52]

International events are frequently formed into complex storylines. A story is a simplified scenario of social action and makes sense only within agreed-upon conventions of social understanding and behavior. At the national level, conventional storylines "are as much a part of communication as language."[53] Both fiction writers and journalists understand story-based syntax and respect it as much as they respect grammar and spelling. This kind of *storyline analysis* is increasingly being used to examine political events. Katz and Dayan even have argued that global media events must be seen as *rituals.*[54]

Most media events are national in character, but in recent times global communications channels have united billions of people in a shared experience. The transformation in international summit meetings is a good case in point. Early summits, for example at Yalta and Potsdam, were secret meetings whose purpose was to create policy away from the view of the public. Summits still create policy, but the summit meeting of today has become a "public, symbolic activity, a political ritual and media event."[55]

Spheres of Influence, Consensus, and Legitimacy

Chomsky and Herman observed that American mass media give attention only to those international news events that are consistent with U.S. foreign policy goals. Those nations that fall outside the U.S. "sphere of influence" tend to be covered negatively. At the same time, media tend to ignore negative aspects of governments of U.S. allies. Chomsky and Herman believe it is more accurate to talk about a "propaganda framework" in regard to news coverage.[56] McLeod believed this applied equally well to media of other nations, namely, that they cover international news with respect for the allegiances of their countries.[57] Thus, we could explain the difference in U.S. media coverage of elections in El Salvador (triumphant vindication of democracy) and Nicaragua (Sandinista intransigence and totalitarian controls).[58]

Hallin argued that media grant credibility only to events within a certain circle of legitimacy.[59] Within the central "sphere of consensus" journalists "do not feel compelled either to present opposing views or to remain disinterested observers. On the contrary, the journalist's role is to serve as an advocate or celebrant of consensus values."[60] In other words, certain topics are simply beyond the range of polite debate. (See Figure 7-6.)

MACRO-LEVEL THEORIES OF GLOBAL COMMUNICATION

Now we turn our attention to large aggregates—nation–states, cultures, economies, and the world system. Some of the macro-level theories of global communication that are easiest to grasp are environmental theories.

Geopolitical and Environmental Theories

Here we find theories that examine the *environment of global communication*.[61] By "environment" we mean not only the earth's physical features and geography, but also all products of human culture, such as resource availability, demographic factors, technological development and the symbolic environment (socio-sphere).

Geopolitical theory looks at the political consequences of geographical variables. Swedish geographer Rudolf Kjellen, the first writer to use the term *geopolitics,* maintained that all states have five things in common: boundaries, a capital, national consciousness, a culture—and *lines of communication*.[62] The lines of communication are essential to spanning the distances within and between territorial units. A nation's geopolitical power depends in part on its channels of communication in the same way its bridges span rivers: They both unite and protect.

Geopolitics plays an important role in the life—and the death—of nations. For example, the Polish people inhabited a contiguous territory and had a common language and ample lines of communication. But without natural land protection, Poland has been the victim of repeated invasion. Some countries have *physical discontinuities,* territories separated by water or by intervening countries. For example, the physical noncontiguity of the two parts of divided Pakistan (before the creation of Bangladesh in 1971) hindered that nation's ability to integrate politically because it impeded the flow of communication, goods, and people.[63] Merritt found that political disintegration increased with distance. Communication was greater among neighboring peoples than among distant peoples. A noncontiguous polity depends on communications to keep its separated parts integrated.[64] For this reason the United

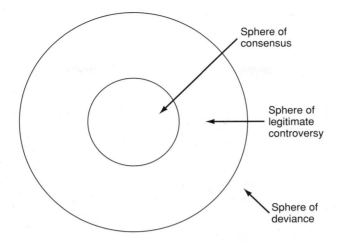

FIGURE 7-6 Hallin's model illustrates spheres of consensus, controversy, and deviance.

SOURCE: From "*The Uncensored War*": *The Media and Vietnam* by Daniel C. Hallin, Copyright © 1986 by Daniel C. Hallin. Reprinted by permission of Oxford University Press, Inc.

States maintains the highest quality undersea cable and satellite links with Alaska and Hawaii.

Geopolitical theorists included communication and information channels as essential variables. Mahan wrote that the success of the British empire was due to its control of the sealanes, especially narrow waterways. Except for the Panama Canal, Britain controlled all of the world's major waterways and choke points. During the time of the British Empire, land transportation channels were largely undeveloped.[65]

Like Mahan, Mackinder saw the intimate relationship between power, technology, and communication. But to Mackinder, the "Heartland" was what mattered. Land channels—not sealanes—were pivotal, particularly in the era of technological advancement in terrestrial communication.[66] (See Figure 7-7.) Today the airplane and the rocket ship make air and space channels key elements in the political power equation. Douhet did for the airplane what Mahan did for the seas and Mackinder did for land. No longer constrained by land-based transportation, air channels could penetrate formerly invulnerable areas.[67]

All these technological developments have an impact on "distance." Afghanistan is not likely to go to war with Bolivia because they are so far apart. But geographical distance between countries is just one measure of distance. *Strategic distance* between two countries is a function of their possession of nuclear-tipped missiles. The *political distance* is a function of their similarity in governing systems. *Technological distance* is a function of their connection through communication systems, transportation, and trade.[68] The interplay of these various "distances" is very apparent in Great Britain's close relationship with and willingness to go to war over the Falklands/Malvinas Islands.

Another important geopolitical variable is population. By the year 2050 there

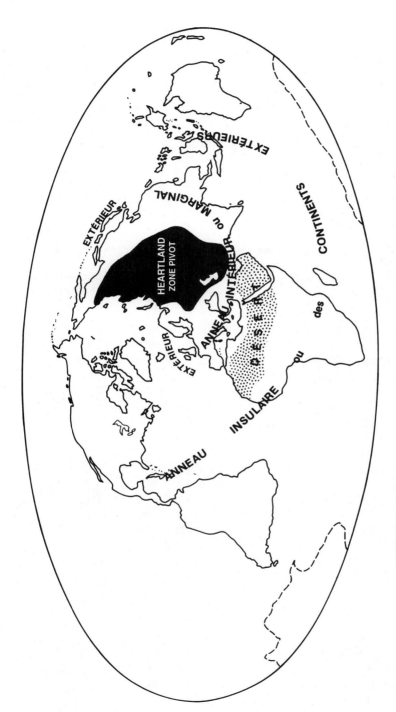

FIGURE 7-7   The World According to Mackinder (1904). Control of the pivotal Heartland zone, the Euro-Asian continental landmass, constituted a potential threat to the maritime powers.

SOURCE: Gérard Chaliand and Jean-Pierre Rageau, *Atlas Strategique* (Paris: Fayard, 1983), p. 21. Reprinted by permission.

may be as many as twelve billion people on our earth.[69] As Wright once observed, population growth has "stimulated global communication, interpenetrated cultures, increased international cooperation and tended to bring the entire human race together into a single community."[70] At the same time, this growth has produced considerable confrontation and friction between cultures that were once isolated from one another. As populations grow, communication interactions increase among and between peoples and cultures. As the weapons of destruction have increased in capacity, so too have both the size of belligerent populations and the size of the territory contested. Today the ocean, the atmosphere, and even outer space have become part of the battlefield. Global—even interplanetary—communication technologies spanning these distances provide the command and control apparatus to manage this planetary geopolitical space. The advent of these C^3I technologies ("Communication, Command, and Control," in military jargon) has forced a reexamination of geopolitical relationships.

The "information as virus" theory has generated a great deal of controversy. This theory arises from *sociobiology,* which holds that natural selection applies to behavior in the same way it applies to genetics.[71] *Memetics* is an information theory that applies biological models to the evolution, spread, and persistence of ideas within, between, and among cultures. One author has called this the "germ theory applied to ideas."[72] Basic to memetic theory are four notions:

1. Ideas (memes) develop according to certain predictable rules.
2. Cultural transmission and spread of ideas of all types (in particular, scientific ideas) embody these rules.
3. There is a distinct similarity of evolution of memetic building blocks to that of genetic building blocks (which raises the obvious question of whether language structure is controlled by human genetic structure).
4. New, unanticipated language and meme structures, can, and possibly already do, exist.[73]

Social movements, in this view, are seen as the results of "infectious ideas" that spread throughout the world in the same way an epidemic spreads. One example is an idea such as "Don't worry, Be happy," which spread quickly throughout popular culture by replicating itself in the mind when heard. Memetic theory might predict when and explain how Shiism (fundamentalist Islam) might spread to Turkey or how liberal democracy might spread throughout Eastern Europe.

Dawkins devised the term "meme" (rhymes with "seem") as an analogy to "gene" in his book *The Selfish Gene.* Memes use human minds to replicate information patterns in the same way genes use cells to copy DNA patterns. Memes are subject to selective evolutionary factors in the same way genes are. Human minds, communication channels, and the huge repertoire of competing and cooperating memes make it possible for some "fittest" (from *survival of the fittest*) memes (such as market capitalism) to have global reach while other, "less fit," memes (such as slavery and feudalism) die out. This theory sees ideological struggle as a fight to the finish between incompatible memes for space within the collective mind. Indeed, the world today is one vast information ecosystem wherein memes of many kinds compete to find host organisms within which to live.

But unlike genes, whose purpose is survival of the organism, some memes, such as the philosophies behind *kamikaze* attacks and suicide bombing, are contrary to human survival. Henson calls these *memeoids* and lists as examples such lethal ideas as the People's Temple in Guyana and Hitler's "master race" theory. However, "most memes, like microorganisms, are either helpful or at least harmless."[74]

Systems Theories

Perhaps the broadest macro-level approach to global communication theory is the study of grand systems.[75] This approach unites systems as diverse as the human nervous system, an automobile motor, a room thermostat, the Hilton hotel chain, or an aquarium fish tank. The flow of information is vital to the survival of systems. All systems communicate within themselves and with other systems. They have feedback mechanisms to make "mid-course corrections." The system of contemporary international affairs depends on the routine communication transactions of the various actors as well as transborder (that is, cross-system) flows such as trade, tourism, investment, technology transfer, and news flows. As systems grow more interdependent, communication interactions grow increasingly more frequent, as does complexity of the system. New technologies have had a tremendous impact on the international system by allowing speedier and higher-quality interactions.

Systems theories owe much to the pioneering information theory known as *cybernetics*.[76] Cybernetics (from the Greek *kybernetes,* meaning "helmsman") is "the systematic study of communication and control in organizations of all kinds. . . . Essentially it represents a shift in the center of interest from drives to steering, and from instincts to systems of decisions, regulation and control."[77] Cybernetics was born when researchers noticed the resemblance between humans and machines in their dependence on information for control. A system needs to receive information on the way in which it needs to change. *Negative feedback* gives information that calls for corrective actions in the opposite direction of an error. Nations depend greatly upon feedback, without which adaptation cannot sensibly take place. Cybernetics is closely related to *information theory*.[78]

We can distinguish successful systems by the way they respond to demands placed upon them and by how they collect, evaluate, and respond to incoming information. Those systems that survive are the ones that competently abstract and code incoming information, store coded symbols, screen certain important information from the rest, recall stored information when needed, and transmit information without succumbing to information overload.[79] "Communication is the cement that makes organizations. Communication alone enables a group to think together, to see together and to act together."[80]

In fact we can say that *the higher the volume of interaction* (defined variously using such communication flows as mail, student exchange, and trade), *the higher the level of integration.*[81] Societies and nation–states now conduct their relations through written and oral communications using elaborate symbol sets and communication rituals. Indeed, "communication and interaction are at the core of global politics."[82] Leaders make state visits, intelligence agencies gather data, diplomats make representations, citizens travel in good will. In crisis situations, nations reach for the "hotline" or diplomats undertake "shuttle diplomacy." The mass media cover issues of peace and war. International organizations exchange information and reach agreements. Colleagues, friends, and relatives write, wire, and call around the world.

As Beer has explained, "[G]lobal communication provides information and contacts, encouraging images, values and patterns of identification that help create and maintain peace and reduce the likelihood of war."[83]

Integration theory examines the volume of interactions between and among political entities that make up a community. It presumes that "cohesiveness among individuals can be measured, and is probably promoted, by the extent of mutual relationship or interactions among them."[84] By analyzing the actual flows of interactions among the constituent units, one can use objective data to make generalizations about integration, friendship, and solidarity, or the lack thereof.[85] The most common measures are flows of mail, telephone, trade, and student exchanges.[86]

One good example of this is the changing mail flows in Europe over several decades of political evolution from fracture to integration. European mail flow before World War II reflected prevailing regional groupings: Tightly-knit mail flow regions existed in Anglo-America, Scandinavia, and Eastern and Southeastern Europe. Until 1937 Germany, the Netherlands, Luxembourg, Belgium, France, and Italy lacked any semblance of being a cohesive mail flow region. In fact, they manifested a strong pattern of indifference to one another. But by the late 1950s social communication as measured by mail flows had increased. "By 1961 the EEC states had finally emerged as a fairly distinct and cohesive region in terms of international mail flows . . . especially significant because it represents one of the few appreciable shifts during the twentieth century in the basic structure of West European mail flows."[87]

One powerful concept in integration theory is *aggregation.* Beer wrote that global communication, international exchange transactions, international law, and international organization all contribute to "aggregation," defined as "the logic of technology that makes larger, relatively integrated units out of smaller elements."[88] Aggregative factors "work to produce fewer and shorter wars. Wars occur, to some extent, because of a failure or lack of aggregation."[89] Using measures of the global flows of satellites, television, radio, journals, magazines, newspapers, letters, telegrams, and telephones, Beer noted that "peace promotes the growth of international transaction and communication. . . . By the same logic, war may have negative effects on international transaction and communication."[90]

One final systems approach is known as *regime theory.* Traditionally, the nation–state was considered the basic unit in the international arena.[91] Recently, however, it is increasingly apparent that nation–states are not the only actors; one new actor is the "regime."[92] Regimes are patterns of cooperation among states; these patterns correspond to a set of principles, norms, rules, and agreements.

What kinds of regimes do we find today? The best illustration of contemporary regimes is the *international trade regime* governed by the General Agreement on Tariffs and Trade (GATT) and the International Monetary Fund (IMF).[93] Also much studied is the *international security regime.* One stable security regime was the Concert of Europe, in which between 1814 and 1822 the great powers did not seek to maximize their individual power positions or take advantage of the temporary weakness or vulnerability of others.[94] Another example is the *international food regime* that governs food trade, food aid, and international financing for rural development and agricultural research.[95]

Is there a global communication regime? Using the definition of regime cited earlier, we can speak of the current, "liberal" *global communications regime,* formed in 1865 originally around the International Telegraphic Union and now extended to the international organizations that regulate global communication.[96] This regime is characterized by its adherence to the "free flow" doctrine and its domination by transnational corporations. The "new world information order" regime stressed national sovereignty, collective self-reliance, and challenge to the status quo.[97]

Systems theory has been criticized because it assumes that systems are stable. Negative feedback is the only feedback generally considered. Recently some authors have focused on morphogenetic, or evolving, systems in which positive as well as negative loops are critical. Systems are seen as dynamic rather than static. Periods of chaos or turbulence are not seen as failures but as required periods of "punctuation," during which a system may reorient itself externally in relation to other systems and respond to changes taking place internally. Order leads to chaos, which leads again to order.[98]

Theories of Power and International Communication

Power can be defined in ways that relate it closely to the process of communication.

> Power is the ability to move the individual or the human collectivity in some desired fashion through "persuasion, purchase, barter, and coercion."[99]
>
> Spykman

> Power may [be comprised of] anything that establishes and maintains the control of man over man. . . . from physical violence to the most subtle psychological ties by which one mind controls another.[100]
>
> Morgenthau

> [Power is] the ability to move others or to get them to do what one wants them to do and not to do what one does not want them to do.[101]
>
> Wolfers

> Power can be *psychological control* over others.[102]
>
> Sullivan

Realist theory has dominated the study of power in international relations for decades. Drawing on Machiavelli and Bismarck, elaborated by Kissinger and Morgenthau, and most incontestable in the two world wars and the Cold War, realism overwhelmed the *idealist theory* of Woodrow Wilson, the League of Nations, and the Kellogg–Briand Pact.[103] Although there is much to differentiate these two approaches, what unites realism and idealism are their *normative* orientations, their study of history, and their focus on public opinion and communication (or lack of communication).

Idealism maintains that the "law of the jungle" in the current nation–state system can be changed through international law and organization and that politics can be made to conform to some ethical standard.[104] The League of Nations, created after World War I under the stewardship of U.S. President Woodrow Wilson, exemplified this orientation in the role it foresaw for the mass media. Wilson called the League "the court of public opinion" in which the "conscience of the world" could render its verdict.[105] "The Press," said one League resolution, "constitutes the most effective means of guiding public opinion towards moral disarmament, which is a concomitant condition of material disarmament."[106] The 1945 UNESCO Constitution rang of idealism, human perfectibility, and the influence of public opinion on international politics: "[S]ince wars begin in the minds of men, it is in the minds of men that the defences of peace must be constructed."

The contrast between idealism and realism could not be greater. Realists maintain that there is no essential harmony of interests among nations. They see the international arena of competing nation–states as being in a "state of nature." International public opinion does not have much influence because the world's moral and political consensus is weak. In such a world, pursuing naked self-interest is more effective and secure than pursuing the idealist goals of human rights, social justice, disarmament, law, and international organization.

Realist theory typically subordinates communication and public opinion to the requirements of power politics. But Tehranian has pointed out that the realist worldview has changed. He has argued that realists today are forced to "consider the vital role that the apparatuses of image making are playing in international relations."[107] He is supported by one noted realist writer John Hertz, who has "reconsidered" his position. Hertz asserted: "It is perhaps no exaggeration to say that today half of power politics consists of 'image making' . . . Today, hardly anything remains in the open conduct of foreign policy that does not have a propaganda or public relations aspect.[108] Image-making, propaganda, public relations: Hertz, the realist, has identified the very components of idealism. His "reconsideration" reflected the fact that the polarity between idealism and realism may be breaking down in the information age.

In the past, propaganda, public relations, and global communication were mere handmaidens of the state. Today they have increasingly become statecraft itself. Indeed, one of the results of the tremendous growth in global communication has been the "ideologization" of international relations.[109] Today a country need not maintain its power over others strictly through armed force. Its dominance can reach around the world through communication and culture—in short, through hegemony. *Hegemony* might be thought of as the penetration of a certain set of beliefs, values, attitudes, and morality that supports "the established order and the class interests that dominate it."[110] In all societies, media expand and promote dominant beliefs and reinforce the coercive power of the state. "To Bottomore the hegemony of a dominant class is created and recreated in a web of institutions, social relations, and ideas."[111] Kolakowski once remarked that "hegemony signifies the control of the intellectual life of society by purely cultural means."[112]

How can global communication channels perpetuate hegemony? The French philosopher Louis Althusser wrote of the role of *ideological state apparatuses* (ISAs) such as schools, the legal system, culture, religion, and the media.[113] ISAs reinforce the dominant class's worldview in the classroom, in the courtroom, and throughout society. Each society also has international ISAs, which direct the "war of ideas" to influence the hearts and minds of people in other parts of the world. These international ISAs include governmental propaganda organs, institutions of public diplomacy, exchanges of scholars and students, and the like.[114]

Theories of Political Economy

If Karl Marx were alive today, he would not write *Das Kapital*, but "Die Information." No longer are agriculture and manufacturing the leading economic sectors; throughout the world, the information economy now dominates our society. Marx was one of the first political economists, and he set the terms of debate for the succeeding century and beyond. Political economic theory of global communication studies the effect of information production, exchange, and consumption on the international political environment.

We divide these theories into three categories—liberal economic theory and modernization theory, Marxist approaches, and structuralism and dependency approaches. Each might analyze global media flows in a different way.

Liberalism arose originally in Europe in the period between the Reformation and the French Revolution as a political philosophy emphasizing individual freedom.[115] Feudalism had given way to Protestantism, the nation–state, commerce, science, cities, and a growing middle class of traders and industrialists (called the *bourgeoisie*). Adam Smith summarized liberal economics in his *Inquiry into the Nature and Causes of the Wealth of Nations.* National wealth, he maintained, came about through human effort in producing commodities. Economic growth worked best within a system of perfect competition. Smith called for a system of natural liberty that would allow competitive, interest-seeking, and self-maximizing individuals to accumulate capital and at the same time to maximize the general welfare. He believed in the "invisible hand" of the market, which obeyed the law of supply and demand.

Today's doctrine of the free flow of information embodies these concepts. It emphasizes an unrestricted flow of information and open competition in the marketplace. It demands elimination of regulations in order to permit greater competition and removal of obstacles to flow. Most important is the concept of information as a commodity. In the information age, the economy is concerned with the creation and application of information to make all forms of production more efficient and to create new wealth. The limiting factor is knowledge. Today power flows to those who create or process information.[116]

Communication and liberal economics had their finest expression in modernization theory. Rostow's famous book *The Stages of Economic Growth* proposed economic stages leading from traditional society, to "takeoff," to sustained growth.[117] Lerner saw the media as an engine of these stages, with four crucial communication-dependent variables important in accelerating the "takeoff" phase of economic growth: urbanization, literacy, mass media exposure, and political participation.[118] The key to the "modernization" process was the growth of mobile personalities possessing the capacity to transmit information in a meaningful manner between individuals and groups, creating national cultures and communities.[119]

Next comes Marxist political economy. It should be noted that the collapse of the Stalinist variety of socialism in Eastern Europe has caused far-reaching rethinking of the future of socialism in general and of the continued vitality of Marxism, on which socialism rests. Yet Marx's method and many of his theories will persist beyond the collapse of Stalinism.

Marxist political economy of communication seeks to reveal how various modes of material production (for example, feudalism, capitalism, socialism, and communism) are encoded in the communication process and the products of information. Such analysis of communication and information seeks to disclose the values, class relations, and power structures of a particular historical or socioeconomic situation. Marxists believe that communication is part and parcel of dominant social relations. In capitalist society, communication follows the dictates of the marketplace. Media are central agents in "mystifying" the public. Media are fetishized to make their commercial character seem natural: People become things. Money "works," capital "produces," and in the same way, media "act." Media conceal their manipulative power by contending they are a force for contentment. To Marxists, media are the new means of social control. Monopoly capitalism has moved from direct coercion, repression, and wage slavery to ideological coercion as the preferred method of class domination. Society has reached the crossover point where information often replaces the military as a means of social control.

Typical research questions that Marxists ask are: Who owns, controls, and operates the media? What social, political, and economic arrangements characterize the media of social communication? What roles do media play in society? What are the functions of various popular media art forms? What ideas, values, notions, concepts, and beliefs are spread by the media, and which are overlooked? How are writers, artists, actors, and other creative people affected by the patterns of ownership and control of the media? What function does communication perform in commodity production, circulation, exchange, and accumulation?

Structuralism and dependency theory depart from the orthodoxy of both liberal economics and Marxism. Structuralism begins with the unbalanced relationship that exists between "center" and "periphery" nations.[120] Even within nations there is a center and a periphery, thus resulting in four categories: the center of the Center (cC), the periphery of the Center (pC), the center of the Periphery (cP), and the periphery of the Periphery (pP). In more concrete terms, the following example is proposed:

cC = New York   cP = Moscow
pC = Appalachia   pP = Kazakhstan

In this analysis, a harmony of interests exist between Moscow and New York. One could even say that Moscow is a "bridgehead" for New York's (Wall Street) expansion into the vast resource markets of Kazakhstan.

In terms of global communication, under this theory we might expect to find strong communication flows and high-capacity, two-way information exchange among the world's cCs, such as between New York and Tokyo. We might also expect to find high capacity, but fewer two-way flows between the cC and the cP, such as between New York and Moscow. Communication between the cC (New York) and the pC (Appalachia) will tend to be low-capacity and one-way; communication between the cP (Moscow) and pP (Kazakhstan) will be even worse. Communication between the pC (Appalachia) and the pP (Kazakhstan) will be virtually nonexistent.

Dependency theory arose in the 1970s as one school of structuralism.[121] It takes its name from the "dependent" relationship between the center and the periphery. Periphery nations are not poor because they lack capital or because they lie at the edge of the capitalist world; they are poor precisely because they have been *integrated* into the capitalist world. Dependency theory sees the international media as powerful agents that promote imported lifestyles from the center to the periphery.[122]

TOWARD AN INTEGRATIVE THEORY OF GLOBAL COMMUNICATION

An integrative theory of global communication would be one that consolidated many of the foregoing partial theories, accommodated their differences, harmonized their

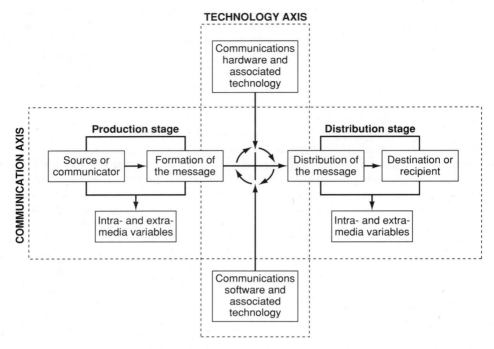

FIGURE 7-8 Mowlana's Model of the International Flow of Information. With a "hardware" and a "software" axis, this integrative model can explain many global communication phenomena.

SOURCE: From *Global Information and World Communication: New Frontiers in International Relations,* by Hamid Mowlana, p. 11. Copyright © 1986 by Longman Publishing Group. Reprinted with permission from Longman Publishing Group.

similarities, and thus explained and predicted global communication phenomena in a unified way. An integrative theory ideally would account for 100 percent of the variation in explaining and predicting these phenomena. This is not an idle occupation for closeted theorists. As world cultures are transformed by science and technology, as a new division of labor arises based on the information economy, and as new transnational actors vie for attention in the global media arena, there has also arisen a sense of urgency to find a unified theory of global communications.

The problem with devising an integrative theory is that there are many types of communication on the international level. There are also many disciplines contributing important theoretical statements about global communication. If a comprehensive theory of global communication ever arose, it would have to encompass biology, psychology, social psychology, sociology, anthropology, history, political science, geography, economics, organizational theory, game theory, strategic theory and decision-making theory, integration theory, and systems theory—not to mention communication theory!

One writer, Hamid Mowlana, has sought to unify these disparate threads. Mowlana begins with the critique that most previous theories are historically biased. They are products of the particular social and historical circumstances in which they arose and in which their authors wrote. Such theories have also relied too heavily on the source and content of global messages. Mowlana calls for a "dynamic paradigm that can take the social, economic, political, and structural variables into account."[123]

Mowlana does this by putting control at the center of his theory. Control has two components: control of message production and control of message distribution. These are not used as economic terms; *production* means message formation, and *distribution* means message dissemination. Control of the distribution process, Mowlana says, "is the most important index of the way in which power is distributed in a communication system."[124]

Mowlana began this quest for a universally applicable and historically dynamic theory of global communication in 1970 with a model that compared mass media systems nonideologically.[125] By 1986 this model had developed to show the communication axis (production and distribution) along one axis and the technology axis (hardware and software, or "know-how") along the other (see Figure 7-8).

Here is where the concept of control is important. The ability to produce a message is no guarantee that the message will be disseminated. Neither is control of the hardware alone. Only when a global communicator controls all four elements (production, distribution, hardware, and "know-how") does the message stand a chance of reaching its audiences. Without this quadripartite power, "effective control . . . will fall to the possessors of certain of the components before others," especially to the controllers of the distribution and the software.[126] Using this model, Mowlana goes on to explain such diverse global communication phenomena as the right to communicate, message cost, structural changes, product differentiation, media domination, cultural pluralism, and the role of the state.[127]

NOTES

1. Claudio Cioffi-Revilla, Richard L. Merritt, and Dina A. Zinnes, "Communication and Interaction in Global Politics," in *Communication and Interaction in Global Politics,* ed. Claudio Cioffi-Revilla, Richard L. Merritt, and Dina A. Zinnes (Newbury Park, CA: Sage, 1987), p. 9.

2. I am indebted to two texts for their inspiration in this chapter: James E. Dougherty and Robert L. Pfaltzgraff, Jr., *Contending Theories of International Relations: A Comprehensive Survey,* 3rd ed. (New York: Harper & Row, 1990); and Denis McQuail, *Mass Communication Theory: An Introduction,* 2nd ed. (Newbury Park, CA: Sage, 1987).

3. Dougherty and Pfaltzgraff, *Contending Theories of International Relations,* p. 15.

4. See Carl G. Hempel, *Fundamentals of Concept Formation in Empirical Science* (Chicago: University of Chicago Press, 1952), p. 36.

5. Paul Sites, *Control: The Basis of Social Order* (New York: Dunellen, 1973), p. 9.

6. One word of caution before proceeding. Micro-level theorists often hesitate to generalize broadly from individual human behavior to the international level. In the past, mistakes were made by assuming that processes operating at the international level were merely the aggregation of processes operating at the individual level. Kelman cautions that there is no separate psychological theory of international relations; psychologists may only contribute insights to a more general theory. See Herbert C. Kelman, "Social–Psychological Approaches to the Study of International Relations," in *International Behavior: A Social–Psychological Analysis,* ed. Herbert C. Kelman (New York: Holt, Rinehart & Winston, 1965).

7. Hadley Cantril, *The Human Dimension: Experiences in Policy Research* (New Brunswick, NJ: Rutgers University Press, 1967), p. 16.

8. See John Anderson, *Cognitive Psychology and Its Implications* (San Francisco: W. H. Freeman, 1980); Peter Lindsay and Donald Norman, *Human Information Processing* (New York:

Academic Press, 1972); and Richard Nisbett and Lee Ross, *Human Inference: Strategies and Shortcomings of Social Judgment* (Englewood Cliffs, NJ: Prentice-Hall, 1980).

9. Kenneth E. Boulding, *The Image: Knowledge in Life and Society* (Ann Arbor, MI: University of Michigan Press, 1956).

10. Daniel Goleman, *Vital Lies, Simple Truths: The Psychology of Self-Deception* (New York: Simon & Schuster, 1985), pp. 18–19.

11. David Knox Perry, "The Mass Media and Inferences about Other Nations," *Communication Research* 12 (4, 1985): 595–614.

12. See Elton B. McNeil, "The Nature of Aggression," *The Nature of Human Conflict*, ed. Elton B. McNeil (Englewood Cliffs, NJ: Prentice-Hall, 1965); John Paul Scott, *Animal Behavior* (Garden City, NY: Doubleday/Anchor, 1963); Konrad Lorenz, *On Aggression,* trans. Marjorie Kerr Wilson (New York: Bantam Books, 1967); and Robert Ardrey, *The Territorial Imperative* (New York: Atheneum, 1966).

13. John Dollard, Leonard W. Doob, Neal E. Miller, et al., *Frustration and Aggression* (New Haven, CT: Yale University Press, 1939).

14. Leon Festinger, *A Theory of Cognitive Dissonance* (Stanford, CA: Stanford University Press, 1957); and Leon Festinger, ed. *Conflict, Decision, and Dissonance* (Stanford, CA: Stanford University Press, 1964).

15. Lloyd DeMause, "The Gulf War as Mental Disorder," *The Nation,* March 11, 1991, pp. 1+.

16. Otto Klineberg, *The Human Dimension in International Relations* (New York: Holt, Rinehart & Winston, 1964), p. 33.

17. Geoffrey K. Roberts, *A Dictionary of Political Analysis* (London: Longman, 1971), s.v. "stereotype."

18. Walter Lippman, *Public Opinion* (New York: Harcourt, Brace, 1922), p. 96.

19. William Buchanan and Hadley Cantril, *How Nations See Each Other* (Urbana, IL: University of Illinois Press, 1953), p. 56.

20. Uri Bronfenbrenner, "The Mirror Image Hypothesis in Soviet–American Relations: A Social Psychologist's Report," *Journal of Social Issues* 17 (3, 1961): 46–48. See also I. L. Child and L. Doob, "Factors Determining National Stereotypes," *Journal of Social Psychology* 17 (1943): 203–219; W. Buchanan and H. Cantril, "National Stereotypes," in *The Process and Effects of Mass Communication,* ed. W. L. Schramm (Urbana, IL: University of Illinois Press, 1955), pp. 191–206; Kenneth Berrien, "Stereotype Similarities and Contrasts," *Journal of Social Psychology* 78 (1969): 173–183; José Miguel Salazar, "National Stereotypes as a Function of Conflict and Territorial Proximity: A Test of the Mirror Image Hypothesis," *Journal of Social Psychology* 101 (1977): 13–19; and Douglas M. McLeod, K. Viswanath, and Young-Chul Yoon, "A Content Analysis of Radio Moscow and the Voice of America: A Test of the 'Sphere of Influence' and the 'Mirror-Image' Hypotheses." Paper presented at the Conference of the International Communication Association, Montreal, 1987.

21. Arthur Gladstone, "The Concept of the Enemy," *Journal of Conflict Resolution* 3 (June 1959): 132.

22. Ralph K. White, "Misperception and the Vietnam War," *Journal of Social Issues* 22 (3, 1966): 218. See also Ralph K. White, *Nobody Wanted War: Misperception in Vietnam and Other Wars* (Garden City, NY: Doubleday, 1968).

23. See Marshall R. Singer, "Identity Groups: We vs. They," in *Weak States in a World of Powers* (New York: Free Press, 1972), pp. 25–30.

24. J. Z. Rubin and B. R. Brown, *The Social Psychology of Bargaining and Negotiation* (New York: Academic Press, 1975), p. 92.

25. Morton Deutsch, *The Resolution of Conflict: Constructive and Destructive Processes* (New Haven, CT: Yale University Press, 1973), cited in Martin Patchen, *Resolving Disputes Between Nations: Coercion or Conciliation?* (Durham, NC: Duke University Press, 1988), p. 51.

26. Thomas W. Milburn, "The Management of Crises," in *International Crises: Insights from Behavioral Research,* ed. Charles F. Hermann (New York: Free Press, 1972), pp. 272–273.

27. Ole R. Holsti, "Time, Alternatives, and Communications: The 1914 and Cuban Missile Crises," in *International Crises,* p. 76.

28. Dina A. Zinnes, Joseph L. Zinnes, and Robert D. McClure, "Hostility in Diplomatic Communication: A Study of the 1914 Crisis," in *International Crises*, pp. 139–162.

29. Francis A. Beer, *Peace Against War: The Ecology of International Violence* (San Francisco: W. H. Freeman, 1981), p. 277.

30. See P. Suedfeld and P. Tetlock, "Integrative Complexity of Communications in International Crises," *Journal of Conflict Resolution* 21 (1977): 169; and R. J. Rummel, *Dimensions of Nations* (Beverly Hills, CA: Sage, 1972), p. 457, cited in Beer, *Peace Against War,* pp. 277 and 282, respectively. See also K. J. Gantzel, G. Kress, and V. Rittberger, *Konflikt—Eskalation—Krise: Sozialwissenschaftliche Studien zum Ausbruch des Ersten Weltkrieges* (Düsseldorf, FRG: Bertelsmann, 1972).

31. Steven J. Brams, *Game Theory and Politics* (New York: Free Press, 1975); Steven J. Brams and Morton D. Davis, "The Verification Problem in Arms Control: A Game-Theoretic Analysis," in *Communication and Interaction in Global Politics,* pp. 141–161; John Conway, *On Numbers and Games* (New York: Academic Press, 1976); Morton D. Davis, *Game Theory: A Nontechnical Introduction* (New York: Basic Books, 1983); Christer Jonsson, *Communication in International Bargaining* (London: Pinter, 1990); Herman Kahn, *Thinking the Unthinkable,* 2nd ed. (New York: Avon, 1966); R. Duncan Luce and Howard Raiffa, *Games and Decisions* (New York: Wiley, 1967); John C. McKinsey, *Introduction to the Theory of Games* (New York: McGraw-Hill, 1952); Guillermo Owen, *Game Theory,* 2nd ed. (New York: Academic Press, 1982); Anatol Rapoport, *Fights, Games, and Debates* (Ann Arbor, MI: University of Michigan Press, 1960); Anatol Rapoport, *Strategy and Consciences* (New York: Schocken Books, 1969); Anatol Rapoport, *Two-Person Game Theory* (Ann Arbor, MI: University of Michigan Press, 1969); and Thomas C. Schelling, *The Strategy of Conflict* (New York: Oxford University Press, 1963).

32. John Von Neumann and Oskar Morgenstern, *The Theory of Games and Economic Behavior* (Princeton, NJ: Princeton University Press, 1944).

33. Schelling, *The Strategy of Conflict*, p. 75. Schelling (pp. 55–56) gives a vivid example of a prominent solution: "Name any amount of money. If you all name the same amount you can have as much as you named." A plurality of American players choose $1 million, the prominent solution.

34. Claude E. Shannon and Warren Weaver, *The Mathematical Theory of Communication* (Urbana, IL: University of Illinois Press, 1949).

35. Claudio Cioffi-Revilla and Richard L. Merritt, "Communication Research and the New World Information Order," *Journal of International Affairs* 35 (2, 1981/1982): 233–234.

36. Ibid., p. 238.

37. Hamid Mowlana, *Global Information and World Communication: New Frontiers in International Relations* (New York: Longman, 1986), p. 11.

38. Gary Gumpert and Robert Cathcart, "Media Stereotyping: Images of the Foreigner," in *Intercultural Communication: A Reader,* ed. Larry A. Samovar and Richard E. Porter (Belmont, CA: Wadsworth, 1982), pp. 348–354.

39. Bruce Westley and David MacLean, "A Conceptual Model for Mass Communication Research," *Journalism Quarterly* 34 (1957): 31–38.

40. Paul F. Lazarsfeld, Bernard Berelson, and Helen Gaudet, *The People's Choice* (New York: Duell, Sloan & Pearce, 1944). See also Elihu Katz, "The Two-Step Flow of Communication: An Up-to-Date Report on an Hypothesis," *Public Opinion Quarterly* 21 (1, 1957): 61–78.

41. Sydney Milgram, "The Small World Problem," *Psychology Today* 1 (1, 1967): 60–67; and Manfred Kochen, ed., *The Small World* (Norwood, NJ: Ablex, 1989).

42. Roland Barthes, *Critical Essays* (Evanston, IL: Northwestern University Press, 1972); Fernande M. De George and Richard De George, eds., *The Structuralists: From Marx to Lévi-Strauss* (Garden City, NY: Anchor Books, 1972); and Michael Lane, ed., *Structuralism: A Reader* (London: Cape, 1970).

43. Leonard Bloomfield, *Language* (London: Allen & Unwin, 1955); Robbins Burling, *Man's Many Voices: Language in Its Cultural Context* (New York: Holt, Rinehart & Winston, 1970); John B. Carroll, *Language and Thought* (Englewood Cliffs, NJ: Prentice-Hall, 1964); Joshua A. Fishman, *Sociolinguistics* (Rowley, MA: Newbury House, 1972); Paul Henle, ed., *Language, Thought, and Culture* (Ann Arbor, MI: University of Michigan Press, 1958); Harry Hoijer, ed., *Language in Culture* (Chicago, IL: University of Chicago Press, 1954); Dell Hymes, ed., *Language in Culture and Society: A Reader in Linguistics and Anthropology* (New York: Harper & Row, 1964); and Edward Sapir, *Selected Writings of Edward Sapir on Language, Culture, and Personality,* ed. David G. Mandelbaum (Berkeley and Los Angeles: University of California Press, 1949).

44. Howard Rheingold, *They Have a Word for It: A Lighthearted Lexicon of Untranslatable Words* (Los Angeles: Tarcher, 1988).

45. David Altheide, *Creating Reality: How T.V. Distorts Events* (Beverly Hills, CA: Sage, 1976); Todd Gitlin, *The Whole World Is Watching* (Berkeley and Los Angeles: University of California Press, 1980); and Gaye Tuchman, *Making News: A Study in the Construction of Reality* (New York: Free Press, 1978).

46. Denise J. Kervin, "Structure and Meaning: A Semiotic Analysis of Network Television News" (Ph.D. diss., University of Wisconsin, Madison, 1985).

47. Robin K. Anderson, "Images of War: Photojournalism, Ideology and Central America," *Latin American Perspectives* 16 (Spring 1989): 96–114.

48. Tim O'Sullivan et al., *Key Concepts in Communication* (London: Methuen, 1983), p. 72.

49. Peter A. Bruck, "Strategies for Peace, Strategies for News Research," *Journal of Communication* 39 (1, 1989): 111, 115.

50. See among many others: Howard H. Frederick, *Cuban-American Radio Wars: Ideology in International Telecommunication* (Norwood, NJ: Ablex, 1986); Ariel Dorfman and Armand Mattelart, *How to Read Donald Duck: Imperialist Ideology in the Disney Comic* (London: International General, 1975); International Commission for the Study of Communication Problems [MacBride Commission], *Many Voices, One World* (Paris: UNESCO, 1980); Anthony Smith, *The Geopolitics of Information* (New York: Oxford University Press, 1980); and Jim Richstad and Michael H. Anderson, *Crisis in International News* (New York: Columbia University Press, 1981).

51. Paul Chilton, *Orwellian Language and the Media* (London: Pluto Press, 1988), p. 45. See also Paul Chilton, ed., *Language and the Nuclear Arms Debate: Nukespeak Today* (Dover, NH: Pinter, 1985); and Stephen Hilgartner, Richard C. Bell, and Rory O'Connor, *Nukespeak: Nuclear Language, Visions, and Mindset* (San Francisco, CA: Sierra Club Books, 1982).

52. Teun A. Van Dijk, "Introduction: Discourse Analysis in (Mass) Communication Research," in *Discourse and Communication: New Approaches to the Analysis of Mass Media Discourse and Communication,* ed. Teun A. van Dijk (New York: Walter de Gruyter, 1985), p. 8. See also Cees Hamelink, "International Communication," in *Discourse and Communication,* pp. 143–159; Hans Heinz Fabris, "Krieg und Frieden in den Medien," *Wiener Zeitung* (Vienna), July 22, 1989; and Bruck, "Strategies for Peace," p. 119.

53. Andrew Arno, "Communication, Conflict, and Storylines: The News Media as Actors in a Cultural Context," in *The News Media in National and International Conflict,* ed. Andrew Arno and Wimal Dissanayake (Boulder, CO: Westview Press, 1984), p. 7.

54. For summarizing this approach, thanks to Daniel C. Hallin and Paolo Mancini, "The Summit as Media Event: The Reagan–Gorbachev Meetings on U.S., Italian, and Soviet Television." Paper

presented at the conference of the International Communication Association, San Francisco, 1989. See also Elihu Katz with Daniel Dayan and Pierre Motyl, "Television Diplomacy: Sadat in Jerusalem." Paper presented at the conference on World Communication: Decisions for the Eighties, Philadelphia, 1980; Elihu Katz with Daniel Dayan and Pierre Motyl, "In Defense of Media Events," in *Communications in the Twenty-First Century,* ed. Robert W. Haight, George Gerbner, and Richard Byrne (New York: Wiley, 1981); Elihu Katz and Daniel Dayan, "Media Events: On the Experience of Not Being There," *Religion* 15 (1985): 305–314.

55. Hallin and Mancini, "The Summit as Media Event."

56. Noam Chomsky and Edward S. Herman, *The Political Economy of Human Rights,* 2 vols. (Boston: South End Press, 1979).

57. McLeod, Viswanath, and Yoon, "Radio Moscow and the Voice of America."

58. Edward S. Herman, "Diversity of News: Marginalizing the Opposition," *Journal of Communication* (Summer 1985): 135–146. This case has also been treated by Walter C. Soderlund, "Canadian and American Press Coverage of the 1984 El Salvador Election." Paper presented at the conference of the Canadian Association of Latin American and Caribbean Studies, Windsor, Ontario, October 1987; Walter C. Soderland, "El Salvador's Civil War as Seen in North and South American Press," *Journalism Quarterly* 63 (1986): 268–274; and Walter C. Soderland, "The 1984 Nicaraguan Election: A Comparison of American and Canadian Press Coverage." Paper presented at the 37th Annual Conference of the International Communication Association, Montreal, Canada, May 1987.

59. Daniel Hallin, *The Uncensored War: The Media in Vietnam* (Berkeley and Los Angeles: University of California Press, 1989), pp. 116–118.

60. Mark Hertsgaard, *On Bended Knee: The Press and the Reagan Presidency* (New York: Farrar, Straus, & Giroux, 1988), p. 93.

61. For further reading, see Dougherty and Pfaltzgraff, *Contending Theories of International Relations,* pp. 53–80; Harold Sprout and Margaret Sprout, *The Ecological Perspective on Human Affairs with Special Reference to International Politics* (Princeton, NJ: Princeton University Press, 1965); Alfred Thayer Mahan, *The Influence of Seapower Upon History, 1660–1783* (Boston: Little, Brown, 1897); Halford Mackinder, *Democratic Ideals and Reality* (New York: Norton, 1962); Nicholas J. Spykman, *The Geography of Peace* (New York: Harcourt, Brace, 1944); and Robert Strausz-Hupé, *Geopolitics: The Struggle for Space and Power* (New York: Putnam, 1942).

62. Rudolf Kjellen, *Der Staat als Lebensform* [The State as a Life Form], trans. M. Langfelt (Leipzig, Germany: S. Hirzel Verlag, 1917), pp. 218–220.

63. Amitai Etzioni, *Political Unification: A Comparative Study of Leaders and Forces* (New York: Holt, 1965), p. 29.

64. Richard L. Merritt, "Noncontiguity and Political Integration," in *Linkage Politics: Essays on the Convergence of National and International Systems,* ed. James N. Rosenau (New York: Free Press, 1969), pp. 237–272.

65. Mahan, *Influence of Seapower, pp. 281–329.*

66. Halford Mackinder, "The Geographical Pivot of History," *Geographical Journal* 23 (April 1904): 434. See also Spykman, *Geography of Peace,* pp. 40, 43; Stephen B. Jones, "Global Strategic Views," *Geographical Review* 45 (October 1955): 492–508; and George F. Kennan, "The Sources of Soviet Conduct," *Foreign Affairs* 25 (July 1947): 566–582.

67. Giulio Douhet, *The Command of the Air,* trans. Dino Ferrari (New York: Coward-McGann, 1942), pp. 10–11.

68. Quincy Wright, *A Study of War,* abr. by Louise Leonard Wright (Chicago: University of Chicago Press, 1964), p. 332; see also Dina A. Zinnes, *Contemporary International Relations Research* (New York: Free Press, 1976), pp. 149–157.

69. United Nations, Population Division of the Department of International Economic and Social Affairs, *Long Range Population Projections: Two Centuries of Population Growth, 1950–2150* (New York: United Nations, 1992).

70. Wright, *Study of War,* p. 293.

71. David Barash, *Sociobiology and Behavior* (New York: Elsevier, 1977); David Barash, *Sociobiology: The Whisperings Within* (New York: Harper & Row, 1979); Arthur L. Caplan, *The Sociobiology Debate* (New York: Harper & Row, 1978); Richard Dawkins, *The Selfish Gene* (New York: Oxford University Press, 1976); Michael Gregory, Anita Silvers, and Diane Sutch, eds., *Sociobiology and Human Nature* (San Francisco: Jossey-Bass, 1978); Edward O. Wilson, *Sociobiology: The New Synthesis* (Cambridge, MA: Belknap Press, 1975); and Edward O. Wilson, *On Human Nature* (Cambridge, MA: Harvard University Press, 1979).

72. Keith Henson, "Memetics: The Science of Information Viruses," *Whole Earth Review* (57, Winter 1987): 50. See also *Journal of Ideas* published by the Institute for Memetic Research, Panama City, FL. Email: moritz@well.sf.ca.us.

73. Elan Moritz, "Memetic Science: I—General Introduction," *Journal of Ideas* 1 (1, 1991): 14.

74. Henson, "Memetics," p. 54.

75. For further reading: John W. Burton, *Systems, States, Diplomacy, and Rules* (Cambridge, England: Cambridge University Press, 1968); David Easton, *The Political System: An Inquiry into the State of Political Science* (New York: Knopf, 1971); Morton A. Kaplan, *System and Process in International Politics* (New York: Wiley, 1957); Charles A. McClelland, *Theory and the International System* (New York: Macmillan, 1966); Richard Rosecrance, *Action and Reaction in World Politics* (Boston: Little, Brown, 1963); Rosenau, *Linkage Politics; and Oran R. Young, Systems of Political Science* (Englewood Cliffs, NJ: Prentice-Hall, 1968).

76. For further reading: W. Ross Ashby, *An Introduction to Cybernetics* (New York: Wiley, 1956; reprint, 1968); Karl W. Deutsch, *The Nerves of Government* (New York: Free Press, 1966); Norbert Wiener, *Cybernetics: Control and Communication in the Animal and the Machine* (Cambridge, MA: MIT. Press, 1948); Walter R. Fuchs, *Cybernetics for the Modern Mind* (New York: Macmillan, 1971); F. H. George, *Cybernetics* (London: St. Paul's House, 1971); and Norbert Wiener, *The Human Use of Human Beings: Cybernetics and Society* (Garden City, NY: Doubleday, 1950).

77. Deutsch, *Nerves of Government,* p. 76.

78. For more on information theory, see R. B. Ash, *Information Theory* (New York: Interscience Publishers, 1965); Julius S. Bendat, *Principles and Applications of Random Noise Theory* (New York: Wiley, 1958); F. Clark, *Information Processing* (Pacific Palisades, CA: Goodyear, 1970); Solomon Kullback, *Information Theory and Statistics* (New York: Dover, 1968); Stephen Littlejohn, *Theories of Human Communication* (Belmont, CA: Wadsworth, 1989); Donald MacKay, *Information, Mechanism, and Meaning* (Cambridge, MA: MIT. Press, 1969); A. R. Meetham, *Encyclopedia of Linguistics, Information, and Control* (New York: Pergamon Press, 1969); and A. M. Rosie, *Information and Communication Theory,* 2nd ed. (New York: Van Nostrand Reinhold, 1973).

79. Deutsch, *Nerves of Government,* pp. 250–254.

80. Ibid., p. 77. This is actually a paraphrase from Wiener, *Cybernetics.*

81. For further reading: Roger W. Cobb and Charles Elder, *International Community: A Regional and Global Study* (New York: Holt, 1970); Karl W. Deutsch et al., *Political Community and the North Atlantic Area* (Princeton, NJ: Princeton University Press, 1957); Carl J. Friedrich, *Trends of Federalism in Theory and Practice* (New York: Praeger, 1968); Ernst Haas, *Beyond the Nation–State: Functionalism and International Organizations* (Stanford, CA: Stanford University Press, 1964); David Mitrany, *A Working Peace System* (Chicago: Quadrangle Books, 1966); Philip Jacob and James Toscano, eds., *The Integration of Political Communities* (Philadelphia: Lippincott, 1964); and Karl W. Deutsch, *Political Community at the International Level: Problems of Definition and Measurement* (Garden City, NY: Doubleday, 1954).

82. Cioffi-Revilla, Merritt, and Zinnes, "Communication and Interaction in Global Politics," in *Communication and Interaction in Global Politics,* p. 9.

83. Beer, *Peace Against War,* p. 132.

84. Philip Jacob and Henry Teune, "The Integrative Process: Guidelines for Analysis of the Bases of Political Community," in *The Integration of Political Communities,* p. 23.

85. Dina A. Zinnes and Robert G. Muncaster, "Transaction Flows and Integrative Processes," in *Communication and Interaction in Global Politics,* pp. 23–48.

86. For example, the Universal Postal Union publishes mail flow figures each year for both international and domestic post. Using these numbers we can compute the *D/I ratio,* or the ratio of domestic to international mail flow, within one country, as well as the rate of mail exchange between two or more countries. Excellent examples of this approach are Karl W. Deutsch, "Transaction Flows as Indicators of Political Cohesion," in *The Integration of Political Communities,* p. 80; and Karl W. Deutsch, "Shifts in the Balance of International Communication Flows," *Public Opinion Quarterly* 20 (Spring 1956): 143–160, reprinted in Karl W. Deutsch, *Tides among Nations* (New York: Free Press, 1979), pp. 153–170.

　　Another empirical way of using information flows to measure political integration is Zipf's predictor of interaction between two populations i and j (I_{ij}). It varies directly with the product of their mass (or size) (M_i and M_j) and inversely with the distance (D) separating them (adjusted by some constant, K):

$$I_{ij} = K\ (M_i M_j/D)$$

Imbalances between the actual and expected levels of interaction, Zipf said, could lead to conflict. See George Kingsley Zipf, *Human Behavior and the Principle of Least Effort* (Cambridge, MA: Addison-Wesley, 1949). Other relevant studies that have drawn on Zipf's research can be found in Cioffi-Revilla and Merritt, "Communication Research and the New World Information Order," pp. 228–229. See also I. Richard Savage and Karl W. Deutsch, "A Statistical Model of the Gross Analysis of Transaction Flows," *Econometrica* 28 (3, 1960): 551–572; and Michael D. Wallace and J. David Singer, "International Networks, 1904–1950: The Small World of Trade and Diplomacy," in *The Small World,* pp. 128–147.

87. Cal Clark and Richard L. Merritt, "European Community and Intra-European Communications: The Evidence of Mail Flows," in *Communication and Interaction in Global Politics,* pp. 220, 231.

88. Beer, *Peace Against War,* pp. 10–12.

89. Ibid., pp. 73–74.

90. Ibid., p. 116.

91. Robert O. Keohane and Joseph S. Nye, eds., *Transnational Relations and World Politics* (Cambridge, MA: Harvard University Press, 1973), p. ix.

92. Stephen D. Krasner, ed., *International Regimes* (Ithaca, NY: Cornell University Press, 1983), p. 2. The concept was introduced by John Gerard Ruggie in "International Responses to Technology: Concepts and Trends," *International Organization* 29 (3, 1975): 570. See also Robert O. Keohane, *After Hegemony: Cooperation and Discord in the World Political Economy* (Princeton, NJ: Princeton University Press, 1984); and John Gerard Ruggie, ed., *The Antimonies of Interdependence* (New York: Columbia University Press, 1983).

93. IMF functions to stabilize foreign exchange and to aid international currency convertibility. GATT is preoccupied with those parts of the international trade regime that have to do with goods (and increasingly with services) moving across national boundaries.

94. Robert Jervis, "Security Regimes," in *International Regimes,* pp. 178–179. There are currently no contemporary examples of international security regimes because they are more difficult to establish than economic regimes. See Roger K. Smith, "Explaining the Non-Proliferation Regime: Anomalies for Contemporary International Relations Theory," *International Organization* 41 (2, 1987): 253.

95. Donald Puchala and Raymond Hopkins, "International Regimes: Lessons from Inductive Analysis," in *International Regimes*, pp. 75–76.

96. Stevina Evuleocha, "International Communication Regimes" (Unpublished article). See also Peter F. Cowhey, "The International Telecommunications Regime: The Political Roots of Regimes for High Technology," *International Organization* 44 (Spring 1990): 168–199.

97. Chin-Chuan Lee, "The Politics of International Communication Regimes: Changing the Rules of the Game," *Gazette* 44 (1989): 77, 85–87.

98. Thanks to Sandra Braman. See Humberto R. Maturana and Francisco J. Varela, *Autopoiesis and Cognition: The Realization of the Living* (Boston: Reidel, 1980); Gregoire Nicolis and Ilya Prigogine, *Exploring Complexity: An Introduction* (New York: W. H. Freeman, 1989); Ilya Prigogine and Isabelle Stengers, *Order Out of Chaos: Man's New Dialogue with Nature,* foreword by Alvin Toffler (Boulder, CO: New Science Library, 1984); Klaus Krippendorff, ed., *Communication and Control in Society* (New York: Gordon and Breach, 1979); and Klaus Krippendorff, *Information Theory: Structural Models for Qualitative Data* (Beverly Hills, CA: Sage, 1986).

99. Nicholas J. Spykman, *America's Strategy in World Politics* (New York: Harcourt Brace Jovanovich, 1942), p. 11.

100. Hans Morgenthau, *Politics among Nations,* 5th ed. (New York: Knopf, 1967), p. 9.

101. Arnold Wolfers, *Discord and Collaboration* (Baltimore, MD: Johns Hopkins Press, 1962), p. 46.

102. Michael P. Sullivan, *International Relations: Theories and Evidence* (Englewood Cliffs, NJ: Prentice-Hall, 1967), p. 160.

103. Signed in Paris by fifteen nations in 1928, the Kellogg–Briand Pact was an agreement to renounce war as an instrument of national policy. Almost every country in the world soon joined the pact, which was hailed as an important step toward peace. See Robert Ferrell, *Peace in Their Time: The Origins of the Kellogg–Briand Pact* (New Haven: Yale, 1952).

104. Dougherty and Pfaltzgraff, *Contending Theories of International Relations*, p. 5.

105. Inis L. Claude, Jr., *Swords into Plowshares,* 3rd rev. ed. (New York: Random House, 1964), p. 47.

106. "Collaboration of the Press in the Organization of Peace," League of Nations Resolution A. 138, Geneva, September 25, 1925, in Kaarle Nordenstreng, Enrique Gonzales Manet, and Wolfgang Kleinwächter, *New International Information and Communication Order: A Sourcebook* (Prague: International Organization of Journalists, 1986), p. 105.

107. Majid Tehranian, "Events, Pseudo-Events, Media Events: Image Politics and the Future of International Diplomacy," in *News Media in National and International Conflict,* p. 45; see also a related essay by Majid Tehranian, "International Communication: A Dialogue of the Deaf?" *Political Communication and Persuasion* 2 (1, 1982): 21–46.

108. John H. Hertz, "Political Realism Revisited," *International Studies Quarterly* 25 (2, June 1981): 187.

109. See Georgi Arbatov, *The War of Ideas in Contemporary International Relations* (Moscow: Progress, 1973); Frederick, *Cuban-American Radio Wars*; William A. Hatchen in collaboration with Marva Hatchen, *The World News Prism: Changing Media, Clashing Ideologies* (Ames, IA: Iowa State University Press, 1981); L. T. Sargent, *Contemporary Political Ideologies: A Comparative Analysis,* 4th ed. (Homewood, IL: Dorsey Press, 1978); A. de Crespigny and J. Cronin, *Ideologies of Politics* (New York: Oxford University Press, 1975); J. Gould and W. H. Truitt, *Political Ideologies* (New York: Macmillan, 1973).

110. Carl Boggs, *Gramsci's Marxism* (London: Pluto Press, 1976), p. 39. See also Abbas Malek and Laura Paige Spiegelberg, "Hegemony and the Media: A Conceptual Framework." Unpublished paper, International Communication Program, The American University, Washington, DC, pp. 6–7.

111. Tom Bottomore, ed., *A Dictionary of Marxist Thought* (Cambridge, MA: Harvard University Press, 1983), p. 201.

112. Leszek Kolakowski, *Main Currents of Marxism: Its Rise, Growth, and Dissolution,* trans. P. S. Falla (Oxford: Clarendon Press, 1978), vol. III, p. 244.

113. Louis Althusser, "Ideology and Ideological State Apparatuses," *Lenin and Philosophy and Other Essays* (New York: Monthly Review Press, 1972), pp. 132–133.

114. See Howard H. Frederick, "A Theory of Inter-Ideological State Propaganda Apparatuses," in *Cuban-American Radio Wars,* pp. 59–61.

115. This should be distinguished from the contemporary American left-of-center political tendency known as *liberalism.* See Dudley Dillard, *The Economics of John Maynard Keynes* (New York: Prentice-Hall, 1948); Daniel Fusfeld, *The Age of the Economist* (New York: Morrow, 1968); Robert Heilbroner, *The Worldly Philosophers,* 5th ed. (New York: Simon & Schuster, 1980); Ingrid Rima, *Development of Economic Analysis,* 4th ed. (Homewood, IL: Irwin, 1986); Paul Samuelson, *Economics,* 12th ed. (New York: McGraw-Hill, 1985); Joseph A. Schumpeter, *Ten Great Economists* (New York: Oxford University Press, 1965); and Leonard Silk, *The Economists* (New York: Basic Books, 1976).

116. Tom Stonier, "Information Revolution: Its Impact on Industrialized Countries," in *The New Economics of Information,* ed. Tom Stonier, Neville Jayaweera, and James Robertson (London: New Economics Foundation, 1989), pp. 7–24.

117. Walt Rostow, *The Stages of Economic Growth: An Anti-Communist Manifesto* (New York: Cambridge University Press, 1960).

118. Daniel Lerner, *The Passing of Traditional Society: Modernizing the Middle East* (Glencoe, IL: Free Press, 1958), pp. 43–75. See also Everett Rogers, *The Diffusion of Innovations* (Glencoe, IL: Free Press, 1962); and Everett Rogers and F. Shoemaker, *Communication of Innovations* (New York: Free Press, 1973).

119. See Lucian Pye and Sidney Verba, eds., *Political Culture and Political Development* (Princeton, NJ: Princeton University Press, 1965); Karl D. Jackson, ed., *Political Power and Communications in Indonesia* (Berkeley and Los Angeles: University of California Press, 1978); Gabriel A. Almond et al., *Crisis, Choice, and Change: Historical Studies of Political Development* (Boston: Little, Brown, 1973); Ithiel de Sola Pool, *Symbols of Internationalism* (Stanford, CA: Stanford University Press, 1951); and Ithiel de Sola Pool, *The Prestige Press: A Comparative Study of Political Symbols* (Cambridge, MA: MIT. Press, 1970). Many thanks to Anantha Sudhaker Babbili, "Ideology of Nationalism and International Discourse." Paper presented at the Conference of the International Association for Mass Communication Research, New Delhi, 1986.

120. See Johan Galtung, "A Structural Theory of Imperialism," in *Dialectics of Third World Development,* ed. I. Vogeler and A. R. DeSouza (New York: Allanheld, Osmun, 1980), pp. 281–297; and Johan Galtung, *The True Worlds: A Transnational Perspective* (New York: Free Press, 1980).

121. James Caporaso, "Dependence and Dependency in the Global System," *International Organization* 32 (1978): 2+; Fernando Henrique Cardozo and Enzo Falleto, *Dependency and Development in Latin America* (Berkeley and Los Angeles: University of California Press, 1979); André G. Frank, *Latin America: Underdevelopment or Revolution* (New York: Monthly Review Press, 1969); and André G. Frank, *Crisis in the Third World* (New York: Holmes and Meier, 1981).

122. Omar Souki Oliveira, "Satellite TV and Dependency: An Empirical Approach," *Gazette* 38 (1986): 127–145; Alan Wells, *Picture-Tube Imperialism?* (New York: Orbis, 1972); Luis R. Beltran, "TV Etchings in the Minds of Latin Americans: Conservatism, Materialism, and Conformism," *Gazette* 24 (1978): 61–85; Armand Mattelart, *Transnationals and the Third World: The Struggle for Culture* (South Hadley, MA: Bergin & Garvey, 1983); Herbert I. Schiller, *Communication and Cultural Domination* (New York: Sharp, 1976); and Omar Souki Oliveira,

"Brazilian Media Usage as a Test of Dependency Theory," *Canadian Journal of Communication* 13 (3–4, 1988): 16–27.

123. Hamid Mowlana and Laurie J. Wilson, *The Passing of Modernity: Communication and the Transformation of Society* (New York: Longman, 1990), p. 91.

124. Mowlana, *Global Information and World Communication*, p. 10.

125. Mowlana, "A Paradigm for Comparative Mass Media Analysis," in *International and Intercultural Communication*, ed. Heinz-Dietrich Fischer and John C. Merrill (New York: Hastings House, 1976), pp. 474–484.

126. Mowlana, *Global Information and World Communication*, p. 12. See also Mowlana and Wilson, *The Passing of Modernity*, p. 91.

127. Mowlana and Wilson, *The Passing of Modernity*, pp. 91–93. Stepping even further back in abstraction, recently Mowlana has been advocating a unified theory of communication as ecology. See Hamid Mowlana, "Civil Society, Information Society, and Islamic Society: A Comparative Perspective," in *Information Society and Civil Society: An International Dialogue on the Changing World Order,* ed. Slavko Splichal, Andrew Calabrese, and Colin Spark (West Lafayette, IN: Purdue University Press, forthcoming); Hamid Mowlana, "New Global Order and Cultural Ecology," in *National Sovereignty and International Communication,* 2nd ed., ed. Kaarle Nordenstreng and Herbert I. Schiller (Norwood, NJ: Ablex, forthcoming).

8

Communication
in War and Peace

THE OPPOSITE OF VIOLENCE IS COMMUNICATION. . . . WHERE
COMMUNICATION ENDS, VIOLENCE STARTS.[1]

We watched in astonishment in 1977 as the Egyptian leader descended from his
airplane to be greeted by Israeli leaders whom Egypt had fought in four wars. Television had not been the mere purveyor of history. In this case, television had actually
brought about the entire event.

Throughout November 1977 Palestinian artillery and Israeli jets traded retaliatory
attacks in Southern Lebanon and Northern Israel. Yet, in a rhetorical flourish, Egyptian President Anwar Sadat stated that his commitment to peace was so great he
was prepared to go even to Israel to discuss it. For his part, Israeli Prime Minister
Menachem Begin responded to that bluster that it would be his pleasure to welcome
Sadat in Israel.

Despite the fact that Sadat and Begin had never spoken directly, on November
14 Walter Cronkite opened his newscast with: "Now all obstacles appear to have
been removed for peace discussions between Egyptian President Sadat and Israeli
Prime Minister Begin . . . ," and he announced that the two leaders had agreed for
Sadat to come to Israel.[2] Actually, this feat of international peacemaking had been
accomplished with considerable help from the editing studios. The interviews had
taken place *four hours apart* via satellite connection to New York, with Sadat speaking first. But Cronkite's editing made it possible for Sadat and Begin to appear to be
speaking together. Satellite television had telescoped the time between the interviews to give the impression that there had been a face-to-face meeting.[3]

Some have criticized Cronkite's feat for overstepping the bounds of ethical journalism, but it demonstrates one unmistakable fact: *Media* and *mediate* have the
same Latin root. To mediate conveys the sense of being an intermediary or concilia-
tor between persons or sides. A *medium* is a means, agency, or instrument through

which a message passes. More than anything, what Cronkite did was focus on how the mass media can affect the course of peace and war.

From the earliest times, rulers have used available communication channels to declare and wage war. They have also relied on channels of communication to propose peace or suggest terms for a truce. From warmaking to peacekeeping, from initial volley to cease-fire, one thing has remained constant until now: "In every case . . . [conflict] is created, maintained, and abolished through the exchanges of messages."[4]

But something has now changed. We have reached a point in human evolution where we can communicate with millions of human beings on the planet and at the same time destroy them. This is no accident, for some of the same technology that has produced the weapons of mass destruction is also the basis of the revolution in the technologies of global communication. As we enter the twenty-first century, we must choose the right path between the technologies of destruction and the technologies of international understanding.

COMMUNICATION, PEACE, AND WAR IN HISTORICAL PERSPECTIVE

This section contains some remarkable examples of communication (and miscommunication) in war.

The Battle of New Orleans Need Not Have Happened

If transatlantic communication had been faster, the War of 1812 need not have happened—or it would have ended sooner.[5] The cause of that conflict was the 1807 British "Order in Council" that forced all U.S. trade with Europe to pass through British ports. At the time, communication between Britain and America was measured in weeks, and Congress declared war on Britain not knowing that Parliament had repealed the order two days before. "Had there been a transatlantic cable to convey the glad tidings . . . the Senate probably would have mustered the necessary four votes to defeat the War Hawks."[6] Even worse, the lack of communication lengthened the war and caused thousands of needless casualties. News of the peace treaty took weeks to arrive, and the British attack on New Orleans went ahead as planned, even though the war had officially ended.

The British Public and Coverage of the Crimean War

In the Crimean War of 1853–1856, Czarist Russia sought to expand its influence in the Balkans at the expense of the declining Ottoman Empire. Britain, in contrast, saw the preservation of the Ottoman Empire as vital for its own imperial interests in the eastern Mediterranean and Asia. In the end, England, France, and Turkey joined to defeat Russia in a war in which far more people died of disease than of battle wounds.[7] The war's only exceptional aspect was that for the first time long-distance telecommunications, namely, the telegraph, exerted an astonishing influence on government decisions and press coverage. Reports sent to the *Times* of London by William Howard Russell marked the beginning of war coverage to mass populations. Russell described the inadequate supplies, disease, and blundering that wrecked any hope for success. Outraged at these reports, British public opinion demanded changes in the field and at home. Russell's reports "helped to topple the British government."[8]

Franco-Prussian War Due to Altered Telegram and Press Leak

Only an armed conflict with France, so Prussian Chancellor Otto von Bismarck thought in 1870, could complete the unification of the fractious German states. But how to provoke that war?[9] It so happened that the French ambassador was visiting the Prussian king on the Ems river near the Dutch border, where the ambassador demanded that the German monarch promise not to interfere in the succession to the Spanish throne. The king politely refused this unreasonable request and sent a rather innocuous telegram to Chancellor Bismarck outlining the results of the meeting.

Bismarck struck on an idea. He altered the contents of the dispatch (the famous "Ems telegram") to give the impression that the French ambassador had insulted the Prussian king and that the ruler had retaliated by insulting the ambassador. He then leaked the story to the press, infuriating both the French and Prussian publics. Bismarck thus maneuvered the French government into a position where it had to either accept a public loss of face or go to war. Fearing public opinion at home, Napoleon III declared war on Prussia and was crushed by a unified German command. Bismarck succeeded in persuading all the German rulers to join together in forming the new German Reich with the king of Prussia as the German emperor.

Yellow Journalism and the Spanish–American–Cuban War

The great New York newspaper circulation wars of the 1890s between William Randolph Hearst's *Morning Journal* and Joseph Pulitzer's *New York World* facilitated the emergence of the United States as a great power; the advent of American overseas imperialism; the domination of the Cuban government; and the acquisition of Puerto Rico, Guam, and the Philippines.[10] This was the period in American newspaper history known as "Yellow Journalism," characterized by biased reporting, distorted or mislabeled pictures and illustrations, and large-type headlines appealing to readers' emotions. The high point of the Hearst–Pulitzer feud was their coverage of the Spanish–American–Cuban War.

When Cuba began a bloody revolt against its Spanish colonial rulers, American expansionists called on President William McKinley to intervene and take Cuba. McKinley hesitated, but public opinion was inflamed by the sensationalist coverage in the two newspapers. When a Spanish general herded Cuban farmers into squalid concentration camps and many civilians died, Hearst's *Journal* dubbed the general the "butcher" of Havana and editorialized for intervention and annexation of Cuba. In 1898 Hearst even published a purloined private letter in which the Spanish ambassador in Washington sharply criticized President McKinley. Then the American battleship *Maine* mysteriously exploded in the Havana harbor. McKinley could no longer resist the surging pressure for intervention, and Congress passed a declaration of war. It is often said that Hearst started the Spanish–American–Cuban War to stimulate newspaper sales. In reality, Hearst was only one of many influential Americans who felt the need to push the nation into competition with the British, French, and Germans for overseas bases.

The Zimmermann Telegram and U.S. Entry into World War I

Before World War I, the German military and diplomatic corps communicated overseas through oceanic cables. After declaring war against Germany in 1914, Britain cut all of them. Germany had to resort to wireless radio, easily tapped by British monitoring stations. In time the British even broke the German code. Stalemated by the Germans, losing lives and ground continuously, the British used this communication stranglehold to lure the United States into the war. In early 1917 the British gave the United States the text of an intercepted and decoded German message known as the "Zimmermann telegram." In this message, the German government asked its ambassador in Mexico to approach the Mexican government with an offer of an alliance, the reward for which would be Mexican possession of Texas, New Mexico, and Arizona. It also announced unrestricted submarine warfare in the Atlantic. Leaked to the press in Washington, the telegram aroused American public opinion in anger and led Congress to support President Wilson's call for war against Germany.[11]

Pearl Harbor and Radar

A breakdown in communication contributed to the success of the Japanese attack on Pearl Harbor on December 7, 1941. At the time, U.S. armed forces were using recently arrived radar devices that could detect ships or airplanes at sea. Two Army privates with no radar training were about to go off duty at 7:00 A.M. on December 7, 1941, when they noticed a huge blip on the screen two hundred kilometers north of Oahu. Thinking that these radar images were a huge flight of enemy planes, they tried to contact headquarters by radio. But no one answered, and minutes later they finally got through by ordinary telephone. The commanding officer, thinking the blip was a group of American bombers arriving from the mainland, told them "not to worry about it."[12] The rest is history.

Vietnam War Provoked by Communications Breakdown?

On August 2, 1964, the U.S. destroyer *Maddox* was cruising a zigzag course off the coast of North Vietnam. Aboard the *Maddox* was the most modern communications and electronics equipment available. That evening violent thunderstorms rocked the Gulf of Tonkin, and the *Maddox*'s equipment was functioning erratically. For the second time in two days, the captain of the *Maddox* received messages that he interpreted to be from North Vietnamese ships on the attack. For the second time he called in American jets and unloaded decoys in all directions to detonate incoming torpedoes. The ship's sonars detected twenty-two incoming torpedoes, none of which struck its target. Actually, none of the sailors saw any Vietnamese ships. Neither had the fighter pilots. Subsequent research has indicated with almost total certainty that the second attack in the Gulf of Tonkin never happened.

Yet President Johnson, seeking a pretext, went on television to say "Repeated acts of violence . . . must be met . . . with positive reply." He immediately went to

Congress to report that U.S. destroyers had again been attacked in the Gulf of Tonkin. Johnson seized upon a fuzzy set of circumstances to fulfill a contingency plan.[13] Under pressure from the President, on August 10, 1964, Congress passed the infamous "Gulf of Tonkin Resolution," giving the President power to commit American forces in Vietnam without Congressional approval.

COMMUNICATION AND THE SPECTRUM OF FOREIGN AFFAIRS

Many textbooks on international relations list four traditional instruments of foreign affairs: diplomacy, trade, communication, and force. One could say that without communication there is no diplomacy—or trade. Indeed, force itself—occupation troops, artillery shells, even missile exchange—is really a message of physical persuasion and coercion. In essence, all foreign policy actions are either communications acts themselves or heavily dependent on communication channels.

One way to visualize the role of communication in global affairs is by drawing a spectrum of communication in peace and war (see Figure 8-1). Although these aspects often overlap, we can divide global communication and information relations generally into five intensities. At one end is *peaceful relations,* the desired state of affairs with routine news flow, satellite telecommunications, transborder data flow, and other channels that have been examined so far throughout this book. Next is *contentious relations,* the commonplace state of less-than-peaceful world affairs, with its flurry of diplomatic communications, public opinion "wars," and interactions between the media and political figures. Then comes *low intensity conflict,* less-than-military means of political, economic, psychological, and diplomatic warfare.[14] *Medium intensity conflicts* are clashes that go beyond this level to armed insurgencies and revolutions. Finally, *high intensity conflict* is fought at the level of conventional arms, tanks and troops, even nuclear weapons.

COMMUNICATION IN CONTENTIOUS GLOBAL RELATIONS
The Language of Conflict

Words can inflict pain, legitimize aggression, justify dehumanization, and rationalize militarism. The violence of language is nowhere so evident as in the case of ethnic slurs. Try calling a Puerto Rican American a "spic," an Asian American a "gook," or an American Jew a "kike."[15] What all these words have in common is the intention to deny the essential humanity of the victim of the slur. Words can legitimize oppression and can rationalize militarism. Chilton describes an atomic-age word game called *Nukespeak,* which is the game nuclear nations play in order to manipulate and mystify the material facts. Words can justify war; words can be weapons of war.

In the Middle East, for example, after a series of Palestinian attacks on civilian targets in Israel in 1978, Israeli pilots bombed Palestinian refugee camps in Lebanon. A British newspaper contained the headline: "Israeli Jets Bomb Terror Camps." Israeli radio had a rule that the Palestine Liberation Organization could never be referred to by name. Only their initials could be used, presumably because the word *liberation* implies a legitimate Palestinian claim to occupied Israeli land. Similarly, Arab newspapers never referred to Palestinians as "terrorists." That word was reserved for members of the so-called Jewish underground.

I
c
r
e
a
s
i
n
g

C
o
n
f
l
i
c
t

Peaceful Relations
News flow
Satellite communications
Transborder data flow
International broadcasting
International organizational communication

Contentious Relations
Diplomacy and communication
Communication and international negotiations
The language of international conflict
Public opinion and the outbreak of war
Media as actors in conflict

Low Intensity Conflict
Public diplomacy
Propaganda
Disinformation
Communication and espionage
Development-sabotage communication
"Electronic penetration"

Medium Intensity Conflict
Communication and terrorism
Communication and revolution

High Intensity Conflict
Communication technology and the military
Military force as communication

FIGURE 8-1   Spectrum of Communication in Peace and War.

In the Middle East, as elsewhere, proper names are laden with political content. None is more controversial than the term used to describe the territories on the West Bank of the Jordan River, captured by Israel from Jordan in the war of 1967. Centrist Israelis call them the "conquered areas," and hard-liners call them the "liberated areas." Right-wing Israelis refer to the territories by their biblical names, Judea and Samaria. Outside of Israel, the territory is usually referred to as "the West Bank," the term used after Jordan annexed the area in 1950. The war of words has even extended to the diplomatic realm. United Nations Resolution 242, often cited as the basis for a permanent settlement, refers to "withdrawal of Israeli armed forces from territories occupied" in the 1967 war. Because the resolution does not refer to *the* territories, it leaves open the question of whether it means full or partial withdrawal.

The language of war is filled with obfuscation and euphemism. Consider these pairs: Friendly fire—Shot by mistake; Assets—Bombs; Collateral damage—Deaths of innocent civilians; Assertive disarmament—Destruction of enemy weapons. Whether innocent or purposeful, these examples of doublespeak cover up the horror of war and make the unspeakable into polite discourse.

Diplomacy and Communication

Diplomats, of course, are caught up in the linguistic context of communication. Diplomacy is "the process and method, the means and the mechanism, by which national governments conduct relations and communicate with one another."[16] As former

Vietnamese diplomat and communication professor Tran Van Dinh has said, "Communication is to diplomacy as blood is to the human body. Whenever communication ceases, the body of international politics, the process of diplomacy, is dead, and the result is violent conflict or atrophy."[17] The central role of communication in diplomacy is enshrined in international law.[18]

Until the first world war, diplomatic communication was carried out by a small group of men from elite nations. The volume of message flow was modest, consisting primarily of face-to-face, hand-delivered, or telegraphic communications. But this century's tremendous political upheavals, coupled with the communications revolution, have brought about a transformation in diplomacy. The sheer volume of diplomatic communication has mushroomed. By the end of World War II there were 115 countries with diplomatic legations; by 1992 there were more than 170, and more on the way. In addition, a large portion of diplomatic communication is channeled through the more than 10,000 nongovernmental and intergovernmental organizations vying for influence in the international arena.

Diplomats rely on extensive communication and information systems. Computer communications, satellite systems, television transmission, international radio broadcasts, spy satellites, electronic monitoring, and detection devices: These and other technologies have transformed the work of the diplomat. The United States Diplomatic Telecommunications Service (DTS) links 260 posts in over 150 countries using commercial and military circuits, high-frequency radio bands, and satellite channels.[19]

Diplomatic communication between governments, like all international communication, is subject to distortion due to cultural differences, ideological divisions, and plain misunderstandings. To avoid this, elaborate rituals have arisen in diplomatic communication to guarantee explicit meaning. Written diplomatic communication often seems stilted to the outsider ("I feel constrained to advise your excellency that my government cannot but acquiesce in the view that . . ."), but it allows diplomats to phrase precise statements without being impolite or belligerent. Diplomats must also be alert to the content "between the lines."[20]

Former Israeli diplomat Abba Eban believes journalists and diplomats have an *antagonistic* relationship—a "built-in conflict of interest"—because "what one seeks to conceal the other seeks to reveal."[21] They also have a *symbiotic* relationship, because the press often functions as the eyes and ears of diplomacy. Embassy workers regularly monitor domestic and foreign press, make recordings, and distribute summaries.[22]

Diplomats usually fear media coverage. Publicity can serve a dysfunctional purpose by undermining a negotiator's public image or public support. Leaks to the press can weaken public trust. Premature disclosure of a settlement may lead to greater inflexibility in negotiations.[23]

But media coverage need not always be the enemy of diplomacy. Media can play a positive, if indirect, part in the settlement of international disputes by paving the way to negotiation. They can facilitate the acceptance of agreements reached. Media can issue reminders that mediation mechanisms are available. They can make sure each side is truly familiar with the other side's position. They can also make the mediator's task easier by conferring prestige on the peacemaker and by reminding opponents of the need to respect international law and to comply with UN resolutions.

Media play varying roles. They can serve as auxiliary channels in diplomatic negotiations. Governments sometimes use mass media as a "trial balloon" to find out whether other governments are interested in negotiating. Media can confer recognition and generate pressure on the opponent, as they did during the 1948 Berlin blockade.[24] But there is also a risk in using the media: A government may suffer "loss of freedom" in national decision making due to media influences. This happens, for example, when the media concentrate attention on making the enemy look evil. As Deutsch points out, "hostile attention in the mass media may tend to harden public opinion to such a degree eventually as to destroy the freedom of choice of the national government concerned."[25] The opposite can also happen. Lack of news coverage can lead to "loss of legitimacy," which constrains a diplomats ability to negotiate.[26]

Communication, Public Opinion, and Peace

Just as diplomats use communications to negotiate peace, political and military leaders use communications to mobilize mass publics for war. They make hostile statements about their adversaries and use communication strategies to influence target populations at home and abroad. Indeed, manipulating the opinion of mass attentive publics has become one of the most important elements in warmaking in the contemporary world.

Quincy Wright showed how this worked in American newspapers before, during, and after World War I (see Figure 8-2). The media developed friendliness toward France and enmity toward Germany well in advance of U.S. entry on the side of the Allies. The shift began in 1911 in the *New York Times* and in 1913 in the *Chicago Tribune.* As the war commenced, the papers increased their hate of Germany and love of France, both of which peaked in 1918.

Writers have studied the connection between communication and war mobilization for years. Deutsch once suggested a way to provide early warning to international conflict: international mass media inspection teams.[27] Large-scale preparation for war is a social process, Deutsch wrote. He argued that "the presence or absence of such psychological preparation can be readily monitored from the statistical analysis of the content of the mass media of communication . . . "[28] In other words, going beyond an internationally agreed-upon threshold of inflammatory material in the media would provide an early warning for war preparations. McClelland recommended that such an advanced warning system could be developed by monitoring intelligence analyses and news flow.[29] Singer likewise suggested a "systematic surveillance of newspapers, magazines, journals, radio, and television in order to ascertain the degree to which a nation might be adhering to, or evading, a disarmament agreement."[30]

Of course, increasing the flow of information between nations does not necessarily prevent disagreement or stop the outbreak of violent confrontation. Yet the chances of conflict increase as information flow declines. The breakdown in communication, though rarely the cause of conflict, is definitely a sign of impending conflict. As Davison warns, "increasing the quality and quantity of communication will not solve the underlying causes of conflict; indeed, in some cases these causes may receive greater salience as a result of more accurate perceptions on both sides."[31]

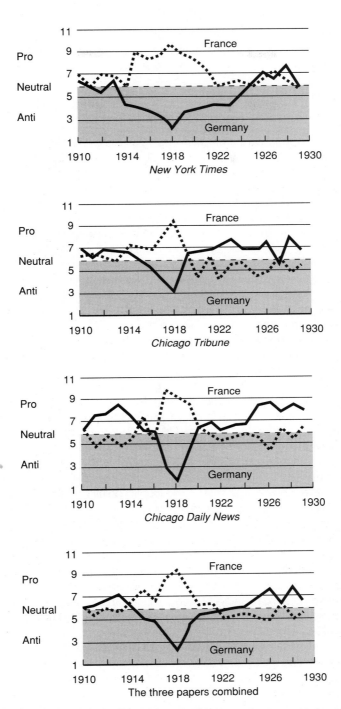

FIGURE 8-2 Wright demonstrated how three newspapers shifted their opinions of France and Germany before, during, and after World War I.

SOURCE: From *A Study of War,* 2nd ed., by Quincy Wright. Copyright © 1965 by University of Chicago Press. Reprinted by permission.

For example, the increased flow and quality of communication between Iran and the United States during and after the 1980 hostage crisis may have ultimately hardened perceptions.

The Media as Actors in Conflict

As Walter Cronkite demonstrated in 1977, news media are not passive observers to international conflict. They have become a political force in their own right, autonomous entities that not only transmit, but frame and interpret events.[32]

Tehranian described seven roles that media play in relation to social conflict. They can be *selfless revolutionaries* serving as collective organizers, agitators, and propagandists, as the "midwife of history." Their counterparts in liberal democratic societies are the *fearless truth seekers,* courageous investigators of social evil and political corruption. In a more socially accountable setting we find media as *responsible agenda setters,* whose task is more to interpret than to report. Less visible but no less powerful are media as *benign gatekeepers,* who select, as the *New York Times*'s motto says, "all the news that's fit to print." In the Third World we often find media as *development promoters*—servants of national unity, independence, and economic progress. The *hidden persuaders* are those media whose commercial interests compel them to manipulate their publics through glorification of business. Finally, Tehranian lists the *sinister manipulators,* media whose ideological bias and allegiance compel them to bend the truth for economic and political gain.[33]

Certain global patterns seem to be emerging in media politics.[34] One interaction pattern is the *appeal to world public opinion.* Antagonists take their dispute to the global public as a means to force changes. Such groups as Amnesty International have used this tactic for years. When an American women's group demanding conversion to a peacetime economy blocked the halls of the Pentagon in 1980, they chanted "The whole world is watching." Chinese students demanding democratic reform in Beijing in 1989 assisted the foreign mass media in their coverage of the movement because they knew that world public opinion was important to their cause. The Russian people, barricading their "White House" in 1991, knew that the global media formed a protective shield of visibility around them.

Another growing pattern is the *international media echo,* when the content of one nation's media becomes news in the media of another country. In this way, the media themselves become significant sources for international exchange of opinion and information. For example, policy shifts by Russian leaders are often reported in the U.S. with excerpts from Radio Moscow's English-language broadcasts. During the hostage crisis between the United States and Iran, American television would run excerpts from televised statements by Iranian leaders.

A disturbing media pattern of frequent *cross-cultural misunderstanding* has also emerged. For example, the "Citizen's Summit" programs were transmitted between the United States and the Soviet Union in the first heady days of Soviet–American rapprochement and Reagan–Gorbachev summitry. The format was the same: a "space bridge" (interactive, large-screen, satellite television broadcasts with simultaneous translation) linking audiences in both countries, moderated by American talk show host Phil Donahue and Soviet journalist Vladimir Pozner. There were high hopes for open and frank discussion, but the programs became "bogged down in confrontational rhetoric saturated with national politics.'' As a result, ''instead of promoting greater understanding between the two cultures, the simulcast tend[ed] to reconfirm dogmatic positions and stereotypes.''[35]

Equally disturbing is the pattern of *governmental censorship and interruption of the free flow of information.* The United States has interrupted news transmissions from Cuba and even blocked the American broadcast of the Pan American Games in Cuba. Israel routinely censors news from the West Bank. The Chinese government eventually pulled the plug on Western news coverage of the Tienanmen massacre. This trend is particularly true of governments threatened by world attention. Yet the effect may sometimes be counterproductive in the end. In 1985 the South African government restricted reporting of the racial strife, ostensibly to prevent the spread of violence and preserve some modicum of normalcy, but also to keep the conflict off the front pages of the world's newspapers. Giffard and Cohen showed that in the short run, instead of declining, the amount of coverage increased. What is more, lacking sensational pictures, television coverage began to give more background and to explain ''why'' rather than just ''what'' happened.[36]

COMMUNICATION IN LOW INTENSITY CONFLICT

From public diplomacy to the use of communication channels in nonmilitary destabilization, statesmen and military leaders have learned their media lessons well.

"Public Diplomacy"

The extensive use of media channels in diplomacy, known as ''public diplomacy,'' began originally in the propaganda campaigns during World War II. Today the term describes activities, directed abroad in the fields of information, education, and culture, whose objective is to influence a foreign government by influencing its citizens.[37]

In the case of the United States, public diplomacy tries to convey positive American values to foreigners, to create a climate of opinion in which American policies can be successfully formulated, executed, and accepted.[38] These activities include overseas radio broadcasts by the Voice of America and Radio Free Europe/Radio Liberty, student and faculty exchanges, placement abroad of noted American speakers, cultural programs and exchanges, and distribution of government-funded periodicals.

Of course, public diplomacy is no American monopoly; it has become a worldwide phenomenon. When Argentina, Indonesia, Korea, the Philippines, and Turkey hired public relations consultants in the United States, their news images in the *New York Times* improved considerably.[39] Israeli diplomats have long been trained in *hasbara* (Hebrew for ''propaganda'').[40] The breakaway Nigeria state of Biafra conducted a systematic national-image campaign in the world media.[41]

Propaganda and Disinformation

Propaganda is the systematic manipulation of symbols such as words, gestures, slogans, flags, and uniforms to alter, control, or otherwise influence the attitudes, values, beliefs, and actions of a foreign population toward the goal of bringing them into conformity with those of the propagandist.[42] Propaganda must have four elements: intentionality, symbolic communication, some medium of communication, and a target population.[43]

The word *propaganda* comes from the title of the *Congregation for Propagating the Faith* [Congregatio de propaganda fide], established by Pope Gregory XV in 1622, which had jurisdiction over missionary work conducted by the Roman Catholic church. The First World War was a watershed in the development of modern propaganda, where entire nations could be mobilized for war through the media of mass propaganda. Most people associate the concept with the Nazi propaganda machine under Joseph Goebbels, Hitler's Minister of Popular Enlightenment and Propaganda, who shrewdly exploited the captive media in a carefully orchestrated campaign supporting the National Socialist party line.[44]

In the English language, the word *propaganda* ordinarily carries a negative connotation and is taken to mean the deliberate dissemination of distorted or biased messages to support one cause or to damage another. Americans generally fear propagandists.[45] However, in other languages propaganda is understood to include advertising, public relations, and opinion molding. The dispute here is whether or not the source of the message aims at the truth. Like the advertiser, the propagandist deliberately selects those particular arguments, symbols, and actions that are expected to have maximum effect on how people react. The propagandist strives to control access to information and will either avoid facts or attempt to undermine any contradictory arguments. Ideally, the journalist and educator, in contrast, strive to give information that can be used independently to collect and evaluate evidence.[46]

Virtually all governments—and many international organizations, religious groups, and nongovernmental agencies—conduct information programs aimed at foreign publics. Most of these entities have large bureaucracies at home and abroad to influence the attitudes and actions of target groups and organizations in another entity, with the purpose of creating favorable attitudes and actions[47] (see Figure 8-3).

There are eight classical propaganda techniques: Name-calling, glittering generalities, transferring existing prejudice to new targets, appealing as "just plain folks," expert testimonials, selective facts, the bandwagon effect, and scapegoating.[48] Although these categories have often been criticized, they have become part of the lexicon of propaganda analysis. The larger the propaganda campaign, the more likely it will use such mass media as television, newspapers, and the radio.

We can divide propaganda into three types based upon the source. *White propaganda* always identifies the source and place of origin of the propaganda message. It disseminates official opinion and cites well-known authorities. In *gray propaganda* the source is not discernible. The correctness of the information is in doubt. In *black propaganda* false information, such as lies, inventions, and deceptions, are disseminated. No source is mentioned.

There is a widespread misbelief that media have enormous propaganda powers, that if information can be placed in the correct channels, aimed at the right audience, there will be a massive change of attitude and behavior. Quite to the contrary, present evidence indicates that propaganda through mass communication channels normally fails to produce marked changes in opinions or actions. What propaganda can do is to *reinforce preexisting beliefs and values* of the audience when several condi-

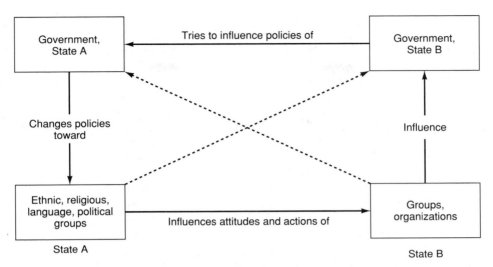

FIGURE 8-3 **Holsti's model shows how governments seek to influence the policies of other countries by influencing the attitudes and actions of groups and organizations within those countries.**

SOURCE: From K.J. Holsti, *International Politics: A Framework for Analysis*, 3rd ed., © 1977, p. 219. Reprinted by permission of Prentice-Hall, Inc., Englewood Cliffs, NJ.

tions are present. Attention must be awakened. Receptiveness must be increased, perhaps by presenting alternative solutions or ideas. The receiver's social and political context must be taken into account. And the receiver's belief system must be reinforced. Attention can be awakened by presenting serious arguments and considering counterarguments. This is the typical model of today's modern propagandist and is the model used by such international radio stations as the Voice of America.[49]

In recent years, governments and organizations have devised a new strategy to influence public information. *Disinformation* "is propaganda plus—the 'plus' being the manipulation of events or deeds so as to maximize the impact of the propaganda message."[50] The objectives of disinformation include inflicting harm on the target, inflicting harm on the agent (channel, medium), discouraging morale, compelling or provoking decisions, pacifying the victim, misleading military capability, winning world or national public opinion, manipulating publics, creating misunderstanding, undermining programs or policies, exploiting discontent, and polluting international relations.[51]

In an era in which many people confuse TV entertainment with news,[52] *disinfotainment* refers to fictional simulations of "reality" that deliberately plant falsehoods or distortions in the public mind. *ABC World News Tonight* brought this phenomenon into sharp focus in 1989 when it presented a "hidden-camera" surveillance picture purporting to show U.S. diplomat Felix Bloch handing a briefcase to a Soviet diplomat. As the picture was shown, correspondent John McWethy cited unnamed U.S. officials saying Bloch had been photographed passing a briefcase to a Soviet agent. What ABC did not say is that the entire scene was a dramatization of the incident.[53]

The impact of disinfotainment lies in the eye of the beholder, as two American television films during the Reagan era showed. In November 1983 the American Broadcasting Company transmitted the three-hour film "The Day After," about the consequences of a nuclear attack on a small town in Kansas. Although peace activists complained that the film understated the likely situation, right-wingers saw the film as an attack on U.S. nuclear policy and as a victory for Soviet propaganda. Conservatives called on ABC to "tell the other side of the story."

Then ABC broadcast a 14½-hour miniseries called "Amerika" about a Soviet invasion. In "Amerika," the new rulers enforce control with troops from the United Nations, now transformed into a Russian pawn. Schoolchildren undergo daily brainwashing, and dissidents are packed off to gulags in the Southwest or sent to mental hospitals for chemically-induced behavior modification. Meanwhile, hard-liners in the Kremlin meet over how to handle an emerging Resistance movement.[54] In the end, it seems that "the social impact of the program, in terms of its influence on political attitudes and images of Russia, [was] rather minimal." Two attitude factors did stand out as being significantly strengthened, though: anticommunism and belief in capitalism.[55]

Communication and Espionage

Espionage is the clandestine collection of information about an adversary's plans or activities.[56] Originally it consisted of sending a person—the spy, or "intelligence operative"—to another country to gather information. The most vexing problem in espionage was communicating that information back home. Censorship of the main public communication channels, especially in wartime or if the spy was already suspect, made this task all but impossible. In ages past, spies have used everything from carrier pigeons to the microdot.[57] World War II marked the introduction of communication technologies in espionage.

Today the work of the human agent is supplemented (and sometimes replaced) by the use of artificial devices, including spy satellites, high-powered cameras, and complex electronic equipment. Remote-sensing satellites can photograph in great detail everything on the surface of the land and sea. Communications satellites intercept local radio signals, and ground sensors—or "people sniffers"—supply knowledge of the movements of troops and supplies. In fact, these electronic devices obtain such reliable information that they have been accepted as a primary means of verifying arms control agreements.

In the United States, the National Security Agency (NSA)—the largest and most secret intelligence agency in the world—has two functions: to protect U.S. government communications and to intercept foreign communications. To protect government communications, it encodes messages and takes other measures to ensure their secrecy. To intercept foreign messages, the NSA concentrates a vast corps of intelligence analysts who use sensitive electronic equipment to monitor, decipher, and translate the communications of foreign governments. We rarely hear of NSA successes because publicity would cause opponents to change their systems.

Development Sabotage Communication

Communication strategies—the same ones used widely in positive economic, social, and political development in the Third World—have become integral to international conflict.[58] Military planners now can choose the same communication "change strategies" devised by the Agency for International Development, the United States

Information Agency, the Central Intelligence Agency, and other governmental agencies and private consulting firms. For example, the "United States Army's 'development' projects in Honduras must be considered within the context of counterinsurgency and 'low intensity warfare.' . . . [They are] a 'public relations' opportunity to win the 'hearts and minds' of the local population."[59]

The use of communication in low intensity warfare does not seek victory on the battlefield as much as it strives to destabilize national will and to sow confusion and doubt in the opponent. It seeks to isolate, divide, and neutralize attentive publics. Behind the doctrine is the realization that the nature of warfare has changed. In the preindustrial age, the object of war was to destroy the opponent's army. In the industrial era, it was to destroy not only the army, but also the economic base that fed, armed, transported, and supplied those forces. In the information age, as former U.S. Secretary of Defense Caspar Weinberger once said, "now we [see] a form of warfare directed at the destruction of hope itself."[60]

Psychological operations (psyops) troops use propaganda and other communication strategies to influence opinions, attitudes, and emotions of neutral and friendly groups. A U.S. Army field manual states that in counterinsurgency operations "psychological operations are directed at exploiting resentments and raising expectations, influencing the population and promoting cooperation among insurgent groups."[61]

Another means of sabotaging peaceful development is called "electronic penetration." Broadcasting is virtually the only global communication medium that cannot be stopped at borders. Jamming is essentially ineffective outside of a small radius and may make the listeners even more interested in hearing the broadcasts. Throughout the world, governments and liberation organizations use radio and other electronic means to influence the public opinion of opposing populations. This is not a new phenomenon. The German–Austrian radio war of the 1930s, the West-German–East-German radio war of the 1960s through 1980s,[62] the Cuban–American radio war to the present day,[63] the Central American radio war of the 1980s,[64] and the Southern Africa radio war:[65] All these illustrate the role of electronic penetration in insurgency environments.[66] Nor is this limited to governments and revolutionary organizations. Fundamentalist churches use shortwave radio and satellite television to compete for the hearts and minds of believers, particularly in Central and South America.[67]

COMMUNICATION IN MEDIUM INTENSITY CONFLICT
Communication and Terrorism

Terrorist actions during the 1970s and 1980s focused attention on the role of the media in terrorism. In 1985 and 1986, for example, U.S. television networks devoted extensive news coverage to the TWA hostage crisis, the *Achille Lauro* hijacking, the Malta debacle, and the Rome and Vienna airport bombings. Such massive attention wittingly or unwittingly gave terrorists a platform. Studies have shown that the networks may be granting legitimacy to terrorist actions and become unwitting participants in the event.[68]

Indeed, terrorism and communication are unalterably linked. As Schmid has written:

Without communication there can be no terrorism [for] violence and propaganda have much in common. Violence aims at behaviour modification by coercion. Propaganda aims at the same by persuasion. Terrorism is a combination of the two. . . . Terrorism can best be understood as a communication strategy. There is a sender, the terrorist, a message generator, the victim, and a receiver, the enemy and his public.[69]

Global news media are faced with a constant dilemma: how to keep the public informed of daily events without becoming, to some degree, propagandists for the terrorists. Is former British Prime Minister Thatcher correct when she says that the media provide the "oxygen of publicity" on which terrorism thrives? Can we speak of the "Robinhoodization" of terrorists? Do media need terrorists (to capture audiences) as much as terrorists need media?

Conventional wisdom would have it that media coverage helps make terrorism a successful political weapon. However, studies of network news programs contradict this by showing that television news generally ignores the motivations, objectives, and long-term goals of the terrorists and prevents their causes from gaining legitimacy with the public.[70] Media do not contribute to raising the level of violence because they want to; most are vehemently opposed to it. Yet their opposition to terrorism "does not exonerate them from being 'used' for propaganda purposes."[71] Television is the terrorist's medium of choice. It not only reports terrorism; it can become part of the story.

Terrorist groups are increasing their publicity skills. They even monitor coverage of their ongoing actions. One "coup" for terrorists was NBC's 1986 interview of Abul Abbas, who allegedly masterminded the seajacking of the Italian cruise liner *Achille Lauro.* Abbas stated that he planned to bring terrorism to the United States to "respond against America, in America itself."[72] There was a tremendous outcry. The State Department accused NBC of being an accomplice to terrorism by giving Abbas publicity. NBC even refused to disclose the country where Abbas was interviewed, defending itself on classic freedom of the press grounds.

How do terrorists use the media? First, there are active uses, such as communicating messages to mass audiences and polarizing public opinion; making converts, winning favorable publicity, and attracting new members to terrorist movements; demanding publication of demands under threat of harm to a victim; verifying demand compliance; spreading false information; and using journalists as negotiators in bargaining situations.

There are also passive uses of the media in terrorism, such as communicating between terrorist groups, obtaining information about the identity and status of hostages, obtaining information on countermeasures by security forces, using media presence as insurance against attack, and obtaining information about public reactions.[73]

Communication and Revolution

For centuries, the battle plans of insurgents have followed the same script: Secure the strategic high ground, attack the main garrison, use clandestine media to attract the support of the people. In many cases the script is now reversed. The high ground is now the transmission tower.

Teheran, 1979. Under the Shah, Iran's mass media were dominated by Western products and values and were firmly within official control. Beauty pageants, sex magazines, interviews with the royal family, Hollywood gossip, and rock music all "westoxified" the population. Denied access to officially controlled media, conservative fundamentalists, as well as radical revolutionaries, turned to traditional channels such as the bazaar and the mosque to spread their messages and organize their resistance. From Paris, Ayatollah Khomeini was able to send his messages through telephone and tape channels to Teheran, where they were copied by the thousands and made their way into the traditional channels.

Manila, 1986. Corazon Aquino was able to rally massive electoral support against dictator Ferdinand Marcos through televised rallies and advertisements. When television also carried pictures of army troops taking ballot boxes, Radio Veritas, the principal voice of the Catholic church, urged people to conduct nonviolent resistance. With live broadcasts around the world, the Philippine people nonviolently laid down their bodies before government troops and demanded the dictator's overthrow.

Prague, 1989. In November Czech police brutally attacked a peaceful demonstration being held in Prague to mark International Students' Day. Czech viewers learned more about the situation from Soviet TV, which was experiencing a period of *glasnost,* than from their own media. Journalists denounced the police attack. Czech TV employees threatened disruptions, and security forces surrounded the broadcast building. But television journalists were able to patch through a live transmission from Wenceslaus Square to inform the people of what took place. This was the beginning of the end of the Czechoslovak regime.

Bucharest, 1990. Romanian viewers were accustomed to seeing pictures of contented workers reporting on their overfulfilled quotas. But one area of Romania had access to "Western" television. The Romanian revolt against the dictator Ceauscescu began first in the region around Timisoara because that area had been flooded by Hungarian television. Not only did television light the flame of revolt in Romania, but people were able to view their own revolution live and unedited on television. They watched the overthrow, trial, and execution of Ceauscescu and his wife. The new regime actually governed briefly from the TV studio.

Moscow, 1991. The "Emergency Committee" seized power as Gorbachev vacationed in the Crimea. Yet communications had so developed under *glasnost* that the coup leaders were unable to "pull the plug." Foreign news reporters interviewed Boris Yeltsin behind the barricades by telephone and satellite television. Computer networks such as Moscow-based "GlasNet" telecommunicated with supporters outside the country. Information flowed through the vast underground communication network, which was first developed with mimeographed *samizdat* publications and now was interconnected in a decentralized web of electronics. The coup leaders did manage to send a surge through the electrical lines in a partially successful attempt to burn out fax machines, computers, and telephones. But with Radio Liberty, Cable News Network, and thousands of telephone lines pouring in information and support, in the end the abortive Soviet coup demonstrated that once the electronic gates are opened, it is hard to close them again.

Throughout the world, communication technologies are accelerating movements toward democracy. No matter how tightly a government controls its official media, determined opponents can circumvent this control with such media. Today there has arisen a worldwide metanetwork of highly decentralized and inexpensive technologies—computer networks, fax machines, amateur radio, packet data satellites, VCRs, video cameras, and the like. For the first time in history, revolutionary forces have the same communication tools previously reserved for the military and governments. They have become effective tools in countering media blackouts, organizing protests, and exchanging information.

The first large-scale impact of these decentralizing technologies on international politics happened on June 4, 1989.[74] When the Chinese government fired on its citizens near Tienanmen Square, Chinese students transmitted the most detailed, vivid reports instantly by fax, telephone, and computer networks to activists throughout the world. They organized protest meetings, fund-raising, speaking tours, and political appeals. Their impact was so immense and immediate that the Chinese government tried to cut telephone links to the exterior and started to monitor computer networks where much of this was taking place.

Another example is the U.S. war with Iraq, where computer networks such as PeaceNet exploded with activity. (PeaceNet is a U.S. computer communications system helping the peace movements cooperate more effectively and efficiently.) While mainstream channels of communication were blocked by Pentagon censorship, PeaceNet was carrying accurate reports of the effects of the Gulf War on the Third World, Israel and the Arab countries, and the worldwide antiwar movement.[75]

COMMUNICATION IN HIGH INTENSITY CONFLICT
Communication Technology and the Military

Military force itself is a powerful communications medium. Von Clausewitz articulated this when he asked and answered his own question: "Is not war merely another kind of writing and language for political thought? It has certainly a grammar of its own, but its logic is not peculiar to itself."[76] Put another way, war and the use of military forces are but dialects of the language of diplomacy, for communication and information are instrumental components in military strategy.[77]

Until recently the difficulties of long-distance communication prevented heads of state and commanders of armed forces from learning about their successes or failures on the battlefield until after the battle was all over. But beginning with the Vietnam war, President Johnson was able personally to choose bombing targets in the morning, then view photoreconnaissance images of the results in the evening.[78] Today the U.S. worldwide military command and control system employs satellites, computers, and ground receiving stations to provide a degree of centralized information unimaginable in the past.[79]

The U.S. government is the single largest user of information systems in the world. Mosco reports that in 1988 the government's budget for information systems accounted for one-tenth ($17 billion) of the entire market for computers, software, and services.[80] For years research and development in the communications industry has been driven by the needs of the military. The Defense Department granted huge contracts to private industry to develop the microchips that have totally transformed the communication industry. Software development has largely been underwritten by the U.S. military. The defense establishment is a major consumer of all this technology—15 percent of all integrated circuits produced in the United States, for example.[81]

The military and intelligence establishment controls about 25 percent of all radio frequencies used within the United States. It is also the largest user of telecommunications equipment, with a total budget exceeding the annual revenues of all commercial broadcasting in the country. Through the Defense Communication Agency and the Defense Telecommunication and Command Control System, the Pentagon operates the world's most powerful system of communications satellites, submarine cables, computers, and terrestrial systems.[82] Computing and communications systems are central to weapons systems, missile guidance, satellite observation, weapons design and testing, military intelligence, and scrambling.[83]

The big powers maintain a platoon of spies in the sky using optical, infrared, and radar detectors. Their combined militaries account for about half of operational satellites worldwide. The Pentagon budget for satellites alone is twice that of NASA, the civilian space agency.[84]

NOTES

1. Frederic Wertham, cited in Alex P. Schmid, "Violence as Communication: The Case of Insurgent Terrorism," in *Elements of World Instability: Armaments, Communication, Food, International Division of Labour* (Frankfurt: Campus Verlag, 1981), p. 147.

2. "Transcript of the Interviews with Sadat and Begin," *New York Times*, November 15, 1977, p. 2.

3. See Les Brown, "TV's Role in Mideast: Almost Diplomacy?," *New York Times*, November 18, 1977, p. 11; "News and Comment," *New Yorker*, January 9, 1978, p. 19; and Elihu Katz with Daniel Dayan and Pierre Motyl, "Television Diplomacy: Sadat in Jerusalem," in *World Communications: A Handbook*, ed. George Gerbner and Marsha Siefert (New York: Longman, 1984), pp. 127–136.

4. Andrew Arno, "Communication, Conflict, and Storylines: The News Media as Actors in a Cultural Context," in *The News Media in National and International Conflict*, ed. Andrew Arno and Wimal Dissanayake (Boulder, CO: Westview Press, 1984), p. 1.

5. Harry L. Coles, *The War of 1812* (Chicago: University of Chicago Press, 1965); Reginald Horsman, *The War of 1812* (New York: Knopf, 1969); John K. Mahon, *The War of 1812* (Gainesville, FL: University of Florida Press, 1972); and Glen Tucker, *Poltroons and Patriots: A Popular Account of the War of 1812*, 2 vols. (Indianapolis, IN: Bobbs-Merrill, 1954).

6. T. A. Bailing, *Diplomatic History of the American People* (New York: Appleton-Century-Crofts, 1964), cited in Colin Cherry, *World Communication: Threat or Promise? A Socio-technical Approach*, rev. ed. (Chichester, England: Wiley, 1978), p. 54.

7. Ann P. Saab, *Origins of the Crimean Alliance* (Charlottesville, VA: University Press of Virginia, 1977); H. W. V. Temperley, *England and the Near East: The Crimea* (London: Cass, 1964); and Philip Warner, *The Crimean War: A Reappraisal* (London: Barker, 1972).

8. Philip Knightley, *The First Casualty: From the Crimea to Vietnam: The War Correspondent as Hero, Propagandist, and Myth Maker* (New York: Harcourt Brace Jovanovich, 1975), p. 5. See also Rupert Furneaux, *News of War: Stories and Adventures of the Great War Correspondents* (London: Max Parrish, 1964); and Joseph J. Mathews, *Reporting the Wars* (Minneapolis, MN: University of Minnesota Press, 1957).

9. See Michael Howard, *The Franco-Prussian War: The German Invasion of France, 1870–71* (London: Methuen, 1981); and Lawrence D. Steefel, *Bismarck, The Hohenzollern Candidacy, and the Origins of the Franco-German War of 1870* (Cambridge, MA: Harvard University Press, 1962).

10. Oliver Carlson and Ernest Sutherland Bates, *Hearst, Lord of San Simeon* (Westport, CT: Greenwood Press, 1970); French E. Chadwick, *The Relations of the United States and Spain: The Spanish–American War,* 2 vols. (New York: Scribner's, 1909); Edwin and Michael Emery, *The Press and America* (Englewood Cliffs, NJ: Prentice-Hall, 1978); Philip S. Foner, *The Spanish–Cuban–American War and the Birth of American Imperialism, 1895–1902,* 2 vols. (New York: Monthly Review Press, 1972); Frank Freidel, *The Splendid Little War* (Boston: Little, Brown, 1958); W. A. Swanberg, *Citizen Hearst* (New York: Scribner's, 1961); and John Tebbel, *The Life and Good Times of William Randolph Hearst* (New York: Dutton, 1952).

11. Barbara W. Tuchman, *The Zimmermann Telegram* (New York: Macmillan, 1958; reprint, 1966).

12. "Testimony of Lt. Col. Kermit A. Tyler before the Army Pearl Harbor Board, August 17, 1944," in *What Happened at Pearl Harbor? Documents Pertaining to the Japanese Attack on December 7, 1941, and Its Background,* ed. Hans Louis Trefousse (New York: Twayne, 1958), p. 98. See also Roberta Wohlstetter, *Pearl Harbor: Warning and Decision* (Stanford, CA: Stanford University Press, 1962), pp. 6–12.

13. Stanley Karnow, *Vietnam: A History* (New York: Viking Press, 1983), p. 373.

14. This definition is slightly different from the Pentagon's definition, which puts "high intensity warfare" at the nuclear level and "medium intensity conflict" at the level of conventional weapons. For more information on low intensity conflict, see the February 1987 edition of *Military Review*; Lilia Bermudez, *Guerra de Baja Intensidad: Reagan contra Centroamérica* (Mexico City: Siglo XXI Editores, 1987); Arthur H. Blair, Jr., et al., "Unconventional Warfare: A Legitimate Tool of Foreign Policy," *Conflict* 4 (1,1983): 59–81; Richard A. Hunt and Richard H. Schultz, Jr., *Lessons from Unconventional War: Reassessing U.S. Strategies for Future Conflicts* (New York: Pergamon Press, 1982); Bill Keller, "Essential, They Say, But 'Repugnant' (Department of Defense Conference on Little Wars—'Low Intensity Conflict')," *New York Times,* January 20, 1986, pp. 12+; Frank Kitson, *Low Intensity Operations: Subversion, Insurgency, Peace-Keeping,* 1st ed. (Harrisburg, PA: Stackpole Books, 1971); Michael T. Klare and Peter Kornbluh, *Low Intensity Warfare: Counterinsurgency, Proinsurgency, and Antiterrorism in the Eighties* (New York: Pantheon Books, 1988); Brad Knickerbocker, "U.S. Military Surveys Central America Turf; Some Officers Say U.S. Unready for Demands of 'Low Intensity Conflict,'" *Christian Science Monitor,* May 15, 1985, p. 1; James Berry Motley, "Grenada: Low Intensity Conflict and the Use of United States Military Power," *World Affairs,* 146 (3, Winter 1983–1984): 221–238; G. Reed, "Low Intensity Conflict: A War for All Seasons," *Black Scholar* 17 (1, 1986): 14–22; Sam C. Sarkesian, *The New Battlefield: America and Low Intensity Conflicts* (Westport, CT: Greenwood Press, 1986); Sam C. Sarkesian and William L. Scully, *U.S. Policy and Low Intensity Conflict* (New Brunswick, NJ: Transaction Books, 1981); and Thomas Walker, *Reagan versus the Sandinistas: The Undeclared War on Nicaragua* (Boulder, CO: Westview Press, 1987).

15. *Spic* is the verb *speak* uttered with a Spanish-speaking immigrant's accent. *Gook* is the word for "country" in Korean. *Kike* comes from the Yiddish word for "circle," *kirkel,* and harks back to the time when illiterate Jewish immigrants signed their names by making a circle, not the cross that immigration officials demanded.

16. *International Encyclopedia of Communications,* 1st ed., s.v. "Diplomacy."

17. Tran Van Dinh, *Communication and Diplomacy in a Changing World* (Norwood, NJ: Ablex, 1987), p. 8.

18. The Vienna Convention on Diplomatic Relations guarantees the right to "free communication on the part of the mission for all official purposes. . . . including diplomatic couriers and messages in code or cipher. . . . The official correspondence shall be inviolable." This includes communications by post, telegraph, and diplomatic pouch. But a "wireless" transmitter requires the consent of the host government. Vienna Convention on Diplomatic Relations, 500 *United Nations Treaty Series* 95, 3(1)(d).

19. See Diane B. Bendahmane and David W. McClintock, eds., *Science, Technology, and Foreign Affairs,* vols. 4 and 5 (Washington, DC: U.S. Department of State, Foreign Service Institute, Center for the Study of Foreign Affairs, 1984); and Thomas J. Ramsey, "International Diplomatic Telecommunications," in *Toward a Law of Global Communications Networks,* ed. Anne W. Branscomb (New York: Longman, 1986), pp. 217–223.

20. K. J. Holsti, *International Politics: A Framework for Analysis,* 3rd. ed. (Englewood Cliffs, NJ: Prentice-Hall, 1977), pp. 188–189.

21. Abba Eban, *The New Diplomacy: International Affairs in the Modern Age* (New York: Random House, 1983), p. 347.

22. Certain international media channels have constant influence on diplomatic personnel around the world—particularly the morning broadcasts of the BBC World Service. Wire services such as Associated Press and Reuters sometimes are the only sources available in world crises. Elite newspapers also are important. In Europe these include *The Times of London, Le Monde, Neue Zürcher Zeitung, Frankfurter Allgemeine Zeitung, The International Herald Tribune, The Economist,* and the European editions of *Time* and *Newsweek.* In New York and Washington, DC, these channels include the *New York Times* and the *Washington Post.* The newspaper with perhaps the best international coverage is the *Los Angeles Times.* Although it is the largest metropolitan paper in the United States, its influence is limited because it is not in a national capital.

23. See the following works by W. Phillips Davison: "News Media and International Negotiation," *Public Opinion Quarterly* 38 (1974): 174–191; *International Political Communication* (New York: Praeger, 1965); *Mass Communication and Conflict Resolution: The Role of the Information Media in the Advancement of International Understanding* (New York: Praeger, 1974); and "Diplomatic Reporting: The Rules of the Game," *Journal of Communication* 25 (1975): 138–146.

24. W. Phillips Davison, "Political Significance of Recognition in the Mass Media: An Illustration from the Berlin Blockade," *Public Opinion Quarterly* 20 (1, 1956): 332.

25. Karl W. Deutsch, "Mass Communications and Loss of Freedom in National Decision-Making: A Possible Approach to Interstate Conflict," *Conflict Resolution* 1 (2, 1957): 202. For example, the 1954 "canned crisis" of Quemoy and the Matsus, islands that had served as points for nationalist Chinese retreat in 1949 and that were still in nationalist (Taiwanese) hands, came about when American news magazines greatly exacerbated a situation that should not have warranted such attention. Daniel J. Leab, "Canned Crisis: U.S. Magazines, Quemoy, and the Matsus," *Journalism Quarterly* 44 (1967): 340.

26. The 1978 United Nations Special Session on Disarmament was an extraordinary opportunity for the nations of the world to take a giant step toward arms reductions and nuclear nonproliferation. Yet coverage was so slight that the session was "among the best-kept secrets of 1978. . . . Most news organizations . . . [gave] the possibility of nuclear annihilation far less coverage than gastronomic matters and far less systematic attention than the television listings." Richard Pollak, "Covering the Unthinkable: The U.N. Disarmament Session and the Press," *The Nation,* May 1, 1982, p. 516.

27. Karl W. Deutsch, "Communications, Arms Inspection, and National Security," in *Preventing World War III,* ed. Quincy Wright, William Evan, and Mortimer Deutsch (New York: Simon & Schuster, 1962), pp. 62–73.

28. Deutsch, "Communications, Arms Inspection, and National Security," p. 65.

29. Charles A. McClelland, "The Anticipation of International Crisis: Prospects for Theory and Research," *International Studies Quarterly* 21 (1, March 1977): 35.

30. J. David Singer, "Media Analysis in Inspection for Disarmament," *Journal of Arms Control* 3 (1, 1965): 248–259.

31. Davison, *Mass Communication and Conflict Resolution,* p. 38.

32. See Elie Abel, "Television in International Conflict," and Andrew Arno, "The News Media as Third Parties in National and International Conflict: Duobus Litigantibus Tertius Gaudet," in *News Media in National and International Conflict,* pp. 63–70 and pp. 229–239, respectively.

33. Majid Tehranian, "International Communication: A Dialogue of the Deaf?" *Political Communication and Persuasion* 2 (1, 1982): 23–25. Tehranian's original formulation treats "journalists," not "media."

34. Andrew Arno, "Communication, Conflict, and Storylines," p. 11.

35. Joyce Evans-Karastamatis, "Citizens' Summit II: Problems in Intercultural Communication." Paper presented at the conference of the International Communication Association, New Orleans, 1988.

36. C. Anthony Giffard and Lisa Cohen, "Television, Censorship, and South Africa." Paper presented at the conference of the Association for Education in Journalism and Mass Education, 1987; and C. Anthony Giffard and Lisa Cohen, "The Impact of Censorship of U.S. Television News Coverage of South Africa," in *Current Issues in International Communication* (New York: Longman, 1990), pp. 122–133.

37. Gifford D. Malone, "Managing Public Diplomacy," *Washington Quarterly* 8 (3, 1985): 199–210.

38. Kenneth L. Adelman, "Speaking of America: Public Diplomacy in Our Time," *Foreign Affairs* 59 (1976): 927.

39. Robert B. Albritton and Jarol B. Manheim, "Public Relations Efforts for the Third World: Images in the News," *Journal of Communication* 35 (2, Spring 1985): 58.

40. Robert I. Friedman, "Selling Israel to America: The Hasbara Project Targets the U.S. Media," *Mother Jones,* February–March 1987, p. 21+.

41. See M. Davis, *Interpreters for Nigeria: The Third World and International Public Relations* (Urbana, IL: University of Illinois Press, 1977); K. Rothmyer, "What Really Happened in Biafra? Why Did Themes Such as Mass Starvation and Genocide Alternately Surface and Fade? A Study of Media Susceptibility to Public Relations Manipulation," *Columbia Journalism Review,* Fall 1970, pp. 43–47; and G. Zieser, "Die Propagandastrategie Biafras im Nigerianischen Bürgerkrieg," *Publizistik* 16 (1971).

42. Adapted from Bruce L. Smith, "Propaganda," *Encyclopedia of the Social Sciences,* ed. D. L. Sills (New York: Macmillan, 1968), p. 579.

43. See also Michael Balfour, *Propaganda in War, 1939–1945: Organizations, Policies, and Publics, in Britain and Germany* (London: Routledge & Kegan Paul, 1979); Leonard W. Doob, *Public Opinion and Propaganda,* 2nd ed. (Hamden, CT: Anchor Books, 1948); Jacques Ellul, *Propaganda: The Formation of Men's Attitudes* (New York: Knopf, 1965); Carl I. Hovland, Irving L. Janis, and Harold H. Kelley, *Communication and Persuasion* (New Haven, CT: Yale University Press, 1953); *International Encyclopedia of Communications,* s.v. "Propaganda"; Paul Kecskemeti, "Propaganda," in *Handbook of Communication,* ed. Ithiel de Sola Pool et al. (Chicago: Rand McNally, 1973); Harold D. Lasswell, Daniel Lerner, and Hans Speier, eds., *Propaganda and Communication in World History,* 3 vols. (Honolulu, HI: University of Hawaii Press, 1979 and 1980); and Daniel Lerner, ed., *Propaganda in War and Crisis* (New York: G. W. Stewart, 1951, reprint 1972).

44. Ernest K. Bramstedt, *Goebbels and National Socialist Propaganda, 1925–1945* (East Lansing, MI: Michigan State University Press, 1965); Joseph Goebbels, *My Part in Germany's Fight,* trans. Kurt Fiedler (London: Hurst & Blackett, 1935); *The Goebbels Diaries, 1942–43,* trans. Louis F. Lochner (New York: Putnam, 1983); and *Final Entries 1945: The Diaries of Joseph Goebbels,* ed. Hugh Trevor-Roper, trans. Richard Barry (New York: Putnam, 1978).

45. Such fear prompted Congress since 1948 to prohibit domestic dissemination of materials produced for overseas information programs. Kenneth L. Adelman, "Speaking of America," p. 914.

46. See the excellent four-article forum "What is Propaganda, Anyway?" in *Propaganda Review* (5, 1989).

47. Doob, *Public Opinion and Propaganda;* Ellul, *Propaganda;* Erich Fromm, *Escape from Freedom* (New York: Farrar & Rinehart, 1941); Alexander L. George, *Propaganda Analysis* (New York: Row, Peterson, 1959); Russell W. Howe and Sarah H. Trott, *The Power Peddlers* (Garden City, NY: Doubleday, 1977); Garth Jowett and Victoria O'Donnell, *Propaganda and Persuasion* (Newbury Park, CA: Sage, 1986); Lasswell, Lerner, and Speier, *Propaganda and Communication in*

World History, vol. 1; Thomas E. Patterson and Robert D. McClure, *The Unseeing Eye: The Myth of Television Power in National Politics* (New York: Putnam, 1976); and Oliver Thomson, *Mass Persuasion in History* (Edinburgh, Scotland: Paul Harris, 1977).

48. Developed by the Institute for Propaganda Analysis and elaborated by Holsti, *International Politics,* pp. 22–30; adapted originally from Alfred McClung Lee and Elizabeth Bryant Lee, *The Fine Art of Propaganda: A Study of Father Coughlin's Speeches* (New York: Harcourt Brace Jovanovich, 1939), pp. 22–25.

49. W. Phillips Davison, "Political Communication as an Instrument of Foreign Policy," *Public Opinion Quarterly* 27 (Spring 1963): 28.

50. L. John Martin, "Disinformation: An Instrumentality in the Propaganda Arsenal," *Political Communication and Persuasion* 2 (1, 1982): 50.

51. The CIA broadly defined disinformation as "a range of practices such as written and oral 'disinformation' (forgeries, false rumors), 'gray' and 'black' propaganda, manipulation or control of foreign media assets, political action and 'agent of influence' operations, clandestine radio stations, semiclandestine use of foreign communist parties and international front and special action organizations, staged or manipulated demonstrations, and even, in the past, blackmail and kidnaping." U.S. Congress, House of Representatives, *Soviet Covert Action,* Hearings before the Subcommittee on Oversight of the Permanent Select Committee on Intelligence, 96th Congress, 2nd Session, February 6 and 19, 1980, p. 63, cited in Martin, "Disinformation," p. 58.

52. Thomas R. Rosenstiel, "Viewers Found to Confuse TV Entertainment with News," *Los Angeles Times,* August 17, 1989, p. A17; Howard Rosenberg, "TV & Reality," *Los Angeles Times,* Calendar Magazine, September 10, 1989, p. 7.

53. "Beware: 'Disinfotainment,'" *Extra!* October/November 1989, p. 3.

54. Harry Waters, "A Storm Over 'Amerika,'" *Newsweek,* November 10, 1986, pp. 91–92.

55. Jin K. Kim, J. Justin Gustainis, and Pirouz Shoar-Ghaffari, " 'Amerika': Selectivity in Exposure Patterns and Attitude Influence." Paper presented at the conference of the International Communication Association, New Orleans, 1988.

56. For more on espionage, see Philip Agee and Louis Wolf, *Dirty Work I—The CIA in Western Europe* (New York: Stuart, 1978) and *Dirty Work II—The CIA in Africa* (New York: Stuart, 1979); Christopher Andrew, *Her Majesty's Secret Service: The Making of the British Intelligence Community* (New York: Viking Press, 1986); James Bamford, *The Puzzle Palace* (Boston: Houghton Mifflin, 1982); Michael R. Beschloss, *Mayday: Eisenhower, Khrushchev, and the U-2 Affair* (New York: Holt, Rinehart, 1986); William Blum, *The CIA, A Forgotten History: U.S. Global Interventions since World War 2* (London and Atlantic Heights, NJ: Zed Press, 1987); Robert L. Borosage and John Marks, *The CIA File* (New York: Grossman, 1976); Andrew Boyle, *The Fourth Man* (New York: Dial Press, 1974); *The CIA's Nicaraguan Manual: Psychological Operations in Guerrilla Warfare* (New York: Vintage, 1985); Ray S. Cline, *Secrets, Spies, and Scholars* (Washington, DC: Acropolis Books, 1976); Richard Deacon, *A History of the British Secret Service* (New York: Taplinger, 1969); Allen W. Dulles, *The Craft of Intelligence* (New York: Holt, Rinehart, 1963; reprint 1977); Ladislas Farago, *The Broken Seal* (New York: Random House, 1967); Howard Frazier, *Uncloaking the CIA* (New York: Free Press, 1978); F. H. Hinsley, ed., *British Intelligence in the Second World War* (London: H.M. Stationery Office, 1979); Allison Ind, *A Short History of Espionage* (London: Hodder & Stoughton, 1965); *International Encyclopedia of Communications,* s.v. "Espionage"; R. V. Jones, *Most Secret War* (London: Hamilton, 1978); Lyman Kirkpatrick, *The U.S. Intelligence Community* (New York: Hill and Wang, 1973); Ronald Lewin, *Ultra Goes to War: The Secret Story* (London: Hutchinson, 1978); Victor Marchetti and John D. Marks, *The CIA and the Cult of Intelligence* (New York: Knopf, 1974); Harry Howe Ransom, *The Intelligence Establishment* (Cambridge, MA: Harvard University Press, 1970); Harry Rositzke, *The CIA's Secret Operations* (New York: Reader's Digest Press, 1977); Frank N. Trager, *National Security and American Society* (Lawrence, KS: University Press of Kansas, 1973); Tuchman, *The Zimmermann Telegram;* F. W. Winterbotham, *The Ultra Secret* (New York: Harper & Row, 1974).

57. Invented during World War II, the microdot reduced a printed page to a dot the size of this typed period.

58. Howard H. Frederick, "'Development Sabotage Communication' in Low Intensity Warfare: Media Strategies against Democracy in Central America," in *Communication For and Against Democracy,* ed. Peter A. Bruck and Marc Raboy (Montreal and New York: Black Rose, 1989), pp. 19–35.

59. John W. Higgins, "Development Communication as 'Public Relations': The U.S. Army in Honduras." Paper presented at the conference of the International Association for Mass Communication Research, Sao Paulo, Brazil, August 16–21, 1992.

60. Caspar W. Weinberger, "Low Intensity Warfare," *Vital Speeches,* February 15, 1986, p. 259.

61. *Army Field Manual 100–20* (on Low Intensity Warfare), cited in Bermudez, *Guerra de Baja Intensidad,* pp. 98, 125. Each psyops group is organized and equipped to carry out a psychological war to help in the theater of operations. Troops and equipment can be loaded quickly into huge aircraft and deployed rapidly to any part of the world. The resources of a strategic battalion include a 50,000-watt AM transmitter, a mobile satellite earth station, sophisticated monitoring equipment, and a mobile printing press. A team of writers can quickly develop written materials with any message. The specific message itself is designed by the intelligence section through public opinion surveys to uncover vulnerable messages with the maximum impact. The groups have enough translators and linguists to handle any language or dialect. Other equipment that can be flown in includes mobile film trucks, jeeps, public address systems, remote sensing equipment, jammers, secure communications systems, and high-speed data burst equipment. See also Peter Kornbluh, "Nicaragua: U.S. Proinsurgency Warfare Against the Sandinistas," in Klare and Kornbluh, *Low Intensity Warfare.*

62. David Marks, "Broadcasting across the Wall: The Free Flow of Information between East and West Germany," *Journal of Communication* 33 (1, 1983): 46–55; Douglas A. Boyd, "Broadcasting between the Two Germanies," *Journalism Quarterly* 60 (1983): 232–239.

63. Howard H. Frederick, *Cuban-American Radio Wars* (Norwood, NJ: Ablex, 1986).

64. Howard H. Frederick, "Electronic Penetration in Low Intensity Warfare: The Case of Nicaragua," Walker, ed., *Reagan versus the Sandinistas,* pp. 123–142.

65. *Neue Deutsche Presse* (GDR), February 1989, pp. 18–19, cited in *Mass Communication Media in the World* 6 (3, 1989): 20.

66. See also Hazel G. Warlaumont, "Strategies in International Radio Wars: A Comparative Approach," *Journal of Broadcasting and Electronic Media* 32 (1, Winter 1988): 43–59.

67. Razelle Frankl, *Televangelism: The Marketing of Popular Religion* (Carbondale, IL: Southern Illinois University Press, 1987), p. 5; Hugo Assman, *La Iglesia Electrónica y Su Impacto en América Latina* (San José, Costa Rica: Editorial DEI, 1987); and David Martin, *Tongues of Fire: The Explosion of Protestantism in Latin America* (Oxford: Basil Blackwell, 1990).

68. David L. Altheide, "Three-in-One News: Network Coverage of Iran," *Journalism Quarterly* 59 (Autumn 1982): 641–645; David L. Altheide, "Impact of Format and Ideology on TV News Coverage of Iran," *Journalism Quarterly* 62 (Summer 1985): 346–351; Dan Nimmo and James E. Combs, *Nightly Horrors: Crisis Coverage by Television Network News* (Knoxville, TN: University of Tennessee Press, 1985), p. 165; David L. Paletz, John Z. Ayanian, and Peter A. Fozzard, "Terrorism on TV News: The IRA, the FALN, and the Red Brigades," in *Television Coverage of International Affairs,* ed. William C. Adams (Norwood, NJ: Ablex, 1982), pp. 143–165; and Tony Atwater, "Network Evening News Coverage of the TWA Hostage Crisis." Paper presented at the conference of the International Communication Association, Montreal, 1987.

69. Alex P. Schmid, "Violence as Communication: The Case of Insurgent Terrorism," in Egbert Jahn, ed., *Elements of World Instability: Armaments, Communication, Food, International Division of Labour* (Frankfurt: Campus Verlag, 1981), pp. 147–167 (The quotation in this chapter comes from pp. 148, 151–152).

70. David L. Paletz, Peter A. Fozzard, and John Z. Ayanian, "The I.R.A., the Red Brigades, and the F.A.L.N. in the *New York Times,*" *Journal of Communication* 32 (2, 1982): 162–171; and Paletz, Ayanian, and Fozzard, "Terrorism on Television News," pp. 143–165.

71. Zoe Che-wei Tan, "Media Publicity and Insurgent Terrorism: A Twenty-Year Balance Sheet." Paper presented at the conference of the International Communication Association, Montreal, 1987.

72. Excerpted from Schmid, "Violence as Communication," p. 163. See also David L. Paletz and Alex R. Schmid, eds., *Terrorism and the Media* (Beverly Hills, CA: Sage, 1992).

73. Excerpted from Schmid, "Violence as Communication," p. 163.

74. John S. Quarterman, *The Matrix: Computer Networks and Conferencing Systems Worldwide* (Bedford, MA: Digital Press, 1990), p. i.

75. For more information, write to PeaceNet, 18 De Boom Street, San Francisco, CA 94107. Voice: 415-442-0220. Fax: 415-546-1794. Internet: peacenet@igc.org Bitnet: peacenet%igc.org@stanford

76. Carl Von Clausewitz, *Vom Kriege* (Bonn: Dümmlers Verlag, 1973), p. 991. Translation by the present author.

77. See Vincent Mosco, "Communication and Information Technology for War and Peace," in Colleen Roach, ed. *Information and Culture in War and Peace* (Newbury Park, CA: Sage, forthcoming); Herbert I. Schiller, *Mass Communication and American Empire* (Boston: Beacon Press, 1969); Dallas Smythe, *Dependency Road* (Norwood, NJ: Ablex, 1981); and Armand Mattelart and Seth Siegelaub, eds., *Communication and Class Struggle, Vol. I: Capitalism, Imperialism* (New York: International General, 1979) and *Vol. II: Liberation, Socialism* (1983).

78. Paul A. Chadwell, "C³I Satellite Systems," *National Defense*, June 1980; and Deborah G. Meyer, "Strategic Satellites: Our Eyes in the Sky," *Armed Forces Journal*, February 1983.

79. Daniel Deudney, *Whole Earth Security: A Geopolitics of Peace* (Washington, DC: Worldwatch Institute, 1983), p. 23.

80. Mosco, "Communication and Information Technology."

81. U.S. Congress, Office of the Budget, *The Benefits and Risks of Federal Funding for Sematech* (Washington, DC: Congressional Budget Office, 1987), as cited in Vincent Mosco, *The Pay-Per Society* (Norwood, NJ: Ablex, 1989), p. 142.

82. Mosco, "Communication and Information Technology," pp. 20–21.

83. Brian Martin, "Computing and War," *Peace and Change* 14 (2, 1989): 203–222.

84. Federation of American Scientists, *What's Up in Space* (Washington, DC: Federation of American Scientists, 1987). See also J. Canan, *War in Space* (New York: Harper & Row, 1982). According to the Stockholm International Peace Research Institute, about 75 percent of satellites in orbit are military satellites. These include reconnaissance, navigation, communications, weather, and geodetic satellites. Frank Barnaby and Ian Williams, "Heavenly Watchdogs," *South,* November 1983, p. 13.

9

Global Communication and Information Law

BETWEEN THE STRONG AND THE WEAK IT IS FREEDOM WHICH
OPPRESSES AND LAW WHICH LIBERATES.

Jean Baptiste Lacordaire

HISTORICAL DEVELOPMENT

Nations have obeyed the international law of communication and information for
more than a century.[1] In fact, this is one of the oldest bodies of continuously
respected international law in the world. Three of the four oldest specialized agencies of the United Nations deal primarily with communication and information: the
International Telecommunications Union (ITU), founded in 1865; the Universal Postal
Union (UPU), 1874; and the World Intellectual Property Organization (WIPO), 1883.[2]

By the second half of the nineteenth century, public opinion had already become
a factor in international relations. States found themselves with a need to persuade
their own populations as well as their opponents. Prussian Chancellor Bismarck and
Emperor Napoleon III were the consummate "great communicators" of their time.
Late nineteenth-century battles for international public opinion led to regulatory
approaches through the law of neutrality. The 1907 *Convention Respecting the
Rights and Duties of Neutral Powers and Persons* included several articles limiting or
controlling propaganda activities.[3]

These early days of global communication and information law were sleepy compared with what was to come. World War I and the Russian Revolution ideologized
international relations and gave a powerful role to the media of international political
communication. The League of Nations dealt with this development very early on.

Meeting for the first time just six days after the Treaty of Versailles came into force, League delegates wanted to break with the past by replacing power politics and secret diplomacy with international cooperation, collective security, and open diplomacy. Delegates envisioned a new role for the press. In a 1925 resolution, still quite applicable today, the League stated: "The Press constitutes the most effective means of guiding public opinion towards moral disarmament, which is a concomitant condition of material disarmament."[4]

Throughout history, one clear pattern is apparent. Every time a new innovation in communication technology appears, sooner or later international law arises to regulate it. Gutenberg's invention of the printing press led John Milton to call for a "right to freedom of expression." Morse's discovery of the telegraph led to the creation of the International Telegraph Convention. The development of wireless radio led quickly to the International Radio Telegraph Convention. The great "radio propaganda wars" of the 1930s led to the famous *International Convention Concerning the Use of Broadcasting in the Cause of Peace,* the first multilateral effort to regulate peacetime propaganda.[5]

DEFINITIONS

International law was traditionally defined as the body of rules governing relations between sovereign states (meaning national governments). In the past, the *subjects* of international law were states, who in turn applied that law to the so-called *objects* of international law, namely citizens (natural persons) and private firms (juridical persons).

But in the present century, other international actors have challenged the supremacy of the state. *International organizations, nongovernmental organizations, and private firms* can now be the subjects of international law. The most significant change, however, is the increasing role of *individuals* in international law. The 1945 United Nations Charter acknowledges individual human beings as personalities in international law. The 1948 Universal Declaration of Human Rights outlines the rights and duties of individuals, and the 1966 Human Rights Covenants enshrine those rights in binding law. As the Nuremberg judges ruled concerning Nazi war criminals, "individuals have international duties which transcend the national obligations of obedience imposed by the individual state."[6]

Modern international law is concerned with such individual struggles as human rights, racial prejudice, and gender discrimination. So the definition of international law now includes *all the institutions and processes governing matters of international concern, and the norms or rules they produce.* This definition allows for the law-creating part played by intergovernmental organizations, multinational corporations, political parties, pressure groups, liberation organizations, and individuals. Extending this definition to the subject of this study, *global communication and information law is comprised of those legal institutions, instruments, and processes that govern communication among and between individuals, peoples, cultures, nations, and technologies.*

Can international law be applied to private media firms and individual communicators? States themselves are of course the subjects of international law; state-controlled or state-financed mass media (for example, government broadcasting stations) are necessarily included here. But for almost two centuries, nations have disputed whether a state is responsible for restraining its private citizens who, for example, might be broadcasting destabilizing propaganda to other countries.[7]

Private media were not subjects of international law in the old definition. But from Article 26 of the 1969 *Vienna Convention on the Law of Treaties,* we can deduce that states today have general obligations in the sphere of international law that they cannot evade by pointing to domestic laws.[8] Furthermore, the modern definition of international law definitely includes individuals as subjects. The manner in which international law is enforced on private media is a matter of a state's sovereign prerogative. The point is that these measures must be promulgated. Private media must comply with laws of the state in which they operate. If international law prohibits propaganda for war or racism, the state has an obligation to regulate the private media in this regard.[9]

PRINCIPLES AND PRACTICE OF INTERNATIONAL LAW

All international law is based on the seven fundamental principles.[10] Members of the United Nations are required to obey them and to compel all subjects under their jurisdiction to act in agreement with them. Later in this chapter, the ways these fundamental principles apply to global communication law will be discussed.

Non-use of force. States may not threaten or use force against the territory or independence of another state or against the rights to self-determination, freedom, and independence of peoples. A war of aggression constitutes a crime against peace. States may not organize mercenary forces or civil strife in another state, nor may they occupy another state through military force or recognize that occupation as legal.

Peaceful settlement of disputes. States must settle their disputes by peaceful means in a way that does not endanger peace and security. States in dispute must seek negotiation, mediation, and settlement and, short of a resolution, must not aggravate the situation.

Nonintervention. No state has the right to intervene directly or indirectly in the internal or external affairs of another state. This includes not only armed intervention, but also any form of economic or political coercion against the political, economic, or cultural integrity of another state. Every state has the inalienable right to choose its own political, economic, social, and cultural system without outside interference.

International cooperation. Whatever their differences may be, states have the duty to cooperate with one another, to maintain peace and security, and to promote economic stability and progress. This means conducting international relations according to the principles of equality and nonintervention, promoting respect for and observance of human rights, and eliminating racial discrimination and religious intolerance.

Equal rights and self-determination of peoples.   All peoples have the right freely to determine their political status and to pursue their economic, social, and cultural development without external interference. States must promote friendly relations, end colonialism, and guarantee respect for and observance of human rights. States must refrain from any threat or use of force that deprives their own or any other people of self-determination, freedom, and independence.

Sovereign equality of states.   The United Nations Charter is based on the sovereign equality of all nations, notwithstanding differences of an economic, social, political, or other nature. This means that states are equal before the law and enjoy the full rights of sovereignty and territorial integrity. All states must respect the political, social, economic, and cultural systems of other states and strive to live in peace with all states.

Good-faith obligations.   States must fulfill in good faith their obligations under recognized international law. States must be aware of such obligations; commitments to the United Nations Charter always take precedence over any other international agreement.

There are three *primary sources of international law*:[11]

International conventions   (often called "treaties"). In formal terms, these treaties bind only *states signatories*.[12] But when a very large number of states adhere to a treaty or accept its terms without becoming signatories, a treaty becomes an independent source of international law.[13]

International custom.   A second primary source of international law is *customary law,* consisting of principles derived from actual behavior of states rather than from formal legislation. Customary law is reflected in such promulgations as governmental statements and proclamations, international conferences, diplomatic exchanges, court decisions, and legislation. There are innumerable customary practices that have become international law, including such areas as sovereignty, diplomatic recognition, consent to sanctions, good-faith obligations, and freedom of the seas.

General principles of international law.   Although less relied upon today, when international law first emerged, "the general principles of law recognized by civilized nations"[14] were the only norms that could be generalized from the national to the international level.

In addition, there are *secondary sources of international law.* They include teachings of legal scholars, decisions of the World Court and other tribunals, and publications of the UN International Law Commission. Especially important secondary sources are *declarations, resolutions, or recommendations* by international intergovernmental organizations. Though not as a rule legally binding,[15] some have led to binding conventions. For example, the nonbinding Universal Declaration of Human Rights led ultimately to the binding 1966 Human Rights Covenants.

States incorporate international legal standards into domestic law in a variety of ways. The route usually leads from signing a convention, to ratification, to implementation in domestic law, and finally to enforcement of those provisions.[16] National legislation provides the legal basis for enforcing international law.[17]

Unfortunately, states can and do violate international law to achieve political ends. Unlike domestic law, international law has no "enforcer" to punish violators. Governments are most likely to uphold international law only when doing so will yield short-term gains. These commitments are often fragile and may be abandoned when they no longer seem to serve national interests.

Before we despair of the effectiveness of international law, we must note that there are countless areas of international relations where international law is respected and observed. There are numerous international legal instruments that regulate areas as diverse as trade and finance, transportation and communication, boundary and territorial law, and diplomatic affairs, just to name a few.

The *International Court of Justice*—or the World Court—is the principal judicial organ of the United Nations. Under international law, states may submit disputes to the Court. There are many other avenues of dispute resolution outside the World Court that otherwise follow international law. These include the United Nations itself, regional organizations, diplomatic conferences, and multilateral commissions, where international law plays a great role in resolving disputes.

HUMAN RIGHTS LAW AND COMMUNICATION

International legal instruments that establish regulatory principles for global communication and information are now surveyed.[18] We begin with three of the four documents that make up the so-called *International Bill of Human Rights.*[19]

The first, written in the crucible of a postfascist Europe dominated by Western liberalism, is the 1948 *Universal Declaration of Human Rights.* Its famous Article 19 declares:

> Everyone has the right to freedom of opinion and expression; this right includes freedom to hold opinions without interference and to seek, receive and impart information and ideas through any media and regardless of frontiers.

The Declaration does not guarantee *absolute* freedom of opinion or expression. Article 19's provisions, like all other human rights safeguarded by the Declaration, are qualified by Article 29, which declares:

> 1. Everyone has duties to the community in which alone the free and full development of his personality is possible.
> 2. In the exercise of his rights and freedoms, everyone shall be subject only to such limitations as are determined by law solely for the purpose of securing due recognition and respect for the rights and freedoms of others and of meeting the just requirements of morality, public order and general welfare in a democratic society.
> 3. These rights and freedoms may in no case be exercised contrary to the purposes and principles of the United Nations.[20]

The other documents of the International Bill of Human Rights are the three 1966 *Human Rights Covenants,* which make the principles set forth in the Universal

Declaration legally binding. For all the emphasis the United States places on human rights, it is disappointing that the United States has not ratified any of these important instruments of international law.[21]

The *International Covenant on Civil and Political Rights* restates the famous formulation of the Universal Declaration in its own Article 19:

1. Everyone shall have the right to hold opinions without interference.
2. Everyone shall have the right to freedom of expression; this right shall include the freedom to seek, receive and impart information and ideas of all kinds, regardless of frontiers, either orally, in writing or in print, in the form of art, or through any other media of his choice.

Here too the exercise of these rights is not absolute:

3. The exercise of the rights provided for in paragraph 2 of this article carries with it special duties and responsibilities. It may therefore be subject to certain restrictions, but these shall only be such as are provided by law and are necessary: (a) for respect of the rights or reputations of others; (b) for the protection of national security or of public order, or of public health or morals.

We see that each of these documents presents two facets in regard to freedom of expression. Freedom brings with it both "rights" and "duties." Here we see the essence of two diverging positions. One view would give states the right freely to disseminate information throughout the world without restrictions. The other would give states the right to stop communication that threatens national security, public order, or morality.

The International Covenant on Civil and Political Rights goes beyond the Universal Declaration of Human Rights in one significant respect. While the Universal Declaration only prescribes, the Covenant on Civil and Political Rights also proscribes; it actually prohibits certain content. Article 20 states unequivocally:

1. Any propaganda for war shall be prohibited by law.
2. Any advocacy of national, racial or religious hatred that constitutes incitement to discrimination, hostility or violence shall be prohibited by law.[22]

The *Optional Protocol to the 1966 International Covenant on Civil and Human Rights* has been ratified by forty governments. This document is very significant in that it allows individual citizens who have experienced violation of their human rights to petition directly to the United Nations Human Rights Commission for redress of grievances (this is called "individual communication").[23]

Beyond the International Bill of Human Rights there are two other human rights documents, neither of which the United States has ratified, that treat communication and information aspects of racism. The 1966 *International Convention on the Elimination of All Forms of Racial Discrimination* condemn[s] all propaganda and all organizations which are based on ideas or theories of superiority of one race or group of persons of one color or ethnic origin, or which attempt to justify or promote racial hatred, discrimination in any form . . .

It also forbids certain information activities. It prohibits

all dissemination of ideas based on racial superiority or hatred, incitement to racial discrimination, as well as all acts of violence or incitement to such acts against any race or group of persons of another color or ethnic origin, and also the provisions of any assistance to racist activities, including the financing thereof; [and]
    organizations, and also organized and all other propaganda activities, which promote and incite racial discrimination, and shall recognize participation in such organizations or activities as an offense punishable by law.[24]

In similar fashion, the 1973 *International Convention on the Suppression and Punishment of the Crime of Apartheid* declares apartheid a crime against humanity and makes individuals as well as institutions and organizations criminally liable. This convention goes on to make it criminally illegal to

a. Commit, participate in, directly incite or conspire in the commission of [the crime of apartheid];
b. Directly abet, encourage or cooperate in the commission of the crime of apartheid.[25]

The one human rights instrument that the United States has finally signed, ratified, and implemented is the 1948 *Convention on the Prevention and Punishment of the Crime of Genocide.* The Genocide Convention prohibits certain communication activities. It makes punishable "direct and public incitement to commit genocide," defined as the "intent to destroy in whole or in part, a national, ethnical, racial or religious group."[26]

Finally, some human right documents treat discrimination against women. The 1979 *Convention on the Elimination of All Forms of Discrimination against Women* commits its signatories to take steps in all areas of life, including information and communication,

to modify or abolish existing laws, regulations, customs and practices which constitute discrimination against women [toward] the elimination of prejudices and customary and all other practices which are based on the idea of the inferiority or the superiority of either of the sexes or on stereotyped roles for men and women; [and] to eliminate any stereotyped concept of roles of men and women.[27]

Many declarations and resolutions apply human rights standards to communication and information. The 1975 Mexico City Conference during *International Women's Year* makes explicit reference to communication:

All means of communication and information as well as all cultural media should regard as a high priority their responsibility for helping to remove the attitudinal and cultural factors that still inhibit the development of women and for projecting in positive terms the value to society of the assumption by women of changing and expanding roles.[28]

The *Nairobi Forward-Looking Strategies for the Advancement of Women* specifies that

all existing impediments to the achievement by women of equality with men should be removed. To this end, efforts should be intensified at all levels to overcome prejudices [and] stereotyped thinking.

It is important to note that unlike prohibitions against racist and genocidal propaganda, international law does not clearly prohibit information content that stereotypes and discriminates against women. On the whole, international law does not impose a duty on governments to eliminate sexist propaganda.

SECURITY, PEACE, AND COMMUNICATION

We have already seen that human rights treaties forbid war propaganda and racial hatred. Many other documents on security and disarmament include provisions addressing the content of communication.

In the 1947 declaration on *Measures to Be Taken Against Propaganda and Inciters of a New War,* the General Assembly

condemns all forms of propaganda, in whatsoever country conducted, which is either designed or likely to provoke, or encourage any threat to the peace, breach of the peace or act of aggression.[29]

The 1970 *Declaration on the Strengthening of International Security* prohibits states from "any attempt aimed at the partial or total disruption of the national unity" and from "organizing, instigating, assisting or participating in acts of civil strife" against another state.[30] The 1978 *Final Document of the Tenth Special Session of the General Assembly on Disarmament* encourages states to

ensure a better flow of information with regard to the various aspects of disarmament, to avoid dissemination of false and tendentious information concerning armaments, and to concentrate on the danger of escalation of the armaments race and on the need for general and complete disarmament under effective international control.[31]

The 1981 *Declaration on the Inadmissibility of Intervention and Interference in the Internal Affairs of States* details the relationship of communication and information activities to national security. Noninterference means:

The right of States and peoples to have free access to information and to develop fully, without interference, their system of information and mass media and to use their information media in order to promote their political, social, economic and cultural interests and aspirations.

The duty of a State to refrain from the promotion, encouragement or support, direct or indirect, of rebellious or secessionist activities within other States . . . ;

The duty of a State to abstain from any defamatory campaign, vilification or hostile propaganda for the purpose of intervening or interfering in the internal affairs of other States.[32]

The 1983 *Declaration on the Condemnation of Nuclear War* specifically

condemns the formulation, propounding, dissemination and propaganda of political and military doctrines and concepts intended to provide 'legitimacy' for the first use of nuclear weapons and in general to justify the 'admissibility' of unleashing nuclear war."[33]

Complementing these instruments on security and disarmament is international law treating peace and international understanding. Most illustrative of this category are the many declarations and resolutions that call on states to encourage media to work in the service of peace, international understanding, and confidence building among the peoples of the world.

The 1965 *Declaration on the Promotion among Youth of the Ideals of Peace, Mutual Respect, and Understanding between Peoples* proclaims that "all means of education . . . instruction and information intended for the young should foster among them the ideals of peace, humanity, liberty and international solidarity."[34]

The 1978 *Declaration on the Preparation of Societies for Life in Peace* "recognize[s] the essential role of . . . the mass media . . . in promoting the cause of peace and understanding among nations," declares that states have the duty to "refrain from propaganda for wars of aggression," and calls upon states to ensure that "media information activities incorporate contents compatible with the task of the preparation for life in peace of entire societies and, in particular, the young generations."[35] The 1984 *Declaration on the Right of Peoples to Peace* "declares that the preservation of the right of peoples to peace and the promotion of its implementation constitute a fundamental obligation of each State."[36]

UNESCO's 1978 *Mass Media Declaration* emphasizes the positive roles that mass media channels should play:

Mass media have an important contribution to make in the strengthening of peace and international understanding and in countering racialism, apartheid and incitement to war [and in] eliminat[ing] ignorance and misunderstanding between peoples, mak[ing] nationals of a country sensitive to the needs and desires of others, to ensur[ing] the respect of the rights and dignity of all nations.

The mass media contribute effectively to the strengthening of peace and international understanding, to the promotion of human rights, and to the establishment of a more just and equitable international economic order.[37]

OUTSIDE THE GENERAL ASSEMBLY

United Nations specialized agencies and other intergovernmental organizations have contributed a great deal to global communication and information law. The most active has been UNESCO.

For decades UNESCO has fought to improve global communication. Indeed, many of the underlying premises of the *Constitution of UNESCO* are based on a "communication analysis" of peace and war. The Constitution's preamble reads:

[S]ince wars begin in the minds of men, it is in the minds of men that the defences of peace must be constructed;

[I]gnorance of each other's ways and lives has been a common cause, throughout the history of mankind, of that suspicion and mistrust between the peoples of the world through which their differences have all too often broken into war.

States Parties . . . are agreed and determined to develop and to increase the means of communication between their peoples and to employ these means for the purposes of mutual understanding and a truer and more perfect knowledge of each other's lives.

UNESCO's fundamental purposes and functions include:

collaborat[ing] in the work of advancing the mutual knowledge and understanding of peoples, through all means of mass communication and to that end . . . recommend[ing] such international agreements as may be necessary to promote the free flow of ideas by word and image.[38]

The discussion in this chapter now turns to how the UNESCO General Conference has dealt with communication and information issues in relation to peace. The 1974 statement on *UNESCO's Contribution to Peace and Its Tasks with Respect to the Promotion of Human Rights and the Elimination of Colonialism and Racialism* calls for strengthening the role of

member States to make wider use of the information media and organs for reaching the general public to intensify the struggle against racialism and apartheid and other violations of human rights and fundamental freedoms . . . [and] to inform the public on the abominable practices of racial segregation.[39]

The 1978 *Declaration on Race and Racial Prejudice* is very concrete about the role of the media:

The mass media and those who control or serve them . . . are urged . . . to promote understanding, tolerance, and friendship among individuals and groups and to contribute to the eradication of racism, racial discrimination and racial prejudice, in particular by refraining from presenting a stereotyped, partial, unilateral or tendentious picture of individuals and of various human groups.[40]

Outside the UN system are numerous regional and transregional organizations and conferences that supplement the work of the United Nations and its specialized organizations. Some of these organizations have constitutions or other constitutive documents whose general statements are relevant for communication and information issues. All have adopted resolutions or declarations that either deal with communication and information specifically or treat related topics, such as disarmament or human rights.

The *Non-Aligned Movement*, made up of ninety-nine nations and two independence movements, has no constitution, but the periodic summit meetings have treated communication and information extensively. A 1976 *Political Declaration* notes with concern

the vast and ever growing gap between communication capacities in non-aligned countries and in the advanced countries, which is a legacy of their colonial past. . . . The emancipation and development of national information media is an integral part of the over-all struggle for political, economic and social independence.[41]

The 1979 *Political Declaration* recognizes that "non-aligned and other developing countries have made notable progress along the path of emancipation and development of national information media" and "considers that the building up of national information media and mass communication systems . . . are essential preconditions . . . for a multi-dimensional flow of information."[42]

Another important international forum for information issues is the *Conference on Security and Cooperation in Europe* (CSCE), composed of more than forty European countries, the United States, and Canada. The CSCE first met in Helsinki, Finland, in 1975, and the *Final Act* of these "Helsinki Accords" has a large section on communication and information. It calls on signatories to

> make it their aim to facilitate the freer and wider dissemination of information of all kinds . . . and to improve the conditions under which journalists . . . exercise their profession.[43]

Periodic follow-up meetings of the Helsinki signatories have monitored compliance of the information section of "Basket Three," which deals with respect for human rights and the movement of people and information.[44]

Turning to regional organizations, the 1950 *Convention for the Protection of Human Rights and Fundamental Freedoms,* ratified by all member states of the Council of Europe, asserts that

> everyone has the right to freedom of expression. This right shall include freedom to hold opinions and to receive and import information and ideas without interference by public authority and regardless of frontiers.

But this important document of the European Community provides a comprehensive list of limitations to free expression:

> The exercise of these freedoms, since it carries with it duties and responsibilities, may be subject to such formalities, conditions, restrictions or penalties as are prescribed by law and are necessary in a democratic society, in the interests of national security, territorial integrity or public safety, for the prevention of disorder or crime, for the protection of health or morals, for the protection of the reputation or rights of others, for preventing the disclosure of information received in confidence, or for maintaining the authority and impartiality of the judiciary.[45]

In the Americas, the 1969 *American Convention on Human Rights,* to which twenty governments in the Western Hemisphere are parties, guarantees in Article 13 that

> everyone shall have the right to freedom of thought and expression [which] shall not be subject to prior censorship but shall be subject to . . . (a) respect for the rights or reputation of others; or (b) the protection of national security, public order, or public health or morals. . . . Any propaganda for war and any advocacy of national, racial or religious hatred that constitute incitements to lawless violence or to any other similar illegal action against any person or group of persons on any grounds including those of race, color, religion, language, or national origin shall be considered as offenses punishable by law.

In Article 14 these American countries pledge the following:

> Anyone injured by inaccurate or offensive statements or ideas disseminated to the public in general by a legally regulated medium of communication has the right to reply or make a correction using the same communications outlet, under such conditions as the law may establish.[46]

This right to reply is reminiscent of the 1952 *Convention on the International Right of Correction,* which required news correspondents and agencies

> to report facts without discrimination and in their proper context and thereby to promote respect for human rights and fundamental freedoms, to further international understanding and cooperation and to contribute to the maintenance of international peace and security. . . .
>
> In cases where a Contracting State contends that a news dispatch capable of injuring its relations with other States or its national prestige or dignity . . . is false or distorted, it may submit its version of the facts . . . to correct the news dispatch in question.[47]

BASIC PRINCIPLES OF INTERNATIONAL COMMUNICATION AND INFORMATION LAW

What fundamental principles about media practice and performance surface in international law? There are at least *thirteen basic principles in global communication and information law.*

Communications media may not be used for war and aggression. The universally respected principle that prohibits the threat or use of force by one state against another forbids not only war of aggression but also propaganda for wars of aggression. This means that propaganda glorifying the threat or use of force in international relations is prohibited by law. States are forbidden from spreading warmongering content themselves, for example, through government-owned and government-operated international radio stations. They are also obligated to stop any war propaganda emanating from their territory by private groups.

Communications media shall not be used to intervene in the internal affairs of another state. This principle forbids all forms of interference or attempted threats against a state or against its political, economic, and cultural elements. This includes organizing, assisting, fomenting, financing, inciting, or tolerating subversive information activities directed toward the overthrow of another state, or interfering in civil strife in another state. It also bans systematically undermining public support for the opponent's inner cohesion, gradually putting another country's state leadership in a state of uncertainty and discouragement, and diminishing the leaders' ability to act under the pressure of a national public opinion undergoing a process of reorientation. This principle prohibits subversive foreign broadcasts that attempt to change another country's governing system or that try to foment discontent and incite unrest.

All dissemination of ideas based on racial superiority or hatred and incitement to racial discrimination are punishable by law. This principle forbids the information activities of all organizations that are based on ideas or theories of superiority of one race or group of persons of one color or ethnic origin, or of organizations that attempt to justify or promote racial hatred or discrimination in any form. Binding international law prohibits all dissemination of these ideas, as well as all organizations that promote and incite racial discrimination. It is a crime against humanity to directly abet, encourage, or cooperate in the commission of racial discrimination.

The direct and public incitement to destroy a national, ethnic, racial, or religious group is punishable by law. This includes using the media to incite another person to destroy in whole or in part a national, ethnic, racial, or religious group. As the Nuremberg Tribunal stated, crimes against humanity include "murder, extermination, enslavement, deportation, and other inhuman acts performed against any civilian population prior to or during the war."

States are obligated to modify social and cultural practices, including information and communication activities, that are based on the inferiority or the superiority of either of the sexes and to eliminate any stereotyped concept of roles of men and women. This means changing media practices that advocate discrimination against women.

Media should play a positive role in educating and enlightening the public toward peace. Throughout international law, media are repeatedly called on to promote a better knowledge of the conditions of life and the organization of peace. Media activities should incorporate contents compatible with the task of the preparation for life in peace. The mass media must contribute effectively to the strengthening of peace and international understanding and to the promotion of human rights.

Peoples enjoy equal rights and self-determination in communication and information. All peoples have the right freely to pursue their chosen system of economic, social, and cultural development. This includes the right to develop local information and communication infrastructures without the interference of external parties, to establish communication policies for the benefit of the people, and to participate in global information relations without discrimination.

States enjoy sovereign equality in the communication and information infrastructures. Every state has an inalienable right to choose its political, social, economic, and cultural systems without interference in any form by another state. States enjoy the full rights of sovereignty and territorial integrity in the area of communication and information. From this we derive the principle of "information sovereignty," which includes: the right to a locally controlled communication infrastructure; the right to an indigenous communication policy; the right to participate as an equal in global information relations; the right to transmit nonbelligerent foreign propaganda; the right to conclude bilateral or multilateral agreements in the area of communication and information; and the obligation to respect the information sovereignty of other states. Every national communication system has juridical expression through an "information authority," especially in its constitutional, penal, civil, press, copyright, post, and telecommunications laws.

Disputes about communication and information must be settled peacefully. The principle that governments must settle their disputes by peaceful means applies to the processes of communication and information. Many global communications activities require advance coordination and, if conflict arises, peaceful resolution through negotiation. This principle implies that conflicts such as unwanted direct satellite broadcasting must be settled by negotiation. If a nation is aggrieved in an area of global information relations, it may call upon the violating nation to settle the dispute in a way that does not endanger peace and security. This duty also implies that states must refrain from and prevent hostile and subversive ideological campaigns.

Communication and information demand global cooperation. Despite their differences, states have a built-in incentive to cooperate in the field of communication. International broadcasters need to coordinate their frequencies to avoid interference. New technologies such as transborder data flow and global satellite television cannot succeed technically without the willingness of states to work cooperatively toward mutually beneficial solutions. Future technologies cannot prosper without cooperation in setting technical standards. Cooperation guarantees technical success and ensures the sovereign equality of states.

Good-faith obligations require states to uphold global communication and information law. States must fulfill in good faith their obligations under recognized international law. States must be aware of such obligations and of obligations to the United Nations Charter and cannot refrain from upholding them by pointing to national law. This applies in all areas of international law, including global communication and information law.

Certain kinds of information content are prohibited. There is an absolute ban on war propaganda. In addition, there are prohibitions of communication content advocating hatred, acts of violence, or hostility among peoples and races. Media may not advocate colonialism, nor may they be used in propaganda against international treaties. This includes all communication activities that attempt to prohibit or impede the fulfillment of in-force treaty obligations among states. In addition, the circulation of obscene publications is forbidden under binding international law.

Certain kinds of information content are encouraged. To begin, the principle of free flow of information is prominent throughout global communication and information law. Everyone has the right to freedom of opinion and expression; this right includes freedom to hold opinions without interference and to seek, receive, and impart information and ideas through any media and regardless of frontiers. Although this right is often abused, it is important to remember that this is one of the fundamental goals of global communication and information law.

THE EVOLVING RIGHT TO COMMUNICATE

International law is constantly evolving. Two new concepts that have attracted considerable attention are *the rights of peoples* and *the right to communicate.*

International law in its modern form deals with the rights of states (national governments) as well as with the rights of individuals. One emerging concept is the rights of "peoples," and this has sparked a debate about where the locus of rights lies.

Two conflicting approaches once dominated this debate. According to one, largely Western, approach, only the rights of individual human beings can be seen as "human rights." Rights vested in larger entities such as churches, trade unions, states, and corporations may be desirable, but they cannot be *human* rights. International law, in this view, does not support such rights as freedom of expression as "collective" rights. Individuals can exercise their human rights in association with other humans. But rights belong to the individual.

The other approach, one heard most frequently in socialist countries, holds that rights belong collectively to society and not to individual citizens. Here the state is supreme and guarantees rights to individuals.[48] The first approach emphasizes personal liberties, such as freedom of expression, association, and travel, whereas the socialist expression of human rights stresses collective freedoms, such as the right to health care, employment, shelter, and education.

A third approach, representing a growing Third World position, lies between the two once-dominant positions. The concept of peoples' rights has a long history and a dynamic present. As early as 1790 the French National Constituent Assembly made reference to both the rights of man [sic] and the rights of peoples. The term has appeared often in post–World War II human rights instruments and UN resolutions. The United Nations Charter itself was adopted in the name of "We the Peoples," and it recognizes the "self-determination of peoples." Both of the great 1966 Covenants, in their first articles, assert that "all peoples have the right of self-determination."

There are two fundamental differences between the concept of people and that of the individual. The crux of the difference lies in cultural differences in the role of the individual in society. As in many cultures, in Africa a person is not an isolated individual, but rather a member of a larger social group. This contrasts with the Western view of the individual, wherein a person is perceived as having a unique identity, and a group is merely a collection of individuals.[49] The other distinction is that a "people" is different from the state, which often cannot be counted upon to protect basic rights.

Sohn summarizes the rights of peoples this way:

One of the main characteristics of humanity is that human beings are social creatures. Consequently, most individuals belong to various units, groups, and communities; they are simultaneously members of such units as a family, religious community, social club, trade union, professional association, racial group, people, nation, and state. It is not surprising, therefore, that international law not only recognizes inalienable rights of individuals, but also recognizes certain collective rights that are exercised jointly by individuals grouped into larger communities, including peoples and nations.[50]

Sohn details such peoples' rights as the right to self-determination, the right to development, and the right to peace. He also mentions the right to food, the right to benefit from or share in the common heritage of mankind, the right to the satisfaction of basic needs, the right to disarmament, and the *right to communicate.*[51]

The African Charter on Human and Peoples' Rights best illustrates how contemporary law now accepts the right of peoples.[52] With cultural differences that deemphasize individuality, this basic human rights document of the African continent treats peoples as much as it treats individuals. Kiwanuka summarizes: "The main attributes of peoplehood are . . . commonality of interests, group identity, distinctiveness and a territorial link."[53]

Applying the concept of peoples' rights to communication, we find that such groups as political parties and trade unions generate and promote ideas independent of individuals or the state. Larger aggregates, such as social communities and peoples, are held together by communication networks, on which they rely to promote and develop their identities both within themselves and vis-a-vis others. As the MacBride Report stated: "Freedom of speech, of the press, of information and of assembly are vital for the realization of human rights. Extension of these communication freedoms to a broader individual and collective right to communicate is an evolving principle in the democratization process."[54]

One of these evolving peoples' rights is the right to communicate.[55] A germ of this evolving right can be seen in the famous formulation of Article 19 of the Universal Declaration of Human Rights:

> Everyone has the right to freedom of opinion and expression; this right includes freedom to hold opinions without interference and to seek, *receive and impart information* and ideas through any media and regardless of frontiers. [Emphasis added]

The Universal Declaration does not call explicitly for the right to communicate. It includes a passive right simply to "receive and impart" information, whereas the right to communicate is a dedication to the interactive spirit of liberty and democracy. The most diverse segments of the population must have access to communication channels.

Toward the end of the 1970s, spurred on by the information debates in the Non-Aligned Movement and UNESCO, human rights advocates began to call for an active right to communicate for individuals and groups who had no access to the large transnational media channels. The "father of the right to communicate" is widely acknowledged to be the Frenchman Jean D'Arcy, who stated first in 1969:

> The time will come when the Universal Declaration of Human Rights will have to encompass a more extensive right than man's right to information, . . . This is the right of man to communicate.[56]

The concept was buoyed especially by the International Commission for the Study of Communication Problems (the MacBride Commission), which commissioned no less than seven separate studies on the issue.[57] The MacBride Commission's final report recommended:

> Communication needs in a democratic society should be met by the extension of specific rights such as the right to be informed, the right to inform, the right to privacy, the right to participate in public communication—all elements of a new concept, the right to communicate.[58]

How to define this new right? One Canadian report described the essential components of the right to communicate as "the rights to hear and be heard, to inform and to be informed."[59] Another author lists the following constituents of a general right to communicate: (1) the right to speak; (2) the right to be heard; (3) the right to a reply; (4) the right to make a reply; and (5) the right to listen. To these have been added: (6) the right to see; (7) the right to be seen; (8) the right to express oneself in writing or in print; (9) the right to express oneself in the form of art; and (10) the right to be selective.[60]

Harms proposes the following language:

> Everyone has the right to communicate. The Components of this comprehensive human right include but are not limited to the following communication rights:

- a right to assemble, a right to participate, and related *association* rights;
- a right to inform, a right to be informed, and related *information* rights;
- a right to privacy, a right to language and related *cultural evolution* rights.

Within the world communication order, the achievement of a right to communicate requires that communication resources be available for the satisfaction of human communication needs.[61]

Active participation in the communication process is the "core of the right to communicate." The right to communicate is partially protected by existing instruments, but, according to a UNESCO consultation of experts, it is also essential

> that adequate channels of communication should exist, using all available and appropriate technology;
> that individuals and groups who wish to use those channels should have fair and equitable access to them, and opportunities for participation in them, without discrimination of any kind;
> that such channels of communication should be available to those who wish to take part in public affairs, or to exercise any other of those of their human rights and fundamental freedoms protected by international law, including the right to health, education, assembly, and association, and to take part in cultural life, enjoy the benefits of scientific progress and its applications, and of the freedom indispensable for scientific research and creative activity;
> that restriction on the exercise of the right to communicate should be strictly confined to those authorized by international law;
> that individuals and groups should be able to participate at all relevant levels and at all stages in communication, including the formulation, application, monitoring and review of communication policies.[62]

The right to communicate seems like a logical next step in the evolution of human rights. It is surprising, then, "that in the 1980s this concept has been roundly denounced by the United States press and government officials as radical and subversive."[63] As Roach points out, the American position completely ignores the fact that the concept arose in the West and was elaborated upon by Americans, Canadians, and French.

A VISION FOR THE FUTURE?

Global communication and information law is one of the oldest bodies of continuously respected international law in the world today. This law establishes widely accepted norms for media practice and governs the daily communication and information relations among states around the globe. Were it not this way, there would be chaos in the airwaves, incomprehensibility over the telephone lines, and anarchy in the geostationary orbit. There is clearly a built-in incentive for states to cooperate.

For the most part, nations respect and honor global communication and information law despite the fact that there is no "enforcer." They do so because it yields short-term gains, for example, in avoiding radio interference with stations in neighboring countries.

When international law demands a more profound commitment, such as the prohibition on war propaganda, states have been known to abandon laws that no longer serve their national interests. This is the case in the United States, for example, when national security interests outweigh legal considerations with regard to Radio Martí, Tele Martí and clandestine *contra* radio stations in Central America.

Because states seem unwilling to enforce the more profound provisions, one can say that the law of communication and information works *imperfectly* at the level of nation–states. At the individual level also—at the level of private citizens and media outlets—work still needs to be done. With few exceptions, international law does not give individuals or organizations any ways of directly enforcing its provisions. In practical terms, if State X refuses to seek a remedy before the World Court for behavior by State Y, private persons (both natural and juridical) in State X have little recourse under international law.

In the United States, the Senate has yet to ratify and enact the important conventions with media provisions, especially the International Covenant on Civil and Political Rights; the International Covenant on Economic, Social, and Cultural Rights; the American Convention on Human Rights; the Convention on the Elimination of All Forms of Racial Discrimination; and the Convention on the Elimination of All Forms of Discrimination against Women.

The Senate has rejected these and other human rights treaties on the grounds that they diminish basic rights guaranteed under the U.S. Constitution, violate the rights of U.S. states, promote world government, enhance communist influence, subject citizens to trial abroad, threaten our form of government, infringe on domestic jurisdiction, and increase international entanglements.[64] It is not surprising that the United States is seen as the chief laggard in international law because of its failure to ratify and enact international law.[65]

As we enter the 1990s, there is a growing realization that *communication and information are central to human rights.* Communication media do not merely defend human rights by reporting violations and victories. There is a growing perception that *the right to communicate* should be added to the Universal Declaration among the *basic human rights* cherished by all peoples. This new right transcends the right to receive information, as guaranteed in the Universal Declaration. Today, communication among nations must be a two-way process in which partners—both individual and collective—carry on a democratic and balanced dialogue in which the mass media operate in the service of peace and global understanding.

There is a huge gap between international law and international practice. Modern national states have been more willing to use their military, economic, and propaganda power than to abide by international law. Yet Lacordaire's sentiments are gaining greater support around the world.

Just like their earthly counterparts, electronic highways require "rules of the road." Regulation is important and necessary for our highly congested communication thoroughfares. To carry this analogy one step further, rules prohibiting drunk drivers from our streets are not meant to limit freedom. They increase the freedom for the good drivers. In the same way, regulations against communications violating international norms are not meant to limit the freedom to communicate. They are meant to strengthen the freedom for responsible communication. In our lifetimes, international law has grown immensely and is respected now more than ever. The evolutionary trend is apparent—and so is the work before us.

NOTES

1. Most of the international legal documents in this chapter appear in one or more of the following principal reference works, referred to as *Nordenstreng et al., Ploman,* and *Bowman,* respectively: Kaarle Nordenstreng, Enrique Gonzales Manet, and Wolfgang Kleinwächter, *New International Information and Communication Order: A Sourcebook* (Prague: International Organization of Journalists, 1986); Edward W. Ploman, ed., *International Law Governing Communications and Information: A Collection of Basic Documents* (Westport, CT: Greenwood Press, 1982); and M. J. Bowman and D. J. Harris, eds., *Multilateral Treaties: Index and Current Status* (London: Butterworth, 1984) and Fifth Cumulative Supplement (Nottingham: University of Nottingham Treaty Centre, 1988). Another important source is "Developments in Regulation," in UNESCO, *World Communication Report* (Paris: UNESCO, 1989), pp. 165–193.

   Documents are *italicized* in the text for their first or primary reference.

   In addition, information on U.S. adherence to a particular treaty is indicated with the code **US = SRE,** where S = signed, R = ratified, and E = entered into force. **US = NS** means that the United States has not signed that particular instrument. **US = S** means that the United States has signed that treaty but has not ratified it.

2. The third oldest United Nations specialized agency is the World Meteorological Organization (WMO), which also relies extensively on communication.

3. Convention Respecting the Rights and Duties of Neutral Powers and Persons in War on Land, October 18, 1907, The Hague (Bowman, T37), **US = SRE.** Article 3 forbade belligerents to establish a telegraph station on the territory of a neutral power for use as a means of communication with belligerent forces, or to use an existing station on neutral territory for an exclusively military purpose. Article 5 required neutral states to punish acts in violation of neutrality only if they have been committed on the neutral state's own territory. Article 8 rejected any requirement for neutral states to forbid or restrict the use of public or private telegraph or telephone cables on behalf of belligerents. Article 9 required any restrictions or prohibitions taken by a neutral power to be applied uniformly to both belligerents.

4. Collaboration of the Press in the Organization of Peace, League of Nations Resolution A. 138, September 25, 1925, Geneva (Nordenstreng et al., 105).

5. International Convention Concerning the Use of Broadcasting in the Cause of Peace, September 23, 1936, Geneva (Nordenstreng et al., 106; Ploman, 169; Bowman, T158), **US = NS.** (The United States was not a member of the League of Nations.) Although the Convention was ignored during World War II, in 1988 this binding international convention still had twenty-nine adherents. David Goldberg, of the University of Glasgow, Scotland, argues that the Convention can be applied also to television transmissions among the adherents. David Goldberg, "A Re-Examination of the International Law of Libel in Inter-State Broadcasting." Paper presented at the Conference of the International Association for Mass Communication Research, Bled, Yugoslavia, August 1990.

6. Cited in Mary M. Kaufman, "The Individual's Duty Under the Law of Nurnberg: The Effect of Knowledge on Justiciability," *The National Lawyers Guild Practitioner* 27 (1, 1968): 15–21.

7. Elizabeth A. Downey, "A Historical Survey of the International Regulation of Propaganda," in *Regulation of Transnational Communications: Michigan Yearbook of International Legal Studies, 1984,* ed. Leslie J. Anderson (New York: Clark Boardman, 1984), p. 342.

8. Vienna Convention on the Law of Treaties, May 23, 1969 (Bowman, T538), **US = S.**

9. One instance of a professional communicator being the subject of international law was the Nazi propagandist, Julius Streicher, editor of the anti-Semitic newspaper *Der Stürmer.* He was accused of crimes against humanity under the 1945 *Charter of the International Military Tribunal* (**US = SRE**), the so-called Nuremberg Tribunal, which had the power to try and punish Axis soldiers who committed crimes against peace, war crimes, and crimes against humanity. Crimes

against humanity included: "murder, extermination, enslavement, deportation, and other inhuman acts performed against any civilian population prior to or during the war; [and] persecution on political, racial, or religious grounds in the perpetration of or in connection with any crime which falls within the jurisdiction of the tribunal." The Nuremberg judges interpreted "crimes against humanity" to include propaganda and incitement to genocide. The Court determined that for more than twenty-five years Streicher had engaged in writing and preaching anti-Semitism and had called for the extermination of the Jewish people in 1938. Based on a content analysis of articles from *Der Stürmer,* the judges further determined that Streicher had aroused the German people to active persecution of the Jewish people. The International Military Tribunal found Streicher guilty and condemned him to death by hanging.

10. These seven principles are elaborated in the United Nations Charter (Nordenstreng et al., 111); and Declaration on Principles of International Law Concerning Friendly Relations and Cooperation among States in Accordance with the Charter of the United Nations of October 25, 1970 (Declaration on Principles) (Nordenstreng et al., p. 155).

11. Statute of the International Court of Justice, June 26, 1945, Article 38(1) (Bowman, T181), **US = DENOUNCED 1986.** In 1988 there were 48 parties to the statute. The United States denounced its membership on April 7, 1986.

12. There is a *continuum of universality* among international conventions. At one pole are the constituent documents, especially charters and constitutions, of modern international intergovernmental organizations, to which most, if not all, states belong. Next come multilateral agreements that lay down legal norms to which most or a large number of states adhere. Then there are multilateral treaties to which a small number of states, perhaps only the states in a particular world region, adhere. Finally there are bilateral agreements, which make up the greatest number of binding international agreements. In global communication and information law, the bulk of agreements are bilateral. For the United States alone, they range from dozens of bilateral agreements on amateur radio reception to a score of agreements on the U.S.–Mexican radio interference situation.

13. This includes such universally respected (but not universally ratified) instruments as the 1949 Geneva Conventions, the 1948 Convention on the Prevention and Punishment of the Crime of Genocide, and the 1969 Vienna Convention on the Law of Treaties.

14. Statute of the International Court of Justice, Article 38(1).

15. Some resolutions, such as UN Security Council resolutions (see UN Charter, Article 25) and various legislative measures promulgated by the International Civil Aviation Organization (ICAO), are actually legally binding.

16. See Branimir M. Jankovič, *Public International Law* (Dobbs Ferry, NY: Transnational, 1984), pp. 287–302; and Paul Sieghart, *The Lawful Rights of Mankind: An Introduction to the International Legal Code of Human Rights* (New York: Oxford University Press, 1985), pp. 50–58.

17. Current international legal procedure allows a state to make *reservations* to a treaty, that is, to exclude or modify the legal effect of certain provisions of the treaty in their application to that state. Reservations must receive the consent of other signatories. In contrast, "statements of interpretation"—deriving from the principle that contracting states should themselves interpret the convention that they conclude with another—do not require such consent. Jankovič, *Public International Law,* pp. 299–302.

18. Many of the instruments cited in this study reach far beyond the areas of our interest. We only refer to the communication and information aspects of them. Space limitations prevent us from examining the context in which these laws and treaties were adopted and the relative importance of communication and information in them compared to other areas of treatment.

19. The fourth instrument of the International Bill of Human Rights is the 1966 *International Covenant on Economic, Social, and Cultural Rights,* entered into force January 1976 (Nordenstreng et al., 144; Ploman, 21; Bowman, T497), **US = S,** which deals slightly with communication and information. Article 13 guarantees everyone the right to education, and Article 15 recognizes the right of everyone to take part in cultural life and to benefit from the "protection of the moral and

material interests resulting from any scientific, literary or artistic production of which he is the author.''

20. Universal Declaration of Human Rights, December 10, 1948, New York (Nordenstreng et al., 121; Ploman, 12).

21. For purposes of this discussion we will not treat the fourth instrument, the International Covenant on Economic, Social, and Cultural Rights, December 1966, New York. It does not contain substantive communication and information provisions.

22. International Covenant on Civil and Political Rights, and Optional Protocol, December 19, 1966, New York. Entered into force March 23, 1976 (Nordenstreng et al., 137; Ploman, 21; Bowman, T498), **US = S.** There were eighty-seven States Parties in 1988.

23. Optional Protocol to the 1966 International Covenant on Civil and Human Rights, December 16, 1966, New York (Bowman, T499), **US = NS.** Only forty states are parties to this Optional Protocol, less than half of those who have signed the parent covenant. See also P. R. Ghandhi, ''The Human Rights Committee and the Right of Individual Communication,'' *British Year Book of International Law* 57 (1986): 201–251.

24. International Convention on the Elimination of All Forms of Racial Discrimination. Adopted by the UN General Assembly December 21, 1965, New York. Concluded May 7, 1966. Entered into force January 4, 1969 (Nordenstreng et al., 136; Ploman, 30; Bowman, T490), **US = S.** There are 127 member states.

25. International Convention on the Suppression and Punishment of the Crime of Apartheid, November 30, 1973 (Nordenstreng et al., 162; Bowman, T638), **US = NS.** In 1988, eighty-six governments were parties to this agreement.

26. Convention on the Prevention and Punishment of the Crime of Genocide, December 9, 1948, New York (Nordenstreng et al., 119; Ploman, 29; Bowman, T225), **US = SRE.** In 1988 there were 97 States Parties. President Reagan signed the bill on November 4, 1988. For the implications of this important development in the realm of First Amendment theory, see Ann Fagan Ginger, ''The New U.S. Criminal Statute, the First Amendment, and the New International Information Order,'' *The National Lawyers Guild Practitioner* 46 (1, 1989): 16–27.

27. Convention on the Elimination of All Forms of Discrimination against Women. Adopted by the UN General Assembly, December 18, 1979, New York. Entered into force September 3, 1981 (Bowman, T769), **US = S.** In 1984, fifty governments were parties to this convention.

28. Declaration of Mexico on the Equality of Women and Their Contribution to Development and Peace, 1975. Adopted by the World Conference of the International Women's Year on July 2, 1975. In *International Human Rights Instruments of the United Nations: 1948–1982* (Pleasantville, NY: UNIFO, 1983), p. 127.

29. Measures to Be Taken against Propaganda and Inciters of a New War, General Assembly Resolution 110 (II), November 1947 (Nordenstreng et al., 113; Ploman, 47).

30. Declaration on the Strengthening of International Security, General Assembly Resolution 2734 (XXV), 1970 (Ploman, 48).

31. Final Document of the Tenth Special Session of the General Assembly on Disarmament, S10/2, May 25, 1978, New York (Nordenstreng et al., 179; Ploman, 49).

32. Declaration on the Inadmissibility of Intervention and Interference in the Internal Affairs of States, UN General Assembly Resolution, December 9, 1981, New York (Nordenstreng et al., 186).

33. Declaration on the Condemnation of Nuclear War, UN General Assembly, December 15, 1983 (Nordenstreng et al., 193).

34. Declaration on the Promotion among Youth of the Ideals of Peace, Mutual Respect, and Understanding between Peoples, General Assembly Resolution 2037 (XX), December 7, 1965 (Nordenstreng et al., 133; Ploman, 52).

35. Declaration on the Preparation of Societies for Life in Peace, General Assembly Resolution 33/73, December 15, 1978 (Nordenstreng et al., 181; Ploman, 54).

36. Declaration on the Right of Peoples to Peace, UN General Assembly, November 12, 1984 (Nordenstreng et al., 194).

37. Declaration on the Fundamental Principles Concerning the Contribution of the Mass Media to Strengthening Peace and International Understanding, to the Promotion of Human Rights, and to Countering Racialism, Apartheid, and Incitement to War [Mass Media Declaration], UNESCO General Conference, Resolution 4/9.3/2, November 28, 1978 (Nordenstreng et al., 225; Ploman, 172).

38. Constitution of the United Nations Educational, Scientific, and Cultural Organization (Nordenstreng et al., 211; Ploman, 71; Bowman, T184), **US = withdrawn, December 31, 1984.** In 1988 there were 158 States Parties.

39. UNESCO's Contribution to Peace and Its Tasks with Respect to the Promotion of Human Rights and the Elimination of Colonialism and Racialism, General Conference 11.1, 1974 (Ploman, 77).

40. Declaration on Race and Racial Prejudice, General Conference Resolution 3/1.1/2, November 27, 1978 (Nordenstreng et al., 230; Ploman, 79).

41. Political Declaration of the Fifth Summit Conference of Non-Aligned Countries, August 1976, Colombo, Sri Lanka (Nordenstreng et al., 288; Ploman, 119).

42. Political Declaration, Sixth Summit Conference of Heads of State or Government of Non-Aligned Countries, Havana, 1979 (Nordenstreng et al., 296; Ploman, 116).

43. The Final Acts of the Conference on Security and Cooperation in Europe (Nordenstreng et al., 333; Ploman, 118).

44. Concluding Document of the Follow-Up Meeting of Representatives of the Participating States of the Conference on Security and Cooperation in Europe, September 1983, Madrid (Nordenstreng et al., 337). The third follow-up meeting completed its work in 1989 in Vienna. A CSCE Information Forum took place in 1989 in London.

45. [Western European] Convention for the Protection of Human Rights and Fundamental Freedoms, November 4, 1950, Rome (Nordenstreng et al., 341; Bowman, T256), **US = NS.**

46. American Convention on Human Rights, November 22, 1969, San José, Costa Rica (Nordenstreng et al., 342; Ploman, 106; Bowman, T547), **US = S.** In 1988 there were 20 parties to this convention.

47. Convention on the International Right of Correction, December 16, 1952, New York, Article II. Entered into force August 1962 (Nordenstreng et al., 126; Bowman, T291), **US = NS.** In 1987 Burkina Fasa became the twelfth party (and the first in twenty years) to join. The other eleven adherents include Cuba, Cyprus, Egypt, El Salvador, Ethiopia, France, Guatemala, Jamaica, Sierra Leone, Uruguay, and Yugoslavia.

48. Desmond Fisher, *The Right to Communicate: A Status Report,* Reports and Papers on Mass Communication, no. 94 (Paris: UNESCO, 1982), p. 24.

49. Dolores Cathcart and Robert Cathcart, "Japanese Social Experience and Concept of Groups," in *Intercultural Communication: A Reader,* ed. Larry A. Samovar and Richard E. Porter (Belmont, CA: Wadsworth, 1988), p. 186.

50. Louis B. Sohn, "The New International Law: Protection of the Rights of Individuals Rather than States," *American University Law Review* 32 (1, 1982): 48.

51. Ibid.

52. African Charter on Human and Peoples' Rights, June 26, 1981, Banjul, Gambia (Nordenstreng et al., 344; Bowman, T806). In 1988 there were thirty-five States Parties.

53. Richard N. Kiwanuka, "The Meaning of 'People' in the African Charter on Human and Peoples' Rights," *American Journal of International Law* 82 (1988): 87–88.

54. International Commission for the Study of Communication Problems [MacBride Commission], *Many Voices, One World* (Paris: UNESCO, 1980), p. 265.

55. Perhaps the best background source on this issue is Fisher, *The Right to Communicate: A Status Report.* Another valuable source is Howard C. Anawalt, "The Right to Communicate," *Denver Journal of International Law and Policy* 13 (2–3, 1984): 219–236.

56. Jean D'Arcy, "Direct Broadcast Satellites and the Right to Communicate," *EBU Review* 118 (November 1969): 14–18.

57. Jean D'Arcy, "The Right to Communicate," International Commission for the Study of Communication Problems, document no. 36 (Paris: UNESCO, 1980); L. S. Harms, "The Right to Communicate: Concept," International Commission for the Study of Communication Problems, document no. 37,1 (Paris: UNESCO, 1980); Desmond Fisher, "The Right to Communicate: Towards a Definition," International Commission for the Study of Communication Problems, document no. 37,2 (Paris: UNESCO, 1980); J. Richstad, "The Right to Communicate: Relationship with the Mass Media," International Commission for the Study of Communication Problems, document no. 38,4 (Paris: UNESCO, 1980); A. A. Cocca, "The Right to Communicate: Some Reflections on Its Legal Foundation," International Commission for the Study of Communication Problems, document no. 38,3 (Paris: UNESCO, 1980); J. Pastecka, "The Right to Communicate: A Socialist Approach," International Commission for the Study of Communication Problems, document no. 39 (Paris: UNESCO, 1980); and Gamal El-Oteifi, "Relation between the Right to Communicate and Planning of Communication," International Commission for the Study of Communication Problems, document no. 39 bis (Paris: UNESCO, 1980). Many of these are contained in *The Right to Communicate: A New Human Right,* ed. Desmond Fisher and L. S. Harms (Dublin: Boole Press, 1983).

58. International Commission for the Study of Communication Problems, *Many Voices, One World,* p. 265.

59. Canadian Telecommunications Commission, *Instant World* (Ottawa: Information Canada, 1971), p. 3.

60. Henry Hindley, "A Right to Communication? A Canadian Approach," in *Evolving Perspectives on the Right to Communicate,* ed. L. S. Harms and Jim Richstad (Honolulu: East–West Center, East–West Communication Institute, 1977), pp. 119–127.

61. Harms, "The Right to Communicate: Concept."

62. UNESCO, "Right to Communicate: Legal Aspects," An Expert Consultation, Bucharest, February 9–12, 1982 (Paris: UNESCO, 1982).

63. Colleen Roach, "U.S. Arguments on the Right to Communicate and People's Rights," *Media Development* 35 (4, 1988): 18.

64. Natalie Hevener Kaufman and David Whiteman, "Opposition to Human Rights Treaties in the United States Senate," *Human Rights Quarterly* 10 (3, 1988): 309–337.

65. William Korey, "Human Rights Treaties: Why is the U.S. Stalling?" *Foreign Affairs* 45 (3, 1967): 414–424.

10

Global Communication as We Enter the Twenty-First Century

Just the blink of an eye ago, or so it seems to anyone born before 1950, our planet was rotating comfortably in its well-established orbit of political and social relations. Peoples and societies were neatly divided into communities identified as much by ideologies and enemy images as by nationality or race.

But suddenly in the mid-1980s, someone pressed the fast-forward button, and life has careened ahead topsy-turvy through a cavalcade of previously inconceivable images. Big Macs are in Moscow. The Berlin Wall crumbles to the sledgehammer. People in Beijing stand up courageously to their own soldiers and tanks. Scud and Patriot missiles battle for supremacy in Mideast skies as billions watch on television.

This final chapter takes the long view on where the world is heading in reference to global communication. In this chapter, some speculative issues are discussed and some predictions made about the course of global communication in the twenty-first century.

GLOBAL COMMUNICATION AND HUMAN UNDERSTANDING

Everyone talks about the information society. Yet there is evidence that global communication has led more to divergence and division than to unity.

To begin, it may not be entirely true that our world has suddenly shifted into fast forward, swept by revolutionary changes. To Krasner, "the idea that the world has fundamentally changed lacks historical perspective." From the Enlightenment to the Age of Revolution, ideas swept across national frontiers in printed and oral form. For hundreds of years up through the beginning of World War I, the global transfer of products, ideas, and capital had been accelerating. In fact, Krasner believes the period between 1914 and about 1970 was more of an *aberrant slump* following centuries of quickening activity. The history of communication provides ample evidence to show that the vigorous global transfer of ideas has been going on for at least four hundred years. What is happening now may simply be that the world is regaining its former high levels of exchange.[1]

To converge or not to converge? That is the question. In the last decade of our century, evidence is mounting that the world is indeed flying apart. National and cultural autonomy are the watchwords of these centrifugal forces. From Quebec to Kashmir to Moldava to Sri Lanka, ethnic and national identities are more important today than the integrative forces of nationalism. We live in a fractured world divided by nationalism, race, gender, ethnic groups, and ideology. New communication technologies cannot reverse this trend. Cherry wondered whether the communications revolution has led us into the "delusion that, as the global network expands, so the walls of our mental villages are being pushed back." There is a world of difference between having a shared experience with people and reading about it, between knowledge by experience and knowledge by reporting.[2]

Be that as it may, something is indeed different. The "world's largest machine," the global communications system, may not have fundamentally altered the course of history. Still, it allows us all to observe and participate in world affairs on an unprecedented scale. For good or for bad, the information and communication revolution has ushered in an era of open diplomacy and public involvement that forever alters the balance of power. So we need to ask ourselves, Has global communication truly led to greater understanding, or has it led people to see the divisions between nations, cultures, and peoples more keenly and with fewer illusions than before?

Does communication have a dark side? Does it in fact spread division, revolt, and disharmony? It may be no coincidence, Carey reminds us, that the world first experienced Balkanization and then global orgies of violence shortly after the birth of the first truly global media, the telegraph, telephone, and undersea cable.[3] Similarly, improvements in modern communications technologies may have led inevitably to greater social isolation and alienation. Rural Free Delivery brought mail to a person's residence, a great convenience. Previously people had to fetch their mail at a central place, usually a general store where they could socialize with their neighbors. As historian Daniel Boorstin writes, "from every farmer's doorstep there now ran a highway to the world, but at the price of dissolving the old face-to-face communities." Radio and television continued the trend while at the same time providing images that deluded listeners and viewers into thinking they were really gregarious.[4]

Recall the famous phrase from the UNESCO Constitution, "that since wars begin in the minds of men, it is in the minds of men that the defences of peace must be constructed." Such optimism is often contradicted by present-day realities. In our era it is obvious that *increasing the quantity and quality of global communication does not necessarily solve the underlying causes of conflict.* Confirming this by surveying 2,500 years of history, Naroll, Bullough, and Naroll found that diplomatic activity and communication "had little if any effect on war frequency."[5]

Early communication research led us to believe that the clearer the message, the less distorted it is by "noise," the greater the chances of full understanding. It is assumed that if people understood each other, they would be more likely to find peaceful solutions to conflict. This does not seem to be true in the present era. Perhaps the best we can say is that "the positive direct effects of international transactions and communications are limited. They may easily be offset by other negative factors in the environment."[6] In some cases, international disharmony may become more conspicuous as a result of more accurate perceptions on both sides. Conflict is rooted "not in the lack of communication but in realistic confrontations over scarce resources such as status, power and economic advantages."[7]

Coser contends that *less communication may often be better communication.* Ignorance serves definite functions in social relations. "The reduction of ignorance, far from being a blessing, may under specifiable conditions be a curse."[8] He maintains there is no empirical foundation for the belief that improved communication leads to greater understanding. Rather, there are many instances in which "if we really knew what motivated other persons, we would become more antagonistic toward them."[9] Coser even believes that "humane concern for the other may dictate a policy of protective withholding of information. . . . Communication is *not* the universal solvent to human predicaments."[10]

Hostile attitudes and stereotypes from previous wars can and do fade away. Widespread negative stereotypes of Germans, Italians, and Russians—products of world war—no longer exist widely in the United States.[11] In the same way, negative stereotypes of Vietnamese and Iranians seem to be fading into the past. Yet Beer reminds us that "though they fade with time, underlying images from the past do not disappear. They remain as psychological foundations for possible future wars. If political tensions reappear, a new escalation of hostile imagery builds on such bases."[12]

So wherein lies the failure of the liberal paradigm so well embodied in the famous "minds of men" phrase in the UNESCO Constitution? For one, it is important to realize that communication requires two interrelated skills: *transmission* and *interpretation.* New communications technologies have resulted in high-speed methods of transmission; information can be transmitted across the globe in seconds. But interpretation—analysis and integration of information, turning information into knowledge—is much slower. It requires those ancient human communication channels of conversation, discussion, interrogation, and persuasion. In our age of global information, high-speed data in no way necessarily lead to knowledge, let alone to wisdom, without these ancient, slow human processes.

In one significant way, though, our world is totally different from our ancestors' world: We now have the capability to communicate with virtually any other human being on our globe. Our communication horizons have truly expanded to encompass the whole world. What were formerly impenetrable obstacles to communication (walls, mountains, oceans) have fallen away. Hardly anything of consequence can occur today without an instantaneous audience of millions of viewers and listeners. Every two years, half the human race is linked by the televised Olympic games. There is a widespread popular belief that our vast information and data system has created what Teilhard de Chardin once called a "noosphere," a living dominion of intelligence. Computer systems are said to have integrated into the so-called ecocomputer network, and people are asking, "How will we directly connect our nervous system to the global computer?"[13]

So it seems that communications technology has both centrifugal and centripetal force. The same technology that can bind vast populations together in a world community can also have a divisive effect. It can bring unprecedented attention to small, threatened groups—from the Basques of Euzkadi to the Aborigines of Australia. Proud groups that would otherwise have had no way to command attention on the world stage today clamor for notice in the hearts and minds of attentive world populations. Profound as communication is, it is a knife that cuts both ways.

NEW CONCEPTS OF CIVIL SOCIETY AND COMMUNICATION

As much as our world is changing, we still use old language and think in old paradigms. We continue to refer to a world of competing nation–states. In fact, while new nations are sprouting up and nationalist movements are challenging the status quo, we may be witnessing the crumbling of national sovereignty. Today a maze of state and mercantile conglomerates carry out the bulk of the world's manufacturing and cultural production, transcending the legal boundaries of the nation–state and often operating outside legal scrutiny.

We must be precise in our choice of words. *International* communication, as this field has been called for decades, in its very etymology presumes the supremacy of the nation–state. *Global* communication, the term preferred in this book, is more expansive and encompasses all planet-girdling channels. But other terms stretch our conceptions even further. Speaking of the need for worldwide human rights, syndicalist, solidarity, and women's movements to communicate, Waterman defines *internationalist* communication as "transterritorial solidarity relations which enrich and empower popular and democratic communities or collectivities by exchanging, sharing, diversifying . . . and synthesising their ideas, skills and arts."[14] Rush defines *global eco-communication* as "the mutual communicative and informative relations among humans, as a species, and between them and their environment. . . . an integrative, realistic, networking force among humans and their concerns for the inclusion and well-being of all planetary species' information and communication systems."[15] There is even increasing interest in how the earth itself communicates with people, in *gaia-communication.*[16]

While on the subject of definitions, we should ask, who are *we* anyway? Who is actually doing the communicating? Are we only technologies and markets, nation–states and corporations? Increasingly the answer is "no." We are *civil society,* and we often find ourselves fighting market and state forces that hinder our self-governance and development. We are individuals and groups of individuals, associations and networks, affiliations and relationships. We are nongovernmental organizations and interest groups, complex infrastructures and confederations of peoples.

In the last decade a new kind of global community has emerged, one that has increasingly become a force in international relations. We speak of the emergence of *global civil society,* that part of our collective lives that is neither market nor government but is so often inundated by them. Still somewhat inarticulate and flexing its muscles, global civil society is best seen in the worldwide "NGO Movement," nongovernmental organizations and citizens advocacy groups uniting to fight planetary problems whose scale confounds local or even national solutions. Previously isolated from one another, nongovernmental organizations (NGOs) are flexing their muscles at the United Nations and other world forums as their power and capacity to communicate increase.

The concept of *civil society* arose with John Locke, the English philosopher and political theorist. Civil society referred to all social transactions in the public and private sphere that were not interfered with by the state. For Locke, civil society was that part of civilization—from the family and the church to cultural life and educa-tion—that was outside the control of government or the market but was increasingly marginalized by them. In most countries, civil society even lacked its own channels of communication. It was speechless and powerless, isolated behind the artifice of national boundaries, rarely able to reach out and gain strength in contact with coun-terparts around the world. Locke's concept of civil society implied a defense of human society at the national level against the power of the state and the inequalities of the marketplace. For Locke, the state existed only so far as it preserved the natural rights of its citizens to life, liberty, and the pursuit of happiness. Locke saw the importance of social movements to protect the public sphere from these com-mercial and governmental interests.

Dutch social theorist Cees J. Hamelink argues the need to take the concept of civil society from the national to the global level. He sees a new phenomenon emerg-ing on the world scene—*global civil society*.[17] From the Earth Summit to GATT, from the United Nations General Assembly to the Commission on Human Rights, global civil society, as embodied in the movement of nongovernmental organizations (NGOs), is finally becoming a force in international relations. The development of communications technologies has vastly transformed the capacity of global civil soci-ety to build coalitions and networks. Today, new forces have emerged on the world stage: the rain forest protection movement, the human rights movement, the cam-paign against the arms trade, alternative news agencies, and planetary computer networks.

Hamelink observes that the very powers that obstruct civil society at the local level, markets and governments, also control most of the world's communication flows. "When channels for expression were left in the hands of those who control either the state or the market, we lost our freedom of speech."[18] Media controlled by market or government have been unable to provide the reliable and diversified infor-mation so essential to democracy. Civil society needs new media to produce and distribute information. It also needs protection against corporations that control large shares of national and planetary economies, and cultural production.

THE EMERGENCE OF WORLD PUBLIC OPINION

In traditional international relations theory there were two kinds of opinion. *Home* opinion—what one's own people thought—always was vital to governmental foreign policy decision making. *Foreign* opinion—what other countries and peoples thought about a particular action—grew increasingly important as communication technolo-gies developed.[19]

A third type of opinion is emerging. Indeed, one way we can confirm the ascen-dance of global civil society is to examine the accumulating evidence for *world* public opinion, a cosmopolitan convergence of interactively communicating national pub-lics. The MacBride Report observed that world public opinion was "still in the pro-cess of formation, and thus fragile, heterogeneous, easily abused."[20] Yet political leaders now find it necessary to pay attention not only to home and foreign public opinion. They increasingly heed the opinion expressed by the world at large.

The emergence of world public opinion is a significant development in human history. In pre-electronic ages, political leaders believed they could control home and foreign public opinion. The news media rarely quoted from editorials or opinion pieces that appeared abroad. But today improved communication technologies, together with sophisticated sampling techniques, now make it possible for governments and the news media to know precisely what foreign publics think. Governments often tailor their actions to foreign publics as well as to their own.

World public opinion has formed around two types of problems: Widespread national problems, such as underdevelopment, hunger, social inequalities, and the energy crisis; and problems that are global in scope, such as cooperation for development, disarmament, and human rights. We can now point to several firm beliefs of the global civil society. World public opinion:

- Desires peace through international law
- Holds governments responsible for averting the horrors of nuclear war
- Opposes torture and inhuman treatment
- Opposes the persecution of minority beliefs
- Opposes discrimination based on race or gender
- Supports the preservation of a sustainable environment
- Supports resolution of conflict through nonviolent means
- Supports action to eliminate hunger and poverty

This is not to say that all people or leaders support these goals, but they are increasingly conscious of them.

One influential locus of world public opinion is the United Nations. Governments attach great importance to the resolutions, declarations, treaties, and covenants of the General Assembly, the Security Council, and the specialized agencies of the United Nations. Another forum where world public opinion operates are summit meetings. Summit meetings "bring into being some semblance of an international public sphere," the key arbiters of which are not national leaders but rather global news organizations.[21] Reporters at summit meetings are increasingly heard to use the term *we* to refer not to the citizens of a particular country, but rather to all of humanity. "Once global society has been invoked, moreover, values considered appropriate to that society tend at least partly to displace more particularistic values of ideology and national sovereignty."[22]

So media have a dual role. They have a moral and political responsibility to report public attitudes and opinions at home and abroad. But they also help people construct images of the world and gain a sense of reality. In fact, "the cumulative body of information provided by their reports stands in for and effectively is the public's knowledge."[23]

PROTECTING THE CULTURAL ENVIRONMENT, PROMOTING PEACE COMMUNICATION

Let us examine the "cultural environment." Just as Earth's physical environment has its moving plates and colliding continents, Earth's cultural environment is dynamically active, with ideas moving about, crashing into one another, and causing social earthquakes and revolutionary eruptions. And just as the physical environment is threatened with toxics and degradation, so too the cultural environment is threatened by monopolistic control, market-driven commercialism, indeed even by toxic ideas such as jingoism and xenophobia.

The cultural environment is a system of symbols, images, words, concepts, stories, and values. Within it, we live out virtually our entire lives. It is a *shared resource* that is (more or less) held in common by the people of a particular society or nation. It shapes our tools, our languages, and our buildings, and they in turn shape our perceptions of the world, our relations with others, and even our images of ourselves.

We need to protect the cultural environment, just as we protect the physical environment. The media lords of the global village cultivate behaviors that drug and kill thousands every day through tobacco and alcohol advertising. They portray our lives as stereotypes, marginalizing, dehumanizing, and stigmatizing us. They inundate us with a cult of media violence that desensitizes, intimidates, and terrorizes us, and, when they call us up, we willingly incinerate, pulverize, and devastate other peoples. Commercial hucksterism lulls and seduces us, blinding us to the role of our own hyper-consumption in the destruction of our planet's environment. Our criminal justice system, the arts, our schools, and the electoral system are crumbling while make-believe media politics masquerades as participatory democracy.

In essence, we need to redefine the terms of political dialogue in our society toward the common good. Using new communication technologies, we need to reinvent democracy. We must move away from what Italian Foreign Minister Gianni De Michelis has called "Newtonian democracy, based on mechanistic understanding of science and culture," one that can be manipulated by the crassest of commercialism. We must build another kind of "democracy based on systems theory—interaction and flexible feedback with no fixed flow of information and power from top to bottom." It is decentralized media that provide us with the most hope—those channels of communication that arise from and reach into grass roots, that provide truly alternative information from the monopolies of knowledge, those that empower and enfranchise the advocates of peace and the protectors of the environment, those that are low-cost and reliable, those that help people to cooperate on a global scale.

What we need is a global system of peace communication to supplant the present system of war communication. Here are some of the communication attributes that characterize these two systems.[24]

In a society grounded in war and preparations for war, media and popular culture play important roles. They perpetuate the belief that war is inevitable. They show violence as a means of upholding the social order. War movies and news reporting encourage military solutions to international and domestic conflict. Mass media promote the belief in the futility of the peace movement and peace activists, the rationality of the government leadership, the superiority of stereotypical male virtues, and conflict resolution through male social and cultural values. Media industries make vast profits from violent themes of conflict. They suffuse mass messages and popular culture with racism and sexism. In a war system, there is an extensive military/industrial/communications complex, with corporations and government actively involved in all three sectors, with media power increasingly centralized in the hands of a few corporations. The high-technology manufacturing industry contributes to military programs.

In a society based in peace, there is widespread belief that communication and information should contribute to peace and international understanding. Media purposely increase the amount of information on peaceful solutions to conflict and help break down stereotypes of racial, ethnic, and national minorities. Journalists and news agencies serve as early warning devices of impending conflict and remind opponents of peaceful solutions to war. They support the principles of the United Nations, including the demilitarization of outer space.

In a society at peace, media confer prestige on the peacemaker and help create modes conducive to reconciliation. They promote a healthy respect for the most diverse cultural traditions and publicize violations of human rights. The widest segments of the population have access to increasingly decentralized media, which help overcome the historic injustices done to women and minorities and promote genuine communication between all races and peoples.

The outlook is grim as we approach the next millennium. As Herbert Schiller warns,

> American informational cultural power now constitutes a crucial, if not the main source of whatever remains of American global authority in the waning years of the 20th century.[25]

In testimony before a Congressional committee, Secretary of State James Baker said that American foreign policy "must look at new ways that we can promote American values and interests through mass media and the global communications network. . . . Mass media and the worldwide information network can play critical roles in our foreign policy."[26]

THE STUDY OF COMMUNICATION FLOURISHES IN A DEMOCRACY

As the momentum toward democracy increases around the world, masses of people will have to learn the ancient arts of communication first identified by Aristotle: how to deliberate policy, how to decide issues involving justice, and how to ensure social stability. Peoples who have experienced decades or centuries of repression at first are inarticulate. Once they find their tongue, they tend to despise and disdain their oppressors. But it takes years to rediscover the lost arts of Aristotle. And these peoples should find the study of communication useful as they undertake the adventures of self-government and of rebuilding their political and cultural lives.[27]

Too often political leaders and citizens treat communication and information as transparent entities. They "look through" the media rather than treating them as independent sources of authority and judgment. The study of global communication phenomena is at most seventy years old, and there is a great need for more analytical thinking about and critical inquiry into planetary communication phenomena. But much of the research has been fragmentary and imbalanced. In the future, students of global communication must broaden and deepen their focus, for the problems facing us today are substantially different in scope and character from any that have faced the world before. These problems are so large in scope and have such geographically dispersed effects as to limit the effectiveness of solutions developed on a local, or even national, scale.

To solve these problems, we need cooperative efforts involving large numbers of people throughout the world. Communication is intrinsic to cooperative effort, and technologies available today, properly supported, can greatly speed and enhance communication and its application toward solving global problems. However, the technological age has also turned information into a commodity, increasingly available only to those with enough resources to afford the mounting costs. This places individuals, nonprofit organizations, and other grass-roots groups at a distinct disadvantage; they are unable to compete with the resources of private industry.

Instead of dealing with value-free questions at the micro-level, global communication research must focus on the macro-level, on communication as a social process. "This means studying media institutions not in isolation but in their relationship to other institutions in broad social, national and international contexts."[28] Just as the media should contribute to the struggle for democracy and independence, so too the study of communication must meet the needs of a democratic society in which people wish to inform, be informed, and participate in public communication.

NOTES

1. Stephen Krasner, cited in Susan Wels, "Global Integration: The Apparent and the Real," *Stanford Magazine*, September 1990, p. 48.

2. Colin Cherry, *World Communication: Threat or Promise? A Socio-technical Approach*, rev. ed. (Chichester: Wiley, 1978), p. 8.

3. James W. Carey, "High Speed Communication in an Unstable World," *Chronicle of Higher Education*, July 27, 1983, p. 48.

4. *International Herald Tribune*, March 11, 1988, p. 5, cited in *Mass Communication Media in the World* (3, 1988): 22.

5. R. Naroll, V. L. Bullough, and F. Naroll, *Military Deterrence in History: A Pilot Cross-Historical Survey* (Albany, NY: State University of New York Press, 1974), pp. 332–335, cited in Francis A. Beer, *Peace Against War: The Ecology of International Violence* (San Francisco: W. H. Freeman, 1981), p. 133.

6. Beer, *Peace Against War*, p. 134.

7. Lewis A. Coser, "Salvation through Communication," in *The News Media in National and International Conflict*, ed. Andrew Arno and Wimal Dissanayake (Boulder, CO: Westview Press, 1984), p. 20.

8. Ibid., p. 21.

9. Ibid.

10. Ibid., pp. 24 and 25.

11. S. Stanley and H. H. Kitano, "Stereotypes as a Measure of Success," *Journal of Social Issues* 29 (2, 1973): 83–98.

12. Beer, *Peace Against War*, p. 277.

13. Stewart Brand, *The Media Lab: Inventing the Future at M.I.T.* (New York: Viking Press, 1987), p. 264.

14. Peter Waterman, *From 'Global Information' to 'Internationalist Communication': Reconceptualising the Democratisation of International Communication*, Working Paper Series no. 39 (The Hague: Institute of Social Studies, 1988), p. 26.

15. Ramona R. Rush, "Global Eco-Communications: Assessing the Communication and Information Environment." Paper presented at the conference of the International Communication Association, San Francisco, 1989; and Ramona R. Rush, "Global Eco-Communications Revisited: Grounding Concepts." Paper presented at the conference of the International Association for Mass Communication Research, Sao Paulo, Brazil, 1992.

16. Michael J. Cohen, *How Nature Works: Regenerating Kinship with Planet Earth* (Walpole, NH: Stillpoint, 1988).

17. Cees J. Hamelink, "Global Communication: Plea for Civil Action," in *Informatics in Food and Nutrition,* ed. B. V. Hofsten (Stockholm: Royal Academy of Sciences, 1991), pp. 5–8.

18. "Communication: The Most Violated Human Right," Inter Press Service dispatch, May 9, 1991.

19. See Evan Luard, *Conflict and Peace in the Modern International System: A Study of the Principles of International Order* (New York: MacMillan Press, 1988), pp. 266–283; Bernard C. Cohen, *The Influence of Non-Governmental Groups on Foreign Policy Making* (Boston: World Peace Foundation, 1959); Joseph Frankel, *The Making of Foreign Policy* (Oxford: Oxford University Press, 1963), pp. 70–83; and B. C. Cohen, *The Press and Foreign Policy* (Princeton, NJ: Princeton University Press, 1963).

20. International Commission for the Study of Communication Problems [MacBride Commission], *Many Voices, One World* (Paris: UNESCO, 1980), p. 198.

21. Daniel C. Hallin and Paolo Mancini, "The Summit as Media Event: The Reagan–Gorbachev Meetings on U.S., Italian, and Soviet Television." Paper presented at the conference of the International Communication Association, San Francisco, 1989, p. 5.

22. Elihu Katz with Daniel Dayan and Pierre Motyl, "In Defense of Media Events," in *Communications in the Twenty-First Century,* ed. Robert W. Haight, George Gerbner, and Richard Byrne (New York: Wiley, 1981), p. 53.

23. Peter A. Bruck, "Acting on Behalf of the Public? The News Media, Arms Control, and Verification," in *A Proxy for Knowledge: The News Media as Agents in Arms Control and Verification,* ed. Peter A. Bruck (Ottawa: Centre for Communication, Culture, and Society, 1988), p. 11.

24. I have been especially influenced by Colleen Roach, "Information Attributes of a War/Peace System" (manuscript); Hamid Mowlana, *Global Information and World Communication: New Frontiers in International Relations* (New York: Longman, 1986), pp. 218–222; Cherry, *World Communication;* and W. Phillips Davison, *Mass Communication and Conflict Resolution: The Role of the Information Media in the Advancement of International Understanding* (New York: Praeger, 1974).

25. Herbert I. Schiller, *The Ideology of International Communications,* monograph series no. 4, ed. Laurien Alexandre (New York: Institute for Media Analysis, 1992), p. 69.

26. "Baker Stresses Focus on Business and Media," Inter Press Service dispatch, March 6, 1992.

27. Michael Osborn, "The Study of Communication Flourishes in a Democratic Environment," *The Chronicle of Higher Education,* January 17, 1990, p. B2.

28. International Commission for the Study of Communication Problems, *Many Voices, One World,* p. 226.

Index

HOWARD H. FREDERICK has taught communications and international relations for more than a decade. Much of the research and writing for this book was carried out while Frederick was a Fulbright Professor of Communication at the University of Salzburg in Austria and an IREX scholar at the University of Leipzig in Germany, vantage points for witnessing the dramatic changes in Eastern Europe. The author of *Cuban-American Radio Wars* (Ablex, 1986) and numerous articles, he has lectured and worked in Europe, Latin America, and the Middle East.

Frederick received his Ph.D. in International Relations from The American University in Washington, D.C. He received his Master of Arts degree in Broadcast Communication Arts from San Francisco State University and his Bachelor's degree in German and Psychology from Stanford University.

Frederick heads the International Communication Section of the International Association for Mass Communication Research (IAMCR/AIERI). He also serves with the Center for Media and Values in Los Angeles and with Radio for Peace International in Costa Rica. He worked at the Institute for Global Communications in San Francisco before coming to the University of California at Irvine, where he currently teaches in the Department of Politics and Society. He may be reached by email at hfrederick@igc.org (Internet).